MEDIA LAW

A PRACTICAL GUIDE TO MANAGING PUBLICATION RISKS

AUSTRALIA
LBC Information Services—Sydney

CANADA AND USA
Carswell—Toronto

NEW ZEALAND
Brooker's—Auckland

SINGAPORE AND MALAYSIA
Sweet & Maxwell Asia
Singapore and Kuala Lumpur

MEDIA LAW

A Practical Guide to Managing
Publication Risks

By

Simon Gallant, LL. B., LL. M
Mishcon de Reya
and Institute of Practitioners in Advertising

Jennifer Epworth, B.A., LL. B., LL. M.
Peter Carter-Ruck and Partners

LONDON
SWEET & MAXWELL
2001

Published in 2001 by
Sweet & Maxwell Limited of
100 Avenue Road
London NW3 3PF
(http://www.sweetandmaxwell.co.uk)
Typeset by Servis Filmsetting Ltd, Manchester
Printed and bound in Great Britain by
MPG Books Ltd, Bodmin, Cornwall.

No natural forests were destroyed to make this product,
only farmed timber was used and replanted.

ISBN 0 421 598 204

A CIP catalogue record for this book is available from
the British Library

TO GILLIAN, CURTIS AND EDEN

TO ASTER, ROBERT AND BARBARA

PREFACE

With any publication, whether it be a television programme, newspaper or book, what the audience perceives is just the tip of a publishing iceberg. The finished product is the culmination of a sometimes lengthy process from the germ of an idea, through stages which will include research, writing, editing and, ultimately, publication. Whilst the author may be chiefly motivated by the desire to say something interesting, provocative or amusing, a responsible publisher should be seeking throughout the production process to balance this creativity with an assessment of legal risk. That is the subject of this text.

The book aims to be a "one-stop shop" in the area of media law, identifying the legal and regulatory issues which have a bearing on content and examining how media organisations can balance these risks against the commercial imperative of producing a product that sells. The text covers the key media sectors—television, newspapers, book publishing, the Internet and advertising—and many more besides. We have attempted to make the book user-friendly by including substantial cross-referencing. You will also find the essential statutes and Codes in the accompanying CD-ROM.

The book is designed to encourage those in the media to look proactively at the risks they face and to develop a more systematic and holistic approach to the management of those risks. But risk management is not about avoiding risks altogether. Simple economics dictate that there can be no profit without risk. By the same token, certain risks are so extreme that no publisher would ever wish to take them. Risk management means a publisher taking the risks he wants to take and avoiding those that could be too damaging.

The potential return, financial or otherwise, will of course be an important factor in assessing whether to run a particular risk. Different organisations will however operate with a greater or lesser degree of risk aversion. A Sunday tabloid will take a different approach from a business broadsheet. Neither approach is right or wrong *per se*. The importance lies in taking an informed decision that is right for the particular organisation.

Parts I and II identify the key areas of law and regulation which impose restrictions on the content of published material. Knowing the law and how the various regulators function must underpin any systematic approach to risk management in this context. Substantial damages can result from a serious libel or copyright infringement; hefty fines or even imprisonment may result from a contempt of court; forfeiture of the right to broadcast could follow from persistent breaches of the Codes of the Independent Television Commission. Even the most trivial complaints will involve management time and possibly legal costs. A company can also suffer a significant loss of reputation because of poor risk management.

Parts III and IV focus on the process leading to publication. Part III looks at how journalists and others go about gathering material in preparation for a story or other publication. It highlights the steps that can be taken at an early stage to prevent complaint or, in the event of complaint, to minimise potential exposure.

Part IV considers the editorial process. It is at this stage that the key elements of risk management must be put in place. It will be for the person exercising editorial control, in conjunction with any legal advisers, to identify the potential risks of publication, the likelihood of them taking place and their potential severity. The organisation will then be in a position to decide on the most appropriate handling procedure. It may choose to avoid the risk by not publishing the contentious allegation, to reduce the risk by diluting the strength of the allegation or to rely on the financial burden passing to a third party (for example, by insurance or the securing of an indemnity). Alternatively, the publisher can decide to proceed in the full knowledge of the risk if it considers the risk to be acceptable.

Part V deals with the situation where a complaint has arisen and how that complaint should be managed to achieve the best possible outcome for the publisher. What the outcome will be naturally varies with the circumstances of the complaint. But a prudent publisher will have systems in place that mean the effective handling of all complaints.

Part VI concentrates on techniques for managing the financial costs of complaints. This means taking steps to budget for possible or actual claims and considering the option of transferring risk by obtaining insurance cover.

The emphasis throughout is trying to provide practical guidance as to best practice for all those involved in the production process, for it is only with an awareness and commitment throughout an organisation that publishing risks can properly be managed. Whilst frequent reference is made to newspapers and television, this text aims to offer insights not just to journalists and producers but to all those working with media organisations, including lawyers, book and web publishers, advertising agencies, insurers and risk managers.

The legal landscape for the media, particularly in the fields of privacy and defamation, is likely to change significantly as a result of the House of Lords judgment in the Reynolds case, the introduction of the Civil Procedure Rules, and the Human Rights Act 1998.

At the time of writing, the Human Rights Act had not yet come into effect. This is expected to happen on October 2, 2000. The courts will have to balance more explicitly the right to free expression against other rights contained in the European Convention on Human Rights, such as the right to a fair trial and the right to a private life. As a result, we would expect the law of confidence to assume greater importance in the area of privacy, whilst prior restraint in defamation cases should become increasingly less common.

At the time of writing, the Independent Television Commission and Radio Authority were reviewing their Codes, in part to ensure compatibility with the Human Rights Act 1998. The reviews will result in revised Codes being published over the coming 12 months. At the same time, government has embarked on a consultation exercise to determine whether—particularly in light of converging technologies—to create a super-regulator for all media. It is not known when this process will end or where it will lead.

We have tried where possible to anticipate the likely impact of these changes but in principle have sought to state the law of England and Wales as at July 1, 2000.

July 2000

Simon Gallant,
Jennifer Epworth,

Postscript: Since July, the Independent Television Commission has issued a revised Code of Programme Sponsorship and the Radio Authority has issued a revised Advertising and Sponsorship Code. Whilst time has not permitted us to amend the references to the previous Codes, the CD-Rom accompanying this book contains the revised Codes.

ACKNOWLEDGMENTS

This book is the product of a two-year research project which was generously funded by the Alexander Maxwell Law Scholarship Trust. It involved interviews with many people working in the media, including in-house lawyers, external solicitors, lawyers working for trade organisations, editors, journalists, representatives of the statutory and industry regulators, and media insurance and underwriting specialists. Secondments were also undertaken at two large national newspaper groups and a news agency to see how their "legalling" procedures worked first-hand.

The project was intended to test the idea that legal standards and practices varied between organisations, but that by and large the media were responsible and had been given a bad press. Its aim was to assess those practices and identify best practice guidelines, where they existed, so that the media as a whole could improve its risk management strategies. Although the bulk of the interviews and secondments were undertaken in 1995–1997, our experience suggests that practices have not altered significantly since that time.

A large number of people contributed to the research for this book. We would particularly like to thank the following for their time and their invaluable help in completing our research:

Diana Aide
Keith Barker
Alastair Brett
Charles Carroll
Don Christopher
Charles Clark
Jane Clementson
Charles Collier-Wright
The late David Dare
Michael Dodd
Cecily Engel
Michael Fay
Lucy Gardner
Richard Gregory
Ajay Gupta
Simon Heilbron
Jane Isaacs
Keith Mathieson
Jane Moore
Richard Murray

Tim Parish
Kate Parkin
Marcus Partington
Stuart Patrick
Tom Petrie
Mark Rebein
Gareth Roscoe
Stephen Rudoff
Mary Russell
Roger Sampson
Peter Smith
John Spencer
Daniel Taylor
Alex Wade
Sally Weatherall
Arthur Wynn Davies

We would like to thank our publishers, Sweet & Maxwell Ltd for their encouragement, particularly during the final stages of the project, and Giles Crown who interviewed the in-house lawyer at the Gannett Media group (owners of USA Today) in the United States. Our thanks go to the Department of Journalism Studies at the University of Sheffield, which provided support during the research stage of the book.

We are also extremely grateful to Alasdair Pepper for reading and commenting on the manuscript and to Ray Blaney (Telewest), Mark Hanna (University of Sheffield), Amanda Levitt (BBH) and Roger Sampson (Sampson & Allen) for their helpful suggestions. Any remaining errors are of course ours alone.

CONTENTS

PART I—THE LAW

PART II – STATUTORY AND INDUSTRY REGULATION

PART III – NEWS AND INFORMATION GATHERING

PART IV—LEGAL EDITING

PART V – COMPLAINT HANDLING

PART VI—FINANCIAL ASPECTS OF CLAIMS MANAGEMENT

Table of Cases

Table of Statutes

Table of Statutory Instruments

Table of European and International Legislation

Table of Regulatory Codes

Part I

THE LAW

Chapter 1

Introduction

1. GENERAL APPROACH IN PARTS I AND II

Part I begins by looking at the provisions of the Human Rights Act which are **1-01** most relevant to media law. The remaining chapters examine the civil and criminal claims that are most likely to be relevant to the content of a publication. In most instances, they give rise to a claim that a member of the public can enforce through the courts: in some, such as contempt or claims for obscenity or offences relating to indecency, it would normally be for the relevant official authorities to institute criminal proceedings.

Part II examines what are essentially regulatory obligations imposed on publishers. Those obligations usually vary depending on the type of media concerned. Often the obligations do not give rise to a legal claim on the part of a member of the public: such a person may be entitled only to have their grievance heard by a non-judicial body. Alternatively, the regulatory body may be the instigator of the complaint and will impose its own sanction against the offending publisher.

2. GENERAL APPROACH TO REMEDIES

The remedies available to claimants in civil proceedings are broadly similar for **1-02** every cause of action. They will be considered in relation to each civil claim dealt with in the text. The most common are injunctions, damages and delivery up of any unlawful article. Each civil claim considered in the text deals with remedies. However, the procedures to obtain interlocutory judgments are beyond the scope of this text,[1] other than summary disposal in the context of defamation claims which can lead to the court requiring an apology or correction to be published.[2] To avoid undue repetition, remedies in relation to intellectual property claims generally are described in Chapter 5. Remedies specific to one cause of action—for example, are dealt with in the relevant chapter.

As a general point, it is worth noting that certain remedies, for example

---

[1] Such as that available under CPR 24.
[2] This procedure is examined in Chap. 3 (4).

injunctions and accounts of profits, are discretionary in nature. In considering whether to grant these remedies the court is entitled to take into consideration such issues as whether the claimant has acquiesced or delayed in bringing proceedings or has "unclean hands".

In the context of complaints handling, Chapter 26 also considers approaches to defending an injunction and alternatives to court proceedings.

Chapter 2

Human Rights Act 1998

---

1. THE EUROPEAN CONVENTION ON HUMAN RIGHTS

The United Kingdom is a signatory to the Convention for the Protection of **2-01** Human Rights and Fundamental Freedoms ("the European Convention on Human Rights"). This is an international agreement binding on the United Kingdom.

In the context of media law, the following are the most relevant provisions:

ARTICLE 8: RIGHT TO RESPECT FOR PRIVATE AND FAMILY LIFE

> "1. Everyone has the right to respect for his private and family life, his **2-02** home and his correspondence.
> 2. There shall be no interference by a public authority with the exercise of this right except such as is in accordance with the law and is necessary in a democratic society in the interests of national security, public safety or the economic well-being of the country, for the prevention of disorder or crime, for the protection of health or morals, or for the protection of the rights and freedoms of others."

This is often described as the right to privacy.

ARTICLE 9: FREEDOM OF THOUGHT, CONSCIENCE AND RELIGION

> "1. Everyone has the right to freedom of thought, conscience and relig- **2-03** ion; this right includes freedom to change his religion or belief and freedom, either alone or in community with others and in public or private, to manifest his religion or belief, in worship, teaching, practice and observance.
> 2. Freedom to manifest one's religion or beliefs shall be subject only to such limitations as are prescribed by law and are necessary in a democratic society in the interests of public safety, for the protection of public order, health or morals, or for the protection of the rights and freedoms of others."

ARTICLE 10: FREEDOM OF EXPRESSION

2-04   "1.   Everyone has the right to freedom of expression. This right shall include freedom to hold opinions and to receive and impart information and ideas without interference by public authority and regardless of frontiers. This Article shall not prevent States from requiring the licensing of broadcasting, television or cinema enterprises.
         2.   The exercise of these freedoms, since it carries with it duties and responsibilities, may be subject to such formalities, conditions, restrictions or penalties as are prescribed by law and are necessary in a democratic society, in the interests of national security, territorial integrity or public safety, for the prevention of disorder or crime, for the protection of health or morals, for the protection of the reputation or rights of others, for preventing the disclosure of information received in confidence, or for maintaining the authority and impartiality of the judiciary."

From the media's viewpoint, this is the most significant convention right and can frequently come into conflict with the rights to privacy, a fair trial and freedom of thought and religion.

ARTICLE 14: PROHIBITION OF DISCRIMINATION

2-05   "The enjoyment of the rights and freedoms set forth in this Convention shall be secured without discrimination on any ground such as sex, race, colour, language, religion, political or other opinion, national or social origin, association with a national minority, property, birth or other status."

2. HUMAN RIGHTS ACT 1998

2-06   The European Convention on Human Rights has not previously been part of domestic law. This has meant that government actions or judicial rulings which were inconsistent with the Convention had to be challenged (by aggrieved litigants) in the European Court of Human Rights rather than in our own courts. The Human Rights Act 1998—which came into force on October 2, 2000 (see CD-ROM accompanying this book) — will change this in several radical ways:

(1) COURT APPROACH TO CONVENTION JURISPRUDENCE

2-07   Section 2(1) provides that a court or tribunal determining a question which has arisen in connection with a Convention right must take into account a range of judgments and opinions, including any judgment, decision, declaration or advisory opinion of the European Court of Human Rights. It must do

6

so whenever made or given, so far as, in the opinion of the court or tribunal, it is relevant to the proceedings in which that question has arisen.

(2) IMPACT ON UNITED KINGDOM LEGISLATION

Section 3(1) provides that, so far as is possible, primary and subordinate leg- **2-08** islation must be read and given effect in a way which is compatible with Convention rights.

If the court is satisfied that the provision is incompatible with a convention right, it may make a declaration of that incompatibility. For these purposes, the court includes the High Court, Court of Appeal and House of Lords.[1] Where a court is considering whether to make a declaration of incompatibility, the Crown is entitled to notice.[2]

(3) CONDUCT OF PUBLIC AUTHORITIES

It is unlawful for a public authority to act in a way which is incompatible with **2-09** a Convention right.[3] A public authority includes (a) a court or tribunal, and (b) any person certain of whose functions are functions of a public nature. It is likely to be given a broad definition and will affect many, if not all, of the content regulators described in Part II of this book.

A person who claims that a public authority has acted (or proposes to act) in a way which is made unlawful may bring proceedings against the authority or rely on the Convention right or rights concerned in any legal proceedings, but only if he is (or would be) a victim of the unlawful act.[4]

Proceedings against the authority must be brought within one year of the date on which the act complained of took place or such longer period as the court or tribunal considers equitable having regard to all the circumstances. This is, however, subject to any rule imposing a stricter time limit in relation to the procedure in question.[5] In certain circumstances the court may award damages to the aggrieved party or other forms of relief.[6]

(4) THE COURT'S APPROACH WHEN FREEDOM OF EXPRESSION MIGHT BE AFFECTED

If a court is considering whether to grant any relief which, if granted, might **2-10** affect the exercise of the Convention right to freedom of expression, it must take into account the matters set out in section 12 of the Act. These include the following:

---

[1] s.4(5) of the Act.
[2] *ibid.*, s.5(1).
[3] *ibid.*, s.6(1).
[4] *ibid.*, s.7(1).
[5] *ibid.*, s.7(5).
[6] *ibid.*, s.8.

Presence of the respondent

2-11 If the person against whom the application for relief is made ("the respondent") is neither present nor represented, no such relief is to be granted unless the court is satisfied:

> (a) that the applicant has taken all practicable steps to notify the respondent; or
>
> (b) that there are compelling reasons why the respondent should not be notified.[7]

Prior restraint

2-12 Publication before trial will not be restrained unless the court is satisfied that the applicant is likely to establish that publication should not be allowed.[8]

Balance between free expression and privacy

2-13 The court must have particular regard to the importance of the Convention right to freedom of expression and, where the proceedings relate to material which the respondent claims, or which appears to the court, to be journalistic, literary or artistic material (or to conduct connected with such material), to —

> (a) the extent to which —
>
> > (i) the material has, or is about to, become available to the public; or
> > (ii) it is, or would be, in the public interest for the material to be published;
>
> (b) any relevant privacy code.[9]

Freedom of thought, conscience and religion

2-14 If a court's determination of any question arising under the Act might affect the exercise by a religious organisation (itself or its members collectively) of the Convention right to freedom of thought, conscience and religion, it must have particular regard to the importance of that right.[10]

3. LIKELY IMPACT OF THE HUMAN RIGHTS ACT 1998

2-15 The Human Rights Act has been dealt with first in this book because, in one sense, it sits above all of the law and regulation which will be described. It does

---

[7] s.12(2) of the Act.
[8] *ibid.*, s.12(3).
[9] *ibid.*, s.12(4). This is likely to include many, if not all, of the codes described in Pt. II.
[10] *ibid.*, s.13.

not amount to a complete body of law in itself but creates a set of principles, particularly in the context of free expression and privacy, which may impact on any area of law or regulation. Nevertheless, the European Court of Human Rights in Strasbourg has developed these principles in case law. Media organisations should familiarise themselves with this body of law. Whilst we have tried to anticipate the impact of the Act wherever possible in the remaining Chapters of the text, it is clear that the legislation will generate a large volume of caselaw. The interrelation between the protection of free expression and the respect for privacy is likely to be the most important battleground for the media. It is generally assumed that the courts will be less inclined to grant prior restraint orders out of deference to the Convention right to free expression. On the other hand, the conflicting demands of respect for privacy may see the development of the law of confidence, or even in due course a separate tort of privacy. It will also be interesting to see how the codes of practice described in Part II assume greater significance in light of section 12(4) of the Act in the context of privacy.[11]

---

[11] See para. 2–13 above.

Chapter 3

Defamation

1. INTRODUCTION

3-01 Defamation is the main cause of action offering protection against attacks on the reputation of an individual or company. It is also an area of law which can frequently give rise to pre-publication legal problems. For those with responsibility for publication, there can often be a difficult balancing exercise in deciding whether and, if so, what to publish. The stakes are often high: a libel action is risky (if it proceeds to trial, the outcome and award of damages are usually determined by a jury), time-consuming, and expensive (damages awards can exceed £100,000, and the costs of a trial can run to many times that much).

Defamation takes two forms: libel and slander. Libel is defamation in written or permanent form (for example, a letter or book) whilst slander is transient in nature (the spoken word being the most common example). However, defamation contained in a television and radio broadcast is classified as libel,[1] as is material contained in a theatrical production.[2]

In general, slander (unlike libel) requires proof of special damage, or quantifiable damage, with a number of limited exceptions. The exceptions are where the allegation concerns the claimant having had a contagious or infectious disease, being unfit for his office or profession, committing a crime punishable by imprisonment, or (if a woman) having been guilty of adulterous or unchaste behaviour.

The distinction is of only marginal relevance to this text, which aims to give guidance to those who will generally be publishing content in permanent form. Exceptions may be those occasions when a journalist discusses an intended article before publication, though such discussions are less likely to give rise to complaint. Clearly the journalist should exercise caution in any such discussions.

2. WHAT DOES A CLAIMANT NEED TO PROVE?

3-02 To succeed in defamation proceedings, a claimant must establish three elements; namely that the publication complained of bears a defamatory

---

[1] Broadcasting Act 1990, s.166(1). Films are also subject to libel law: *Youssoupoff v. Metro-Goldwyn-Mayer Pictures Ltd* (1934) 40 T.L.R. 581.
[2] Theatres Act 1968, s.4(1).

meaning, that it refers to himself and that it has been published to a third party. These elements are now considered in more detail.

(1) WHAT IS A DEFAMATORY MEANING?

The publication complained of must bear a defamatory meaning. The courts **3-03**
have formulated a number of tests as to what constitutes defamation. These
tests, none of which is comprehensive or has precedence over the others,[3]
include the publication of a statement which would tend to:

(a) lower a person in the estimation of right-thinking members of society
      generally[4];

(b) cause a person to be shunned or avoided[5];

(c) expose a person to hatred, ridicule or contempt; or

(d) disparage a person in his business, trade, office or profession.

Defamation cases are generally heard by a judge sitting with a jury.[6] Each has
their own function. The judge determines as a matter of law whether the publication is *capable* of bearing a defamatory meaning; it is then for the jury to
consider whether the publication is *in fact* defamatory in the circumstances of
the case.

To ascertain the meaning of a publication, the court will consider it in
context. For example, if the publication is in the form of an article, the statement must be defamatory in the context of the article as a whole. Words not
in themselves defamatory may be found to be so as a result of their juxtaposition with other material; conversely, a defamatory meaning may be removed
by the context.[7] The court will therefore take into account such matters as the
layout, illustrations and headlines of a publication in determining its meaning.

Context also means that the meaning attributed to words will differ according to the time and place of publication: altered standards of morality mean
that, although in the past it has been held to be defamatory to allege that
someone is homosexual,[8] it might not be regarded as such by a jury today.

---

[3] See *Berkoff v. Burchill* [1996] 4 All E.R. 1008.
[4] *Sim v. Stretch* (1936) 52 T.L.R. 669.
[5] *Youssoupoff v. Metro-Goldwyn-Mayer Pictures Ltd* (1934) 50 T.L.R. 581.
[6] There is a right to trial by jury, unless the court decides that the trial requires prolonged examination of documents or accounts, expert knowledge, or scientific or local examination which
cannot conveniently be made by a jury and would increase the expense of the trial. See s.69(1)
of the Supreme Court Act 1981 (CPR 9A–325); s.66(3) of the County Courts Act 1984 (CPR
9A–624); *Beta Construction v. Channel 4* [1990] 1 W.L.R. 1042.
[7] *Charleston v. News Group Newspapers* [1995] 2 A.C. 65: although the article's accompanying
photograph comprised the heads of actors from the *Neighbours* television programme superimposed on to a naked couple, the article explained that the actors were the victims of the
maker of a pornographic computer game from which the photograph had been taken.
[8] *Kerr v. Kennedy* [1942] 1 K.B. 409; *Liberace v. Daily Mirror Newspapers, The Times*, June 17,
18, 1959.

The courts have recognised that there may be different levels of meaning in a publication. A claimant may complain about any such meaning. There are three relevant categories of meaning:

Natural and ordinary meaning

3-04 This is the meaning of the publication as construed by the ordinary, reasonable, and fair-minded reader.[9] If several meanings can be read into a statement, the general rule is that the meaning to be accepted will be the most damaging meaning attributable to the words by the ordinary reader.[10] The "ordinary reader" has been characterised by the courts as not unusually suspicious or avid for scandal,[11] but not unusually naive.[12] Although he does not readily jump to conclusions,[13] the courts recognise that the ordinary reader may not read a publication carefully or critically,[14] and may be affected by his first impression of it.[15] It will also be assumed that the ordinary reader possesses ordinary knowledge and experience of worldly affairs,[16] and that he knows the meaning of slang and colloquial terms.[17]

Inferential meaning

3-05 This arises where the words have a meaning that can be "read between the lines" without any specialist knowledge. It is sometimes referred to as a "false" innuendo.

Innuendo meaning

3-06 This is a meaning which becomes clear to the reader who has knowledge of certain additional facts or special knowledge. This kind of meaning is also referred to as a "true" or "legal" innuendo. If a claimant wishes to raise a true innuendo as part of his case, he must plead that meaning, prove the special facts giving rise to the innuendo, and establish that those facts were known to those to whom the defamatory statement was published.[18]

The classic innuendo case is that of *Tolley v. Fry & Sons Ltd.*[19] This involved an amateur golfer named Tolley being featured in an advertisement for a chocolate bar without his consent. The defamatory innuendo meaning arose from the imputation that those with knowledge of the golfing world

---

[9] Lord Bridge in *Charleston v. News Group Newspapers* [1995] 2 A.C. 65 at 71.
[10] *Lord Reid in Lewis v. Daily Telegraph* [1964] A.C. 234.
[11] *Hartt v. Newspaper Publishing, The Independent*, October 27, 1989.
[12] *Lewis v. Daily Telegraph* [1964] A.C. 234.
[13] *Mapp v. News Group Newspapers* [1998] 2 W.L.R. 260.
[14] *Morgan v. Odhams Press Ltd* [1971] 1 W.L.R. 1239.
[15] *Hayward v. Thompson* [1982] Q.B. 47.
[16] *Lewis v. Daily Telegraph* [1964] A.C. 234.
[17] *Winyard v. Tatler Publishing Co Ltd, The Independent*, August 16, 1991.
[18] A false innuendo does not need not be pleaded separately; nor are any particulars required.
[19] [1931] All E.R. 131.

would assume that Tolley had violated his amateur status by appearing in the advertisement.

(2) IDENTIFICATION OF THE CLAIMANT

Unless the defamatory words were published "of and concerning" the clai-   **3-07**
mant, he will not succeed in his claim.[20] Normally the claimant will be named in the words complained of, so this is often not an issue. It is worth remembering, however, that a claimant could succeed if the description of him in the publication is such that the reasonable person could identify him, even if he is not named.

Media organisations will be liable even in cases of inadvertent identification if, for example, the publication was intended to refer to a person other than the claimant but with the same name. This was illustrated in the celebrated case of *Hulton v. Jones.*[21] Here, a barrister named Artemus Jones successfully sued over a newspaper article which referred to a fictitious character called Artemus Jones, a supposed churchwarden from Peckham who had committed adultery. The court found that the ignorance of the newspaper as to the existence of the real Artemus Jones was no defence, as was the lack of intention to defame him.[22] It is for this reason that particular care should be taken when identifying those convicted in criminal proceedings: a claimant of the same name may be libelled if he is reasonably identified (albeit wrongly) as the person convicted of an offence.[23]

The law does not allow an individual to sue for defamation of a body of people unless the reasonable reader would conclude that a particular individual was "pointed to" within that group.[24] Whether sufficient reference to the claimant has been made depends largely on the size of the group or class and the nature of the allegation made. From a practical point of view, the smaller the group, the more likely it is that an individual claimant will succeed. A statement which refers to an identifiable group may even be interpreted as referring to the whole group; a larger group may be so large that no individuals are identifiable. *Riches v. News Group Newspapers*[25] involved an article which reported hostage-taking by a man who believed 10 detectives from the Banbury police force had attacked and raped his wife. Ten members of the police force sued and recovered damages even though none had been individually named.[26]

(3) PUBLICATION TO A THIRD PARTY

A libel or slander must be communicated to a third party to be actionable. This   **3-08**
is very seldom an issue of any substance. It should be borne in mind, however,

---

[20] *Knupffer v London Express* [1944] AC 116.
[21] [1910] All E.R. 29.
[22] The limited circumstances in which innocence can be a defence are outlined at para. 5(5) below.
[23] *Newstead v. London Express Newspapers* [1940] 1 K.B. 377.
[24] *Eastwood v. Holmes* (1858) 1 F. & F. 347.
[25] [1986] 1 Q.B. 265.
[26] See also *Aiken v. Police Review Publishing Co*, unreported, April 12, 1995.

that every republication gives rise to a separate cause of action as if each was a fresh defamatory publication.[27] The fact that material has already been published by another source does not therefore protect a subsequent publisher from incurring liability for defamatory content.[28] Problems can be encountered in this area by, for example, publishing defamatory letters to the editor in the editor's newspaper or including material from cuttings of previously defamatory articles. Liability for republication of defamatory material by reference is also possible, for example, if an author cites a defamatory work or directs his readers to it.[29]

3. PARTIES PERMITTED TO BRING DEFAMATION PROCEEDINGS

3-09   Any living individual can sue for defamation, including minors (if proceedings are brought by their "next friend"), bankrupts (if they sue through their trustee in bankruptcy), foreign citizens and people suffering from mental disorders. A corporation can also sue if it suffers financial loss or loss of goodwill as a result of a defamatory publication,[30] as may any of its directors in their personal capacity if they have been defamed by the words complained of. Although not recognised as a legal entity, a partnership may sue in the firm name if the words were defamatory of the firm as a body.

Proceedings cannot be brought on behalf of a deceased person or his estate.[31] Similarly, neither an unincorporated association nor a trade union[32] may sue, though if the publication reflects on an individual member of such a body, that individual may bring proceedings. Local authorities and governmental bodies are also prohibited from bringing defamation actions due to the likely inhibiting effect on freedom of expression.[33]

4. PARTIES THAT MAY BE SUED FOR DEFAMATION

3-10   Generally, each and every person who is "a publisher" can be sued for defamation. This includes almost everyone in the chain of publication, for example,

---

[27] The liability of republishers may be reduced by the defence of innocent dissemination: see 5(5) below.

[28] *Lewis v. Walter* (1821) 4 B. & Ald. 205.

[29] *Lawrence v. Newbury* (1891) 64 L.T. 797.

[30] A company cannot have hurt feelings: *Lewis v. Daily Telegraph* [1964] A.C. 234.

[31] Although the estate may bring a claim for malicious falsehood: *Hatchard v. Mege* (1887) 18 Q.B.D. 771.

[32] *EEPTU v. Times Newspapers* [1980] Q.B. 585. However, the law as stated in this decision is doubted in *Gatley on Libel and Slander* (9th ed., Sweet and Maxwell), p. 188.

[33] *Derbyshire C.C. v. Times Newspapers* [1993] A.C. 534. However, an individual within a local authority or government body is permitted to sue in his own name if identifiable from the defamatory words.

authors, sub-editors, editors, producers, publishers, broadcasters, printers, distributors, newsagents or booksellers.[34]

As a general rule of thumb, any person who can sue for defamation can also be sued if responsible for a publication. There are exceptions. Trade unions cannot sue but may be sued[35]; unincorporated associations cannot be sued, but their individual members remain liable for any defamatory publication for which they are responsible.

5. DEFENCES

Once it is established that the defamatory words referred to the claimant and were published to a third party, the burden of proof then shifts to the defendant to establish the existence of one or more defences on the balance of probabilities.[36] In practice, this means that the publication of the defamatory words gives rise to a presumption that the defendant has defamed the claimant and will have to compensate him, unless the defendant can collect and present the evidence necessary to prove a defence as assessed by the jury. The key defences to a claim are now considered.

3-11

(1) JUSTIFICATION (OR TRUTH)

Justification, or proof that the defamatory words are true "in substance and in fact", is a complete defence to defamation: the intention and conduct of the publisher are irrelevant.[37] The defendant does not have to prove the factual accuracy of each and every word or allegation: he must establish the truth of the "sting", or the main defamatory gist of the publication. A defendant is assisted in this by the Defamation Act 1952, which provides that he can succeed in a justification defence, even if he has failed to prove one of two or more allegations against a claimant, if that allegation is trivial in relation to the allegation or allegations which have been proved true.[38]

A defendant will have to be prepared to demonstrate the truth of each defamatory statement that forms part of "the sting", any reasonable interpretation of those statements, and any innuendos underpinning them. It is for this reason that a defendant will be obliged to state in its defence the precise meanings of the words it is seeking to justify.[39] On the other hand, it is not enough

3-12

---

[34] But see 5(5) below: these parties may be able to rely on the defence of innocent dissemination.

[35] Employment Act 1982, s.15(1).

[36] This is an area of defamation law which is likely to be affected by the Human Rights Act 1998. Under the European Convention, restrictions on freedom of expression are permitted in respect of reputation. However, the courts will interpret these restrictions narrowly, so defences to defamation may have to be widened: see Chap. 2.

[37] An exception to this general rule is contained in s.8 of the Rehabilitation of Offenders Act 1974. This provides that malice will defeat a plea of justification if the defamatory allegation was to the effect that the claimant had a conviction which had become spent under the Act.

[38] s.5. The Act is reproduced on the accompanying CD-ROM.

[39] *Lucas-Box v. News Group Newspapers* [1986] 1 W.L.R. 147.

for a defendant to justify merely that he was repeating a rumour. He must prove the sting of the libel itself.

The factor crucial to the success of a justification defence is the quality of the evidence which purports to substantiate it.[40] As the English legal system tends to place greater credence on the oral evidence of witnesses,[41] one of the vital elements of a defence is obtaining credible witnesses to the truth of the journalist's story. Those witnesses must be able to remember events that may have taken place several years previously and withstand the rigours of cross-examination. However, in the celebrated "McLibel" case, the Court of Appeal[42] established that it was sufficient if a defendant pleading justification anticipated being in possession of the necessary evidence at the date of trial; at the time of serving the defence the defendant needed only reasonable evidence to support the plea and reasonable grounds to suppose that the necessary evidence would be available at trial.

(2) FAIR COMMENT

3-13   This defence, which is also a complete defence to libel if proved, aims to protect freedom of expression by allowing the publication of fair and honest opinion. However, the defence is complex and will not succeed unless each of the following elements is established:

(a) Comment, not fact

3-14   The statement must be opinion, as distinct from a statement of fact. As a rule of thumb, the latter is provable by evidence, whereas the former cannot be true or false. However, it is frequently difficult to distinguish fact and comment. In seeking to do so, the court must consider how the words would strike the ordinary, reasonable reader[43] and look to the context of the publication.

(b) The comment must be fair

3-15   The test as to "fairness" is an objective one: the jury will be directed to decide whether the opinion is one which could be held by an honest or fair-minded person.[44] The courts have recognised that a fair-minded person need not be reasonable: he may hold strong or violent views, or prejudiced or exaggerated views. The test is not whether the jury agrees with the views expressed. Consequently, the defence protects the expression of a broad range of opinion.

The requirement of fairness does not feature highly in practice, as the more

---

[40] As to best practice for gathering evidence, see Chap. 21.
[41] This remains the case under the Woolf reforms for evidence as to fact at trials, but at any other hearings written evidence is of equal weight: CPR 32.2.
[42] *McDonald's Corporation v. Steele* [1995] 3 All E.R. 615.
[43] *Grech v. Odhams Press* [1958] 1 Q.B. 276.
[44] *Merivale v. Carson* (1887) 20 Q.B.D. 275.

16

crucial elements of the defence are that the material concerned is comment and that the comment is based on fact. Malice is also a more important factor: comment made maliciously will invariably be unfair.

(c) Based on fact

The comment must be based on true facts. This requirement means that fair comment is often pleaded alongside a defence of justification; the particulars of justification form the factual basis for the comment. **3-16**

In most cases, a defendant relying on fair comment will be required to establish the substantial truth of the facts on which the comment is based. This is partially the effect of the Defamation Act 1952 which provides that the defence may succeed even if the defendant does not prove every allegation to be true, provided the expression of opinion is fair comment based on those facts which are proved by the defendant to be true.[45]

Fair comment may also arise, even if the underlying facts are incorrectly stated, if publication took place on a privileged occasion and the defendant provided a fair and accurate account of the occasion on which the statement was made.[46]

(d) On a matter of public interest

The comment must be on a matter of public interest, though the limits of what is in the public interest are widely drawn. In particular it is generally regarded as including any matter which: **3-17**

> ". . . is such as to affect people at large, so that they may be legitimately interested in or concerned at what is going on or what may happen to them or to others; then it is a matter of public interest on which everyone of entitled to make fair comment."[47]

Accordingly, much comment about public figures, companies or institutions and private companies whose activities affect the public will be in the public interest. The media also has considerable latitude to criticise artistic, dramatic or musical works.

(e) Made without malice

A defence of fair comment is destroyed if a publisher acted with malice. For this reason, media companies may be wary of raising the defence—malice can **3-18**

---

[45] Defamation Act 1952, s.6. The European Court of Human Rights takes a less strict view of the need to prove the truth of underlying facts: see *Bergens Tidende v. Norway*, May, 2, 2000. It remains to be seen whether the English courts will adopt a similar approach in light of the Human Rights Act 1998.

[46] *Brent Walker Group plc v. Time Out* [1991] 2 Q.B. 33.

[47] Lord Denning in *London Artists v. Littler* [1969] 2 Q.B. 375.

open an unwelcoming can of worms, broadening the case into areas such as the journalist's conduct and state of mind.

"Malice" in this context has a wider meaning than in everyday language and exists either (a) where a publisher did not have an honest belief in the truth of the material published or (b) his sole or dominant motive at the time he published the material was an improper one.[48]

As far as honest belief is concerned, the test is generally whether the defendant knew that what he published was false, or was indifferent as to whether it was true or false. The standard for proving indifference on the part of a publisher is reasonably high: a publisher is not indifferent merely because he is careless, impulsive or irrational in publishing the material.

In relation to improper motive, this is usually a desire to injure the claimant, though, for example, it could be established in other ways, if the defendant was seeking to advance his own interests. It might also be the case that a publisher both lacked an honest belief in the publication and had an improper motive in publishing it. However, an improper motive may constitute malice even if the defendant believes what he published was true.[49]

Malice is notoriously difficult to prove. The burden of proving it falls on the claimant.[50] The claimant is rarely in a position to give evidence as to the defendant's motivation or state of mind, so he must persuade the court to draw inferences from the defendant's conduct in preparing and publishing the defamatory material.

A failure to make reasonable inquiries to check information is not necessarily evidence of malice, but it may be inferred if the failure amounted to a journalist having been reckless or improperly motivated. The same principle applies where factual inaccuracies appear in a story. The tone and manner of presentation of a story may be considered in relation to malice, because it may be alleged that a media outlet is motivated by the improper motive of commercial gain at the expense of the claimant's reputation. Wildly exaggerated comment may constitute malice, even if it does not exceed the limits of fair comment, if the publisher was acting recklessly or with an improper motive.[51] However, the courts will make considerable allowance for strong opinions and criticism on the part of the media.[52]

Post-publication conduct is not strictly relevant—the court is concerned with the defendant's state of mind at the time of publication—but such conduct may influence a jury's thinking. It will, however, be a relevant issue when assessing damages.[53]

---

[48] See *Horrocks v. Lowe* [1975] A.C. 135.
[49] Although the House of Lords stated that judges and juries should be slow to come to this conclusion because a positive belief in the truth of a publication will usually protect a defendant.
[50] *Telnikoff v. Matusevitch* [1992] 2 A.C. 343.
[51] *Thomas v. Bradbury, Agnew Ltd* [1906] 2 K.B. 627.
[52] See *Broadway Approvals Ltd v. Odhams Press Ltd* [1965] 2 All E.R. 523. This is particularly the case in relation to a privileged right to reply: see below. The privilege will not be lost if the sole or dominant motive of the person is to reply to an attack.
[53] See 7, below.

(3) PRIVILEGE

Privilege, like fair comment, aims to protect freedom of expression. It recog-   **3-19**
nises that, for reasons of public policy and convenience, there should be occasions on which people are able to speak freely without threat of litigation.[54]
Privilege therefore acts as a bar to libel actions for certain categories of
subject-matter,[55] regardless of whether the publication in question is defamatory or untrue. Along with justification, it is one of the most important and
commonly relied on defences.

Privilege falls into two categories: absolute and qualified. The essential
difference between them is that absolute privilege is a complete bar to libel
actions, whilst qualified privilege will fail if the claimant can show that the
publisher acted with malice.[56]

Absolute privilege

The main situations in which absolute privilege may arise are considered
below.

(a) Reports of court proceedings[57]

The main importance of absolute privilege from the media's point of view is   **3-20**
the complete protection it affords to fair, accurate and contemporaneously
published[58] reports of the following public proceedings:

- any court in the United Kingdom[59];

- the European Court of Justice, or any court attached to that court;

- the European Court of Human Rights; and

- certain international criminal tribunals.

Reports must be substantially accurate and give equal prominence to both
sides of the story. A fair summary is sufficient, rather than a verbatim

---

[54] Parke B. in *Toogood v. Spyring* (1834) 1 C.M. & R. 181 at 193.
[55] The categories of privilege are not closed and may be extended in the public interest: *Science Research Council v. Nasse* [1979] 3 W.L.R. 762.
[56] The test for malice as described in relation to fair comment is essentially the same for qualified privilege. Privilege will also be defeated if a defendant reports a conviction which has become spent under the Rehabilitation of Offenders Act 1974 but is referred to in court and held to be inadmissible evidence.
[57] Defamation Act 1996, s.14. A "court" is any tribunal or body exercising the judicial power of the state. This category of privilege also exists at common law: see para. 3–24 below.
[58] A report which is required to be postponed by statute or court order shall be treated as published contemporaneously if it is published as soon as practicable after publication is permitted: Defamation Act 1996, s.14(2).
[59] Publication must also not be prohibited by an order under the Contempt of Court Act 1981 or any other reporting restrictions: see Chap. 4.

account.[60] Where a trial lasts more than one day, reports of each day of the proceedings must be published separately at the time.[61] This does not mean that every day of a trial must be reported, but media organisations must attempt to ensure that the overall impression of the proceedings is not detrimental to one party or another. For example, a failure to include in a report a rebuttal by one party to a claim made by another may render an article unfair.[62] The burden of proving that a report is fair and accurate lies on the defendant.

Generally a report is treated as being published contemporaneously with proceedings if it is published as soon as possible after the reported statements are made. This will normally be in the next available issue or broadcast following or during the proceedings. Fair and accurate reports which are not published contemporaneously may still be protected by qualified privilege (see below).

It should be emphasised that this category is the only form of absolute privilege attaching to reports of defamatory statements; the following two categories of absolute privilege protect only the maker of the relevant statement, though again reports of these statements may still attract qualified privilege.

(b) Statements made in the course of judicial proceedings[63]

3-21 This privilege extends to statements of case, witness statements and other documents created for use in the proceedings, although wider publication will not be protected unless the documents are publicly available.[64] The evidence of a witness is also protected, unless he makes statements outside the witness box and outside his capacity as a witness.[65] The privilege is not confined to court proceedings but extends to tribunals exercising judicial functions.[66] Whether proceedings are judicial or not is determined by their similarity to court proceedings.[67] Proceedings not sufficiently like court proceedings may still be protected by qualified privilege.

(c) Statements made in parliamentary proceedings

3-22 This category of privilege derives from section 9 of the Bill of Rights 1688, which provides that parliamentary debates and proceedings ought not to be questioned in any court or place outside Parliament. It includes anything said or done in the course of, or for the purposes of or incidental to, proceedings in the Houses of Commons and Lords and committees of either House.[68] The

---

[60] See *Tsikata v. Newspaper Publishing* [1997] 1 All E.R. 655.
[61] *Kimber v. Press Association* [1893] 1 Q.B. 65.
[62] *Kingshott v. Associated Kent* [1991] 1 Q.B. 88.
[63] This class of privilege was confirmed by the House of Lords in *Taylor v SFO* [1999] 2 A.C. 177.
[64] *Stern v. Piper* [1996] 3 All E.R. 385. See also *Smeaton v. Butcher, The Times*, 17 May 2000.
[66] *Seaman v. Netherclift* (1876) 2 C.P.D. 53.
[66] *Mahon v. Rahn (No. 2)* [2000] 2 All E.R. (Comm) 1.
[67] See *Trapp v. Mackie* [1979] 1 W.L.R. 377.
[68] Defamation Act 1996, s.13.

privilege extends to the official daily reports of parliamentary proceedings in *Hansard*, as well as evidence given before any proceedings, and documents presented to or prepared for proceedings.

Parliamentary privilege may now be waived under the Defamation Act 1996. This provision was prompted by M.P. Neil Hamilton's defamation action against *The Guardian* over allegations that he had accepted payment to ask questions in Parliament. In a similar situation, a Member of Parliament would now be permitted to waive parliamentary privilege so that evidence could be given and questions asked about that M.P.'s conduct in Parliament without the privilege being infringed.

Qualified privilege

Qualified privilege can arise in one of three ways:

(a) Reports of proceedings covered by Schedule 1 to the Defamation Act 1996   **3-23**

Schedule 1 to the Defamation Act 1996 is divided into Parts I and II, each of which lists publications which may be covered by qualified privilege. To obtain the protection of qualified privilege under Schedule 1, the following requirements must be met:

• the report must be fair and accurate;

• the report must relate to a matter of public concern, publication of which must be for the public benefit; and

• publication of the matter must not be prohibited by law.[69]

Part I applies to fair and accurate reports of public proceedings in legislatures, courts, government-appointed public inquiries, international organisations or international conferences anywhere in the world. It also covers the fair and accurate publication of documents authorised by those bodies, as well as any documents open to public inspection. The report does not need to be contemporaneous.

Part II covers a fair and accurate:

(a) copy of or extract from notices or matter issued for public information by the legislatures or governments of European Union Member States or authorities performing governmental functions,[70] the European Parliament, European Commission, international organisations or international conferences;

(b) copy of or extract from documents made available by courts in European Union Member States or the European Court of Justice;

---

[69] See s.15 of and Sched. 1 to the Defamation Act 1996.
[70] Authorities performing "governmental functions" include the police: Defamation Act 1996, Sched. 1, Pt. II, para. 9(2).

(c) report of public proceedings of local authorities, justices of the peace and other bodies set up by statute in the United Kingdom or other European Union Member States;

(d) report of proceedings at lawful public meetings in European Union Member States held for the furtherance or discussion of a matter of public concern, whether admission to the meeting is general or restricted;

(e) report of proceedings at general meetings of public companies formed in the United Kingdom or other European Union Member States, and copy of or extract from certain documents circulated to the members of such companies; and

(f) report of findings or decisions of a broad range of business, sporting, cultural and charitable associations in the United Kingdom or other European Union Member States.

Qualified privilege in respect of material covered by Part II differs from that in Part I in that it will be defeated if the claimant was not given a right to reply to the defamatory allegation by way of a reasonable letter or statement. Further, such a reply must be published in a "suitable manner", which means that the reply must be published in the same manner as the article complained of.[71]

(b) Reports of parliamentary and judicial proceedings

3-24 Fair and accurate reports of parliamentary and judicial proceedings are protected by qualified privilege at common law, whether published contemporaneously or not.[72] However, the common law in this area has been overtaken by the extension of privilege in the Defamation Act 1996 (as described in (a) above).

(c) Defamatory statements made under a legal, social or moral duty or interest to a person who has corresponding duty or interest in receiving them[73]

3-25 The objective of this head of qualified privilege is to recognise that there are informal occasions, outside the grandeur of Parliament, the courts and the like, when the publication of defamatory statements should be protected for reasons of public policy. The extent to which the privilege applies has occupied a great deal of court time and it is beyond the scope of this text to examine all of the cases in this area. It is, however, worth examining the more important principles to be derived from the case law and to see how the more difficult decisions have revolved around the desire of the press to defend important stories, particularly with a political flavour, on the basis of a right to inform the public.

---

[71] Defamation Act 1996, s.15(2).
[72] *Kimber v. Press Association* [1893] 1 Q.B. 65.
[73] See Lord Atkinson in *Adam v. Ward* [1917] A.C. 309.

It is clear from the cases that whether a social or moral duty exists will depend on the circumstances of each case. The courts have set no limits to the interests to which the defence might apply,[74] except that "interest" means a legitimate common interest, *i.e.* not ". . . as a matter of gossip or curiosity, but as a matter of substance apart from its mere quality as news".[75] The important element of the defence is that where there is a duty to make the statement, there must at the same time be an interest in receiving it.

Classic examples where a duty and interest have been found are the giving of a job or credit reference, reports to the police or other authorities regarding the commission of crime or wrongdoing, and the distribution within an organisation of internal memoranda regarding organisation business (*e.g.* mismanagement or employee misconduct). Statements by voters as to the suitability of candidates for public office have also been protected,[76] as have statements made during an election address at a local election.[77]

Qualified privilege also protects the right of a person defamed in a publication to make defamatory statements in a reply to that attack, provided they are made in good faith and are relevant and proportionate to the initial publication.[78] The reply must also be by way of answer or explanation rather than retaliation, but the courts allow the person making his reply a reasonable amount of latitude in defending himself. The person replying may only do so in the media if the initial libel was published in public or in the media.[79]

The defence was used successfully in *Watts v. Times Newspapers Ltd.*[80] That case concerned an article in which the claimant was accused of plagiarism. The article was illustrated with a photograph, not of the claimant, but of another man who shared the same name. *The Sunday Times* agreed to publish an apology to the man and a correction, following which the claimant brought a defamation action against *The Sunday Times* in respect of both the original article and the correction. Although *The Sunday Times* joined the man's solicitors in the action, because they had authorised the publication of the correction, it was held that the man and his solicitors were protected by qualified privilege on the basis that he was replying to an attack.

The extent to which the defendant has circulated the publication is also a relevant factor in determining whether the occasion is privileged. The defence

---

[74] *Beach v. Freeson* [1972] 1 Q.B. 14.
[75] Higgins J. in *Howe v. Lees* (1910) 11 C.L.R. 361 at 398.
[76] *Bruce v. Leisk* (1892) 19 R. 482.
[77] *Braddock v. Bevins* [1948] 1 K.B. 580.
[78] *Dwyer v. Esmonde* (1877) Ir R. 11 C.L. 542.
[79] The solicitor of a claimant in a defamation action is protected by qualified privilege when replying in the media to an attack on the claimant, provided that reply is within the scope of the solicitor's authority and duty: *Regan v. Taylor*, [2000] E.M.L.R. 549. That case was brought by the editor of the magazine *Scallywag* against a solicitor over statements to the effect that *Scallywag* was a disgrace to the profession of journalism. The solicitor was responding to allegations made by the magazine against the solicitor's client. The Court of Appeal in that case suggested that a modern solicitor may express views to the media which would be indorsed by his client if it was within the scope of his general instructions to deal with the media.
[80] [1996] 1 All E.R. 152.

will be lost if the defamatory publication is disseminated to people who do not have a corresponding duty or interest in receiving it.

The media has sought to establish in a number of cases that it has a duty to communicate material of legitimate public interest to members of the public who have an interest in receiving that information.[81] Such attempts have previously generally failed, particularly when raised by national newspapers, because the courts have found that it is not enough that a publication should be of general interest to the public. It was only in extreme situations, such as those involving danger to the public from a suspected terrorist or from the contamination of food or drink, that the public would have the legitimate interest necessary to provide the media for a defence to defamation.[82] Regional or specialist publications had more prospects of success because of their more limited readership.

The recent case of *Reynolds v. Times Newspapers Limited*,[83] however, represents a significant development in this area of the law. The judgment of Lord Nicholls in the case indicates that the law of privilege will, in the future, afford greater protection to media outlets when they communicate information to the public at large. The case concerned a defamation action brought by Albert Reynolds, the former Taoiseach (Prime Minister) of Ireland, against *The Sunday Times* for having alleged that Mr Reynolds had deliberately and dishonestly mislead both the Irish Parliament's Dail (House of Representatives) and his Cabinet colleagues by lying to them and withholding information in the run-up to his resignation in November 1994.

Although Lord Nicholls in the *Reynolds* case concluded that the common law test of duty and interest remained sound,[84] he recognised that the courts should have particular regard to the importance of freedom of expression and the press's "vital functions as a bloodhound as well as a watchdog". He stated that:

> "The court should be slow to conclude that a publication was not in the public interest and, therefore, the public had no right to know, especially when the information is in the field of political discussion. Any lingering doubts should be resolved in favour of publication."

In assessing whether a publication gives rise to qualified privilege, his judgment indicated that the court's attention should be focused on two issues:

• Whether the information containing the defamatory allegation was a subject of real public interest: were the particular members of the public who received it entitled to know the particular information? Politics, economics and issues of law and order are likely to be regarded by the courts as such subjects; celebrity "kiss and tell" stories are less likely to be regarded as such.

---

[81] See, for example, *Bennett v. Guardian Newspapers Ltd*, *The Times*, December 28, 1995.

[82] *Blackshaw v. Lord* [1983] 2 All E.R. 311.

[83] [1999] 3 W.L.R. 1010.

[84] Lord Nicholls rejected the idea that "political information" should form a separate category of privilege.

- What steps were taken by the media organisation in the preparation and publication of the story?

In deciding whether privilege should apply, the court is required to take into account all the circumstances of publication, including the nature, status and source of the material. To that end, Lord Nicholls cited 10 factors which were illustrative of what could be taken into account by a court in deciding whether a media outlet had a defence of qualified privilege. He emphasised that the weight to be given to the following factors, if any, would vary from case to case. The factors were:

(1) The seriousness of the allegation. The more serious the charge, the more the public is misinformed and the individual harmed if the allegation is not true.

(2) The nature of the allegation, and the extent to which the subject-matter is a matter of public concern.

(3) The source of the information. Some informants have no direct knowledge of events. Some have their own axes to grind, or are being paid for their stories.

(4) The steps taken to verify the information.

(5) The status of the information. The allegation may already have been the subject of an investigation which commands respect.

(6) The urgency of the matter. News is often a perishable commodity.

(7) Whether comment was sought from the claimant. He may have information others do not possess or have not disclosed. An approach to the claimant will not always be necessary.

(8) Whether the article contained the gist of the claimant's side of the story.

(9) The tone of the article. A newspaper can raise queries or call for an investigation. It need not adopt allegations as statements of fact.

(10) The circumstances of the publication, including the timing.

The Sunday Times failed to establish qualified privilege at trial in the *Reynolds* case, largely because of its failure to include in the article Mr Reynolds' own explanation of his behaviour as given to the Dail. According to the newspaper it was left out because the journalist who wrote the article had rejected Mr Reynolds' explanation and concluded that he had been deliberately misleading. Lord Nicholls stated that:

"It goes without saying that a journalist is entitled and bound to reach his own conclusions and to express them honestly and fearlessly. He is entitled to disbelieve and refute explanations given. But this cannot be a good reason for omitting, from a hard-hitting article making serious allegations against a named individual, all mention of that person's explanation . . . An article which fails to do so faces an uphill task in claiming privilege if the allegation proves to be false and the unreported explanation proves to be true."

Reynolds was subsequently followed in *GKR Karate Ltd v. Yorkshire Post Newspapers.*[85] The defendants succeeded in their privilege defence in an action brought by the claimant, which promoted and taught karate in the Leeds area, over allegations made by the *Leeds Weekly News* concerning the claimant's business practices.

The judge in the *GKR* case closely investigated the activities of the relevant journalist to see whether he had met the standard of the "reasonable and responsible journalist". The article had been initiated by a Leeds resident who had contacted the journalist, who had made a shorthand note of the conversation. The journalist then rang the chief instructor at Leeds Sports Centre to obtain his views on the claimant's activities and, again, took shorthand notes of the conversation. The journalist was referred to the governing body of English karate for their comments on the claimant. A shorthand note of those comments later went astray. The journalist also called the claimant, which relied on a telephone paging service. She left a message for the claimant to contact her, but never received a reply. The judge rejected the submission that the journalist had been indifferent to accuracy or truth, and concluded that she honestly believed her story to be based on reliable evidence.[86]

(4) LEAVE AND LICENCE (OR CONSENT)

3-26   Where a claimant has consented to the publication of a defamatory allegation, the defendant will have a complete defence to the claim. The most obvious example of this is a media report of an interview with the claimant: by consenting to the interview, the interviewee is likely to have waived his rights in respect of defamatory statements made by himself, provided he was aware of what he was consenting to. However, the defence might fail if the claimant was misled about the context in which his words were to be reported or about the nature of the intended piece.

If it wishes to rely on this defence, therefore, the media organisation must be careful to ensure that the claimant consents to publication of the specific allegations in the specific medium: a generalised indication of agreement will not be as likely to be covered as a written release in respect of the specific words, or at least to the gist of specific allegations, for use in a particular publication.

---

[85] [2000] E.M.L.R. 410. The decision of Popplewell J. was approved by the Court of Appeal ([2000] E.M.L.R. 396).

[86] Some commentators found this decision surprising as the journalist's enquiries were not thorough and she failed to include in the article some information which was helpful to the defendant. It may be a case restricted to its own facts. In *James Gilbert Limited v. Webb and MGN Limited* [2000] E.M.L.R. 680, Eady J. rejected the defence when he found that the steps taken by *The Sunday Mirror* to verify the information published were wholly inadequate.

(5) INNOCENT DISSEMINATION

As already noted, English law has made all of those in the publication process **3-27** responsible for defamation. The sole exception previously was the common law defence for the distributor of printed material, such as a newsvendor or librarian, provided he could show that he did not know and had no reason to believe that the publication contained the libel complained of, and that this lack of knowledge was not due to negligence.[87]

The Internet has, however, been a powerful catalyst for change. Those involved in the distribution of defamatory material may well have no ability to control the content of vast quantities of data passing through their computers. The common law defence has become of less significance because of a new statutory defence, introduced in section 1 of the Defamation Act 1996, which codifies and broadens the range of protection for innocent distributors.

The defence will be available if the defendant shows that:

(a) he was not the author,[88] editor[89] or publisher[90] of the statement complained of[91];

(b) he took reasonable care in relation to its publication, and

(c) he did not know, and had no reason to believe, that what he did caused or contributed to the publication of a defamatory statement.[92]

The impact of this provision is considered in more detail below.

Distributors who can rely on the defence

A person is not considered the author, editor or publisher of a statement if he **3-28** is only involved:

• in printing, producing, distributing or selling printed material containing the statement;

• in processing, making copies of, distributing, exhibiting or selling a sound recording (as defined in Part I of the Copyright, Designs and Patents Act 1988) containing the statement;

---

[87] *Vizetelly v. Mudie's Library* [1900] 2 Q.B. 170.
[88] "Author" means the originator of the statement, but does not include a person who did not intend that his statement be published at all: Defamation Act 1996, s.1(2).
[89] "Editor" means a person having editorial or equivalent responsibility for the content of the statement or the decision to publish it: Defamation Act 1996, s.1(2).
[90] "Publisher" means a commercial publisher, or a person whose business is issuing material to the public, or a section of the public, and who issues material containing the statement in the course of that business: Defamation Act 1996, s.1(2).
[91] Authors, editors and publishers remain liable for the acts of their employees or agents who publish defamatory material. The latter must, therefore, meet the same standards as authors, editors and publishers in order to successfully claim the defence: see Defamation Act 1996, s.1(4).
[92] Defamation Act 1996, s.1(1).

- in processing, making copies of, distributing or selling any electronic medium in or on which the statement is recorded, or in operating or providing any equipment, system or service by means of which any statement is retrieved, copied, distributed or made available in electronic form;

- as the broadcaster of a live programme containing the statement in circumstances in which he has no effective control[93] over the maker of the statement;

- as the operator of or provider of access to a communications system by means of which the statement is transmitted, or made available, by a person over whom he has no effective control.[94]

The last two categories are aimed at live broadcasters and Internet Service Providers (ISPs) respectively. In any case not specifically covered by the above categories, the court is permitted to decide by way of analogy whether a person is to be considered the author, editor or publisher of a statement. The definitions of those personnel are, therefore, left open under the Defamation Act in order to cope with further technological developments.

Reasonable care

3-29 In determining whether a person took reasonable care, or had reason to believe that what he did caused or contributed to the publication of a defamatory statement, the following factors will be considered by the court:

(a) the extent of his responsibility for the content of the statement or the decision to publish it;

(b) the nature or circumstances of the publication; and

(c) the previous conduct or character of the author, editor or publisher.[95]

Decided cases

3-30 The defence was relied on in *Godfrey v. Demon Internet Ltd*,[96] one of the first defamation cases involving the Internet to come before the courts in England and Wales. The case concerned a posting defamatory of the claimant which was placed by a person claiming to be Dr Godfrey on an Internet newsgroup carried by the defendant ISP. The claimant complained by fax to the defendant's managing director, informing him that the posting was a forgery and requesting that the defendant remove the posting from its Usenet news server. Although the defendant received the fax, the posting remained on the news server for a further 10 days.

---

[93] There is no definition of "effective control" in the Defamation Act 1996.
[94] Defamation Act 1996, s.1(3) .
[95] Defamation Act 1996, s.1(5).
[96] [1999] 4 All E.R. 342.

In considering section 1 of the Defamation Act 1996, the court found that the defendant was clearly not the publisher of the defamatory posting. However, the defendant was unable to rely on the defence because it failed to establish that it had taken reasonable care in respect of the publication, or that it had not known nor had reason to believe that what it did caused or contributed to the publication of the defamatory statement. This was because the defendant had been informed of the existence of the defamatory posting, but had taken no steps to remove it.

The defence has not yet been fully tested in any case in relation to live broadcasting, however, the defence may be available to protect broadcasters from unforeseen defamatory statements made by participants in live chat shows and radio phone-ins.

(6) EXPIRATION OF THE LIMITATION PERIOD

Under the Defamation Act 1996, a claimant must commence a defamation **3-31** action within a year of the date of publication.[97] However, for the publications before the date on which that provision came into effect,[98] the previous rule applies: defamation proceedings must be brought within three years.[99]

The court may allow a claimant to commence an action outside the limitation period under certain circumstances.[1] In exercising this discretion, the court must take into account the extent of prejudice thereby caused to the case of the claimant and the defendant. It must also consider the particular facts of the case, including:

(a) the length of, and reasons for, delay on the part of the claimant;

(b) where the reason, or one of the reasons, for delay was that facts relevant to the cause of action did not become known to the claimant until after the end of the limitation period:

   •   the date on which any such facts did become known to him;
   •   the extent to which he acted promptly and reasonably once he knew whether or not the facts in question might be capable of giving rise to an action; and

(c) the extent to which, having regard to the delay, relevant evidence is likely:

   •   to be unavailable; or
   •   to be less cogent than if the action had been brought within the limitation period.

For example, the claimant might only have became aware of the publication after the limitation period had ended, or there may have been intervening

---

[97] s.5(2).
[98] September 4, 1996.
[99] Defamation Act 1980, s.4A.
[1] See Limitation Act 1980, s.32A substituted by Defamation Act 1996, s.5(4).

disciplinary or criminal proceedings against him. However, a claimant must act quickly to commence proceedings once he becomes aware of the relevant publication or the intervening proceedings have ended.

(7) OFFER OF AMENDS

3-32 This defence is intended to provide a defendant who has made an innocent mistake with a means of extricating himself from a defamation action quickly and perhaps more cheaply than he otherwise would. It might also be an attractive alternative to a defendant who realises from the outset that his case is weak, or that the "pain" of litigation would outweigh any reason for seeking to defend the action.[2]

An offer of amends must be made before the service of a defence, and either before or after proceedings are issued.[3] The offer must:

- be in writing;

- be expressed to be an offer of amends under Defamation Act 1996, s.2; and

- state whether it is a "qualified offer".[4]

An offer of amends must have certain features under the Act. They are:

(a) the making of a suitable correction of the statement complained of and a sufficient apology to the aggrieved party;

(b) the publication of the correction and apology in a manner that is reasonable and practicable in the circumstances; and

(c) the payment to the aggrieved party of such compensation (if any) and such costs, as may be agreed or determined to be payable.[5]

There is no requirement under the Act for the defendant to set out in the offer the specific steps by which he proposes to fulfil the offer. Consequently, an offer of amends is likely to be very brief and in a standard form.

If the claimant accepts the offer, he cannot proceed, or proceed any further, with defamation proceedings against the defendant. If the parties reach agreement on terms between themselves, the court will only intervene if its approval is needed (for example, for the reading of a statement in open court) or if a

---

[2] Although introduced in the Defamation Act 1996, the relevant provisions only came into effect on February 28, 2000.
[3] Defamation Act 1996, s.2(6).
[4] A "qualified offer" may be made where the claimant alleges that a defamatory statement has a certain meaning, but the defendant claims the statement bears a less serious meaning. The defendant can make a qualified offer of amends in respect of the less serious meaning for which he is willing to apologise: Defamation Act 1996, s.2(2).
[5] Defamation Act 1996, s.2(4). It should be noted that an offer of amends will not contain an injunction or undertaking in respect of repetition of the defamatory statement.

party subsequently defaults.[6] However, if the parties cannot reach agreement on how to fulfil the offer, the court's intervention may be needed.[7] The court cannot compel the defendant to publish a certain apology or correction in a certain way, but it can order the payment of damages and costs. In determining those sums, the courts may take into account the defendant's conduct in failing to agree terms.[8]

If the offer of amends is rejected the action will continue and the defendant can either:

- rely on the offer of amends as a substantive defence (if he does so, he cannot rely on any other defence); or

- abandon the offer of amends and rely on another defence instead.[9]

If the defendant relies on the offer as a defence, the only issue for a court will be whether the offer was validly made, and whether it was properly rejected. A claimant is entitled to reject an offer of amends if he can establish that the defendant knew or had reason to believe that the statement complained of:

- referred to the aggrieved party or was likely to be understood as referring to him; and

- was both false and defamatory of that party.[10]

Even if the defence fails, the fact that the defendant made an offer of amends may mitigate the damages awarded against the defendant.[11]

6. PUBLICATIONS WITH AN INTERNATIONAL ELEMENT

England and Wales has long been a favoured forum for claimants in defama- **3-33**
tion cases. This was traditionally because of the relatively high level of damages awards and the absence of a public figure defence.[12] These attractions have admittedly been lessened in recent times by the measures introduced to reduce damages[13] and by the *Reynolds* decision but, notwithstanding these changes, London will continue to be sought after as a good place to sue.

In managing this demand, the courts and Parliament have developed a

---

[6] Defamation Act 1996, s.3(3).
[7] Such proceedings will be determined by judge alone: Defamation Act 1996, s.3(10).
[8] Defamation Act 1996, s.3(5).
[9] In this situation, the defendant can still rely on the offer of amends in mitigation of any damages awarded against him: Defamation Act 1996, s.4(5).
[10] Defamation Act 1996, s.4(3).
[11] *ibid.*, s.4(5)
[12] cf. *New York Times v. Sullivan* (1964) 376 U.S. 254.
[13] See 7(c) below.

sophisticated approach to determining whether a case should be allowed to proceed.[14] This section summarises the key principles.

As a general point, however, if a publication is to take place overseas, the publisher should consider the possibility of being sued for breaches of local law and it may be appropriate to seek local advice in advance of publication.

(1) CASES GOVERNED BY THE BRUSSELS AND LUGANO CONVENTIONS

3-34 The Member States of the European Union signed the Brussels Convention[15] to govern the recognition and enforcement of judgments of their respective courts. The Convention delineates the rules which must be followed in allocating jurisdiction. The Brussels Convention became part of United Kingdom law under the Civil Jurisdiction and Judgements Act 1982. It was extended to members of the European Free Trade Association (EFTA) by the Lugano Convention.[16]

Defamation cases are governed by Article 5(3), which provides that a person domiciled in a Contracting State may be sued in the courts for the place where the harmful event occurred.

In *Shevill v. Presse Alliance*,[17] the House of Lords considered a libel claim brought in England against a French newspaper. Whilst the circulation in France was some 200,000 copies, compared to just 230 copies in England, the claimant was able to sue in England and Wales in respect of the English publication. That was because a "harmful event" occurred within the jurisdiction. The claimant would also have had the alternative option of suing the publisher in France for all the harm caused by the publication.

(2) NON-CONVENTION CASES

3-35 Whereas the rules for allocating jurisdiction in Convention cases are strict, the courts have a far wider discretion in other cases.[18] If the claimant wishes to serve proceedings on a defendant outside the jurisdiction, the court will need to consider the question of *forum non conveniens*, that is, in which forum the case could most suitably be tried for the interests of all the parties and for the ends of justice.[19]

The leading case in this area is *The Spiliada*.[20] The court must consider what is the "natural forum" which has the most real and substantial connection

---

[14] Similar issues can and do arise with other media-related causes of actions. However, this happens much less frequently.
[15] The Convention on Jurisdiction and Enforcement of Judgments in Civil and Commercial Matters.
[16] The Lugano Convention on Jurisdiction and the Enforcement of Judgments in Civil Matters.
[17] [1992] A.C. 18.
[18] The relevant rules of court appear at CPR 6.19–21.
[19] Once served, defendant may seek a stay of proceedings on the grounds of *forum non conveniens*.
[20] *Spiliada Maritime Corp v. Consulex Ltd* (1987) A.C. 460. See also *Chadha v. Dow Jones* [1999] E.M.L.R. 724

with the dispute. Factors that the courts will take into account include convenience and expense, the availability of witnesses and documents, where the parties reside, carry on business or enjoy a reputation, and the extent of publication in the United Kingdom compared with anywhere else in the world.

The recent House of Lords decision in *Berezovsky v. Michaels*, in confirming that two prominent Russian businessmen could sue the publisher of an American magazine, Forbes, in England, applied the Spiliada test. Despite the fact that fewer than 2000 copies were distributed here, England was clearly the most appropriate forum because the claimants had a substantial connection with England[21] and there had been substantial (i.e. more than minimal) publication here.

(3) THE DOUBLE ACTIONABILITY RULE

Quite apart from whether a court has jurisdiction under (1) or (2) above, in cases where the publication complained of took place abroad, an action will only lie in England and Wales if the publication was civilly actionable under the law of the country where it was published. This is known as the double actionability rule or the rule in *Boys v. Chaplin*.[22] The rule was abolished for other torts by the Private International Law (Miscellaneous Provisions) Act 1995 but retained for defamation.[23]

3-36

7. REMEDIES

(1) DAMAGES

Damages is often the principal remedy for a person who has been defamed. They will usually be assessed by a jury after receiving guidance on the law from a judge. Damages can be awarded on several bases, depending on the circumstances of the case. The principal distinction is between general damages (which are at large) and special damages (which are intended to compensate for actual losses). General damages may themselves either be compensatory or exemplary (punitive). These concepts are considered in more detail below.[24]

3-37

(a) General damages

Compensatory damages

These are intended to compensate a claimant for the distress caused by the publication and for the injury to his reputation. They are also designed to

3-38

---

[21] [2000] 1 W.L.R. 1004.
[22] [1971] A.C. 356.
[23] s.9 of the 1995 Act.
[24] This section should be read in conjunction with the practical considerations described in Chapter 26 at 3(4) when settling claims.

vindicate the claimant's good name by demonstrating publicly that an allegation is unfounded. Compensatory damages are not intended to punish the publisher.

The amount of compensation generally increases with the following factors:

* the status and reputation of the claimant[25];

* the seriousness of the defamation[26];

* the extent, prominence and influence of the publication[27];

* the extent to which the defendant has persisted with the allegations (*e.g.* the failure or refusal to publish a retraction, correction, or apology).

Compensatory damages may be increased if the jury believes that the defendant's behaviour since publication has aggravated the claimant's injury. Nourse L.J. in *Sutcliffe v. Pressdram Ltd* identified a number of instances in which aggravated damages may be appropriate[28]:

* failure to make a sufficient apology or withdraw the allegation;

* repetition of the libel;

* conduct calculated to deter the plaintiff from proceeding;

* persisting with the libel, for example, by way of prolonged or hostile cross-examination of the plaintiff, or by pursuing a plea of justification which is bound to fail;

* general conduct either of the preliminaries or the trial itself in a manner calculated to attract wide publicity; or

* the persecution of the plaintiff by other means.

Aggravated damages may also be appropriate if the defendant has acted with malice or if he has published other unpleasant allegations about the claimant.[29] These other allegations need not concern the same subject-matter,

---

[25] The general presumption is that a claimant has a good reputation. However, if the presumption is successfully rebutted, the damages awarded may be reduced accordingly: see below.

[26] It was stated in *John v. MGN Ltd* [1996] 3 W.L.R. 593 that this was the most important factor in assessing compensatory damages. The more closely the libel touched on the claimant's personal integrity, professional reputation, honour, courage, loyalty and the core attributes of his personality, the more serious it was likely to be.

[27] For example, greater damages are likely to be awarded where a defamatory report is published on the front page of a national newspaper than would be awarded for a publication to a small number of people.

[28] [1991] 1 Q.B. 153 at 184.

[29] Continuing to publish allegations about a claimant with the intention of deterring him from proceeding with a defamation action may also be contempt of court: *Sutcliffe v. Pressdram Ltd* [1991]1 Q.B. 153.

though a publisher can reduce the impact of this aggravating factor by proving the truth of the other allegations.

Aggravated damages cannot be awarded by a jury unless a claimant has specifically pleaded them. If he has, he must include in his claim particulars detailing what conduct of the defendant's is relied on in aggravation. Publishers should be aware that this will subject their conduct, the conduct of journalists, the information-gathering process, supporting documentation, and their solicitors to close scrutiny. For example, breaches of regulatory or industry codes may be aggravating factors.

Just as certain factors in a case may aggravate damages, a non-confrontational approach may also be relied on in mitigation of damages. The publication of an apology (particularly one in agreed terms) by a defendant is likely to mitigate damages.[30] The conduct of the claimant towards the defendant may also reduce the level of damages.[31] This might arise where the claimant has delayed commencing proceedings: this could be regarded as failure on the claimant's part to limit the injury caused by the publication, or as an indication that the injury claimed is not genuine. A publisher can also rely in mitigation on the fact that the claimant has recovered damages from other defendants in respect of the same allegation.[32]

It is possible to rely on a claimant's bad reputation in mitigation of damages,[33] but the circumstances in which a defendant can do this are limited. First, a defendant cannot point to a specific occasion on which the claimant behaved disreputably: he must call a witness who is willing to state that the claimant is generally disreputable.[34] An exception to this is where the claimant has a conviction for a serious crime.[35]

Secondly, the claimant must have a bad reputation in the area of life to which the defamatory allegation relates.[36] If reliance is placed on a criminal conviction, it must be in the same area of the claimant's life as the defamatory allegation.

Thirdly, the evidence as to general bad reputation must date from the time of publication, or beforehand.[37] Evidence of bad reputation since publication is not admissible.

Despite the restrictions on what a defendant may plead as to the claimant's reputation, he is permitted to cross-examine the claimant as to credit,[38] which may incidentally allow in evidence regarding disreputable incidents involving the claimant.

---

[30] *Kiam v. Neil* [1996] E.M.L.R. 493.
[31] *Cassell & Co. Ltd v. Broome* [1972] A.C. 1027.
[32] Defamation Act 1952, s.12.
[33] *Scott v. Sampson* (1882) 8 Q.B.D. 491.
[34] *Plato Films v. Spiedel* [1961] A.C. 1090.
[35] *Goody v. Odhams Press* [1967] 1 Q.B. 333.
[36] *Plato Films v. Spiedel* [1961] A.C. 1090.
[37] *Associated Newspaper v. Dingle* [1964] A.C. 371.
[38] The purpose of cross-examination "as to credit" is to ask the witness about matters not directly relevant to the issues in the case in order that the jury can discern whether that witness is to be believed about issues which *are* relevant to the case.

Exemplary damages

3-39   A jury may, in limited circumstances, award exemplary damages in addition to compensatory damages.[39] They are intended to be punitive in nature, a deterrent to the defendant and others who aim to profit from defaming people. They must be pleaded by the claimant with particulars.

Awards are only made if a jury is satisfied that a defendant:

*   published an allegation, knowing it was untrue or being reckless as to its truth; and

*   hoped or expected that the financial advantage of publication would outweigh the penalty.[40]

In addition to those factors, exemplary damages should be awarded only where compensatory damages are not sufficient to punish the defendant's conduct and deter him from repeating it.[41]

The fact that the defendant is a professional publisher, and therefore makes profit out of publication, is not enough to justify exemplary damages *per se*. However, a defendant need not have made a detailed cost-benefit calculation to be liable. What is needed is clear evidence that the publisher took a calculated risk that the amount of damages and associated costs payable in respect of the publication would be outweighed by the profits to be earned. Part of this calculation might involve an assessment of whether the claimant was a person who was likely to sue or not.

In deciding whether there is such evidence, a court might consider whether the publication in question was promoted in a particularly prominent way. For example, in the case of a newspaper article, features such as an eye-catching headline, an "exclusive" caption, and its position on the front page, may be such evidence.[42] The financial resources of the defendant are relevant in assessing the level of exemplary damages and can be put to a jury.[43]

(b) Special damages

3-40   A claimant may be awarded special damages where he can demonstrate actual financial loss suffered as a direct consequence of the defamatory

---

[39] *Rookes v. Barnard* [1964] A.C. 1129; *Broome v. Cassell* [1972] A.C. 1027.

[40] *John v. MGN Ltd* [1996] 3 W.L.R. 593. Exemplary damages might also be available to a claimant who had been defamed by a government servant if, in defaming the claimant, that servant had exceeded his powers and acted in a way which was "oppressive, arbitrary or unconstitutional": *Rookes v. Barnard*, above.

[41] *Rookes v. Barnard* [1964] A.C. 1129.

[42] *Riches v. News Group Newspapers Ltd* [1986] Q.B. 256.

[43] The resources of the defendant are not relevant in assessing compensatory damages. However, it is widely speculated that juries tend to award greater damages against media defendants than they do against individual defendants. There may therefore already be an inbuilt element of punishment in some compensatory awards. The Court of Appeal has, nevertheless, stated that an exemplary damages award should not exceed the minimum amount necessary to punish the defendant and act as a deterrent: *John v. MGN Ltd* [1996] 3 W.L.R. 593.

publication.[44] Special damages, and the particular losses which form the basis for such a claim, must be pleaded in detail by a claimant. This often places a greater disclosure burden on the claimant than is the case with general damages. The main challenge for a claimant pleading special damages is to establish a direct connection between the publication and his losses. This is often difficult, and it may harm the claimant's case as a whole in the eyes of a jury if he fails on a special damages claim.

(c) Amount of damages

The unpredictability of jury awards is one of the distinguishing features of defamation, and was most evident in the large sums awarded in some cases in the 1980s and early 1990s. However, there is evidence that jury awards have diminished, and should continue to diminish, as a result of several legal developments. **3-41**

Initially, section 8 of the Courts and Legal Services Act 1990 was introduced. The section allows the Court of Appeal to substitute its own award for that of a jury where the jury's award is excessive or inadequate, instead of ordering a new trial. However, it does not permit the Court of Appeal to set aside a jury award merely because it would have awarded the claimant a lesser sum.

In *Sutcliffe v. Pressdram*[45] the Court of Appeal ruled that juries could be referred to the purchasing power of any award that they might make: for example, by reference to the value of a good holiday, a car or a house.

Neither of these changes made a significant impact and juries continued to award excessively high damages. Matters came to a head in *Elton John v. MGN Ltd*[46] where a jury award of £350,000 (in relation to a *Sunday Mirror* article alleging that the claimant had lied about overcoming bulimia) was reduced by the Court of Appeal to £75,000.

This and several other decisions have led to a sea change in practice. Rather than groping for a decision, juries may be given more guidance as to the proper level of damages to be awarded.[47] They may also be referred to other defamation awards where the Court of Appeal has approved an award or substituted its own award.[48]

Perhaps most significantly of all, juries may also be guided by the levels of damages in personal injury cases. This comparison is regarded as being useful because damages in personal injury cases are awarded for loss of amenity and

---

[44] General damages may cover the situation where a claimant has suffered a general loss of business. However, special damages will be appropriate where he can point to particular examples of lost income (*e.g.* loss of employment or customer contracts).

[45] [1991] 1 Q.B. 153.

[46] [1996] 3 W.L.R. 593. See also *Rantzen v. MGN Ltd* [1994] Q.B. 670, where damages were reduced by the Court of Appeal from £250,000 to £110,000.

[47] It was suggested in the *Elton John* case that counsel should propose figures which represent the upper and lower ends of a bracket of damages. However, it must be made clear to the jury that it is not bound by suggestions made either by the judge or counsel, and may award a sum outside any bracket suggested.

[48] Although such guidance may be helpful, the Court of Appeal has not adjudicated on many awards yet, and the differing facts of most cases make it difficult comparing like with like.

for pain and suffering. These losses are in some sense similar to the nebulous losses flowing from damage to reputation.

Unlike defamation, standard levels of damages for certain categories of personal injuries have developed through case law, so damages awards tend to be more predictable.[49] The maximum personal injuries awards for loss of amenity and pain and suffering are £140,000 to £200,000 for the worst injuries, such as quadriplegia or severe brain damage. By referring to such figures, the effect may be to place a cap on the level of general damages awarded for defamation. However, juries should not regard awards for defamation and personal injury as the same thing: the injuries suffered are obviously very different, and damages for defamation should contain an element for vindication.

(2) Injunction

3-42   The second key remedy is to obtain an injunction preventing further repetition of the defamatory statement. It is a particularly powerful tool because a party breaching an injunction (or which has given undertakings to the court instead of an injunction) will be in contempt of court.

A claimant may apply to the court for an injunction to prevent publication pending trial. This is called an interim injunction and is usually made in haste to prevent a media organisation proceeding with a scheduled publication. There has, however, been a longstanding presumption adopted by the courts against prior restraint of publication in the interests of free speech and the public interest. So if a publisher claimed that he intended to justify the allegations complained of, or that the publication was protected by another defence such as fair comment or qualified privilege, the courts would be reluctant to grant an injunction.[50] This presumption has recently been further strengthened by the Human Rights Act 1998.[51]

Once a trial has concluded, different considerations will apply. If the claimant is successful, a final or permanent injunction will generally be granted restraining the defendant from publishing or further publishing the words complained of or any similar words.[52]

(3) Reading a statement in open court

3-43   A successful claimant may wish to have read in open court before a judge a statement which is intended to vindicate his reputation. This is described in more detail in Chapter 26 at 3 in the context of handling complaints.

---

[49] See Kemp and Kemp, *The Quantum of Damages* (Sweet & Maxwell) and Judicial Studies Board's *Guidelines for the Assessment of General Damages in Personal Injury Cases* for standard tariffs in personal injury cases. Note that personal injury damages for pain, suffering and loss of amenity were recently increased by the Court of Appeal in *Heil v. Rankin* [2000] 2 W.L.R. 1173.

[50] *Bonnard v. Perryman* (1891) 2 Chap. 269.

[51] See Chap. 2 at 2(4) and Chaps. 21 at 3.

[52] The court is also empowered to make such an order under the summary procedure: see Defamation Act 1996, s.9(1)(d).

(4) Summary disposal

Summary disposal allows a court (a) to dismiss a claim if it has no realistic prospect of success and there is no reason why it should be tried, or (b) to give judgment for the claimant if there is no defence to the claim which has a realistic prospect of success and there is no other reason why the claim should be tried.[53] Disposal in this manner may be done on the application of either party or by the court of its own motion. **3-44**

Whilst the procedures to obtain interlocutory judgements are generally outside the scope of this book, the summary disposal procedure is worth mentioning because the following summary relief may be available to a claimant:

(a)   a declaration that the statement was false and defamatory of the claimant;

(b)   an order that the defendant publish or cause to be published a suitable correction and apology;

(c)   damages not exceeding the sum of £10,000;

(d)   an order restraining the defendant from publishing or further publishing the matter complained of.[54]

It is for the parties to agree the content of any correction and apology and the time, manner, form and place of publication. If the parties cannot agree on the content, the court may direct the defendant to publish or cause to be published a summary of the court's judgment in the case as agreed by the parties or settled by the court. If they cannot agree on the time, manner, form or place of publication, the court may direct the defendant to take "such reasonable and practicable steps as the court considers appropriate".[55]

There is also likely to be an interrelationship between summary disposal and offer of amends. CPR 53 relating to defamation claims[56] states that, on any application for summary disposal, the court may direct the defendant to elect whether or not to make an offer of amends.[57] If this direction is made because the claimant is in a particularly strong position, the defendant may be wise to make such an offer. Conversely, if an offer of amends is made and rejected, a defendant would be more likely to obtain summary disposal of the claim.

8. MALICIOUS FALSEHOOD AND RELATED CLAIMS

(1) GENERAL REQUIREMENTS

A separate action may lie in malicious falsehood against the publisher of a false statement which, though not defamatory, is likely to cause the claimant **3-45**

---

[53] Defamation Act 1996, s.8. The procedure came into effect on February 28, 2000.
[54] Defamation Act 1996, s.9(1).
[55] Defamation Act 1996, s.9(2).
[56] CPR 53 and the accompanying Practice Directions also came into force on February 28, 2000.
[57] CPR 53.2(4).

financial harm. The cause of action is included here because of its close relationship with defamation, which commonly concerns the making of false statements. Indeed, in some circumstances the facts of a case will satisfy the requirements for both actions.

To succeed in a claim for malicious falsehood, a claimant must establish:

(1) that the words published were false;

(2) that they were published maliciously; and

(3) that the publication has caused the claimant special damage.

Where the false statement disparages the claimant's title to his property, the cause of action is known as slander of title. Where the false statement disparages his goods, it is known as slander of goods. Both causes of action, however, fall broadly within the scope of malicious falsehood.

Malice is used in a similar way here as in the context of defamation.[58] The maker of the statement must have had a dominant dishonest or improper motive to injure the claimant without just cause or excuse and either known that the statement was false or been reckless as to whether the statement was true or not.[59]

The requirement to prove special damage is not necessary if either (a) the words were calculated to cause pecuniary damage to the claimant and were published in writing or other permanent form, or (b) they were calculated to cause damage to the claimant in respect of any office, profession, calling, trade or business held or carried on by him at the time of the publication.[60]

Malicious falsehood is a relatively rare cause of action: with defamation there is no need to prove malice. However, there are two particular reasons why such a claim might be brought: first, where the statement is false but not defamatory; and secondly, because of a loophole which allows claimants to obtain legal aid for malicious falsehood but not for defamation.[61]

The most high profile case in recent years involving an individual was *Kaye v Robertson*.[62] This concerned a well-known actor who had been injured in a car accident and been "interviewed" by a newspaper reporter who had gained access to his hospital room. Kaye sought an injunction to restrain publication of an article and photographs which were to be used to imply that the newspaper had obtained the actor's consent to the interview. The words were found to be false, because the actor had not been in a condition to consent, and the actor found to have suffered special damage, because the value of his right to sell his story to other newspapers would have been reduced by publication of the article in question.

There have also been a spate of cases in recent years where trade rivals have

---

[58] See 5(2)(e) above.
[59] *Kaye v. Robertson* [1991] F.S.R. 62.
[60] Defamation Act 1952, s.3(1).
[61] *Joyce v. Sengupta* [1993] 1 W.L.R. 337.
[62] [1991] F.S.R. 62.

sought to rely on malicious falsehood (sometimes in addition to claims for trade mark infringement and passing off) as a way of preventing the publication of comparative advertising. In this context the false statement must be more than mere "puff". The courts do not want to be seen to be indorsing the goods or services of one business over another as part of ongoing commercial rivalry.[63] In addition, they recognise that the public expects a certain amount of exaggeration in advertising.[64] But the court's approach will vary according to the circumstances of the case: statements in respect of some goods and services may be regarded more seriously than others. For example, claims in respect of pharmaceutical products are less likely to be "puff" than are those made about domestic products, such as flour.[65]

As with defamation, the limitation period for malicious falsehood is generally one year.[66]

(2) REMEDIES

The principal remedies are damages and injunctions. Damages (including   **3-46** aggravated damages) are available for injury to feelings.[67] However, injunctions can be difficult to obtain. As in defamation actions, they will rarely be granted if the defendant intends to plead justification in respect of the allegations made (unless the allegations are clearly false and maliciously published).

In the *Macmillan Magazines case*,[68] Neuberger J. refused to grant an injunction because both sides had an arguable case, the defendant intended to justify its allegations, and the granting of an injunction would have interfered with the defendant's right to free expression. This approach is likely to be more common given the impact of the Human Rights Act 1998.[69]

An injunction was, however, granted in another comparative advertising case, *Compaq Computer Corporation v. Dell Computer Corporation*.[70] The court found that there was a serious question to be tried and that Dell (which had effectively represented that its computers were the same as Compaq's, except that they were cheaper) could easily alter the advertisements in question pending trial.

9. CRIMINAL LIBEL

The publication of defamatory statements in permanent form can be a crime   **3-47** at common law. The libel must be serious, but need not involve the public inter-

---

[63] *White v. Mellin* [1895] A.C. 154.
[64] *Vodaphone Group plc v. Orange Personal Communications Ltd* [1997] F.S.R. 34.
[65] *Ciba-Geigy plc v. Parke Davis & Co. Ltd* [1994] F.S.R. 8.
[66] Defamation Act 1996, s.5.
[67] *Khodaparast v. Shad* [2000] 1 W.L.R. 618.
[68] *MacMillan Magazines Ltd v. RCN Publishing Co Ltd* [1998] F.S.R. 9.
[69] See Chap. 2.
[70] [1992] F.S.R. 93.

est or be likely to breach the peace.[71] Leave to prosecute those involved in the publication of a paid-for newspaper must be obtained from a judge in chambers.[72]

It is a rare form of procedure and will only to be resorted to in exceptional circumstances, namely where the libel was so serious that a defendant should be punished by the state itself.[73]

The defences to a prosecution are broadly the same as those in a civil claim, but a defendant who pleads justification must show that publication was for the public benefit.[74] It will be interesting to see how the crime survives in the light of the Human Rights Act 1998.[75]

There is a separate crime of seditious libel where publication takes place of seditious matter.

---

[71] *Gleaves v. Deakin* [1980] A.C. 477.
[72] Law of Libel Amendment Act 1888, s.8.
[73] *Goldsmith v. Sperrings* [1977] 1 W.L.R. 478.
[74] Libel Act 1843, s.6.
[75] In *Dalban v. Romania* (Application No.28114/95) (1999), the European Court of Human Rights held that a conviction of the applicant journalist for criminal libel constituted a violation of Art.10 of the European Convention on Human Rights.

Chapter 4

Restrictions on court reporting

1. INTRODUCTION

This chapter examines the key provisions which restrict the media's ability to **4-01** report on court proceedings.[1] The provisions aim to strike a balance between two interests: a fair trial on the one hand and the right to free expression on the other.[2]

The most significant impediment is contempt of court. In general terms, the law of contempt aims to ensure the effective administration of justice. It applies broadly to the proceedings of any judicial tribunal or body.[3]

The law of contempt seeks to achieve the effective administration of justice by punishing interference with court proceedings[4] and non-compliance with court orders or undertakings.[5]

Interference can cover a wide range of activities. In terms of direct interference, it would be contempt to create a disturbance in a court room which would disrupt the smooth running of a trial.[6] Less direct interference, which

---

[1] For additional guidance, see Judicial Studies Board, "Reporting Restrictions in the Crown Court" (May 2000), which can be downloaded from www.jsboard.co.uk/represt.htm

[2] The tension between these two positions can be seen in the provisions of the European Convention on Human Rights and the Human Rights Act 1998. Art. 6 guarantees the right to a fair trial; Art. 10 contains the potentially incompatible right to free expression.

[3] The Contempt of Court Act 1981 applies to any tribunal or body exercising the judicial power of the state (s.19). This extends to the lands tribunals, employment tribunals, and mental health tribunals, but does not include local valuation courts or the General Medical Council: see *Attorney-General v. BBC* [1981] A.C. 303; *Peach Grey and Co. v. Sommers* [1995] 2 All E.R. 513; *Pickering v. Liverpool Daily Post and Echo Newspapers plc* [1991] 2 A.C. 370; *GMC v. BBC* [1998] 3 All E.R. 426. Those reporting on the proceedings of other tribunals should take advice on their status for the purposes of the Contempt of Court Act 1981 and common law contempt.

[4] This is called criminal contempt.

[5] This is called civil contempt. Chap. 23 looks at ways of developing a system to ensure compliance with orders and undertakings

[6] This is called "contempt in the face of the court". Such interference may include assaulting or threatening people in court, shouting, singing or protesting in court, or insulting the judge. It may also be contempt to disrupt proceedings by taking photographs or making sketches, although these activities (and the publication of the resulting photographs or sketches) are prohibited under Criminal Justice Act 1925, s.41. The prohibition also applies to television filming: *Re St Andrews, Heddington* [1978] Fam. 121.

take place outside the court room, may also amount to contempt. One of the essential elements of the justice system is that a court decision should be based only on the evidence presented to it, uninfluenced by outside pressures. It may therefore be a contempt to publish prejudicial material about a defendant which the jury did not hear in court. We will be concentrating on the risks of publishing material which interferes with court proceedings.

In addition to contempt, this Chapter will examine other provisions of general application in criminal cases, measures aimed to protect those involved in sexual offences and special provisions aimed at children.

2. CONTEMPT OF COURT

4-02   In this section we shall review the circumstances in which a contempt can arise. This will principally involve an examination of the Contempt of Court Act 1981. Reference will also be made to the common law which has some residual role to play in exceptional circumstances.

(1) PUBLICATIONS INTERFERING WITH COURT PROCEEDINGS: WHEN CONTEMPT CAN ARISE

4-03   Contempt in this context is a long-established concept. Until the Contempt of Court Act 1981 was introduced, however, it was governed by common law rather than statute. The Act was intended to effect a "permanent shift" in favour of freedom of speech,[7] by making the law of contempt less wide and restrictive of the media.

Contempt of court was a strict liability offence under the common law, and this rule was retained under the Contempt of Court Act 1981. This means that conduct will be treated as a contempt when it tends to interfere with the course of justice in particular proceedings, regardless of intent to do so.[8] The harshness of the strict liability rule is mitigated under the Act, however, by providing that there will be no contempt unless proceedings are "active"[9] and the publication in question[10] creates a substantial risk that the course of justice in the relevant proceedings will be seriously impeded or prejudiced.[11] These provisos are considered in turn below.

"Active"

4-04   A publication can only fall foul of the Act if the relevant proceedings are active. Whether proceedings are active depends on the type of proceedings

---

[7] See Lloyd L.J. in *Attorney-General v. Newspaper Publishing Plc* [1988] Ch. 333.
[8] Contempt of Court Act 1981, s.1.
[9] Contempt of Court Act 1981, s.2(3).
[10] "Publication" includes any speech, writing, programme included in a programme service, or other communication in whatever form, which is addressed to the public at large or any section of the public: Contempt of Court Act 1981, s.2(1).
[11] Contempt of Court Act 1981, s.2(2).

involved. For the purpose of criminal proceedings, the active period begins when a warrant or summons to appear is issued, an arrest takes place, an indictment is served, or a person is charged orally. The period ends with acquittal, sentence, any other decision which puts a stop to proceedings, or if proceedings are discontinued.[12]

In civil proceedings other than appeals, proceedings become active when a date for the trial or hearing is fixed (in the High Court, when the case is set down for trial) or, if no such arrangements are made, from the time the hearing begins. Proceedings cease to be active when the proceedings are disposed of, discontinued or withdrawn.[13] Appeals become active proceedings when a party applies for leave to appeal and cease to be active when they are disposed of, abandoned, discontinued or withdrawn.[14]

"Substantial risk" of serious prejudice

There can only be a contempt under the Act if it is proved beyond reasonable doubt that the publication created a "substantial risk that the course of justice in the proceedings in question will be seriously impeded or prejudiced".[15]   **4-05**

It should be stated at the outset that the degree of risk and seriousness of prejudice will be affected by the tribunal hearing the case. It is generally accepted, for example, that professional judges (including stipendiary magistrates) are not capable of being prejudiced by what they read in the media as a result of their professional experience.[16] Consequently, it is very rare that a publication would tend to prejudice civil proceedings, as they are heard by a judge alone rather than a jury.[17] At the other end of the spectrum, lay people like juries and witnesses are considered particularly susceptible to the influence of the media due to their lack of experience and legal knowledge. Lay magistrates are in a slightly different category. Whilst not as susceptible as juries or witnesses, they are viewed as being vulnerable to prejudice owing to their lack of legal qualifications. As magistrates now receive more legal training, they may begin to be regarded more as professional judges in the context of contempt.

The type of tribunal likely to hear the case, therefore, gives an important lead to the media in assessing the risk of being in contempt, particularly if a judge will be hearing the case without a jury. However, the media faces considerable difficulty in deciding whether a publication is likely to create a substantial risk of serious prejudice. The principles of "substantial risk" and "serious prejudice" can only be explained by reference to decided cases, yet the principles are applied differently according to the circumstances of individual cases and inevitably the conclusion reached by a court is often down to a

---

[12] Contempt of Court Act 1981, Sched. 1, paras. 3–5.
[13] Contempt of Court Act 1981, Sched. 1, paras. 12–13.
[14] Contempt of Court Act 1981, Sched. 1, para. 15.
[15] Contempt of Court Act 1981, s.2(2). Note we have used the formula of "substantial risk of serious prejudice" in this section as shorthand for the full wording in the Act.
[16] *R. v. Duffy, ex p. Nash* [1960] 2 Q.B. 188; *Attorney-General v. BBC* [1981] A.C. 303.
[17] The exception is a defamation trial, which is usually heard by a jury.

matter of impression.[18] No guidance can be sought from the court or the Attorney-General prior to publication.

Notwithstanding this difficulty, the court identified three key factors in the important case of *Attorney-General v. MGN Ltd*[19] to be considered in deciding whether there has been a substantial risk of serious prejudice.

(a) The likelihood of the publication coming to the attention of a potential juror

4-06   The court will have regard to the geographical circumstances of a case. The fact that publication takes place in local media which does not circulate in the catchment area from which jurors are likely to be drawn may reduce the risk of prejudice. The court might also take into account the size and nature of the communities affected by the publicity: it may influence a smaller, close-knit community to a greater extent that those in a larger urban area. The risk of prejudice also grows with the extent of distribution or circulation of the prejudicial material in the trial area. Media outlets with high sales or audiences over wide areas will be at greatest risk.

This factor was considered in *Attorney-General v. Independent TV News Ltd*,[20] a case where ITN was prosecuted for contempt, together with four newspaper proprietors. The prosecution followed media coverage of the arrest of two men in 1992 for the murder of a special police constable in which one of the men, Paul Magee, was referred to as an IRA killer and terrorist and the circumstances of his previous conviction and escape from prison were outlined.

The court took notice of the fact that the circulations in London (where the trial took place) of the editions of the newspapers in which the offending articles appeared were only 2,485 in the case of the *Daily Mail*, 1,000 in the case of *Today*, 1,850 in the case of the *Daily Express*, and 146 in the case of the *Northern Echo* (a Leeds newspaper). In the case of the *Northern Echo*, the court commented that it would be impossible to find the newspaper in contempt in view of its limited circulation.[21] According to the court, the offending ITN bulletin was brief, broadcast only once, and ephemeral in nature because it was a television broadcast. The court held that, based on these factors and the lapse of nine months before trial, the risk of prejudice was remote.

(b) The likely impact of the publication on an ordinary reader at the time of publication

4-07   The content and presentation of an article or broadcast have commonly been considered by the courts when assessing the risk of prejudice. The memorable

---

[18] See Leggatt L.J in *Attorney-General v. Independent TV News Ltd* [1995] 2 All E.R. 370.

[19] [1997] 1 All E.R. 456.

[20] [1995] 2 All E.R. 370.

[21] According to T. Welsh and W. Greenwood, *McNae's Essential Law for Journalists* (15th ed., 1999), some editors have taken the *ITN* judgment to mean that regional newspapers have greater latitude to report freely on crime which is to be tried outside their circulation area.

or colourful facts of a case publicised prior to or during a trial may render its content more likely to be recalled by a juror at trial. For example, one of the reasons for the decision in the *ITN* case above was that broadcasts concerning the IRA were so frequent that an individual one was less memorable as a result.

If the striking facts reported concern the accused's character, the risk of prejudice is likely to be greater. This is especially so where the media has reported that the accused has previous convictions, particularly if they are for offences similar to those with which he is charged, for a jury may conclude that the accused has a propensity to behave in that way.

This was considered in *Attorney-General v. Associated Newspapers Ltd*[22] where the London trial of six men accused of escaping from Whitemoor Prison was stayed twice as a result of prejudicial media coverage of the men's criminal records. On the first occasion, the trial was postponed until such time as people's memories had faded and, when the trial recommenced with a new jury, the judge warned the media to restrict their reporting to what was said in the presence of the jury. Shortly afterwards, the *Evening Standard* published an article which featured the photographs of three of the defendants and their terrorist convictions. Despite the fact that the jury must have been aware during the trial that the defendants had been convicted of serious crimes, the Divisional Court fined the *Evening Standard* for contempt on the basis that the article in question was so gripping that it was "something different".

In a similar vein, the publication is likely to be prejudicial if it implies guilt or (less commonly) innocence or if it comments on the merits of the case. A direct assertion of guilt or innocence is serious, as is the publication of a confession. The publication of a photograph is likely to be a contempt if it implies guilt or casts doubt on the evidence of witnesses where identification is in issue. The record fine of £100,000 imposed on *The Sun* and its editor in *Attorney-General v. News International Plc and McKenzie*[23] exemplifies the seriousness with which the courts regard contempts of this sort.

In that case a photograph identifying the defendant in a murder investigation was published two days before an identification parade was due to be held to establish whether witnesses to a shooting were able to identify a suspect. The judge, in considering the penalty, said that if publication of the photographs had been intentional it would have been a contempt that would "necessarily attract an effective prison sentence and a fine of at least seven figures". He also stated that the penalty must "discourage others who might place at risk the integrity of the criminal justice system . . . and underline the individual responsibility of the Editor".

A further issue in this context is how the courts deal with the impact of collective or cumulative pre-trial publicity for the purposes of assessing the risk of prejudice. This matter came up for consideration in *Attorney-General v. MGN Ltd*,[24] which concerned the prosecution for contempt of five newspaper

---

[22] October 31, 1997 (Lexis).
[23] July 5, 1994 (Lexis).
[24] *Attorney-General v. MGN Ltd* [1997] 1 All E.R. 456.

proprietors in connection with the trial of Geoffrey Knights, the partner of former *Eastenders* star, Gillian Taylforth. Knights had been charged with assault, but his trial was stayed on the ground that it had been unfairly prejudiced by a number of articles which were published by five tabloid newspapers around the time of his arrest. However, the Attorney-General claimed that, even before the numerous publications in question at the time of arrest, there existed in relation to Knights a "climate" of prejudice created by considerable earlier publicity regarding Knights's previous convictions and conduct.

The Divisional Court ruled that each of the publications should be considered separately rather than in aggregate. It also held that evidence of additional risk of prejudice on the part of each media outlet was required in cases where it was argued that cumulative pre-trial publicity had already created prejudice.[25]

(c) The residual impact of the publication on a notional juror at the time of the trial

4-08   This factor is crucial and involves considering such issues as:

- the length of time between publication and the likely trial date;

- the focusing effect for a juror of listening to evidence in a trial over a prolonged period of time; and

- the likely effect on jurors of the judge's directions.

The courts have reasoned in many contempt cases that the closer the proximity of prejudicial media coverage to the trial of a particular case, the more likely it is that a juror will remember and be unduly influenced by it. Conversely, the delay between publication and the date of the hearing (sometimes called the "fade factor") has become a major factor in contempt cases.[26]

Adverse publicity which arises during, and particularly at the outset of, a trial is regarded as an extremely serious contempt, but similar coverage a number of months in advance of the trial might not satisfy the test for contempt.

The fade factor is well-illustrated by *Attorney-General v. News Group Newspapers*.[27] In that case the Court of Appeal discharged an injunction obtained by the cricketer, Ian Botham, which had been ordered because Botham became aware that a newspaper intended to republish allegations of drug-taking on his part which were shortly to become the subject of a libel trial. The Court of Appeal decided that the risk of prejudice was not sufficient

---

[25] The dismissal of this contempt case led the National Heritage Committee to recommend in a 1997 report that Contempt of Court Act 1981, s.2 be widened to cover, in addition to individual publications, the collective effect of media coverage. (National Heritage Committee, Second Report, "Press Activity Affecting Court Cases", January 22, 1997, H.C. No. 86, 1996–97). The Government accepted the recommendation in principle, but has not yet amended the Act.

[26] See Chap. 24 at 2 for advice on the practical impact of the fade factor.

[27] [1987] 1 Q.B. 1.

to justify a contempt conviction, based on the period of time (10 or 11 months) likely to elapse between publication and trial.

In another case, *Attorney-General v. Unger*,[28] the fade factor operated in respect of a publication which took place shortly after arrest, even though there was only a two-month delay between publication and trial.

However, it should be remembered that the presence of the fade factor may not be decisive. For example, the producers of the television programme *Have I Got News For You* were fined for contempt for allowing the transmission of a programme in which derogatory remarks were made about the Maxwell brothers six months before their trial.[29]

There is a presumption in contempt law that jurors will decide cases only according to the evidence before the court, and that they will pay attention to a judge's directions to disregard what they hear or read about a case in the media. The courts have noted that the drama of a trial tends to cause all those concerned to focus on the evidence of the witnesses and the submissions of counsel. As Lawton J. stated in *R. v. Kray*[30]:

> "I have enough confidence in my fellow-countrymen to think that they have got the newspapers sized up just as they have got other public institutions sized up, and they are capable in normal circumstances of looking at a matter fairly and without prejudice even though they have to disregard what they may have read in a newspaper."

Considerable care is required, however, as decisions can vary depending on the case. In remarking on Lawton J.'s pronouncement in the *Kray* case, Staughton L.J. said in *R v. Attorney-General, ex p. BBC and Jones*[31]:

> ". . . I am not as confident as he of the ability of jurors to disregard matters . . . If one juror told his fellows that he knew as a fact that the man before them had a long history of violence and serious offences and was on home leave from prison at the time of the alleged offence and, what is more, was shortly thereafter going to start a siege involving ten hostages, I am not absolutely sure that the other 11 member [*sic*] of the jury would persuade him and themselves that all that had to be disregarded."

In conclusion, the case law shows that proceedings have been seriously prejudiced when the outcome of a trial has been affected: the prejudice must be such that it could tip the verdict one way or another. However, a publication will not be treated as a contempt if the risk of prejudice is merely incidental.[32] For a "substantial risk" of such prejudice to arise, the risk involved must be a real

---

[28] [1998] 1 Cr. App. R. 308.
[29] *Attorney-General v. Hat Trick Productions* [1997] E.M.L.R. 76.
[30] [1969] 53 Cr. App. Rep. 412.
[31] December 1, 1995 (Lexis).
[32] *Attorney-General v. English* [1983] A.C. 116; *Attorney-General v. Guardian Newspapers*, July 23, 1999 (Lawtel).

or practical one and more than merely remote or minimal.[33] On this basis, it is not surprising to find that the fact that a trial has been stayed because of a prejudicial article is a telling pointer as to whether the publisher of that article is in contempt.[34]

(2) CONTEMPT AT COMMON LAW

4-09 Despite the Contempt of Court Act 1981, it still remains possible for a journalist or publisher to commit contempt at common law. The Act states in terms that nothing in its provisions "restricts liability for contempt of court in respect of conduct intended to impede or prejudice the administration of justice", *i.e.* where there has been a 'deliberate' contempt.[35] Since the application of the strict liability rule to active proceedings does not arise in the common law, a contempt may be committed even in circumstances where proceedings are neither pending nor imminent. Even common law contempt, however, is unlikely to be committed unless proceedings are reasonably likely to occur.[36]

Because the intention to create prejudice must be proved beyond reasonable doubt, common law contempt is difficult to prove and prosecutions have been rare since the Act was introduced. The requirement of intent is satisfied if the publisher must have foreseen that a publication would create a real risk of prejudice to a fair trial.[37] It might arise, for example, where a newspaper is running a high profile campaign to encourage the prosecution of a suspect where no arrests have yet been made. Care should be taken when running such campaigns.

A media outlet should also take care when publishing material which is known to be the subject of an injunction against another media outlet. This situation arose in 1987 when *The Independent* published extracts from Peter Wright's book *Spycatcher*, in respect of which the Government had obtained injunctions against *The Guardian* and *The Observer* on the grounds of confidentiality. Contempt proceedings were initiated against *The Independent* on the basis that it had intentionally interfered with the course of justice by placing subject-matter in the public domain which was intended to be kept confidential until trial by virtue of the injunctions. It was immaterial that the editor of *The Independent* did not wish to prejudice proceedings, or that he considered publication of the material to be in the public interest.[38]

---

[33] *Attorney-General v. English* [1983] A.C. 116; *Attorney-General v. News Group Newspapers Ltd* [1987] Q.B. 1; *MGN Pension Trustees Limited v. Bank of America National Trust and Saving Association* [1995] E.M.L.R. 99; *Attorney-General v. Guardian Newspapers Ltd* [1992] 3 All E.R. 38.

[34] A recent example is *Attorney-General v. Birmingham Post and Mail Ltd* [1998] 4 All E.R. 49.

[35] Contempt of Court Act 1981, s.6(c).

[36] *Attorney-General v. News Group Newspapers Ltd* [1988] 2 All E.R. 906.

[37] *Attorney-General v. News Group Newspapers* [1988] 2 All E.R. 906.

[38] *Attorney-General v. Newspaper Publishing plc* [1987] 3 All E.R. 276.

(3) DEFENCES AND EXCEPTIONS

Although there are no "defences" to strict liability contempt under the Act, **4-10** there are a number of exceptions. These are as follows.

(a) Innocent publication or distribution

A person is not guilty of contempt if at the time of publication (having taken **4-11** all reasonable care) he does not know and has no reason to suspect that relevant proceedings are active.[39] The same defence attaches to a distributor of the publication if at the time of distribution (having taken all reasonable care) he did not know that the publication contained such matter and had no reason to suspect that it was likely to do so.[40]

Although neither the Act nor case law stipulates what a defendant must do in order to rely on this defence, it is clear that he must show that he has exercised reasonable care prior to publication.[41] A journalist is, therefore, advised to check with the police as to whether proceedings are active (or what stage their inquiries have reached), and make a note of the time and the name of the police officer with whom he checked.[42]

(b) Fair and accurate report of legal proceedings

A person is not guilty of contempt where the publication in question is a: **4-12**

- fair and accurate report of legal proceedings held in public;
- published contemporaneously; and
- in good faith.[43]

It should be noted that, even if a publication does not satisfy one of the requirements listed above, it will not be a contempt unless the publication creates a substantial risk of serious prejudice.

There are, however, circumstances in which a fair, accurate and contemporaneous report could prejudice proceedings: if, for example, the media is ordered not to report proceedings which take place in the jury's absence, or to report any details extraneous to proceedings even if the information is already in the public domain. Care should also be taken that, where a defendant has been charged with a number of offences, any guilty pleas are not reported in such a way as to prejudice a trial for offences which the defendant has not admitted.

---

[39] Contempt of Court Act 1981, s.3(1).
[40] Contempt of Court Act 1981, s.3(2).
[41] The burden is on the defendant to prove the defence on the balance of probabilities: *R v. Carr-Briant* [1943] 1 K.B. 607.
[42] See Chap. 24 at 2.
[43] Contempt of Court Act 1981, s.4(1). Such publications are also afforded the defence of qualified privilege under Defamation Act 1996, s.14: see Chap. 3 at 3. Contempt of Court Act 1981, s.4(3), provides that a report which is subject to a postponement order under s.4(2) will be treated as being published contemporaneously if it is published as soon as practicable after the order expires.

(c) Discussion of public affairs

4-13   A publication forming part of a discussion in good faith of public affairs or other matters of general public interest will not be treated as a contempt of court if the risk of prejudice to particular legal proceedings is merely incidental to the discussion.[44] This provision was included in the Act to give greater weight to freedom of expression by allowing the media to comment more freely on matters of public importance when pending legal proceedings might otherwise stifle argument.

Section 5 is not a "defence" in the strict sense because it is for the prosecution to prove that it does not apply. The prosecution must show not only that the publication created a substantial risk of serious prejudice, but also that the prejudice was not incidental to a discussion of public affairs. It is also not a public interest defence, because it does not allow the media to comment on the facts of a specific case.

The first case in which the exception was found to apply was that of *Attorney-General v. English*.[45] A journalist, writing in support of a pro-life parliamentary candidate in *The Daily Mail*, suggested that it was common practice for doctors to allow severely disabled babies to die. The article was published on the third day of the trial of a Dr Arthur who had been charged with the murder of a baby who had had Down's Syndrome. The House of Lords ruled that the risk of prejudice was no more than an incidental consequence of expounding the article's main theme, the author's support for the platform of the pro-life candidate, and there was no express mention of the *Arthur* case.

In a subsequent case, the provision was found to extend to a publication that contained a direct reference to the accused, Michael Fagan, who was tried for having broken into and stolen from Buckingham Palace.[46] *The Mail on Sunday*'s allegation that Fagan had had a homosexual encounter with the Queen's bodyguard was said to have been part of a discussion about the Queen's personal safety which was regarded by the court as a matter of public concern, and therefore not contempt.

In *Attorney-General v. TVS Television Ltd and H. W. Southey & Sons Ltd*[47] the Divisional Court said that the test as to whether a risk was merely incidental was to examine the subject-matter of the publication and see how closely it related to the matters at issue in particular proceedings. The case also highlighted another factor in the court's assessment of whether the risk of prejudice is incidental: whether public discussion began before the publication in question. If the article merely comments on a pre-existing topic of public debate, it is more likely that the prejudice caused has been incidental.[48]

---

[44] Contempt of Court Act 1981, s.5.

[45] [1983] 1 A.C. 116.

[46] *Attorney-General v. Times Newspapers Ltd, The Times*, February 12, 1983.

[47] *The Times*, July 7, 1989.

[48] See Lord Reid in *Attorney-General v. Times Newspapers Ltd* [1974] A.C. 273.

(4) MISCELLANEOUS PROVISIONS IN THE CONTEMPT OF COURT ACT 1981

(a) Postponement orders

A court may, where it is necessary for avoiding a substantial risk of prejudice **4-14** to the administration of justice in those proceedings, or in any other pending or imminent proceedings, order that the publication of any report of the proceedings be postponed for such period as the court thinks necessary.[49] Postponement orders have frequently been made in cases where the defendant has pleaded guilty to part of an indictment but has yet to be tried on the remaining counts, where several defendants have been charged and are being tried successively, and where there is a *voire dire* (or "trial within a trial") which takes place in the absence of the jury.

In assessing whether a postponement order should be granted, the courts should consider whether the risk of prejudice to the administration of justice is a substantial one: a small or remote risk is not sufficient.[50] According to Lord Denning in *R v. Horsham Justices ex, p. Farquharson*, the courts should not often make such orders because the likelihood of the average juror being influenced by the media is so slight that it can usually be disregarded as insubstantial.[51]

In addition to considering whether there is a substantial risk of prejudice, the court must make a postponement order only if it is "necessary", *i.e.* more than merely desirable or convenient.[52] They should not be made, for example, to protect the interests of the parties or national security. The court should take into account the balance to be struck between the right to a fair trial, press freedom and the principle of open justice, in assessing whether an order is necessary to avoid the risk.[53] It should also consider reasonable alternatives to the making of an order, such as moving or delaying the trial, the giving of directions by the judge to the jury, or denying the jury access to media reports.[54] Postponement orders cannot be made in respect of publication of events which take place outside the courtroom, such as the arrest of the accused.[55]

(b) Indefinite banning order

This section allows the court to prohibit the publication of a name or other **4-15** matter in connection with proceedings before it.[56] This power may be used to

---

[49] Contempt of Court Act 1981, s.4(2). "Pending" and "imminent" are not defined in the Act, but proceedings are "pending" once a person has been charged and "imminent" before that time.

[50] Although s.4(2) refers to a "substantial risk of prejudice" and s.2(2) refers to a "substantial risk" that proceedings will be "seriously" prejudiced, it is generally accepted that the risk of prejudice must be serious for a postponement order to be made.

[51] [1982] Q.B. 762.

[52] *R. v. Reigate Justices, ex p. Argus Newspapers* (1983) 147 J.P. 385.

[53] *R. v. Beck, ex p. Daily Telegraph plc* [1993] 2 All E.R. 177; *Ex p. Telegraph plc* [1993] 2 All E.R. 971.

[54] *Re Central Independent Television plc* [1991] 1 All E.R. 347.

[55] *R. v. Rhuddlan Justices ex parte HTV Ltd* [1986] Crim L.R. 329.

[56] Contempt of Court Act 1981, s.11.

protect the identity of, for example, blackmail victims, informants or those involved with national security. It should not be used to protect privacy or avoid embarrassment,[57] nor should an order be made to withhold a name from publication if that name has already been mentioned in open court.[58]

Failure to comply with either a postponement or banning order under the Act is contempt, regardless of whether the breach created a substantial risk of serious prejudice.[59] This is because non-compliance with a court order is not a contempt relating to publications under the Act: it is a separate form of contempt at common law which aims to protect the administration of justice (see introduction above).

Breach of an order will, therefore, only be a contempt if the person in question:

- knew of the existence of the order, or was reckless as to its existence; or

- intended to interfere with the administration of justice, or was reckless in that regard.

(c) Jury deliberations

4-16   Under the Act, it is a contempt to obtain, disclose or solicit any particulars of statements made, opinions expressed, arguments advanced or votes cast by members of a jury in the course of their deliberations in any legal proceedings.[60] As is clear from the wording above, the offence is committed by a juror who discloses information, as well as by a journalist who obtains or solicits them, regardless of any risk of prejudice to proceedings.[61] The media is allowed to publish details of jurors' views after proceedings have concluded, provided they do not relate to statements made, opinions expressed, arguments advanced or votes cast during the jury's deliberations.

There are only two limited exceptions to the prohibition. First, publication is permitted of disclosures made in court in order to enable the jury to arrive at a verdict. This exception is intended to allow the court, for example, to help the jury with additional guidance or to inquire as to how votes have been split where a majority verdict has been reached.[62] Secondly, the Act provides for publication of disclosures in subsequent proceedings where an offence has been alleged in relation to the jury's activities in the original proceedings.[63] These provisions have been widely criticised for not having exempted academic research into the workings of juries.

---

[57] *R. v. Westminster City Council, ex p. Castelli and Tristan-Garcia, The Times*, August 14, 1995.
[58] *R. v. Arundel Justices, ex p. Westminster Press* [1985] 1 W.L.R. 708.
[59] *R. v. Horsham Justices, ex p. Farquharson* [1982] Q.B. 762.
[60] Contempt of Court Act 1981, s.8(1).
[61] *Attorney-General v. Associated Newspapers Ltd* [1994] 2 A.C. 238.
[62] Contempt of Court Act 1981, s.8(2)(a); *R. v. Young* [1995] Q.B. 324.
[63] Contempt of Court Act 1981, s.8(2)(b).

(d) Tape recordings

It is a contempt to use a tape recorder in court or publish such recordings **4-17** without the court's permission.[64] If the court's consent is obtained, it is also a contempt to use the recording in any way other than that to which the court has consented.

(5) CHALLENGES TO ORDERS MADE UNDER THE CONTEMPT OF COURT ACT 1981

Journalists and media organisations have no right under the Contempt of **4-18** Court Act to oppose the making of a banning or postponement order. This has led to criticism that the courts are too concerned to protect defendants and do not give adequate weight to free speech. This may change with the introduction of the Human Rights Act 1998.

In spite of the lack of formal standing under the Act, the courts do have a discretion to hear representations from the media because it represents the public interest in having a particular case reported.[65] The higher courts have also emphasised the importance of open justice wherever possible.[66]

A Practice Direction issued by the Lord Chief Justice in 1982 also attempted to address the media's concerns about the making of contempt orders by directing that an order should be recorded in writing and state:

• the precise scope of the order

• the specific purpose for which the order was made; and

• the time at which it will cease to have effect.[67]

Orders should also be reduced to writing as soon as possible after they are made, and notified by the court to the public.[68] For example, it has been suggested that the court should fax the details of orders to the Press Association which would then hold them for the reference of other media outlets.[69] If a reporter is in any doubt about the validity of an order, he should find out under what section of the Act it has been made and report his concerns to his editor. The Practice Direction stated that the press should normally be given notice of the order and that court staff should be prepared to answer questions about the case.[70]

---

[64] Contempt of Court Act 1981, s.9. See also the Practice Direction on Tape Recorders (1981) 1 W.L.R. 1526.
[65] *R. v. Clerkenwell Metropolitan Stipendiary Magistrates, ex p. Telegraph plc* [1993] 2 W.L.R. 233.
[66] *Attorney-General v. Leveller Magazine* [1979] A.C. 440.
[67] Practice Direction (Contempt of Court Act: Reports of Proceedings: Postponement Orders) [1983] 1 All E.R. 64.
[68] *Re Central Independent Television plc* [1991] 1 All E.R. 347.
[69] *Attorney-General v. Guardian Newspapers* [1992] 1 W.L.R. 874.
[70] Court Business Rules also suggest prominent display of the notice and insertion into the Daily List.

Apart from receiving this general information, the media may intervene using one of the following routes:

- if the order has not yet been made, the court may be willing to make a limited order and give the media time (perhaps a day or two) to prepare legal representation and arguments against the making of a full order. Alternatively, the matter might be raised at an earlier stage: during a preliminary hearing or when the court is giving directions for the management of the case leading up to trial[71];

- it may make an informal request (orally in court, or by writing to the court or clerk) for the court to state under which section of the Act the order was made, or that the court reconsider its decision;

- it may request that the court exercise its discretion to hear formal representations from the media organisation's solicitor or counsel as to why the order should be revoked or varied;

- if the disputed order was made by a magistrates' court and an informal approach has failed, a media organisation may consider initiating a judicial review by applying to the Divisional Court of the Queen's Bench Division of the High Court. This option may be costly, as it will generally involve instructing counsel;

- if the disputed order was made by a Crown Court judge, leave to appeal may be given by the Court of Appeal under section 159 of the Criminal Justice Act 1988. In addition to appeals against orders in the context of the Contempt of Court Act, the section allows aggrieved persons to appeal against orders restricting admission to or reporting of proceedings.[72] This route will also be expensive and, even if the appeal is successful, the media organisation will not be awarded its costs. In addition, the trial may be over before the appeal is concluded: although the Court of Appeal has the power to halt the trial temporarily and to confirm, reverse or vary the order made, the trial will not be stayed until the appeal is decided.

(6) PENALTIES

4-19   If a journalist or publisher is found guilty of contempt of court, the penalties can be severe. A publisher can be fined an unlimited amount and will usually have to bear the prosecution's costs. Under the Act, individuals can be sentenced to up to two years' imprisonment.[73] An appeal lies to the House of Lords, but permission must first be obtained from the Divisional Court or the House of Lords.[74]

---

[71] *R. v. Beck, ex p. Daily Telegraph plc* [1993] 2 All E.R. 177.
[72] This is referred to at 3(2) below in the context of orders made under Children and Young Persons Act 1933, s.39.
[73] Contempt of Court Act 1981, s.14(1).
[74] Administration of Justice Act 1960, s.12.

3. OTHER REPORTING RESTRICTIONS

(1) CRIMINAL CASES: PROVISIONS OF GENERAL APPLICATION

(a) Magistrates' Courts: preliminary hearings

Criminal offences are determined by either magistrates' or Crown Courts, **4-20**
though virtually all criminal cases start in the magistrates' court. There are two
types of criminal offences that may be dealt with by the Crown Court:
indictable-only offences (which must be tried there) and either-way offences
(which may be tried in the Crown Court or a magistrates' court).

Whether an either-way offence is heard by a magistrates' court or a Crown
Court depends on the plea the defendant enters when he is first brought before
the magistrates. If he pleads not guilty or enters no plea, the magistrate must
decide whether the case should be tried in the Crown Court or summarily.[75]
Even if the magistrate believes it should be tried summarily, the accused may
exercise his right to trial by jury. If he does, his case will be tried by a Crown
Court. If the accused pleads not guilty to the charge, he will be tried by the
magistrate.[76]

Before cases can be transferred to the Crown Court, a magistrates' court
composed of examining justices must commit the accused for trial following
preliminary proceedings called a committal. Restrictions are imposed on
reporting of the committal (and any remand hearings prior to it) in order that
the trial jury is not subsequently prejudiced by prosecution material which
emerges from the those hearings. The media are, therefore, restricted to reporting only the following information:

(i)   the identity of the court and names of the examining justices;

(ii)   the names, addresses and occupations of the parties and witnesses and
the ages of the accused and witnesses;

(iii) the offence or offences, or a summary of them, with which the accused
is or are charged;

(iv) the names of the legal representatives engaged in the proceedings;

(v)   any decision of the court to commit the accused or any of the accused
for trial, and any decision of the court on the disposal of the case of any
accused not committed;

(vi) where the court commits the accused or any of the accused for trial, the
charge or charges, or a summary of them, on which he is committed and
the court to which he is committed;

(vii) where the committal proceedings are adjourned, the date and place to
which they are adjourned;

---

[75] Magistrates' Courts Act 1980, s.19.
[76] See Magistrates' Courts Act 1980, s.17A as amended by Criminal Procedure and Investigations
Act 1996.

(viii) any arrangements as to bail on committal or adjournment;

(ix) whether legal aid was granted to the accused or any of the accused.[77]

The penalty for breaching these restrictions is a fine, which may be imposed on the proprietor, editor or publisher of a newspaper or periodical, the publisher of any other written report and, in the case of the inclusion of a report or picture in a programme service, any body corporate which provides the service and any person having functions in relation to the programme corresponding to those of an editor of a newspaper.[78] No prosecution can be brought for breach of these restrictions without the consent of the Attorney-General.

As an example of what can go wrong, the editor and owners of *The Citizen* in Gloucester were each fined £4,500 in 1996 following the newspaper's report of Fred West's committal: the report accurately reported the committal, but referred to West having admitted killing his daughter.

There are certain exceptions to the above restrictions, where the media is free to report any details aired during the committal. They are:

• if the magistrate decides not to commit the accused for trial and dismisses the charges (for example, because there is insufficient evidence);

• if the case is tried summarily, rather than in the Crown Court;

• if the accused requests that reporting restrictions be lifted (if there is more than one accused and they do not all agree that reporting restrictions should be lifted, the court may decide to lift them if it is in the interests of justice)[79]; or

• where the Crown Court trial of the accused or the last person charged with him has been concluded.

The Crime and Disorder Act 1998 introduced a new "transfer for trial" procedure for indictable-only offences to replace committals: if a person is charged with such an offence, the magistrate must send him to be tried by a Crown Court.[80] This provision, though not yet in force nationwide, is expected to have come into effect by the end of 2000.

Under the new procedure, although there is no committal hearing, the accused may apply for the charge to be dismissed on the basis that there is insufficient evidence for a jury to convict him.[81] Only the information listed below may be reported in respect of applications for dismissal of indictable-only offences:

---

[77] Magistrates' Courts Act 1980, s.8(4).

[78] Magistrates' Courts Act 1980, s.8(5). The reporter responsible for the story will not be liable under the Act.

[79] Even if reporting restrictions under the Magistrates' Court Act are lifted, a reporter should be careful not to report information which would be in contempt of court by caused a substantial risk of serious prejudice to the trial. The court also retains the power to make an order under Contempt of Court Act, s.4(2) to postpone reporting.

[80] Crime and Disorder Act 1998, s.51.

[81] Crime and Disorder Act 1998, Sched. 3, para. 2.

(i)   the identity of the court and the name of the judge;

(ii)   the names, ages, home addresses and occupations of the accused and witnesses;

(iii)   the offence or offences, or a summary of them, with which the accused is or are charged;

(iv)   the names of counsel and solicitors engaged in the proceedings;

(v)   where proceedings are adjourned, the date and place to which they are adjourned;

(vi)   the arrangements as to bail;

(vii)   whether legal aid was granted to the accused or any of the accused.[82]

Liability for breach of the restrictions in respect of applications for dismissal attaches to the same personnel as for breaches of the committal restrictions.[83]

The judge hearing the application for dismissal may lift the restrictions. However, if there is more than one defendant and they do not all agree to the lifting of the restrictions, the judge may only do so if it is in the interest of justice to do so. If the application succeeds, the media is not subject to the reporting restrictions above. However, if the application fails, it cannot be reported until the end of the trial of the defendant or the last person charged with him.

(b) Crown Courts

Reporting restrictions can arise in the Crown Court in a number of ways. The **4-21** key provisions are considered in this section.[84]

Pre-trial hearings

Rulings at pre-trial hearings (together with orders for variation and discharge **4-22** of such rulings) may not be reported until the conclusion of the trial of all of the defendants concerned.[85] The court may in its discretion lift the restrictions in whole or part if it considers that it is in the interests of justice to do so.

Preparatory hearings

Automatic reporting restrictions also apply in respect of preparatory hearings **4-23** involving serious fraud[86] or where the case is a long or complex one.[87]

---

[82] Crime and Disorder Act 1998, Sched. 3, para. 3(8).

[83] Crime and Disorder Act 1998, Sched. 3, para. 3(10).

[84] A useful summary of the law can be found in the Judicial Studies Board paper, "Reporting Restrictions in the Crown Court" (2000) and in Archbold 2000 at 20-7 to 20-10 and 20-266–270.

[85] ss. 41 and 42 of the Criminal Procedure and Investigations Act 1996.

[86] Criminal Justice Act 1987, s.11.

[87] Criminal Procedure and Investigations Act 1996, ss.37 and 38.

In relation to these hearings, any report of proceedings must be limited to the following:

- the identity of the court and the name of the judge;

- the names, ages, home addresses and occupations of the accused and the witnesses;

- any relevant business information;[88]

- the offence or offences, or a summary of them, with which the accused is or are charged;

- the names of counsel and solicitors in the proceedings;

- where the proceedings are adjourned, the date and place to which they are adjourned;

- any arrangements as to bail;

- whether legal aid was granted to the accused or any of the accused.[89]

The restrictions must be lifted if the defendant applies for them to be lifted. If there is more than one defendant and they do not all agree that the restrictions should be lifted, the court may lift the restrictions if it dermines that it is in the interests of justice to do so. Otherwise, the restrictions last until the defendant's application to dismiss is successful, or until the end of the defendant's trial (or where others have been charged with the defendant, until the last person's application is successful or his trial ends).

Dismissal proceedings where there has been no committal

4-24   Similar restrictions to those for preparatory hearings apply to unsuccessful applications for dismissal in cases for trial where there has been no committal proceeding. These include serious fraud cases,[90] sexual offences involving violence or cruelty against children,[91] and indictable only cases automatically sent for trial.[92]

Postponing reports of derogatory assertions made in pleas in mitigation

4-25   The Crown Court may postpone reporting of derogatory assertions about a named or identifiable person which have been newly made in mitigation and sentencing appeals and reviews.[93] It may do so if the assertions are believed on

---

[88] The categories of information regarded as "relevant business information" are outlined in Criminal Justice Act 1987, s.11(14). They include the name and address of any business which the accused was carrying on, whether on his own account, in partnership or as a director of a company.
[89] Criminal Justice Act 1987, s.11(12).
[90] Criminal Justice Act 1987, s.11
[91] Criminal Justice Act 1991, s.53 and Sched. 6, para. 6.
[92] Crime and Disorder Act 1998, Sched. 3, para. 3.
[93] Criminal Procedure and Investigations Act 1996, s.58.

substantial grounds to be false or irrelevant and it is considering them following conviction or on appeal against a sentence imposed by a Magistrates' Court.

(c) Protecting adult witnesses

There are a number of provisions in the Youth Justice and Criminal Evidence   **4-26**
1998 which aim to protect witnesses in criminal cases. The key provisions are
set out below. However, they will only come into force by order of the
Secretary of State[94] and no such order had been made at the time of writing.

*Power to restrict reports about adult witnesses in criminal proceedings (section
46)*

A party to criminal proceedings may apply to the court to give a reporting   **4-27**
direction in relation to a witness in the proceedings (other than the accused)
who is 18 or over.

    A direction may be made if it would improve the quality of the evidence of
the witness or his co-operation.

    A direction, if granted, will be to the effect that no matter relating to the
witness shall during his lifetime be included in any publication if it is likely to
lead members of the public to identify him as being a witness in the proceedings.[95]

*Restrictions on reporting special measures directions and directions prohibiting
cross-examination (section 47)*

The courts are given power in Part II of the Act to provide special measures   **4-28**
to witnesses in criminal proceedings. They may do so on the grounds that they
are under 17, suffer from a physical or mental disability, or by reason of fear
or distress on the part of the witness in connection with testifying.[96]

    The courts have also been given power to direct that a defendant may not
cross-examine a witness in person.[97]

    If a direction has been made under either power, that fact may not be published nor may the details of any application for such a direction.[98] The court
has a discretion, however, to lift or vary the effect of this provision.[99]

Penalties

Section 49 deals with the offences and penalties to be applied to breaches of   **4-29**
sections 46 and 47. A court may impose a fine on conviction.[1] Offences under

---

[94] s.68(3) of the Act.
[95] *ibid.*, s.46(7). The court may in certain circumstances dispense with the restrictions imposed by
a reporting direction: s.47(9).
[96] *ibid.*, ss.17–19.
[97] *ibid.*, s.36.
[98] *ibid.*, s.47(1) and (2).
[99] *ibid.*, s.47(3).
[1] *ibid.*, s.47(5).

section 47 may only be instituted with the consent of the Attorney-General.[2] Section 50 makes provisions for a number of defences that may be available to the media.[3]

(2) SEXUAL OFFENCES

4-30   There are a number of provisions protecting those involved in sexual offences. It should be noted however that, with the restrictions relating to children to be considered at (3) below, the law is in a state of flux because of the Youth Justice and Criminal Evidence Act 1999. This will make significant changes to the current position[4] but the changes are not effective until an order is made by the Secretary of State. At the time of writing no such orders had been made.

(a) Provisions dealing with anonymity

4-31   Reporting restrictions in respect of sexual offences apply to rape offences[5] and a large number of other sexual offences under the Sexual Offences (Amendment) Act 1992.[6] The legislation provides that there is an automatic ban on identifying the complainant during his or her lifetime.[7] There is no similar anonymity for the accused under the legislation, unless his identification would necessarily lead to the identification of the complainant, and the courts have no power to make such an order.

The restrictions take two forms, according to the stage which the case has reached.

After an allegation of rape is made

4-32   Once it has been alleged that a rape offence or offence under the 1992 Act has been committed against a person, no report should be published during that person's lifetime which includes the person's name or address or any still or moving picture of that person if it is likely to lead to the identification of that person as the alleged victim of such an offence.[8]

---

[2] *ibid.*, s.49(6).
[3] See (2)(c) above.
[4] Sched. 2 provides for (amongst other things) the abolition of ss.4 and 5 of the Sexual Offences (Amendment) Act 1976 and amendments to ss.1 to 7 of the Sexual Offences (Amendment) Act 1992. Once implemented, the new law will be contained primarily in the amended 1992 Act.
[5] These are defined in the Sexual Offences (Amendment) Act 1976 as: rape; attempted rape; aiding, abetting, counselling or procuring rape or attempted rape; incitement to rape; conspiracy to rape; burglary with intent to rape.
[6] See Sexual Offences Act 1956, ss.2–16; Mental Health Act 1959, s.128; Indecency with Children Act 1960, s.1; Criminal Law Act 1977, s.54; an attempt to commit the preceding offences: Sexual Offences (Amendment) Act 1992, s.2. Restrictions also apply to any offence involving a conspiracy or incitement to commit the preceding offences: Criminal Justice and Public Order Act 1994, Sched. 9.
[7] Rape includes male rape and rape by a man of his wife: Criminal Justice and Public Order Act 1994, s.142.
[8] Sexual Offences (Amendment) Act 1976, s.4(1); Sexual Offences (Amendment) Act 1992, s.1(1).

These limited restrictions allow, for example, the police to publicise certain other details regarding the alleged victim which might assist in its investigation of the complaint.

After a person has been accused of committing a rape

After a person has been accused of a rape offence or an offence under the 1992 **4-33** Act, nothing should be published during the complainant's lifetime which would be likely to lead to that person being identified as the complainant.

A person is "accused" of an offence when:

- an information is laid alleging that he has committed the offence;

- he appears before a court charged with the offence;

- a court before which he is appearing commits him for trial on a new charge alleging the offence; or

- a bill of indictment charging him with the offence is preferred before a court.[9]

The restrictions stay in place for the lifetime of the complainant even if the complaint does not proceed any further than the making of the allegation or is withdrawn, or if the accused is not eventually tried for a rape offence or one of the 1992 Act offences.

However, anonymity relates to the complainant only in so far as it would allow people to identify that person as the alleged victim of one of the relevant offences; the restrictions would not apply if a story was about the complainant in an unrelated situation. Nor would the restrictions be valid in respect of any criminal proceedings brought against the complainant. The restrictions will, however, continue to apply for the purposes of a civil trial to which the victim is a party.

(b) Power of court to vary restrictions

The trial judge or any appeal court has a discretionary power to order the **4-34** lifting of reporting restrictions before trial if the accused, or other person against whom the complainant is expected to give evidence, applies to the court for a dispensation and satisfies the judge that:

- it is required for the purpose of inducing persons who are likely to be needed as witnesses at the trial to come forward; and

- that the conduct of the applicant's defence is likely to be substantially prejudiced if the direction is not given.[10]

---

[9] Sexual Offences (Amendment) Act 1976, s.4(6); Sexual Offences (Amendment) Act 1992, s.6(3).
[10] Offences (Amendment) Act 1976, s.4(2); Sexual Offences (Amendment) Act 1992, s.3.

A dispensation may also be granted at trial if the effect of the reporting restrictions is shown to:

- impose a substantial and unreasonable restriction upon the reporting of the trial; and

- it is in the public interest to remove or relax the restriction.[11]

(c) Defences

4-35 It is a defence to having breached the reporting restrictions in respect of sexual offences that:

- at the time of the alleged breach, the party was not aware, and neither suspected nor had reason to suspect, that the publication or programme in question included the matter in question[12]; or

- the appearance of the publication or programme in question was one in respect of which the complainant had given written consent.[13]

Written consent must be given for each publication, and such consent will not be a defence if it is proved that any person interfered unreasonably with the peace or comfort of the person giving consent with the intention of obtaining it.[14]

(d) Penalties

4-36 The penalty for breaching these restrictions is a fine, which may be imposed on the proprietor, editor or publisher of a newspaper or periodical, the publisher of any other written report and, in the case of the inclusion of a report or picture in a programme service, any body corporate which provides the service and any person having functions in relation to the programme corresponding to those of an editor of a newspaper.[15]

Where a breach on the part of a body corporate is proved to have been committed with the consent or connivance of, or to be attributable to any neglect on the part of, a director, manager, secretary or other similar officer of the body corporate, or person purporting to act in such a capacity, the officer as well as the body corporate is liable for the offence.[16]

---

[11] Sexual Offences (Amendment) Act 1976, s.4(3); Sexual Offences (Amendment) Act 1992, s.3(2).

[12] Sexual Offences (Amendment) Act 1976, s.5(5); Sexual Offences (Amendment) Act 1992, s.5(5).

[13] Sexual Offences (Amendment) Act 1976, s.4(5A); Sexual Offences (Amendment) Act 1992, s.5(2).

[14] Sexual Offences (Amendment) Act 1976, s.4(5B); Sexual Offences (Amendment) Act 1992, s.5(3).

[15] Sexual Offences (Amendment) Act 1976, s.4(5); Sexual Offences (Amendment) Act 1992, s.5.

[16] Sexual Offences (Amendment) Act 1976, s.5(4); Sexual Offences (Amendment) Act 1992, s.5(6).

No prosecution can be brought for breach of these restrictions without the consent of the Attorney-General.

(3) CHILDREN

This area of law is somewhat in flux. The Youth Justice and Criminal   **4-37**
Evidence Act 1999 will make significant changes but the provisions of relevance to this text will only become effective once the Secretary of State has made orders bringing them into force. At the time of writing no such orders had been made.

The approach taken in this section is to describe (at (a) and (b)) the law as it currently affects reporting of youth and adult courts referring, where appropriate, to the direct impact of the new law. There is an examination at (c) of some further provisions which will be implemented by the 1999 Act. The section concludes at (d) by referring to a number of issues which arise in family proceedings.

(a) In youth courts

Young people under 18 at the time an offence was committed are tried, not in   **4-38**
the regular adult courts, but in youth courts. According to the law, a young person is one aged between 14 and 18.[17] The general public are excluded from youth court hearings[18]; the exceptions are court officers, the parties and their witnesses and legal representatives, reporters from newspapers and news agencies, and others authorised by the court to be present.[19]

Even though journalists may be present, they must not publish:

- any report which reveals the name, address, or school of any child or young person concerned in the proceedings or includes any particulars likely to lead to the identification of any child or young person concerned in the proceedings; or

- any picture of any child or young person concerned in the proceedings.

This obligation derives from section 49 of the Children and Young Persons Act 1933.[20] For these purposes a child or young person is "concerned" in the proceedings if he is a person against or in respect of whom the proceedings are taken, or a witness in the proceedings.[21]

Particular note should be taken of the words "or any particulars likely to lead to the identification of a child or young person" because it may not be

---

[17] Children and Young Persons Act 1933, s.107(1) as amended by Criminal Justice Act 1991.
[18] The full list of proceedings covered by this provision appears at s.49(2), *ibid.*
[19] Children and Young Persons Act 1933, s.47.
[20] Children and Young Persons Act 1933, s.49 as amended by Criminal Justice and Public Order Act 1994.
[21] *ibid.*, s.49(4).

sufficient merely to remove references to a child's or young person's name, address or school: including other details which apply only to a small number of people may allow readers to readily identify the child or young person regardless. The restrictions apply even if the main purpose of the story is not a report of youth court proceedings. For example, a reference to a child or young person having been the subject of proceedings in the youth court may be enough to incur liability under the Act.

The restrictions do not prevent the identification of adults involved in youth court proceedings, as long as that reference does not provide particulars which identify a child or young person. The restrictions continue to apply if the defendant appeals from the youth court to the Crown Court or High Court, or if an application is heard for the varying or revocation of suspension orders made in the youth court.

Liability for breach of youth court reporting restrictions attaches to the same parties responsible for breaches of the reporting restrictions in committal proceedings (see 1 above).

A youth court may dispense with the above reporting restrictions if it is satisfied that:

(a) it is appropriate to do so for the purpose of avoiding injustice to a child or young person; or

(b) as respects a child or young person who is unlawfully at large and is charged with or has been convicted of a violent offence, a sexual offence,[22] or an offence punishable in the case of a person aged 21 or over with imprisonment for 14 years or more, it is necessary to dispense with them to apprehend him, bring him before a court, or return him to the place in which he was in custody.[23]

A youth court also has the power to dispense with any or all of the above restrictions on the conviction of an offender, if it is satisfied that it would be in the public interest and if the proceedings before it are related to:

• the prosecution or conviction of the offender;

• the manner in which he, or his parent or guardian, should be dealt with in respect of the offence;

• the enforcement, amendment, variation, revocation or discharge of any order made in respect of the offence;

• where an attendance centre order is made in respect of the offence, the enforcement of any rules made under section 16(3) of the Criminal Justice Act 1982; or

---

[22] "Violent offence" and "sexual offence" are defined as in Criminal Justice Act 1991, s.31(1).
[23] *ibid.*, Ground (b) will only apply on an application by the Director of Public Prosecutions, s.49(5)

- where a secure training order is made, the enforcement of any requirements imposed under section 3(7) of the Criminal Justice and Public
Order Act 1994.[24]

Before ruling, the court must hear the parties to the proceedings as to whether
they wish the restrictions to remain in place after conviction or not.[25]

An application for a waiver of the restrictions imposed under the Children
and Young Persons Act 1933 may be made by the media, and a number of
such applications have succeeded in recent times. Home Office guidance suggests that a waiver may be justified in the case of persistent or serious offenders
affecting large numbers of the public, or where it is thought that publicity
would help prevent further offending. A waiver would be less likely in cases
where there was a risk that the young person or his family would be attacked
or harassed, where the young person or victim was particularly vulnerable, or
where there was little chance of repeat offending.

It should be noted that paragraph 3 of Schedule 2 to the Youth Justice and
Criminal Evidence Act 1999 anticipates changes to the provisions of section
49. These changes reflect, in broad terms, the approach anticipated at (c)
below. For example, the amended section 49(1) will state:

> "No matter relating to any child or young person concerned in proceed-
> ings to which this section applies shall while he is under the age of 18 be
> included in any publication if it is likely to lead members of the public to
> identify him as someone concerned in the proceedings."

As previously stated, these changes have not yet come into effect.

(b) In adult courts

Unlike youth courts, there is no automatic ban on the identification of children and young people involved in proceedings in adult courts. However,
section 39 of the Children and Young Persons Act 1933 provides that, in relation to any proceedings in any court, the court may impose an order that the
media shall not publish:

4-39

- any report that reveals the name, address, or school, or any particulars
calculated to lead to the identification of any child or young person concerned in the proceedings, either as being the person by or against or in
respect of whom the proceedings are taken, or as being a witness
therein;

- any picture of any child or young person concerned in the proceedings.

---

[24] Children and Young Persons Act 1933, s.49(4A).
[25] *ibid.*, s.49(4B).

These restrictions currently apply to both criminal and civil proceedings.[26] Although section 39 refers to the restrictions applying to "any proceedings", the provision is intended to refer only to the proceedings in the court making the order.[27] This means that an order made, for example, in the magistrates' court, does not cover the case if it is transferred to the Crown Court. However, the Crown Court may make a section 39 order of its own.

The words "lead to" in section 39 suggest that the provision covers the situation where the information in the report, combined with information previously in the public domain, enables the reader to identify the child or young person. This is known as "jigsaw identification". It may occur, for example, in a child abuse case involving a father and his child where one news report names the defendant but does not state his relationship to the child, while another news report does not name the defendant but contains details of the offence. Anyone reading both reports is likely to be able to identify the child by putting together the "jigsaw pieces".[28]

In 1993 most newspapers and broadcasters adopted common rules to prevent the problem arising. The general approach is that the media may identify the adult but will not identify the child. The word "incest" will not be used where a child victim might be identified.[29]

Although the courts often make a "blanket" section 39 order where a child or young person is involved in a case, setting out the wording above to cover any means of identifying him, there are limitations on the making of such orders. It has been held that the mere fact that the proceedings concern a child or young person does not necessarily make a section 39 order appropriate: there must be a good reason for the order.[30] In making an order, it has been accepted by the courts that the public have an interest in knowing the identity of those who have committed crimes, particularly those which are "serious and detestable".[31] The courts should give consideration to the seriousness of the crime, whether the identification of the offender would act as a deterrent to others, the offender's age, and whether identification would be likely to damage the offender before he reached adulthood.[32]

Where the courts impose section 39 orders unreasonably, the media can challenge them in the same way as challenges can be made to postponement or banning orders.[33]

The courts are not permitted to make a section 39 order in respect of an

---

[26] Sched. 2, para. 2 to the Youth Justice and Criminal Evidence Act 1999 will amend this provision so that in future it will only apply to civil proceedings. Reports of criminal proceedings (other than in a youth court) would then be dealt with in accordance with the regime described in (c) below. However, the provision will only become effective after an order of the Secretary of State. No such order had been made at the time of writing.

[27] *R. v. Lee* [1993] 1 W.L.R. 103.

[28] The same problem can arise in sexual offences cases not involving children: see (3) below.

[29] See Press Complaints Commission Code of Practice, cl. 7; Chap. 37 at 4.4, BBC Producers' Guidelines; Independent Television Commission Programme Code, cl. 2.7; Radio Authority Programme Code, cl. 4.7.

[30] *R. v. Lee* [1993] 1 W.L.R. 103.

[31] *R. v. Central Criminal Court, ex p. Godwin and Crook* [1995] 1 All E.R. 537.

[32] *R. v. Inner London Crown Court, ex p. Barnes (Anthony)*, *The Times*, August 7, 1995.

[33] See 5 above. This includes the use of the provision at s.159 of the Criminal Justice Act 1988.

adult defendant on the grounds that that to do so would identify a child or young person.[34] It has also been accepted by the courts that section 39 should not be used to protect the identity of a dead child.[35] The courts have rejected applications for section 39 orders in respect of very young children unlikely to be affected in the long term by resulting publicity, and in cases where it was ascertained that the real reason for the application was to protect the adult's identity. It may also be unreasonable for courts to grant section 39 orders in respect of young people whose identity has already been made public as a consequence of previous news coverage.

The guidelines which should be followed by courts in making section 39 orders are as follows:

- the terms of the order should be clear and ascertainable by those affected by it;

- the identity of the child to whom the order relates should be clear;

- the order should be written up as soon as it is made orally;

- copies of the order should be made available in the court office for representatives of the press to inspect; and

- the order should be noted in the daily list to alert press who were not present when it was made to its existence.[36]

(c) Additional provisions in the Youth Justice and Criminal Evidence Act 1999

This legislation makes provision for new reporting restrictions in relation to children and young people. As stated earlier these have not yet come into force. This section identifies the key provisions not dealt with at (a) and (b).   **4-40**

Restrictions on reporting alleged offences before proceedings

No matter relating to any person involved in an alleged criminal offence[37] shall, while he is under the age of 18, be included in any publication if it is likely to lead members of the public to identify him as a person involved in the offence.[38] A person is "involved" in the offence if he is the person by whom the offence is alleged to have been committed.   **4-41**

The restrictions may be extended by statutory instrument to cover a person against or in respect of whom the offence is alleged to have been committed,

---

[34] *R. v. Southwark Crown Court, ex p. Godwin* [1992] Q.B. 190.
[35] See, *Ex p. Crook* [1995] 1 W.L.R. 139.
[36] Glidewell L.J. in *R. v. Central Criminal Court, ex p. Godwin and Crook* [1995] 1 All E.R. 537.
[37] Or an alleged civil offence committed by someone subject to service law.
[38] Youth Justice and Criminal Evidence Act 1999, ss.44(1) and (2).

or a person who is alleged to have been a witness to the commission of the offence.[39]

Matters likely to lead to the identification of a person are stated to include:

- his name and address;

- the identity of any school or educational establishment attended by him;

- the identity of any place of work; and

- any still or moving picture of him.[40]

The Act provides for the appropriate criminal court to dispense with the restrictions if it is satisfied that it is in the interests of justice to do so, but it should take into account the young person's welfare.[41] These restrictions cease to apply in any event once there are proceedings in a court in respect of the offence.

Restrictions on reporting criminal proceedings

4-42   Section 45 of the 1999 Act, when implemented, will impose restrictions on reporting criminal proceedings involving persons under 18. The section will not affect the law relating to reports of youth courts: this would still be governed by section 49 of the Children and Young Persons Act 1933, albeit subject to possible amendments under the 1999 Act as described at (a) above. Further the section will only apply to criminal proceedings: as described at (b) above, section 39 would continue to operate for civil proceedings only.

Under section 45, a court may direct that no matter relating to any person concerned in the proceedings shall while he is under the age of 18 be included in any publication if it is likely to lead members of the public to identify him as a person concerned in the proceedings.[42] This provision applies to a person against or in respect of whom the proceedings are taken, or a witness in the proceedings.[43] The matters which are likely to identify a young person are set out in section 45(8) and include the same as are contained in section 44(6).

The court may dispense with the restrictions either (a) in the interests of justice, or (b) if their effect is to impose a substantial and unreasonable restriction on the reporting of the proceedings and it is in the public interest to remove or relax that restriction.[44] In either case the court must have regard to the welfare of the person concerned.[45]

---

[39] *ibid.*, s.44(4) This sub-section does not affect the anonymity of the victims of certain sexual offences under Sexual Offences (Amendment) Act 1992, s.1.

[40] *ibid.*, s.44(6).

[41] *ibid.*, s.44(7). There is a right of appeal from a magistrates' court decision to the Crown Court.

[42] *ibid.*, s.45(3).

[43] *ibid.*, s.45(7). It appears that, as under current legislation, there will be no power to make an order to prevent identification of a deceased child (see Judicial Studies Board paper at 4.1(i)(b).

[44] ss.45(4) and (5). The dispensation under (b) is not available only because proceedings have been determined or abandoned.

[45] *ibid.*, s.45(6).

The Act provides that, in deciding whether something is in the public interest, the court must have regard to the following factors:

(i) the interest in the open reporting of crime, the open reporting of matters relating to human health or safety, and the prevention and exposure of miscarriages of justice;

(ii) the welfare of any person in relation to whom the relevant restrictions imposed by or under this chapter apply or would apply; and

(iii) any views expressed by an appropriate person[46] on behalf of a person within (ii) above who is under the age of 16 ("the protected person"), or by a person within (ii) who has attained that age.[47]

Penalties for breach of sections 44 and 45

Breach of these reporting restrictions is a summary offence, though prosecution requires the consent of the Attorney-General. Liability attaches to the same parties responsible for breaches of the reporting restrictions in committal proceedings (see 3(1) above). However, where a breach on the part of a body corporate is proved to have been committed with the consent or connivance of, or to be attributable to any neglect on the part of an officer,[48] the officer as well as the body corporate is liable for the offence.[49]   **4-43**

There are several defences to offences under the Act. For example, it is a defence if it is proved that the parties liable above were not aware, and neither suspected not had reason to suspect, at the time of the alleged offence that the publication included the matter or report in question.[50] Conviction can lead to the imposition of a fine.[51]

(d) Family proceedings

These are heard in the magistrates' court, the county court and the Family Division of the High Court.   **4-44**

In relation to the magistrates' court, the general public is excluded from family proceedings involving children. However, newspaper or news agency reporters are permitted to attend them,[52] unless they are adoption proceedings or the court exercises the right to hear proceedings in private to protect the child's privacy.[53]

---

[46] An "appropriate person" is (in England, Wales and Northern Ireland) a person who is a parent or guardian of the protected person: Youth Justice and Criminal Evidence Act 1999, s.52(3).

[47] Youth Justice and Criminal Evidence Act 1999, s.52(2).

[48] An "officer" means a director, manager, secretary or other similar officer of the body, or a person purporting to act in any such capacity: Youth Justice and Criminal Evidence Act 1999, s.51(2).

[49] *ibid.*, s.51.

[50] *ibid.*, s.50(1). There are other defences in s.50, including a defence that the witness (if an adult) consented.

[51] *ibid.*, s.49(5).

[52] Magistrates Courts Act 1980, s.69.

[53] Magistrates Courts Act 1980, s.144.

In fact a wide variety of hearings relating to family cases involving children do take place in private, *i.e.* in chambers or *in camera*. Although the publication of information relating to proceedings before any court sitting in private shall not of itself be contempt of court, it is contempt to publish such information if the proceedings relate to minors or are brought under the Children Act 1989.[54]

Even if the media is permitted to report family proceedings, certain reporting restrictions will still apply. Reports of family proceedings in the magistrates' court may contain only the following material:

- the names, addresses and occupations of parties and witnesses;

- the grounds of the application, and a concise statement of the charges, defences and counter-charges in support of which evidence has been given;

- submissions on any point of law arising in the course of the proceedings and the decision of the court on the submissions;

- the decision of the court, and any observations made by the court in giving it.[55]

However, these restrictions may be narrowed even further when children are involved. The Children Act 1989 provides that no report should contain material which is intended or likely to identify:

- any child as being involved in proceedings before a magistrates' court in which any power under the Children Act may be exercised by the court; or

- an address or school as being that of a child involved in any such proceedings.[56]

It is a defence under the Children Act for any publisher that he did not know and had no reason to suspect that that published material was intended or likely to identify the child. The court or the Lord Chancellor may dispense with the restrictions if he is satisfied that the welfare of the child requires it.

As has been observed elsewhere, the combined effect of the two statutes is such that it is "difficult for a meaningful story to be compiled".[57]

---

[54] Administration of Justice Act 1960, s.12.
[55] Magistrates Courts Act 1980, s.71.
[56] Children Act 1989, s.97.
[57] T. Welsh and W. Greenwood, *McNae's Essential Law for Journalists* (15th ed., 1999).

Chapter 5

Copyright, moral rights and rights in performance

1. INTRODUCTION

This chapter examines how the law can protect the fruits of creative endea- **5-01**
vour. It is a subject of particular interest to media organisations: the assets
created can be worth more than the bricks and mortar from which the
company operates. At the same time, media companies, working in a competitive environment, need to ensure that they do not infringe the rights of a third
party.

    The rights attaching to creative output are together known as intellectual
property. For our purposes, the key rights are copyright (which, in general
terms, protects the physical embodiment of a creative idea) and trade marks
and passing off (which, as shall be seen in Chapter 6, protect a company's
brand). This chapter will consider copyright and its lesser known cousins—
moral rights and rights in performance.[1]

2. WHEN IS A COPYRIGHT CREATED?

Copyright is the right to exclusive use of ideas, or intellectual property, as they **5-02**
are originally expressed by their author. That right stems both from the creative input of the person who uses their skill and time (whether that be to
produce books, scripts, music, drawings, films, computer programs or other
such work) and from the investment of those who commercially exploit the
work (through, for example, publication, broadcast, recording or distribution).

    Once a work has been created, it will automatically be protected by copy-
right. No formal steps, such as registration, are required to be taken.[2] The
crucial characteristic of copyright is that it safeguards the expression of ideas,

---

[1] Other types of intellectual property right, including patents and design rights, are usually of
less relevance to publishers.
[2] There is no obligation to use the © symbol, but it reminds third parties of an owner's rights. It
may also give rise to punitive damages claims in the United States.

not ideas or information in themselves. So there is no copyright in news and current affairs *per se*, although the original expression of a news story may be protected. Moreover, whether the work has any quality or merit in a creative sense is immaterial to the existence of copyright.[3]

To attract copyright protection, an article must fall into one of the categories of work set out in the Copyright, Designs and Patents Act 1988 ("the Act").[4] Although a work must fall within one of these categories, the categories are not mutually exclusive: in the sense that a single article may consist of several distinct copyright works.[5] The categories of work are set out below.

(1) ORIGINAL LITERARY, DRAMATIC, MUSICAL, OR ARTISTIC WORKS

These works must be "original". The meaning of 'original' in this context is that they must be the product of the author's skill and labour and be expressed in an original form, rather than necessarily contain new ideas.[6] For example, the fact that there is copyright in a specific photograph does not prevent another photographer taking a photograph of the same scene.[7] The example also illustrates the point that copyright is not an exclusive right: two photographers can take photographs of the same scene, and each will have copyright in his own photograph because he has used his own skill and labour to produce that photograph.

Whether sufficient skill and labour has been used in the production of the work is a question for the court to determine, having considered the facts of the case.[8] If there is originality in the selection, interpretation or arrangement of pre-existing material, copyright will exist in that derived work.[9] However, where there is no copyright in the pre-existing material itself, the court will have to determine whether the author has expended sufficient independent skill and labour for copyright protection to attach to his work.[10] There is copyright even in a work which infringes another's copyright, provided sufficient

---

[3] Save for works of artistic craftsmanship: see para. 5-07, below.

[4] Copyright, Designs and Patents Act (CDPA), s.1.

[5] For example, a music CD may consist of a sound recording, a literary work in the form of song lyrics, a musical work in the form of song compositions and an artistic work and typographical arrangement in the form of the album cover. There would be a separate copyright in the broadcast of any songs from the CD.

[6] See *Ladbroke (Football) Ltd v. William Hill (Football) Ltd* [1964] 1 W.L.R. 273; *University of London Press v. University Tutorial Group* [1916] 2 Ch. 601.

[7] *Creation Records Ltd v. News Group Newspapers Ltd* [1997] E.M.L.R. 444. Copyright in a specific photograph may be copied by a mechanical copying process. It may also be copied by recreating a photograph of a scene using features copied from the photograph, although this would be a matter of degree: see *Krisarts S.A. v. Briarfine Ltd* [1977] F.S.R. 557. See also *Antiquesportfolio.com plc v. Rodney Fitch & Co. Ltd*, Times Law Reports, July 21, 2000.

[8] *Biotrading & Financing v. Biohit* [1996] F.S.R. 393; [1998] F.S.R. 109, C.A.

[9] An example is a translation, which has a copyright separate to that of the copyright work it translates: see *Byrne v. Statist Co.* [1914] K.B. 622. Other examples of works which commonly include pre-existing material include directories, databases and compilations.

[10] See *Cala Homes (South) v. Alfred McAlpine Homes East Ltd* [1995] F.S.R. 818: this case examined whether an architect had employed sufficient skill and labour in creating a new design which incorporated features from pre-existing designs.

original skill and labour was expended by the infringer himself in preparing that work.

Literary work

The Act defines a literary work[11] as any work, other than a dramatic or musical work, which is written, spoken or sung. It includes a table or compilation, a computer program, preparatory material for a computer program and a data-base.   **5-03**

Literary works have been held to include sheets of election results,[12] foot-ball fixtures lists,[13] the rules of and a coupon for a football competition,[14] tele-vision programme listings,[15] a series of book-keeping forms,[16] and a trade catalogue.[17] A record of spoken words is also a literary work, so that copyright in a secretary's or reporter's notes of spoken words not previously recorded belongs to the speaker.[18]

The courts have denied copyright protection to certain literary works found to have been lacking in effort or originality, such as single words or titles,[19] advertising slogans,[20] and simple two-sentence instructions regarding the use of a product.[21]

Databases

Databases deserve special mention. A database is defined in section 3A(1) of the Act as "a collection of independent works, data or other materials which (a) are arranged in a systematic or methodical way, and (b) which are individ-ually accessible by electronic or other means".   **5-04**

As we have seen, they may be protected as a literary work. To be so pro-tected, however, the database must satisfy a particular threshold as regards originality; namely it will be original "if, and only if, by reason of the selec-tion or arrangement of the contents of the database the database constitutes the author's own intellectual creation".[22]

If the threshold has not been satisfied, the database may still be protected by a separate right known as the "database right". This will subsist "if there has been a substantial investment in obtaining, verifying or presenting the

---

[11] s.3(1) of the Act.
[12] *Press Association Ltd v. Northern and Midland Reporting Agency* [1905–10] Mac. C.C. 306.
[13] *Football League Ltd v. Littlewoods Pools Ltd* [1959] Ch. 637.
[14] *Ladbroke (Football) Ltd v. William Hill (Football) Ltd* [1964] 1 W.L.R. 273.
[15] *Independent Television Publications v. Time Out Ltd* [1984] E.R.S. 64.
[16] *Kalamazoo (Aus.) Pty Ltd v. Compact Business Systems Pty Ltd* [1990] 1 Qd. R. 231.
[17] *A-One Accessory Imports Pty Ltd v. Off Road Imports Pty Ltd* [1996] E.I.P.R. 11 D-321.
[18] *Donoghue v. Allied Newspapers Ltd* [1938] Ch. 106. See para. 5-34 relating to the use of such a record for the reporting of current events.
[19] *Exxon Corporation v. Exxon Insurance Consultants International Ltd* [1982] R.P.C. 69.
[20] *Sinanide v. La Maison Kosmeo* (1928) 139 L.T. 365.
[21] *Noah v. Shuba* [1991] F.S.R. 14: there was no copyright in the phrase "Follow clinic procedure for aftercare. If proper procedures are followed, no risk of viral infections can occur".
[22] *ibid.*, s.3A (2). s.3A was inserted by the Copyright and Rights in Databases Regulations 1997 (S.I. 1997 No. 3032).

contents of the database".[23] Unlike copyright, the right only subsists, effectively, where the maker is a European Union national or habitually lives in the European Union.[24] The other principal difference is that the database right expires 15 years from the end of the calendar years in which the making of the database was completed.[25] Literary works generally survive for 70 years from the end of the calendar year in which the author dies.[26]

Dramatic work

5-05   A dramatic work includes a work consisting of dance or mime,[27] as well as plays and screenplays. Such a work should be intended to be performed and the subject-matter must be precise and certain. A New Zealand decision illustrated that a game show format will not constitute a dramatic work if the elements of the programme as a whole are not capable of performance.[28] Similarly, there is no copyright in a live event, such as a football match.

A dramatic work must involve action. It has been held, for instance, that the assembling of a rock group with props to be photographed for the cover of an album was not a dramatic work because the necessary element of action was missing.[29]

In *Norowzian v. Arks Limited* (No. 2), the Court of Appeal found that a film can be a dramatic work within the meaning of the Act.[30] In that case, the claimant film director sued an advertising agency for passing off and copyright infringement in respect of a short film entitled *Joy*, which the claimant alleged had been copied in an advertisement named *Anticipation* made by the agency for Guinness. *Joy* featured a man dancing to African guitar music against a background of a canvas sheet, was filmed with the camera in a fixed position, and was edited using a technique known as "jump cutting". The effect of the "jump cutting" was that the man appeared to perform movements in the film which would not have been possible in reality.

The court held that the natural and ordinary meaning of "dramatic work" was a work of action, without or without words or music, which is capable of being performed before an audience. *Joy* was a dramatic work because it fell within this definition. However, in order for a film to constitute a recording of a dramatic work, the work so recorded must be, or be capable of being, physically performed. The Court of Appeal held that *Joy* failed this test because the "jump cutting" produced a work that could not be peformed by anyone. The benefit of the judgment for film directors was reduced by the Court's approach to the question of whether *Anticipation* had copied a substantial part of *Joy*. It was impossible for the Court to say whether such copying had

---

[23] reg. 13(1) of the Copyright and Rights in Databases Regulations 1997.
[24] For the precise criterion, see reg. 18, *ibid.*
[25] reg. 17(1), *ibid.*
[26] CPDA 1988, s.12(2). See 6 below.
[27] *ibid.*, s.3(1).
[28] *Green v. Broadcasting Corporation of New Zealand* [1989] R.P.C. 700.
[29] *Creation Records v. News Group Newspapers* [1997] E.M.L.R. 444.
[30] [2000] E.M.L.R. 67.

taken place because, although there was a striking similarity between the filming and editing styles and techniques used by the directors of the two films, there is no copyright in mere style or technique.

Musical work

A musical work means a work consisting of music, exclusive of any words or action intended to be sung, spoken or performed with the music.[31] Consequently, lyrics and choreography are literary and dramatic works respectively, but the sounds which accompany them are a musical work.   **5-06**

Artistic work

An artistic work means[32]:   **5-07**

(a) a graphic work,[33] photograph, sculpture or collage, irrespective of artistic quality,

(b) a work of architecture being a building or a model for a building, or

(c) a work of artistic craftsmanship.

To be considered a work of artistic craftsmanship, a work must possess both artistic quality and craftsmanship. "Artistic quality" means that the object has aesthetic appeal, which is an objective judgment made by the court.[34]

(2) SOUND RECORDINGS, FILMS, BROADCASTS AND CABLE PROGRAMMES[35]

These works are often referred to as "derivative" copyrights because they tend to be based on or contain underlying literary, dramatic, musical or artistic works.[36] Despite this, the works have a separate copyright.[37]   **5-08**

    A "sound recording" is a recording of sounds, or a recording of the whole

---

[31] s.3(1) of the Act.

[32] *ibid.*, s.4(1).

[33] A graphic work includes any painting, drawing, diagram, map, chart, plan, engraving, etching, lithograph, woodcut or similar work: *ibid.*, s.4(2).

[34] *George Hensher v. Restawhile* [1976] A.C. 64. See *Merlot v. Mothercare Plc* [1984] F.S.R. 358: a basic commodity (in this case, clothing for a mother and child) cannot be a work of artistic craftsmanship because it lacks aesthetic appeal. Purely utilitarian articles may be protected by design right under the Copyright, Designs and Patents Act 1988 or may be registrable under the Registered Designs Act 1949.

[35] See ss.5A–7 inclusive of the Act.

[36] Sporting events are not protected by copyright *per se*. Coverage of such events is governed by contractual arrangements which allow a broadcaster to enter the relevant sports ground. Once the event takes place, copyright will then arises in the film, sound recording, broadcast or cable transmission of it. Copyright and performers' rights may also arise in relation to any commentary to the event.

[37] s.1(1)(b) of the Act.

or any part of a literary, dramatic or musical work, from which sounds reproducing the work or part may be produced. Such a recording is a sound recording regardless of the medium on which the recording is made or the method by which the sounds are reproduced or produced.[38]

A "film" is a recording on any medium from which a moving image may by any means be produced. A soundtrack accompanying a film shall be treated as part of the film for the purpose of the Act.[39] This definition covers video recordings, video games and other multimedia products.

A "broadcast" is a transmission by wireless telegraphy of visual images, sounds or other information which is capable of being lawfully received by members of the public or is transmitted for presentation to members of the public.[40] This definition covers both terrestrial and satellite broadcasts.

For the purposes of the Act, a cable programme is one which forms part of a cable programme service, such a service being one which consists wholly or mainly in the sending of visual images, sounds or other information by means of a telecommunications system aimed at the public.[41] This definition covers websites on the Internet, but excludes email because it is not transmitted to the public.

(3) TYPOGRAPHICAL ARRANGEMENT OF A PUBLISHED EDITION

5-09 This category of copyright work applies to a published edition of the whole or part of a literary, dramatic or musical work.[42]

3. QUALIFYING REQUIREMENTS FOR COPYRIGHT PROTECTION

5-10 To attract copyright protection, a work must satisfy one of the following requirements[43]:

(1) its author is a "qualifying person": usually this will mean a British citizen, subject or resident, or a United Kingdom corporation[44];

(2) the work was first published in the United Kingdom (or in another country to which the Act extends);

(3) in the case of a broadcast or cable programme, it was made in or sent from the United Kingdom (or another country to which the Act extends).

It is only in rare cases that a work will fail to satisfy one of these requirements.

---

[38] s.5A of the Act.
[39] *ibid.*, s.5B.
[40] *ibid.*, s.6.
[41] *ibid.*, s.7.
[42] *ibid.*, s.8.
[43] See, *ibid*, ss.153–156.
[44] Orders may be made to recognise persons or corporations in other countries.

4. WHO IS THE OWNER OF COPYRIGHT?

(1) LITERARY, DRAMATIC, MUSICAL AND ARTISTIC WORKS

The author, that is the person who creates the copyright work,[45] will generally **5-11** be the first owner of copyright.[46] The author is not necessarily the person who physically recorded the work;[47] an author must have originated or contributed specific elements of a work which are original and distinctive.

As mentioned above, the author of spoken words is the owner of copyright in those words, regardless of whether the speaker has recorded them before they are spoken or whether they are recorded by another as they are spoken. However, a journalist who expends sufficient independent skill and labour in preparing that record will possess a separate copyright in it as a literary work,[48] and any person who arranges a sound recording of the spoken words would also be the author of that recording.[49]

There are two main exceptions to the general rule that the author is the first owner of copyright. The first is where the author has contracted to assign future copyright to another person. In that case, copyright will vest in the assignee as soon as it comes into existence.

The second exception is where a literary, dramatic, musical or artistic work has been created by an employee in the course of his employment, in which case his employer will be the first owner of copyright, subject to any agreement to the contrary.[50]

Care should be taken with works created before the Act came into force.[51] Under the previous copyright legislation, copyright was "split" between the print journalist and his employer. In relation to copyright works created in the course of an employment contract at a newspaper, magazine or periodical, the proprietor of such a publication owned copyright only to the extent that he could prevent its publication in another newspaper, magazine or periodical. In all other respects, the author of the work owned the copyright.[52] Similarly, copyright in certain commissioned work was owned by the commissioner. This rule applied only to the taking of photographs,[53] the painting or drawing of portraits, and the making of engravings.[54]

---

[45] s.9(1) of the Act.
[46] *ibid.*, s.11(1).
[47] A shorthand writer or amanuensis will not be the author of a copyright work: *Donoghue v. Allied Newspapers Ltd* [1938] Ch. 106.
[48] *Walter v. Lane* [1900] A.C. 539: *The Times* was held to own the copyright in a publication based on its reporter's verbatim shorthand notes of Lord Rosebery's speeches.
[49] It is, however, good practice to obtain the speaker's consent: see para. 5-30 relating to the use of such a record for the reporting of current events.
[50] s.11(2) of the Act. This does not apply to Crown copyright, parliamentary copyright or the copyright of certain international organisations:, *ibid.*, s 11(3).
[51] This paragraph relates specifically to works created between June 1, 1957 and August 1, 1989.
[52] Copyright Act 1956, s.4(2).
[53] *ibid.*, s.48 provided that the "author" of a photograph was the person who owned the material on which it was taken. Therefore, although the photographer was the author of a photograph, copyright was owned by the person who commissioned the photograph.
[54] *ibid.*, 1956, s.4(3).

(2) OTHER COPYRIGHT WORKS

5-12 In the case of a sound recording, the author is the producer,[55] *i.e.* the person who undertakes the arrangements necessary for the making of the recording.

Film authorship is more complex. Different rules apply depending on when the film was made. In relation to films made on or after July 1, 1994, the author will be the producer and principal director.[56]

The author of a broadcast is the person making the broadcast, *i.e.* either the person responsible to any extent for its contents (if he is transmitting the programme) or the person who makes the arrangements necessary for transmission (if he is the person providing the programme).[57] The author of a cable programme is the provider of the cable programme service in which a programme is included.[58] The author of a typographical arrangement is the publisher of the arrangement.[59]

(3) JOINT AUTHORSHIP

5-13 There are frequently occasions when a work has two or more authors. The following elements are required for a work of joint authorship:

(a) Each party must be an "author" in that he has contributed to the form of the copyright work. Joint authors do not necessarily have to make equal contributions, and they may make contributions of different kinds, but they must both have exercised sufficient skill and labour in the copyright material as it is finally expressed. The contribution of ideas such as titles, incidents, catch lines and the odd word where others had written the material has been held not to be sufficient.[60] Similarly, the revision of a work and suggestion of minor amendments will not give rise to joint authorship, nor will a situation where a "ghostwriter" is the author of a work for which another provides autobiographical material.[61]

(b) The parties must collaborate on the work so that the contribution of each author is not distinct from that of the other author or authors.[62]

(c) The collaboration must be in pursuit of a common design.[63] If the authors of a work are responsible for separate and distinct portions of a

---

[55] s.9(2)(aa) of the Act.
[56] *ibid.*, s.9(2)(ab). Although this provision applies to films made after July 1, 1994, it came into effect on December 1, 1996. Certain transitional rules therefore apply to films made between those two dates. For films made before July 1, 1994, the author will be the producer only. Films made prior to June 1, 1957 were not entitled to copyright as films, but as photographs and dramatic works.
[57] ss.9(2)(b) and 6(3) of the Act.
[58] *ibid.*, s.9(2)(c).
[59] *ibid.*, s.9(2)(d).
[60] *Tate v. Thomas* [1921] 1 Ch. 503.
[61] *Evans v. E. Hulton & Co. Ltd* [1923–28] Mac. C.C. 51. Although where a subject is closely involved in the drafting and substantial amendment of a biography, the subject may be a joint author: *Heptulla v. Orient Longman Ltd* [1989] F.S.R. 598.
[62] s.10(1) of the Act.
[63] *Levy v. Rutley* (1871) L.R. 6 C.P. 523.

copyright work, they are not joint authors, but co-authors. An example is a musical work in which one author has created the song and the other the lyrics. The distinction between joint authors and co-authors may be relevant to a number of issues, including the duration, ownership and infringement of copyright in that work.

5. COMMERCIAL EXPLOITATION OF COPYRIGHT

Copyright can be sold, licensed, transferred as a gift, or otherwise dealt with by its owner.[64] The most common transactions are effected by assignment (which passes ownership) or licence (conferring only the right to use the copyright work on certain conditions).

    5-14

Unlike an assignment, a licence can be exclusive or non-exclusive. An exclusive licence entitles the licensee to exercise any right that would otherwise be exercisable by the licensor to the exclusion of all others, including the licensor. Assignments and exclusive licences must be in writing and signed by or on behalf of the transferor.[65] An assignee or exclusive licensee is permitted to sue to protect their copyright, but a non-exclusive licensee does not have such a right, so any proceedings must be brought by their licensor.

Implied licences may arise in certain circumstances. For example, a person who sends a letter to the editor of a newspaper confers an implied licence to publish the letter on at least one occasion.

Methods of exploitation differ from one copyright owner to another. Some may wish to negotiate licences on an individual basis, while others may want to licence their copyrights on a "bulk" basis via collection agencies such as the Copyright Licensing Agency (reprographic rights), the Performing Rights Society Limited (rights in performance) and the Mechanical Copyright Protection Society (rights to reproduce lyrics and musical works on records).

6. HOW LONG DOES COPYRIGHT LAST?

The duration of copyright varies depending on the copyright work in question.[66] Copyright in literary, dramatic, musical and artistic works generally lasts for 70 years from the end of the calendar year in which the author dies.[67] If the work was one of joint authorship, copyright expires 70 years from the end of the year in which the last author dies.[68]

    5-15

In relation to a sound recording, copyright lasts for 50 years from the end of the calendar year in which it was made or, if it was not immediately released, from the end of the year in which it was released.[69] Copyright in films

---

[64] s.90(1) of the Act.
[65] *ibid.*, s.90(3).
[66] The law is contained in ss.12–14 of the Act, as amended by the Copyright and Rights in Performances Regulations 1995 (S.I. 1995 No. 3297). The Regulations came into force on January 1, 1996.
[67] s.12(2) of the Act.
[68] *ibid.*, s.12(8).
[69] s.13A of the Act.

made on or after January 1, 1996 expires 70 years from the end of the calendar year of the death of the last of the principal director, the author of the screenplay, the author of the dialogue or the composer of music specially created for and used in the film.[70]

For broadcasts and cable programmes, copyright ends 50 years from the end of the calendar year in which the broadcast was made or the programme included in a cable programme service.[71] Copyright in a typographical arrangement of a published work lasts until 25 years from the end of the calendar year in which that work was first published.[72]

In respect of works in which copyright had expired before July 1, 1995, the Copyright and Rights in Performances Regulations 1995[73] provides for the copyright in those works to be "revived". This means that for works the authors of which had died between 1925 and 1945, the period of copyright has been lengthened to 70 years from the end of the year in which the author died, as though the Regulations were in force when the work was first recorded.

7. HOW IS COPYRIGHT INFRINGED?

INTRODUCTION

5-16 The Act provides that a copyright owner has the exclusive right to do certain acts in the United Kingdom with the copyright work. These acts, referred to as "restricted acts", are considered below. Before looking at these acts, a number of general points should be made:

(1) Copyright in a work is infringed by a person who without the licence of the copyright owner does, or authorises another to do, any of the acts restricted by copyright.[74]

(2) Where one of the restricted acts is alleged to have been done, it must have been done in relation to the work as a whole or any substantial part of it, and either directly or indirectly.[75] Whether the whole of a work has been infringed is usually clear, but whether there has been infringement of a "substantial part" can be a more difficult question. "Substantial" refers to the quality and importance of the work infringed, rather than to quantity.[76] Although the court may take account of the physical amount of work infringed, infringement of a "substantial part" means infringement

---

[70] *ibid.*, s.13B. Copyright in films made between August 1, 1989 and January 1, 1996 lasts for 50 years from the end of the calendar year in which it was made or released. For films made between June 1, 1957 and August 1, 1989, copyright depended on whether the film was registrable under the Cinematograph Films Act 1938 or Films Act 1960: if registrable, copyright lasts 50 years from the end of the year of registration.

[71] CDPA, s.14(2).

[72] *ibid.*, s.15.

[73] See n. 66, above.

[74] CDPA, s.16(2).

[75] *ibid.*, s.16(3).

[76] *Ladbroke (Football) Ltd v. William Hill (Football) Ltd* [1964] 1 W.L.R. 273.

of a significant or distinctive part of the work as produced by the author's skill and labour, rather than commonly-known material.[77] Even a parody or satirical work may be an infringement if it incorporates a substantial part of the work it is satirising.[78] With music sampling, even a short sample may constitute infringement if the extract was particularly recognisable. As a result, a licence from the copyright owner is generally necessary if his work is to be sampled.

EXCLUSIVE RIGHTS OF THE COPYRIGHT OWNER[79]

(a) Copying the work[80]

Two elements must be proved to establish infringement, namely: **5-17**

- the copyright work must have been reproduced in a material form[81] in such a way that there is an objective similarity between the copyright work and the copy;

- the similarity must arise from the claimant's work having been copied by the defendant.[82]

Whether a sufficient degree of similarity is present is a question of fact to be determined by the court, having compared the original with the copy. There is no infringement if both works have been derived from the same source, the similarity between them is coincidental, or the claimant's work was actually a copy of the defendant's (rather than vice versa).[83] There will also be no infringement if the similarities between copyright works are commonplace.[84]

In relation to literary, dramatic, musical or artistic works, the copying need not be exact. Minor differences between the original and a copy will therefore not prevent infringement having occurred. For example, literary works such as abstracts, study notes, precis and abridgements are vulnerable to copyright infringement in so far as they reproduce or paraphrase other literary works.[85]

In relation to literary works, it is not an infringement to copy the style of the work unless the language of the original is reproduced. In contrast, infringement of copyright in dramatic works may arise if substantial parts of the plot, characterisation or incidents contained in the original have been copied, since those aspects are likely to be as significant as the actual words

---

[77] For example, the taking of four crucial lines from Rudyard Kipling's 32-line poem 'If' was an infringement: *Kipling v. Genatosan Ltd* [1917–23] Mac. C.C. 203.

[78] *Williamson Music Ltd v. The Pearson Partnership Ltd* [1987] F.S.R. 97.

[79] These are instances of primary infringement; *cf.* secondary infringement below.

[80] ss.16(1) and 17 of the Act

[81] *ibid.*, s.17(2). This includes storing the work in any medium by electronic means, and making copies which are transient or incidental to some other use of the work (CDPA, s.17(6)).

[82] *Francis Day & Hunter Ltd v. Bron* [1963] Ch. 587.

[83] *Corelli v. Gray* (1913) 29 T.L.R. 570.

[84] *EMI Music Publishing Ltd v. Papathanasiou* [1993] E.M.L.R. 306.

[85] See *Sillitoe v. McGraw-Hill Book Co. (U.K.) Ltd* [1983] F.S.R. 545: study notes were an infringement because they reproduced 5–10 per cent of two novels and a play.

used. In the case of artistic works, copying includes the making of a copy in three dimensions of a two-dimensional work, and the making of a copy in two dimensions of a three-dimensional work.[86]

In addition to copying of the whole or a substantial part of a film, broadcast, or cable programme, making a photograph of the whole or a substantial part of any image forming part of those works will be an infringement.[87]

(b) Issuing copies of the work to the public[88]

5-18 This is the act of putting into circulation in the United Kingdom or elsewhere copies of a work not previously circulated. The Act excludes subsequent distribution, sale, hire or importation of copies previously put into circulation.

(c) Renting or lending copies of the work to the public[89]

5-19 This provision applies to literary, dramatic, musical or artistic works, sound recordings and films. "Rental" is defined as making a copy available for use, on terms that it will or may be returned, otherwise than for direct or indirect economic or commercial advantage, through an establishment which is accessible to the public. "Lending" is making a copy available for use, on terms that it will or may be returned, otherwise than for direct or indirect commercial advantage, through an establishment which is accessible to the public.

(d) Performing, showing or playing the work in public[90]

(e) Broadcasting the work, or including it in a cable programme service[91]

(f) Making an adaptation of the work or doing any of the above in relation to an adaptation[92]

5-20 Adaptation, in relation to a literary or dramatic work, means[93]:

- a translation;
- a version of a dramatic work in which it is converted into a non-dramatic work or, as the case may be, of a non-dramatic work in which it is converted into a dramatic work; or
- a version of the work in which the story or action is conveyed wholly or mainly by means of pictures in a form suitable for reproduction in a book, or in a newspaper, magazine, or similar periodical.

---

[86] s.17(3) of the Act.
[87] *ibid.*, s.17(4).
[88] *ibid.*, ss.16(1) and 18.
[89] *ibid.*, ss.16(1) and 18A.
[90] *ibid.*, ss.16(1) and 19.
[91] *ibid.*, ss.16(1) and 20.
[92] *ibid.*, ss.16(1) and 21.
[93] *ibid.*, s.21(3)(a).

An adaptation of a musical work is defined as the arrangement or transcription of the work.[94]

SECONDARY INFRINGEMENT OF COPYRIGHT

In addition to the restricted acts described above, there are a number of further **5-21** acts which may amount to copyright infringement. Unlike the acts considered so far, where liability will attach irrespective of intention, a defendant will only be found liable for a secondary infringement if he has the requisite degree of knowledge. More particularly, he must be shown to have known, or have had reason to believe, that the article with which he was dealing was an infringing copy.

The acts which amount to secondary infringement are as follows.

(a) Importing an infringing copy

The copyright in a work is infringed by a person who, without the licence of **5-22** the copyright owner, imports into the United Kingdom, otherwise than for his private and domestic use, an article which is, and which he knows or has reason to believe is, an infringing copy of the work.[95]

(b) Possessing or dealing with an infringing copy

The copyright in a work is infringed by a person who, without the licence of **5-23** the copyright owner —

(a) possesses in the course or business,

(b) sells or lets for hire, or offers or exposes for sale or hire,

(c) in the course of a business exhibits in public or distributes, or

(d) distributes otherwise than in the course of a business to such an extent as to affect prejudicially the owner of the copyright,

an article which is, and which he knows or has reason to believe is, an infringing copy of the work.[96]

(c) Providing the means to make an infringing copy

Copyright in a work is infringed by a person who, without the licence of the **5-24** copyright owner —

(a) makes,

(b) imports into the United Kingdom,

(c) possesses in the course of business, or

(d) sells or lets for hire, or offers or exposes for sale or hire,

---

[94] s.21(3)(b) of the Act.
[95] *ibid.*, s.22.
[96] *ibid.*, s.23.

an article specifically designed or adapted for making copies of that work, knowing or having reason to believe that it is to be used to make infringing copies.[97]

(d) Permitting the use of premises for infringing performance

5-25   Where copyright in a literary, dramatic or musical work is infringed by a performance at a public place of entertainment, a person may also be liable for infringement if he gave permission for that place to be used for the performance, unless he believed on reasonable grounds that the performance would not infringe copyright.[98]

(e) Providing apparatus for an infringing performance

5-26   Where copyright is infringed by the public performance, playing or showing of a work by means of an apparatus for playing sound recordings, showing films, or receiving visual images or sounds conveyed by electronic means, the following persons are also liable for infringement if they knew or had reason to believe that the apparatus or what they supplied (or a copy made from it) was likely to be used so as to infringe copyright:

- the person who supplied the apparatus, or any substantial part of it;

- an occupier of premises who gave permission for the apparatus to be brought on to the premises;

- a person who supplied a copy of a sound recording or film used to infringe copyright.[99]

8. DEFENCES

5-27   There are a number of defences ("permitted acts") which may protect a person from liability for copyright infringement. These are exceptional occasions when the public interest requires that a third party ought to be allowed to use copyright material without being sued. The key defences of relevance to us are now considered.[1]

(1) FAIR DEALING

There are several instances when fair dealing with another's copyright work will be permitted.

---

[97] s.24(1) of the Act. There is a separate provision dealing with unlawful transmission by means of a telecommunications system: *ibid.*, s 24(2).

[98] *ibid.*, s.25.

[99] *ibid.*, s.26.

[1] There are other defences in the Act concerning, for example, copying in educational establishments and libraries, which are beyond the scope of this text.

(a) Research and private study[2]

Fair dealing with a literary,[3] dramatic, musical, or artistic work for the pur-   **5-28**
poses of research or private study does not infringe copyright in that work or,
in the case of a published edition, the typographical arrangement.[4]

This provision is designed to give students and researchers access to copyright material. The defence is restricted to fair dealing by the student or
researcher himself: a librarian infringes copyright by copying a work if he
knows or has reason to believe that it will result in copies of substantially the
same material being provided to more than one person at substantially the
same time and for substantially the same purpose.[5] Fair dealing, therefore,
does not permit multiple copies to be made of copyright material.

(b) Criticism, review and news reporting[6]

Criticism or review

Use of a work for the purpose of criticism or review, of that or another work   **5-29**
or a performance of a work, constitutes fair dealing, provided that it is accompanied by sufficient acknowledgement of the copyright owner's rights.

"Sufficient acknowledgement" is defined to mean an acknowledgement
identifying the work in question by its title or other description and identifying the author, unless the author is anonymous or, in the case of an unpublished work, it is not possible to ascertain the identity of the author by
reasonable inquiry.[7]

The identity of the author must be clear to the relevant audience: it has been
held that displaying the claimant's name and logo in the extract used is
sufficient acknowledgement if that is the means by which the claimant usually
identifies themselves to its viewers.[8] It should be stressed that it is the author,
and not the copyright owner, who should be acknowledged.[9]

The criticism or review may relate to any aspect of the work or a performance of the work. It also covers the situation where a work is used as a means
of comparison with another work in the process of criticism or review.
Criticism has been defined as the art of analysing and judging the quality of
a work, and review as the results of that process.[10] The concepts of criticism

---

[2] s.29 of the Act.
[3] In the case of a database, fair dealing for the purposes of research (excluding research for a
commercial purpose) or private study does not infringe copyright provided that the source is
indicated: ss.29(1A) and 29(5) of the Act. In relation to a computer program, it is not fair
dealing to convert a program in a low level language into a higher level language version, or to
copy such a computer program while converting it: s.29(4) of the Act.
[4] The defence does not extend to secondary copyrights such as sound recordings or films.
[5] For further provisions governing fair dealing by libraries and archives, see *ibid.*, ss.37–43.
[6] *ibid.*, s.30.
[7] *ibid.*, s.178.
[8] *Pro Sieben Media AG v. Carlton U.K. Television Ltd* [1999] 1 W.L.R. 605.
[9] *Express Newspapers Plc v. News (U.K.) Ltd* [1990] F.S.R. 359.
[10] *Dr Garis v. Neville Jeffress Pidler Pty Ltd* (1990) 18 I.P.R. 292.

and review have been broadly applied by the courts: they have been interpreted to extend beyond the author's style to issues such as the content of the work, the values or philosophy which underpin a work, or even a decision to withdraw a work from circulation.[11]

The test as to whether a copyright work is used for criticism or review is not onerous for a defendant. A defence of fair dealing was upheld in *Time Warner Entertainment Ltd v. Channel 4 Television Corporation Plc*, which concerned the use of extracts from the film *A Clockwork Orange* which amounted to 12 minutes (or 8 per cent of the film) in the defendant's 30-minute programme.[12] The court held that criticism of a work need not be confined to style: it can extend to the ideas in a work, and its social and moral consequences. Criticism in the programme of the decision to withdraw the film from circulation in the United Kingdom amounted to criticism of the work itself, since the content of the film and the decision to withdraw it were inseparable.

The defence of fair dealing was also successfully claimed in *Pro Sieban Media A.G. v. Carlton U.K. Television Ltd.*[13] That case concerned the alleged infringement of a German broadcast concerning Mandy Allwood and her partner, who became well known in the United Kingdom as a result of Ms Allwood's pregnancy with octuplets following fertility treatment. The couple became the subject of particular controversy because they engaged the services of P.R. consultant Max Clifford, who negotiated for them high profile contracts for interviews with certain media outlets. One of these outlets was the German broadcaster Pro Sieben, and a 30-second extract of the resulting interview was used by the defendant in a programme about chequebook journalism.

In the *Pro Sieben* case, the Court of Appeal reversed a first instance decision in which the defence of fair dealing had been rejected because the programme-maker had not proved that the purpose of the inclusion of the extract was to criticise or review the German broadcast. The Court of Appeal ruled that the fair dealing defences involved not only an objective assessment of whether the copyright material had been used for one of the purposes allowed by the Act, but a subjective assessment of the defendant's intentions and motives in order to assess whether the dealing had been fair. Insufficient weight had been given by the trial judge to the defendant's pleaded case that the programme was intended to criticise various works which were the fruits of chequebook journalism, of which the claimant's report was one. The Court of Appeal concluded that the purpose of the programme was the criticism of works of chequebook journalism in general, and Ms Allwood's story in particular. The use of the extract was short, did not include any of Ms Allwood's spoken words, and did not compete with Pro Sieben's exploitation of its rights in the broadcast.

---

[11] *Hubbard v. Vosper* [1972] 2 Q.B. 84; *Time Warner Entertainment Ltd v. Channel 4 Television Corporation Plc* [1994] E.M.L.R. 1.

[12] [1994] E.M.L.R. 1.

[13] [1999] 1 W.L.R. 605 *cf. Hyde Park Residence Limited v. Yelland* [2000] E.M.L.R. 363.

Reporting current events

Fair dealing may also apply to a work for the purpose of reporting current **5-30** events.[14] Again, a sufficient acknowledgement is required, except that no acknowledgement is required in relation to the reporting of current events by means of a sound recording, film, broadcast or cable programme.

"Current events" has been given a liberal interpretation, and is not confined to media reports of very recent occurrences, but it is narrower than the term "news". While "news" might extend beyond current events to information which was not previously known or is of historical interest, reporting of "current events" must relate to genuinely current events. In the *Marks and Spencer* case, an internal cuttings service for senior management was not regarded as sufficiently in the public interest.[15] In the *Pro Sieben* case,[16] it was suggested that the volume and intensity of media interest was sufficient to bring the media coverage at issue in that case within the scope of "current events".

The defence extends to sporting events such as the World Cup in the same way as any other newsworthy event.[17] However, United Kingdom broadcasters have agreed to a voluntary code of conduct relating to the televising of sporting events which governs the use between them of sports excerpts/highlights in news programmes.[18] The code contains guidelines as to what constitutes acceptable use in respect of such excerpts. As such, broadcasters may prefer to rely on the terms of the code (or seek permission from the relevant broadcaster), rather than on fair dealing.

Fair dealing may protect the press practice of "borrowing" other newspaper's stories, rephrasing them and including them in their own pages. *The Daily Star* was held to have had an arguable defence of fair dealing when it incorporated into its own article large extracts (including quotations) from a *Today* exclusive concerning Marina Ogilvy. It was held that it would not be in the public interest for a newspaper to have a monopoly on a "scoop" which should be disseminated to the public at large.[19]

---

[14] Photographs are excluded from the operation of the defence. This means that the permission of the copyright owner will almost always be required in relation to the publication, broadcast or similar use of photographs.

[15] *Newspaper Licensing Agency v. Marks and Spencer*, [1999] E.M.L.R. 369. The Court of Appeal did not strictly need to reach a view on the question of fair dealing for the purpose of reporting current events. The three judges, however, all expressed their view that public policy did not require the defence to apply when the copying was purely in the commercial interests of Marks and Spencer rather than in the public interest. Gibson L.J. rejected the defence on the grounds that the copying was not for the purpose of reporting current events; Chadwick and Gibson L.JJ. did so on the basis that the use was not fair. Marks and Spencer won the case in any event because the court held by a majority that they had not copied a substantial part of the typographical arrangement of a published edition, the sole copyright work relied on by the Newspaper Licensing Agency.

[16] [1999] 1 W.L.R. 605.

[17] *BBC v. British Satellite Broadcasting* [1991] 3 All E.R. 833.

[18] Major Spectator Sports Voluntary Code of Conduct 1996. The current agreement is due to run to 2001. It is also subscribed to by the governing bodies of most major sports, such as the Football Association and the Lawn Tennis Association.

[19] *Express Newspapers Plc v. News (U.K.) Ltd* [1990] F.S.R. 359.

What is fair?

5-31   Another important factor in the application of this defence is that the dealing must be fair: a defendant will not be able to rely on fair dealing if his use of the work goes far beyond what is necessary for the purpose at hand.

Lord Denning stated in *Hubbard v. Vosper* that whether use of a work was fair would be a matter of impression, but he outlined three (non-exhaustive) factors which should be considered in determining the question:

(i)   The number and extent of quotations and extracts. The question should be asked whether the quotations and extracts are too many and too long to be fair. Substantial extracts and quotations may be used to facilitate a criticism of a work, and it has been suggested that the whole original work may be reproduced if it is short.[20]

(ii)   The use that has been made of the quotations and extracts. Consideration should be given to any motive behind the use of the work. For example, where a defendant's work is in competition with the infringed work, or the dealing has prevented the copyright owner from financially exploiting his rights, the use may be unfair.

Despite this factor, BSB was found to have a defence of fair dealing when it had used extracts of BBC World Cup football coverage in its own sports reports.[21] The judge held that BSB's use had been fair because of the shortness of the extracts, the fact that they were replayed no more than four times in 24 hours in genuine news bulletins, and the fact that BSB had acknowledged that they were the BBC's (despite the lack of statutory requirement for such an acknowledgement).

(iii)   The proportion of quotations and extracts should be compared to the proportion of criticism or review in the defendant's work.

Another factor which may be relevant to fairness is the manner in which the copyright work was obtained. In *Beloff v. Pressdram*[22] a memo which was leaked in breach of confidence could not form the basis for a fair dealing defence. In contrast, subsequent cases have shown that the way in which a previously unpublished work had been obtained for use would be unlikely to make that use unfair.[23]

However, a Court will also take into account the motives of the alleged infringer and, in the context of reporting current events, whether the use was necessary for that purpose. In *Hyde Park Residence v. Yelland*,[24] *The Sun* newspaper failed to establish the defence when it published video stills of a visit by the Princess of Wales and Dodi Fayed to Mohammed Al Fayed's villa in Paris,

---

[20]   *per* Megaw L.J. in *Hubbard v. Vosper* [1972] 2 Q.B. 84.
[21]   *BBC v. British Satellite Broadcasting* [1991] 3 All E.R. 833.
[22]   [1973] 1 All E.R. 241.
[23]   *Time Warner Entertainment Ltd v. Channel 4 Television Corporation Plc* [1994] E.M.L.R. 1. See also *Hubbard v. Vosper* [1972] 2 Q.B. 84.
[24]   [2000] E.M.L.R. 363.

the day before they were killed in 1997. Mohammed Fayed had claimed that the couple had visited his villa on the occasion in question for about two hours, and that they were preparing to get married and live there. *The Sun's* article sought to refute Fayed's account and maintained that the couple had only stayed at the villa for 28 minutes.

In rejecting the defence of fair dealing for the purpose of reporting current events, the Court found that the newspaper had failed to meet "the objective standard of the fair-minded and honest person". The fact that the copyright work had not previously been published or reported to the public was an important indication that the dealing was not fair. A fair-minded and honest person would not pay for dishonestly taken stills and publish them when they were relevant only to the fact that Diana and Dodi stayed at the villa for 28 minutes (something which was already known and did not disprove Mohammed Al Fayed's marriage allegations anyway). Further, the use of the stills was excessive as the "timing" information could have been contained in the article without use of the pictures.

In the *Marks & Spencer* case (see above), although it was not required to reach a decision on the issue of fair dealing, a majority of the Court of Appeal indicated that an internal press clippings service was not fair dealing. Mance L.J. rejected the defence on the basis that he did not believe that the defence should extend to reporting of current events for private commercial purposes. His fellow judge, Gibson L.J., formed the view that, whilst the defence should fail on the grounds that it was not for the purpose of reporting current events, he considered the use to be fair: the use was not in competition with the claimant's and the copies were being used purely internally.[25]

Commercial research is expressly excluded from the ambit of the fair dealing defence relating to research and private study.[26]

(2) PUBLIC INTEREST

A public interest defence exists at common law in relation to copyright **5-32** infringement, as it does with breach of confidence.[27] Although this defence is not expressly referred to in the Act, the Act appears to recognise its existence by asserting that the provisions of the Act should not interfere with "any rule of law preventing or restricting the enforcement of copyright, on grounds of public interest or otherwise".[28]

In *Hyde Park Residence v. Yelland*[29], *The Sun* attempted to defend their publication of the video stills on the basis of public interest, in addition to fair dealing. The Court found that there was no public interest in the publication of the pictures since the information could have been made available by the newspaper without infringement of copyright, and was in the public domain anyway.

[25] *Newspaper Licensing Agency v. Marks & Spencer* [1999] E.M.L.R. 369.
[26] s.29(5) of the Act.
[27] See Chap. 7 relating to breach of confidence for a more detailed analysis of this defence.
[28] *ibid.*, s.171(3).
[29] [2000] E.M.L.R. 363.

The court went on to state that it would be entitled to refuse a public interest defence if a work was:

- immoral, scandalous or contrary to family life;

- injurious to public life, public health and safety or the administration of justice (or incited or encouraged others to act in such a way).

It is unclear after *Yelland* how frequently the media will be able to rely on the public interest defence.

(3) INCIDENTAL INCLUSION OF COPYRIGHT MATERIAL

5-33 Copyright in a work is not infringed by its incidental inclusion in an artistic work, sound recording, film, broadcast or cable programme.[30] The deliberate inclusion of a musical work, for example, in another work will not be regarded as incidental inclusion.[31]

(4) USE OF NOTES OR RECORDINGS OF SPOKEN WORDS

5-34 As has already been explained, copyright in spoken words which are recorded belongs to the speaker.[32] This provision would invariably have made reporters' use of their notes of spoken words an infringement of copyright, except that the Act also contains a defence which enables the media to report what someone has said without liability.

Where a record of spoken words is made, in writing or otherwise, for the purpose of

(a) reporting current events, or

(b) broadcasting or including in a cable programme service the whole work or part of the work,

it is not an infringement of any copyright in the words as a literary work to use the record or material taken from it (or to copy the record, or any such material, and use the copy) for that purpose, provided the following conditions are met:

- the record is a direct record of the spoken words and is not taken from a previous record or from a broadcast or cable programme;

- the making of the record was not prohibited by the speaker and, where copyright already subsisted in the work, did not infringe copyright;

- the use made of the record or material taken from it is not of a kind prohibited by or on behalf of the speaker or copyright owner before the record was made; and

---

[30] *ibid.*, s.31(1).
[31] *ibid.*, s.31(3).
[32] *ibid.*, s.3.

- the use is by or with the authority of a person who is lawfully in possession of the record.[33]

(5) COPYRIGHT RELATING TO PUBLIC ADMINISTRATION

Copyright is not infringed by anything done for the purposes of parliamentary or judicial proceedings, Royal Commissions, statutory inquiries, or for the purpose of reporting such proceedings (if they are held in public).[34] This defence does not, however, authorise the copying of a work which is a published report of such proceedings, such as law reports or *Hansard*. However, some commentators consider that the government is unlikely to enforce its copyright in respect of *Hansard* or certain other material such as Bills, Acts of Parliament, statutory instruments, and Select Committee reports, which it is clearly in the public interest to disseminate.[35]   **5-35**

Information which is open to public inspection as a matter of statutory requirement or on a statutory register may also be copied without liability for infringement, provided it is done with the authority of the appropriate person[36] and not intended to be publicly distributed.[37]

(6) WORKS ON PUBLIC DISPLAY

Copyright in buildings, sculptures, models for buildings or works of artistic craftsmanship which are permanently situated in a public place or premises open to the public is not infringed if such a work is: **5-36**

- represented in a graphic work;
- photographed or filmed; or
- broadcast or included in a cable programme service.[38]

9. REMEDIES

There are a range of remedies which may be available to the copyright owner in any proceedings.[39] The following are among the key remedies.

(1) INJUNCTION[40]

An application may be made to the court for an interim injunction to restrain another's use of infringing material before trial, and such an injunction   **5-37**

---

[33] s.58 of the Act.

[34] *ibid.*, s.45–6.

[35] G. Robertson and A. Nicol, *Media Law* (3rd ed., 1992, Penguin), p. 240.

[36] The "appropriate person" is the person required to make the material open to public inspection or, as the case may be, the person maintaining the register: s.47(6) of the Act.

[37] *ibid.*, s.47.

[38] s.62 of the Act.

[39] The key provision dealing with remedies can be found at ss.96 to 115 of the Act. Claims may be brought by copyright owners and exclusive licensees: ss.96 and 101.

[40] *ibid.*, s.96(2).

commonly lasts until trial or until varied by the court. It may be applied for *ex parte*, or without notice to the alleged infringer. The normal grounds for the making of an injunction will apply, so that the applicant will have to persuade the court that he has an arguable claim, that there is a serious question to be tried, and that, on the balance of convenience, the injunction should be granted.[41] The court may also consider factors such as the seriousness of the infringement, the probability of damage, the chance of repetition, or unreasonable delay by the applicant. He will also have to show that damages would be an inadequate remedy if the injunction was not granted. A final injunction may be made after the trial of the action.

(2) SEARCH ORDERS[42]

5-38   A search order allows the person who has obtained the order to enter the premises of the alleged infringer, and to copy or retain material relevant to the action. Such orders may be appropriate in the case of pirated or counterfeit goods, where it may be difficult to obtain and/or preserve evidence of infringement.

(3) DAMAGES

5-39   A copyright owner may claim damages as compensation for the losses caused to the value of his copyright work by infringement.[43] This is generally calculated as the amount of profits which could have been made but for the infringer's action, or the reasonable licence fee which the copyright owner would have charged the infringer if he had sought the owner's permission to use the material.

In addition to the "normal" compensatory damages,[44] the court may award such additional damages as the circumstances of the case may require, having particular regard to:

(a)   the flagrancy of the infringement; and

(b)   any benefit accruing to the defendant by reason of the infringement.[45]

This provision is designed to punish repeated infringements or particularly scandalous or deceitful infringement.[46] This would include a deliberate

---

[41] *American Cyanamid v. Ethicon Ltd* [1975] A.C. 396.

[42] See CPR 25.1 (1)(h) and Civil Procedure Act 1997, s.7. These were known as *Anton Piller* orders prior to the introduction of the CPR: see *Anton Piller K.G. v. Manufacturing Processes Ltd* [1976] Ch. 55.

[43] s.96(2) of the Act.

[44] Whether additional damages are awarded is at the court's discretion, but they can only be awarded where normal compensatory damages under s.96(2) are also awarded: see *Redrow Homes Ltd v. Bett Bros plc* [1998] 1 All E.R. 385.

[45] s.97 of the Act.

[46] In *Williams v. Settle* [1960] 1 W.L.R. 1072 a photographer sold to the press without permission a wedding photograph of a man who had been murdered. Although this case pre-dates the Act, the judge referred to the flagrancy of the infringement in that it illustrated a total disregard for the claimant's feelings as well as his copyright.

infringement in relation to which the defendant had calculated that he would reap a financial benefit in excess of the damages he would have to pay the copyright owner. Other factors to be considered might include the defendant's general conduct and motives, the claimant's response, and injury to the claimant's feelings.[47] Additional damages are compensatory in nature and have some similarities with aggravated damages for defamation.[48]

A claimant will not be entitled to damages from a defendant who did not know, and had no reason to believe, at the time of the infringement that copyright subsisted in the work.[49] However, this exception is a narrow one: it will not protect infringers who are mistaken as to the identity of the copyright owner, or infringers who are ignorant of the law of copyright. Reasonable care must have been taken by the infringer in order for the exception to apply, so appropriate copyright checks must have been made. The exception will not apply to other remedies such as an injunction or delivery up.

(4) ACCOUNT OF PROFITS

A successful claimant may, at his election, seek an account of profits in lieu of damages.[50] Whether this remedy is awarded is at the court's discretion, and will therefore depend on the facts of the case and whether the owner's rights can be protected in some other way.

5-40

If awarded, the claimant will be entitled to receive the infringer's net profits. It is not a particularly popular remedy because, unlike damages, it gives the defendant an opportunity to reduce the amount to be claimed by producing details of his overheads which need to be taken into account before the award is made.

(5) DELIVERY UP

The court may order the delivery up of an infringing copy or article to the copyright owner or some other person if the infringer:

5-41

(i)   has an infringing copy of a work in his possession, custody or control in the course of a business; or

(ii)   has in his possession, custody or control an article specifically designed or adapted for making copies of a particular copyright work, knowing or having reason to believe that it has been or is to be used to make infringing copies.[51]

---

[47] *Ravenscroft v. Herbert* [1980] R.P.C. 193.
[48] See Chap. 2 at 7.
[49] s.97(1) of the Act. This exception does not extend to other remedies for copyright infringement.
[50] *ibid.*, s.96(2). The account would be in lieu of both compensatory and additional damages: *Redrow Homes Ltd v. Bett Bros plc* [1998] 1 All E.R. 385.
[51] s.99 of the Act.

In general, such an application must be made within six years of the infringing copy or article in question being made.[52] Delivery up, like an account, is a discretionary remedy and the court will take into consideration whether the claimant's rights can be protected in some other way.[53]

(6) FORFEITURE AND DESTRUCTION

5-42 The court may order infringing articles to be forfeited to the copyright owner, destroyed or otherwise dealt with as it thinks fit.[54] Again, this is a discretionary remedy.

(7) CRIMINAL SANCTIONS

5-43 Copyright infringement, like trade mark infringement, may amount to a breach of the criminal as well as the civil law. It is beyond the scope of this text to consider these circumstances in detail other than to note that a defendant may be liable to fines or imprisonment if he knows or has reason to believe that the articles with which he is dealing were infringing copies of a copyright work.[55]

10. MORAL RIGHTS

(1) INTRODUCTION

5-44 The author of a literary, dramatic, musical or artistic work, or the director of a film, may be entitled to the protection of certain moral rights.[56] These rights were first introduced in the 1988 Act. They enable an author who is no longer the owner of a copyright work to continue to exercise a degree of control over his work.

Unlike copyright, moral rights are not assignable: they are binding on whoever owns or is the licensee of the work.[57] Moral rights may, however, be waived. In practice, an assignment of copyright may be made contingent on such a waiver being secured.[58] The waiver may relate to a specific work, to works generally, to existing or future works, may be conditional or unconditional, and may be subject to revocation.[59]

Moral rights subsist for as long as copyright lasts, save that the right to object to false attribution (see 2(c) below) expires 20 years after the author's death.[60]

---

[52] *ibid.*, s.113.
[53] In certain limited circumstances, it may be possible to seize and detain infringing copies of a work which are immediately available for sale or hire: *ibid.*, s.100. The police must be notified.
[54] *ibid.*, ss.114.
[55] See ss.107–111 of the Act.
[56] The rights of joint authors are protected by *ibid.*, s.88.
[57] *ibid.*, s.94. The exception is death, when moral rights are assignable to the author's or director's estate: *ibid.*, s.95.
[58] *ibid.*, s.87. Such a waiver should ideally be in writing and signed, but an oral waiver may be implied or arise by way of estoppel: see *ibid.*, s.87 (4).
[59] *ibid.*, s.87(3).

The paternity and integrity rights (see 2(a) and 2(b) below) apply in relation to works in existence when the Act came into force on August 1, 1989, but not if the author died before the commencement of the Act. Similarly the right to privacy (see 2(d) below) does not apply in respect of films made or photographs taken before the commencement date.[61]

(2) THE FOUR CLASSES OF MORAL RIGHTS

The four types of moral rights created by the Act are as follows.

(a) The right to be identified as the author or director (the "paternity right")[62]

The author of a copyright literary, dramatic, musical or artistic work, and the director of a copyright film, has the right to be identified as the author or director of the work in certain specified circumstances.[63] These are intended to include circumstances whenever the work, or a substantial part of the work,[64] is commercially published, performed, exhibited or otherwise exploited.[65]   **5-45**

The right is not infringed unless it has been asserted in one of the ways provided for in the Act.[66] For example, it may be contained in an agreement to assign or licence copyright in a work, or it may be made by making it a condition of an agreement to publicly exhibit a work that the author's name is placed on the frame or mount to which the work is attached.

Assuming the right has been asserted and not waived, the identification of the author or director must be clear, reasonably prominent and made in relation to each copy or of the work (or any substantial part of it) which is publicly promoted or otherwise likely to bring his identity to the notice of a person seeing or hearing the work. If the particular form of identification is not chosen by the author or director, any reasonable form of identification may be used.[67]

There are a number of important exceptions to the right in the Act,[68] including:

(i)   computer programs;

(ii)   typeface designs;

(iii)   computer-generated works; and

(iv)   works done by or with the authority of the copyright owner where copyright in the work originally vested in the author's or director's employer.[69]

---

[60]   *ibid.*, s.86.
[61]   *ibid.*, Sched. 1, para. 24.
[62]   *ibid.*, ss.77–9.
[63]   *ibid.*, s.77 (1). The right extends to adaptations of a work.
[64]   s.89(1) of the Act.
[65]   See s.77 for a precise description of the various forms of exploitation which will give rise to the right.
[66]   s.78 of the Act.
[67]   ss.77 and 89(1) of the Act.
[68]   See *ibid.*, s.79.
[69]   See s.11(2) of the Act in relation to works produced in course of employment.

It should also be noted that the right will not apply in certain circumstances where a defence to copyright infringement would be available.[70] This includes:

(i)   fair dealing for the purpose of reporting current events by means of a sound recording, film, broadcast or cable programme;

(ii) incidental inclusion of work in an artistic work, sound recording, film, broadcast or cable programme;

(iii) parliamentary and judicial proceedings;

(iv) Royal Commissions and statutory inquiries.

The right does not apply in relation to the publication in —

(a)   a newspaper, magazine, or similar periodical, or

(b)   an encyclopaedia, dictionary, yearbook or other collective work of reference,

of a literary, dramatic, musical or artistic work made for the purposes of such publication or made available with the consent of the author for the purposes of such a publication.[71] This provision prevents journalists relying on the paternity right to insist on a byline or credit for work broadcast or published.

Similarly the work does not apply in relation to works of Crown or parliamentary copyright or to works in which copyright first vested in an international organisation by virtue of section 168 of the Act.

(b) The right to object to derogatory treatment (the "integrity right")[72]

5-46   The author of a literary, dramatic, musical or artistic work and the director of a film are entitled in certain circumstances not to have their work, or any part of their work, subjected to derogatory treatment.

"Treatment" is defined as any addition to, deletion from or alteration to or adaptation of the work, other than:

(i)   a translation of a literary or dramatic work;

(ii) an arrangement or transcription of a musical work involving no more than a change of key or register.[73]

Treatment is derogatory if it amounts to a distortion or mutilation of the work or is otherwise prejudicial to the honour or reputation of the author or director.[74]

---

[70] *ibid.*, s.79(4).
[71] s.79(b) of the Act
[72] *ibid.*, s.80.
[73] *ibid.*, s.80 (2)(a).
[74] *ibid.*, s.80 (2)(b).

The circumstances in which the right will be infringed are specified in the Act.[75] They include circumstances where the work, or any part of the work, is commercially published, broadcast, performed, exhibited or otherwise exploited.[76]

The exceptions to the right are similar to those attaching to the paternity right,[77] including the following:

(i) computer programs;

(ii) computer-generated works;

(iii) works made for the purpose of reporting current events;

(iv) in relation to the publication in —
    (a) a newspaper, magazine or similar periodical, or
    (b) an encyclopedia, dictionary, yearbook or other collective work of reference of a literary, dramatic, musical or artistic work made for the purposes of such publication or made available with the consent of the author for the purposes of such publication.

Further, there is no infringement of the right if a work is altered for legal reasons

• to avoid the commission of an offence;

• to comply with a duty imposed by or under an enactment, or

• in the case of the BBC, to avoid including anything in a programme which offends against good taste or decency or which is likely to incite crime or lead to disorder, or to be offensive to public feeling,

provided, where the author or director is identified at the time of the relevant act or has previously been identified in or on published copies of the work, that there is a sufficient disclaimer.

(c) The right to object to false attribution[78]

A person has a right not to have a literary, dramatic, musical or artistic work falsely attributed to him as author, and not to have a film falsely attributed to him as a director. The right applies to a whole work or any part of it,[79] and it extends to adaptations and copies of works.

"Attribution" means an express or implied statement as to who is the author or director of a work, and infringement occurs when falsely attributed works are commercially exploited in the ways described in the Act.[80] In order to

5-47

---

[75] See *ibid.*, ss.80 and 83.
[76] *ibid.*, s.89(2).
[77] *ibid.*, s.81.
[78] s.84 of the Act.
[79] *ibid.*, s.89(2).
[80] See *ibid.*, s.84.

establish infringement, a claimant must prove that the notional reasonable reader would understand the material in question to contain a false attribution of authorship to the claimant.[81]

There is no exception to the false attribution right for works published in newspapers and periodicals as applies in the case of paternity and integrity rights; for example, a newspaper proprietor would be liable for infringement of a journalist's moral right if an incorrect byline was placed on an article.

(d) The right to privacy of photographs and films[82]

5-48 A person who for private and domestic purposes commissions the taking of a photograph or the making of a film has (where copyright subsists in the resulting work) a right not to have:

(i)   copies of the work issued to the public;

(ii) the work exhibited or shown to the public;

(iii) the work broadcast or included in a cable programme service.

Anyone who authorises one or more of these acts infringes that right, even if that person is the copyright owner of the photograph or film.[83]

The Act includes the following exceptions to the right:

(i)   incidental inclusion of work in an artistic work, film, broadcast or cable programme;

(ii) parliamentary and judicial proceedings;

(iii) Royal Commissions and statutory inquiries;

(iv) acts done under statutory authority.[84]

(3) REMEDIES[85]

5-49 An infringement of moral rights is actionable as a breach of statutory duty owed to the person entitled to that right. General and special damages are available, and an injunction may be granted to restrain threatened future breaches.[86]

---

[81] *Clark v. Associated Newspapers Ltd* [1998] 1 All E.R. 959.

[82] CDPA, s.85.

[83] s.85(1) of the Act. This right also applies in respect of a substantial part of the work: *ibid.*, s.89(1). The person who commissioned the photograph may also have an action in breach of contract or breach of confidence against the person who made unauthorised use of such a photograph or film: see Chap. 7 in relation to breach of confidence.

[84] *ibid.*, s.85(2).

[85] *ibid.*, s.103.

[86] Delay in bringing a claim based on the paternity right may be taken into account: *ibid.*, s.95(6).

11. RIGHTS IN PERFORMANCE

(1) INTRODUCTION

The rights described in this section protect performers, by requiring consent **5-50** to the exploitation of their performances (performers' rights), and persons having recording rights in relation to a performance (recording rights). The rights were first conferred by the Copyright Designs and Patents Act 1988 Act. As we shall see below, performers' rights were later extended to create a new class of performer's property right.[87]

The rights exist independently of copyright and moral rights.[88] They apply to performances, but not infringements, taking place before the Act came into force.[89] The rights last for 50 years from the end of the calendar year in which the performance takes place or, if during that period a recording of that performance is released, 50 years from the end of the calendar year of release.[90]

At the outset it is necessary to describe what is meant by "performance" and "recording". "Performance" is defined to mean

(a) a dramatic performance (which includes dance and mime),

(b) a musical performance,

(c) a reading or recitation of a literary work, or

(d) a performance of a variety act or any similar presentation,

which is a live performance given by one or more individuals.[91]

Like copyright, a performance must be one that qualifies under the Act, either because it is given by a "qualifying individual"[92] or takes place in a "qualifying country".[93]

"Recording" in relation to a performance means a film or sound recording:

(a) made directly from the live performance;

(b) made from a broadcast of, or cable programme including, the performance; or

(c) made, directly or indirectly, from another recording of the performance.

---

[87] Council Directive 92/100 on rental right and lending right and on certain rights related to copyright in the field of intellectual property (the Rental and Lending Directive) [1992] O.J. L346/61.

[88] *ibid.*, s.180(4).

[89] The sections of Pt. II of the CPDA 1998 referred to in this chapter have come into force at varying times, due to the amendments effected by the Duration of Copyright and Rights in Performances Regulations 1995 (S.I. 1995 No. 3297) and the Copyright and Related Rights Regulations 1996 (S.I. 1996 No. 2967).

[90] s.191(2) of the Act. A recording is released when it is first published, played or shown in public, broadcast, or included in a cable programme service: s.191(3).

[91] *ibid.*, s.180(2). This definition does not extend to sportsmen, but a performer's consent is nevertheless commonly obtained from those taking parts in sport events.

[92] *ibid.*, s.206. This will usually mean a citizen, subject of or individual resident in the U.K.

[93] *ibid.*, s.206. This will usually mean in the U.K. or E.U.

101

(2) RIGHTS OF PERFORMERS

There are two distinct forms of performers' rights: non-property and property rights.

(i) Perfomers' non-property rights

5-51   A performer's rights are infringed by a person who, without his consent:

(a)   makes, other than for his private or domestic use, a recording of the whole or any substantial part of a qualifying performance directly from a live performance or directly from a broadcast or cable transmission of a live performance[94];

(b)   broadcasts live, or includes live in a cable programme service, the whole or any substantial part of a qualifying performance[95];

(c)   shows or plays in public, or broadcasts or includes in a cable programme service, the whole or any substantial part of a qualifying performance by means of a recording which was, and which that person knows or has reason to believe was, made without the performer's consent[96];

(d)   either
   (i)   imports into the United Kingdom otherwise than for his private or domestic use, or
   (ii)   in the course of a business possesses, sells or lets for hire, offers or exposes for sale or hire, or distributes

   a recording of a qualifying performance which is, and which he knows or has reason to believe is, an illicit recording.[97]

(ii) Performers' property rights[98]

5-52   A performer's rights are infringed by a person who, without his consent:

(a)   makes, otherwise than for his private and domestic use, a copy of a recording of the whole or any substantial part of a qualifying performance ("the reproduction right")[99];

(b)   issues to the public copies of a recording of the whole or any substantial part of a qualifying performance ("the distribution right")[1];

---

[94]   *ibid.*, s.182(1)(a) and (c).
[95]   *ibid.*, s.182(1)(b).
[96]   s.183 of the Act.
[97]   *ibid.*, s.184.
[98]   *ibid.*, See ss.182A–182C as inserted by the Copyright and Related Rights Regulations 1996 (S.I. 1996 No. 2967).
[99]   *ibid.*, s.182A(1). It is immaterial, for the purposes of the reproduction right, whether the copy is made directly or indirectly: *ibid.*, s.182A(2).
[1]   *ibid.*, s.182B.

(c)   rents or lends to the public copies of a recording of the whole or any sub-stantial part of a qualifying performance ("the rental and lending rights").[2]

Unlike non-property performers rights,[3] the performers' property rights can be transferred and assigned.[4] An assignment must be in writing signed by the assignor.[5]

In addition, a performer is entitled to equitable remuneration from the copyright owner of a commercially published sound recording when the whole or a substantial part of a qualifying performance is played in public or included in a broadcast or cable programme service.[6] This right cannot be excluded or restricted by agreement, and it cannot be assigned except to a col-lecting society, which may enforce the right on a performer's behalf. If the amount of remuneration cannot be agreed between the copyright owner and the performer, the Copyright Tribunal may determine the amount payable. An application can also be made to the Tribunal to vary the amount.

(3) RIGHTS OF PERSONS HAVING RECORDING RIGHTS

The Act provides rights to a person who has recording rights in respect of a   **5-53**
performance.[7] In summary this means a person who is party to and has the benefit of an exclusive recording contract to which the performance is subject, or to whom the benefit of such a contract has been assigned, and who is a qualifying person.[8]

An "exclusive recording contract" means a contract between a performer and another person under which that person is entitled to the exclusion of all other persons (including the performer) to make recordings of one or more of his performances with a view to their commercial exploitation.[9]

A person infringes the rights of a person having recording rights in relation to a performance:

(a)   by, without his consent or that of the performer, making a recording of the whole or any substantial part of a performance otherwise than for private or domestic use[10];

(b)   by, without his consent or, in the case of a qualifying performance, that of the performer, showing or playing in public, or broadcasting or including in a cable programme service, the whole or any substantial part of a

---

[2]   *ibid.*, s.182C.
[3]   *ibid.*, 192A. Although perfomers' non-property rights are tranmissible on death.
[4]   *ibid.*, s.191B(1).
[5]   *ibid.*, s.191B (3).
[6]   *ibid.*, s.182D.
[7]   See s.185(2) and (3) of the Act for definition of "person having recording rights".
[8]   "Qualifying person" is defined in s 206 of the Act. It includes a "qualifying individual" (as defined at 3 above).
[9]   *ibid.*, s.185(1).
[10]   *ibid.*, s.186(1).

performance by means of a recording which was, and which that person knows or has reason to believe was, made without the appropriate consent[11];

(c) by, without his consent or, in the case of a qualifying performance, that of the performer, importing into the United Kingdom otherwise than for his private and domestic use, or in the course of business possesses, selling or letting for hire, offering or exposing for sale or hire, or distributing, a recording of the performance which is, and which that person knows or has reason to believe is, an illicit recording.[12]

(4) REMEDIES

5-54 An infringement of a performer's non-property rights and of the recording rights are treated as breaches of statutory duty.[13] The main remedies are an injunction and damages.

However, damages for infringement of a performer's rights under section 182 (see (2)(i)(a) above) or of the person with recording rights under section 186 (see (3)(a) above) will not be awarded if the defendant shows that he believed on reasonable grounds that consent had been given.[14]

Similarly, damages for infringement by importing, possessing or dealing with an illicit recording under sections 184 and 188 (see (2)(i)(d) and (3)(c) respectively above) will not exceed a reasonable payment in respect of the act complained of if the recording was innocently obtained.[15]

An infringement of the performers' property rights is treated in the same way as an infringement of other property rights, such as copyright. The remedies available include damages (including additional damages), injunctions and accounts.[16] Damages will not be awarded if it is shown that the defendant did not know, and had no reason to believe that the rights subsisted in the recording.[17]

There are further remedies which may apply to any infringement of rights in performance. These include orders for delivery up of illicit recordings of a performance[19] and for seizure of illicit recordings which immediately available for sale or hire (if the police have been informed of the proposed seizure).[19]

The Act also creates a number of criminal offences relating to making, dealing with or using illicit recordings.[20]

---

[11] *ibid.*, s.187(1). "Appropriate consent" refers to the consent of the performer or the person who, at the time the consent was given, had recording rights in relation to the performance: *ibid.*, s.187(2).

[12] *ibid.*, s.188(1).

[13] *ibid.*, s.194.

[14] ss.182(3) and 186(2) of the Act respectively.

[15] ss.184(2) and (3) and 188(2) and (3) of the Act respectively.

[16] *ibid.*, s.191I.

[17] *ibid.*, s.191J. This exception is unlikely to apply in the majority of cases.

[18] *ibid.*, s.195.

[19] *ibid.*, s.196.

[20] *ibid.*, ss.198–202.

Chapter 6

Trade marks and passing off

---

1. INTRODUCTION

Building and protecting brands is at the heart of most successful businesses.   **6-01**
By associating a business with particular names, signs, packaging or other elements, companies and individuals can secure further custom in the future. But
such businesses, driven by the value of their goodwill, will inevitably attract
imitators. This chapter examines how brands may be protected from preda-
tory third parties by the law of trade marks and passing off.[1]

It must be said at the outset that these areas of law are encountered only infrequently by many of those involved in publishing contentious material, or at
least cause relatively few problems. Newspaper articles or book titles may refer
to a brand or an individual but, as we shall see, such use is normally permitted.[2]
When television or radio programmes, particularly dramas, refer to brands,
that is a matter which should be treated with caution by the broadcaster.[3]

Where trade marks and passing off can create real difficulties, however, is in
the context of advertising. Advertisers may seek to run campaigns which are
similar to those of their competitors; or they may wish to identify their rival's
product in the course of comparing that product with their own. If taken too
far—and we shall look at the limits placed on such advertising—claims may
be brought not just against the advertiser but also against its agency and the
media owner concerned.[4]

Trade marks may be registered or unregistered. This chapter examines registered marks and then goes on to consider unregistered marks in the context
of claims for passing off. As we shall see, a business launching proceedings to
protect its brand will tend to be in a stronger position if it does so on the basis

---

[1] Brands may also be protected by copyright laws in certain circumstances: the design of a
company logo may, for example, amount to an artistic work. See Chap. 5 on copyright protection generally.

[2] *Clark v. Associated Newspapers Ltd* [1998] 1 All E.R. 959, was a recent case where such use was
not permitted.

[3] Though such references tend to give rise to libel concerns inadvertent libel is considered in
Chap. 2.

[4] Advertisers must also be aware of the provision relating to the use of rival brands contained in
the Codes described in Pt. II. These include the Independent Television Commission's Code of
Advertising Standards and Practice (Chap. 13) and the Committee of Advertising Practice's
Advertising Code (Chap.17).

of a registered mark, rather than proving the extent of its goodwill to a court from scratch as it is required to do in a passing off claim.

2. REGISTERED TRADE MARKS

6-02 Most of the law concerning registered trade marks is contained in the Trade Marks Act 1994 ("the Act"). This legislation grants rights to those who have successfully applied for registration of their marks to the Trade Marks Registry of the Patent Office.

(1) WHAT TYPES OF TRADE MARK CAN BE REGISTERED?

6-03 A trade mark is given a wide definition for the purposes of the Act as:

". . . any sign capable of being represented graphically which is capable of distinguishing goods or services of one undertaking from those of other undertakings . . ."[5]

The Act specifies that a trade mark includes words (including personal names), designs, letters, or numerals or the shape of goods or their packaging. Depending on the circumstances, other distinctive elements such as colours, colour combinations, sounds and smells may be registrable.

(2) APPLYING FOR REGISTRATION

6-04 An application for registration is made to the Trade Marks Registry at the Patent Office and should include a statement of the goods and services in relation to which the mark will be used. For this purpose, all goods and services are classified and the applicant must nominate in which of 42 classes his mark will be used.

(3) GROUNDS FOR REFUSING REGISTRATION

Registration may be refused on either absolute or relative grounds.

Absolute grounds for refusal of registration

6-05 There are certain types of mark which will not be registered under the Act.[6] These include:

(a) Those which do not have a distinctive character.

---

[5] Trade Marks Act 1994, s.1(1).
[6] *ibid.*, s.3.

106

(b)   Those which consist merely of signs or representations as to kind, quality, quantity, intended purpose, value, geographical origin, the time the goods were produced or the services rendered, or other characteristics.

(c)   Those which consist exclusively of signs or indications which have become customary in current language or industry practice.

(d)   Those which are contrary to public policy, accepted principles of morality or of such a nature as to deceive the public.

(e)   Those which would otherwise be prohibited under United Kingdom or Community law.

(f)   Those which fall into the category of "specially protected emblems"; for example, royal insignia, national flags, the emblems of international organisations and the Olympic symbol.[7]

(g)   Those for which the application was made in bad faith.

In respect of (a), (b) and (c) above, registration will not be refused if the mark, by the time an application is made, has become distinctive through use.

Relative grounds for refusal of registration

There are other occasions when the Patent Office will refuse registration if the trade mark, once registered, would conflict with another earlier mark.[8] The situations covered by this provision may be summarised as follows[9]:   **6-06**

(a)   a trade mark shall not be registered if it is identical with an earlier trade mark and the goods or services for which the trade mark is applied for are identical with those for which the earlier trade mark is protected;

(b)   a trade mark shall not be registered if because—

   (i)   the mark is identical with an earlier mark and is to be registered for goods or services similar to those for which the earlier trade mark is protected, or
   (ii)   the mark is similar to an earlier mark and is to be registered for goods or services identical with or similar to those for which the earlier trade mark is protected,

   there exists a likelihood of confusion on the part of the public, which includes the likelihood of association with the earlier trade mark;

---

[7] Trade Marks Act 1994, s.4.
[8] An "earlier" mark is defined in Trade Marks Act 1994, s.6. It includes a registered U.K. or European Community trade mark.
[9] See Trade Marks Act 1994, s.5.

(c) a trade mark which—

   (i)   is identical with or similar to an earlier mark, and
   (ii) is to be registered for goods or services which are not similar to those for which the earlier trade mark is protected,

   shall not be registered if, and to the extent that, the earlier trade mark has a reputation in the United Kingdom (or in the case of a Community trade mark in the European Community) and the use of the later mark without due cause would take unfair advantage of, or be detrimental to, the distinctive character or repute of the earlier trade mark;

(d) A trade mark shall not be registered if, or to the extent that, its use is liable to be prevented by a third party bringing a claim based on (*inter alia*) passing off, copyright, design right or registered designs.

The Patent Office may still allow a registration, notwithstanding an earlier right, if the applicant can show that there has been honest concurrent use of his mark.[10]

(4) REGISTRATION OUTSIDE THE UNITED KINGDOM

6-07   Trade mark registration provides an essentially national remedy to the trade mark proprietor. So, for example, a French trade mark would not of itself provide a remedy for what would otherwise be infringing acts within the United Kingdom. There are, however, two important procedures which allow for international registrations. They are significantly different in approach. Briefly, they may be summarised as follows.

The Community trade mark

6-08   Since April 1, 1996[11] it has been possible to make a single application for trade mark registration which will afford protection throughout the European Union. The application can be filed either at the European Union Trade Mark Office in Alicante, Spain or at the applicant's national Trade Mark Registry. The procedure and requirements for registration are similar to those under the Trade Marks Act 1994, as are the rights and obligations of the proprietor. So, for example, a successful filing made in France for a Community trade mark will afford protection for United Kingdom infringements.

The benefit of the Community system is that, for a single fee, the trade mark proprietor obtains protection in every European Union state. One reason for not applying in this way, however, is that the application may well fail if a search or opposition reveals an earlier conflicting mark in a single European Union country.[12]

---

[10] Trade Marks Act 1994, s.7.
[11] Following the implementation of the Community Trade Mark Regulation: Regulation 40/94.
[12] A rejected Community application can be converted into a national application.

The Madrid Agreement and Protocol

Protection of trade marks on an international basis is further made possible   **6-09**
by two treaties: the Madrid Agreement[13] and the Madrid Protocol.[14]
Registration is applied for at the applicant's home registry and then forwarded
to the World Intellectual Property Organisation (WIPO) in Geneva. The
system which has emerged from these agreements is not like Community registration: whereas a successful Community filing affords protection in all
European Union states, this is an international application which results in a
series of national registrations. The outcome of those applications may vary
between each country.

(5) EFFECTS OF REGISTRATION

The proprietor of a registered trade mark has exclusive rights in the mark.[15] The   **6-10**
acts which amount to infringement, if done without his consent, are as follows[16]:

(1)   using in the course of trade a sign which is identical with the trade mark
      in relation to goods or services which are identical with those for which
      it is registered;

(2)   using in the course of trade a sign where because—

      (a)   the sign is identical with the trade mark and is used in relation to
            goods or services similar to those for which the trade mark is regis-
            tered, or
      (b)   the sign is similar to the trade mark and is used in relation to goods
            or services identical with or similar to those for which the trade mark
            is registered,

      there exists a likelihood of confusion on the part of the public, which
      includes the likelihood of association with the trade mark;

(3)   using in the course of trade a sign which—

      (a)   is identical with or similar to the trade mark, and
      (b)   is used in relation to goods or services which are not similar to those
            for which the trade mark is registered,

      where the trade mark has a reputation in the United Kingdom and the
      use of the sign, being without due course, takes unfair advantage of, or

---

[13] Madrid Agreement Concerning the International Registration of Marks of April 14, 1891.
[14] The Protocol relating to the Madrid Agreement Concerning the International Registration of
Marks of June 28, 1989. The Trade Marks (International Registration) Order 1996 (S.I. 1996
No. 714) came into force on March 11, 1996 and gives effect to the Protocol in the U.K.
[15] See Trade Marks Act 1994, s.9. The rights originate from the date of application, though proceedings cannot be begun before the date of registration: *ibid.*, s 9(3)(a).
[16] *ibid.*, s.10.

is detrimental to, the distinctive character or the repute of the trade mark.

It will be apparent that the criterion to be satisfied by a trade mark proprietor in successfully bringing proceedings mirror very closely the relative grounds for refusing registration of a mark.[17]

A recent case illustrates the point that threatened infringement of a trade mark may entitle a trade mark proprietor to obtain an injunction.[18] In *British Telecommunications plc v. One In A Million Ltd*[19] the defendant was a dealer in Internet domain names and had acquired the domains of BT and other well-known businesses without their consent. The domain names did not relate to active websites but were acquired with a view to being sold to the trade mark proprietors, or at least to block the use of that name by the proprietors. The court found that there was a threatened use sufficient to grant an injunction.[20]

It should also be noted that groundless threats of proceedings for infringement of registered trade mark may allow the victim of the threat to institute proceedings.[21]

(6) WHO CAN BE SUED?

6-11   A person uses a sign

"... if, in particular, he:

(a)   affixes it to goods or the packaging thereof;

(b)   offers or exposes goods for sale, puts them on the market or stocks them for those purposes under the sign, or offers or supplies services under the sign;

(c)   imports or exports goods under the sign; or

(d)   uses the sign on business papers or in advertising."[22]

Persons caught by this provision, which is not an exhaustive statement of what amounts to use, will be treated as primary infringers.

Persons who are more peripherally involved may be able to claim that their use was innocent. The relevant provision is section 10(5) of the Act which states:

"A person who applies a registered trade mark to material intended to be used for labelling or packaging goods, as a business paper, or for advertising goods and services, shall be treated as a party to any use of the

---

[17] See 2(3) above.
[18] It may also be possible to invoke the Uniform Domain Dispute Resolution Policy operated by ICANN: see Chap. 20 at 2.
[19] [1998] 4 All E.R. 476.
[20] The injunction was also granted on the grounds of passing off.
[21] Trade Marks Act 1994, s.21.

material which infringes the registered trade mark if when he applied the mark he knew or had reason to believe that the application of the mark was not duly authorised by the proprietor or a licensee."

Printers and publishers may be able to rely on this provision. It is more difficult for advertising agencies to do so.

(7) DEFENCES (OR "EXCEPTIONS" TO LIABILITY)

Though the Act does not use the word "defence", there are a number of pro-   **6-12**
visions which amount, in effect, to defences. It is beyond the scope of this text to examine these provisions in detail, but the key provisions (particularly those affecting advertisers) are set out below. In addition there may be more formal grounds on which to defend a claim—for example, by proving that one or more of the elements of infringement are not present, that the trade mark registration is invalid or that the registration has been revoked.

Identifying goods or services as the proprietor's

There will be no infringement if a person uses a trade mark for the purpose of   **6-13**
identifying goods or services as those of the proprietor or a licensee.[23] There is a proviso to this provision, however, to the effect that the section will not prevent there being an infringement if the use is ". . . otherwise than in accordance with honest practices in commercial and industrial matters" and "without due cause takes unfair advantage of, or is detrimental to, the distinctive character or character or repute of the trade mark".

This provision can be relied on by advertisers when carrying out comparative advertising and represents a considerable relaxation of the law compared with previous legislation. It was first examined in *Barclays Bank v. RBS Advanta*,[24] a case where Barclays complained about an advertisement by the defendant which sought to compare the relative merits of the companies' credit cards. In refusing an injunction, Laddie J. provided some guidance on the section including the following:

(i)   The onus of proving the proviso factors falls on the claimant.

(ii) The test as to whether use of the mark was honest is an objective one: would the use be considered honest by the reasonable man? If it would, there is no infringement. In applying the test, the court should overlook the emphasis placed on the benefits of the advertiser's product at the expense of the competitor's because the public expects hyperbole in advertising. Laddie J. cited, as an example of an advertisement that was not honest, one that was "significantly misleading".

---

[22] Trade Marks Act 1994, s.10(4).
[23] Trade Marks Act 1994, s.10(6).
[24] [1996] R.P.C. 307.

(iii) The court will not look at whether the advertiser has adhered to the advertising industry's codes in determining whether the advertiser has acted "in accordance with honest practices in industrial and commercial matters".[25]

(iv) To amount to an infringement, the advertisement must confer an advantage on the advertiser, or cause damage to the competitor, which is more than minimal.

This decision was followed by *Vodaphone Group plc v. Orange Personal Communications Services Ltd*,[26] a case involving comparative advertising in the telecommunications sector. Orange deployed advertising stating that "on average Orange users save £20 every month" and referred to Vodaphone's "equivalent tariffs" as a means of comparison. The court approved the approach of Laddie J. on the issue of honesty in comparative advertising, stating that the test was whether a reasonable man would take the claim seriously and that the more precise and specific the claim was, the more likely it was to be taken seriously. An advertisement was "otherwise than in accordance with honest practices" if it was objectively misleading to a substantial proportion of the reasonable audience.

Whether these decisions, and indeed section 10(6) of the Trade Marks Act, will remain good law in the context of comparative advertising has been thrown into some doubt by the Control of Misleading Advertisements (Amendment) Regulations 2000. These Regulations, which came into force on April 23, 2000, implement the European Union Directive on Comparative Advertising.[27] The purpose of the Directive was to harmonise comparative advertising laws across the European Union: in several Member States, this had not previously been possible. However, it remains to be seen whether the United Kingdom Regulations are more stringent than the provisions in section 10(6).

Regulation 5 inserts a new Regulation 4A in the Control of Misleading Advertisements Regulations 1988. It states that a comparative advertisement shall, so far as the comparison is concerned, be permitted only when the following conditions are met:

- it is not misleading;

- it compares goods or services meeting the same needs or intended for the same purpose;

---

[25] It is nonetheless good practice to adhere to the codes: see Part II of this text.

[26] [1997] F.S.R. 34. See also *British Telecommunications plc v. A.T. & T. Communications (U.K.) Ltd* [1997] E.I.P.R. D-134 and *Cable & Wireless plc v. B.T. plc* [1998] F.S.R. 383. For an example of comparative advertising being carried other otherwise than in accordance with honest practices, see *Emaco Ltd & Aktiebolaget Electrolux v. Dyson Appliances Ltd*, *The Times*, February 8, 1999, in which both Electrolux and Dyson published false statements about the other's vacuum cleaners.

[27] Council Directive 97/55. Responsibility for enforcement falls to the Director-General of the Office of Fair Trading, the Independent Television Commission and the Radio Authority. The Committee of Advertising Practice will also refer instances of persistent breach of its Codes to the Director-General of the OFT.

- it objectively compares one or more material, relevant, verifiable and representative features of those goods and services, which may include price;

- it does not create confusion in the marketplace between the advertiser and a competitor or between the advertiser's trade marks, trade names, other distinguishing marks, goods or services and those of a competitor;

- it does not discredit or denigrate the trade marks, trade names, other distinguishing marks, goods, services, activities, or circumstances of a competitor;

- for products with designation of origin, it relates in each case to products with the same designation;

- it does not take unfair advantage of the reputation of a trade mark, trade name or other distinguishing marks of a competitor or of the designation of origin of competing products; and

- it does not present goods or services as imitations or replicas of goods or services bearing a protected trade mark or trade name.

The Regulations also require that, in the case of a comparative advertisement referring to a special offer, such an advertisement is not permitted unless it indicates in a clear and unequivocal way the date on which the offer ends or, where appropriate, that the special offer is subject to the availability of the goods and services and, where the special offer has not yet begun, the date of the start of the period during which the special price or other specific conditions shall apply.

Use by a person of his own name or address

A registered trade mark is not infringed by the use by a person of his own **6-14** name or address, provided the use is in accordance with honest practices in industrial or commercial matters.[28]

The legislative intention behind this provision was that a trader using his own name should not have to "look over his shoulder to make sure that a registered trade mark is not in the way".[29] A company may rely on the full name by which it is usually known in the marketplace, and that name does not have to be its full corporate title (*i.e.* it can exclude "limited", "plc", "corporation", etc.) in order to be protected by the defence.[30] In accordance with the proviso mentioned above, the defendant must establish that he has used his own name in good faith in order to succeed in this defence.[31]

---

[28] Trade Marks Act 1994, s.11(2)(a).
[29] *Mercury Communications Ltd v. Mercury Interactive (U.K.) Ltd* [1995] F.S.R. 850. The court pointed out that, although such a trader would not be liable for trade mark infringement, he might be liable for passing off.
[30] *NAD Electronics Inc. v. NAD Computer Systems Ltd* [1997] F.S.R. 380.
[31] This requirement originally derived from Trade Marks Act 1938, s.8(a), under which the defendant had to prove that his use of the name was bona fide, but is thought to accord with the "honest practices" proviso in the 1994 Act: Morcom, Roughton and Graham, *The Modern Law of Trade Marks* (1999).

In the *NAD* case, for example, the defendant failed to do so because its use of the "NAD" name after it had been informed of the claimant's complaint had not been in good faith, especially as it had changed the mark to make it even more like the mark complained of.[32]

The use of indications concerning characteristics of goods or services

6-15 A registered trade mark is not infringed by the use of indications concerning the kind, quality, quantity, intended purpose, value, geographical origin, the time of production of goods or of rendering of services, or other characteristics of goods or services, provided the use is in accordance with honest practices in industrial or commercial matters.[33]

The impact of section 11(2)(b) was illustrated by the *Wet Wet Wet* case.[34] This concerned trade mark infringement proceedings against the publishers of a book about the well-known pop band called *A Sweet Little Mystery — Wet Wet Wet — The Inside Story*. Lord McCluskey held that the use of the trade mark "Wet Wet Wet" in the book fell within section 11(2)(b) because the words were an indication of the main character of the book. He observed that it would be a bizarre result of the Trade Marks Act if it could be used to prevent publishers from using the protected name in the title of a book about the company or product.

The section was examined again in *British Sugar plc v. James Robertson & Sons Ltd* (the *Treat* case).[35] The claimant, the maker of the ice cream syrup "Silver Spoon Treat", alleged that the maker of a sweet spread called "Robertson's Toffee Treat" had infringed its trade mark. The action failed because the defendant's use of the "Treat" mark was descriptive, or an "indication", within the meaning of section 11(2)(b).

It was held in *European Ltd v. Economist Newspapers Ltd*[36] that, if a descriptive word was so similar to a trade mark as to cause confusion, it would be contrary to "honest practices" to use that word, and therefore the defendant would not be able to rely on section 11(2)(b) as a "defence".

There can be considerable overlap between the availability of this "defence" and that available under section 10(6) of the Act which, as we have seen above, allows a mark to be used to identify goods or services to be identified as those of the proprietor. The inclusion in section 11(2)(b) of the "honest practices" proviso means that there is also considerable overlap with case law relating to section 10(6). It is necessary to consider the impact of the Control of Misleading Advertisements (Amendment) Regulations 2000 when considering the effect of section 11(2)(b).

---

[32] *NAD Electronics Inc. v. NAD Computer Systems Ltd* (1997) F.S.R. 380.

[33] Trade Marks Act 1994, s.11(2)(b).

[34] *Bravado Merchandising Services Ltd v. Mainstream Publishing (Edinburgh) Ltd* [1996] F.S.R. 205.

[35] [1996] R.P.C. 281.

[36] [1996] F.S.R. 431. In the case, *The European* newspaper failed in an action against *The Economist* to prevent publication of a weekly newspaper called *The European Voice* on the basis that the marks were not sufficiently similar, so the judge did not need to consider whether the defendant could rely on s.11(2)(b).

Use to indicate the intended purpose of a product or service

A registered trade mark is not infringed by the use of the trade mark where it **6-16** is necessary to indicate the intended purpose of a product or service (in particular, as accessories or spare parts), provided the use is in accordance with honest practices in industrial or commercial matters.[37]

Earlier right

Another exception arises where the alleged infringer is the user of an earlier **6-17** unregistered mark which has been used continuously in relation to goods or services in a particular locality, such that the earlier mark would be protected by a rule of law such as passing off.[38]

Exhaustion of rights

There will be no infringement in the case of parallel imports, where goods **6-18** bearing the United Kingdom proprietor's trade mark are placed on markets elsewhere in the European Union by him or with his consent, unless the owner has some legitimate reason to object (for example, the goods have been altered or impaired in some way).[39] This provision illustrates the "exhaustion of rights" principle: a trade mark proprietor is entitled to be the first to market goods under his mark, but once they have been sold he can no longer exercise his rights over the use of the mark so as to prevent their importation or exportation to other European Union states.

(8) REMEDIES

The remedies available for a trade mark infringement are broadly the same **6-19** as those where copyright has been infringed. General provisions described in relation to copyright remedies apply equally to trade mark infringements.

The 1994 Act provides for damages, an account of profits, injunctive relief and any other relief that would be available in respect of the infringement of any other property right orders.[40] This would include search orders.

Trade mark proprietors are also able to obtain special relief under the Act. These include:

- the erasure, removal or obliteration of an offending sign[41];

- the delivery up of infringing goods[42]; and

---

[37] Trade Marks Act 1994, s.11(2)(c).
[38] *ibid.*, s.11(3).
[39] *ibid.*, s.12.
[40] *ibid.*, s.14(2).
[41] *ibid.*, s.15(1).
[42] *ibid.*, ss.16 and 18.

- the destruction or forfeiture of infringing goods, materials or articles.[43]

In the *One in a Million* case—described at (5) above—the court ordered a domain name to be transferred to the trade mark proprietor.[44]

It should be noted that the Trade Marks Act also creates certain criminal offences aimed at counterfeit or pirated goods.[45]

3. PASSING OFF

(1) INTRODUCTION

6-20 Unlike proceedings based on registered trade marks, there are no prior formalities to be completed to institute a claim for passing off. It is, however, necessary for a claimant to demonstrate that he has built up a brand which, on the facts of the case, will give him protection against third parties who seek to pass off their goods or services as the claimant's. To succeed, he will need to show that there is goodwill associated with his goods or services, a misrepresentation by the defendant leading to confusion or deception, and damage to his business.[46] These elements are considered below.

Although the tort of passing off is well established in the common law, it has been extended over the years to safeguard not just names or trade marks, but also slogans, packaging, celebrity indorsements and, more recently, the use of domain names.[47] It is a further means of imposing honest standards on advertising and other business conduct in those instances where it oversteps the mark between fair and unfair competition.

(2) GOODWILL

General considerations

6-21 Goodwill has been defined as the benefit and advantage of the good name, reputation and connection of a business, the attractive force which brings in custom, and the characteristic which distinguishes an established business from a start-up business.[48] Broadly, goodwill will exist if a business has had substantial sales and substantial promotion of its goods or services.

In assessing whether sufficient goodwill has been accumulated for the purposes of passing off, the court will consider factors such as the inherent distinctiveness of the claimant's trade mark, the quality of his goods or services,

---

[43] Trade Marks Act 1994, ss.15(2) and 19(1).
[44] [1998] 4 All E.R. 476.
[45] Trade Marks Act 1994, ss.92–101.
[46] *Reckitt & Colman Products Ltd v. Borden Inc.* [1990] 1 All E.R. 873.
[47] *British Telecommunications plc v. One In A Million Ltd* [1998] 4 All E.R. 476.
[48] *Lord MacNaughten in IRC v. Muller & Co's Margarine Ltd* [1901] A.C. 217.

the nature and extent of use of the trade mark (for example, the period and geographical area of use, and the value and volume of sales), and the nature and extent of advertising of the goods or services.

These are regarded as factors which lead consumers to choose one product over another. As the consumer will come to associate certain characteristics with a given trade mark over time, so that product's goodwill will become embodied or represented by the trade mark. As a result, it is not necessary that the consumer knows or cares about the manufacturer or trade mark owner, so long as he understands the trade mark to indicate a particular origin, *i.e.* the claimant.[49]

As goodwill is not an exclusive right, it may be a "defence" to a passing off action that the claimant and defendant have concurrent rights to a trade mark. The parties may honestly share the trade mark, for example, because several parties share in the goodwill of a business, or because a trader has continued to use a trade mark in a locality despite the use of a similar mark elsewhere.

Descriptive, not distinctive

On the other hand, a claimant will fail if his mark is not distinctive, but merely **6-22** a descriptive or generic term. This was well illustrated in *Barnsley Brewery Co. Ltd v. RBNB*[50] where the claimant was refused an injunction to prevent another brewery using the name "Barnsley Bitter" because the average customer was not likely to assume that "Barnsley Bitter" was brewed by the claimant and no one else.

Goodwill may also be lost if a product name becomes a generic description of goods of that type. "Hoover" and "Thermos" could be examples. The owner of such a brand name would have to prove that the name still induced consumers to buy that product, rather than other products.[51]

Reputation in the United Kingdom

Goodwill must be shown to exist in the United Kingdom for a claimant to **6-23** succeed in a passing off action. The business concerned must generally be carried on, and have customers, in this country.

This was seen in the case of *Anheuser-Busch Inc v. Budejovicky Budvar NP.*[52] Anheuser-Busch, the American beer brewer, sought to establish passing off by the defendant Czech brewer on the basis that they sold beer at United States military and diplomatic institutions in the United Kingdom. The claimant failed in its action because it did not have sufficient goodwill amongst the general public in the United Kingdom.[53] In another case, the owner of the

---

[49] *United Biscuits (U.K.) Ltd v. Asda Stores Ltd* [1997] R.P.C. 513.
[50] [1997] F.S.R. 462.
[51] *Sypha Sounds Sales Ltd v. Tape Recorders (Electronics) Ltd* [1961] R.P.C. 27.
[52] [1984] F.S.R. 413.
[53] See also *Jian Tools for Sales Inc v. Roderick Manhattan Group Ltd* [1995] F.S.R. 924, although that case concerned the grant of an injunction, for which the judge found the claimant had sufficient customers in the U.K. to show goodwill.

"Crazy Horse Saloon" in Paris failed in a claim for passing off: the court found that, although promotional literature for the Saloon was distributed in this country, it lacked a real connection with the United Kingdom.[54]

However, this aspect of the law relating to goodwill depends on the circumstances of the case. An injunction was granted to the Sheraton Corporation of America, even though it had no business in the United Kingdom save for a booking office for its hotels abroad.[55] The songwriter Pete Waterman also succeeded against the United Kingdom licensee of a New York recording studio which was using Waterman's mark "The Hit Factory". Although the New York studio had customers in the United Kingdom, it had no place of business here. Nevertheless, the judge found that the presence of customers in the United Kingdom was sufficient to prove local goodwill.

In *Mecklermedia Corp. v. D.C. Congress GmbH*[56] an injunction was granted against a German company's promotion of its trade show and exhibitions under the claimant's "Internet World" mark, despite that fact that the show and exhibitions took place outside the United Kingdom. This was because they were promoted in the United Kingdom on the Internet and thereby interfered with the claimant's goodwill. This case can therefore be distinguished from those just described: the claimant clearly had a goodwill in the United Kingdom.

Anticipatory goodwill

6-24   Goodwill may also exist where a business is not, technically, being carried on. For instance, advance advertising and publicity prior to the launch of a business has been held to generate the goodwill.[57] In *Pontiac Marina Pte Ltd v. CDL Hotels International Ltd*, an injunction was obtained by the claimant owner of the yet-to-be-opened "Millenia" hotel to prevent the defendant promoting the launch of its own "Millenium Hotels and Resorts".[58]

Conversely, goodwill has also been held to remain attached to businesses, even though they have ceased using a particular mark, or even trading, a number of years earlier.[59]

Class actions

6-25   Passing off has been extended by the courts to cover more general circumstances where the goodwill in a name or mark vests in more than one person or business. Producers in a geographical area have used passing off to protect

---

[54] *Bernadin (Alain) et Cie v. Pavilion Properties Ltd* [1967] R.P.C. 581.

[55] *Sheraton Corporation of America v. Sheraton Motels Ltd* [1964] R.P.C. 202.

[56] [1998] Ch. 40.

[57] *Fletcher Challenge Ltd v. Fletcher Challenge Pty Ltd* [1982] F.S.R. 1; *Glaxo plc and Wellcome plc v. Glaxo Wellcome Ltd* [1996] F.S.R. 388 (those cases involved advance publicity of company mergers).

[58] [1997] F.S.R. 725.

[59] *Ad-Lib Club Ltd v. Granville* [1971] 2 All E.R. 300; *Thermawear Ltd v. Vedonis Ltd* [1982] R.P.C. 44. On the other hand, no protection will be given where the mark or name has been abandoned.

their collective goodwill: for example, champagne producers in the Champagne region of France[60] and chocolate manufacturers in Switzerland.[61] Producers who manufacture goods to a certain recipe[62] or to accord with certain industry standards[63] have also relied on passing off.

Although passing off normally attaches to business or trading activities, it has also been applied by the courts to non-traders whose trade marks have been misrepresented. Passing off has been successfully claimed by professional and charitable bodies,[64] non-profit associations and chambers of commerce.[65] It has also been held to apply to professionals, artists[66] and authors.[67]

(3) MISREPRESENTATION

Types of misrepresentation

The claimant must establish that there has been a misrepresentation, either express or implied, by the defendant that gives rise to actual or likely confusion or deception as to the origin of the goods or services in question. The confusion or deception may be on the part of actual or potential customers, suppliers or fellow traders.   **6-26**

Misrepresentations take a number of forms. The most obvious is to the effect that the defendant's goods or services are in fact the claimant's.[68] Other forms of misrepresentation are to the effect that the defendant's goods or services are of the same kind or quality as the claimant's,[69] that second-hand goods of the claimant's are new,[70] that superceded goods are the claimant's current products,[71] or that altered or adulterated goods were manufactured in that form by the claimant.[72]

Another common misrepresentation is that there is an association between the defendant's goods or services and those of the claimant. Such an association is not established if the defendant merely fashions his goods in such a way that the consumer is reminded of the claimant's product. The link with the claimant's product must be so precise as to imply an association between the claimant and the defendant; for example, that the claimant exercised some sort

---

[60] *Taittinger S.A. v. Allbev Ltd* [1993] F.S.R. 641.
[61] *Chocosuisse Union des Fabricants Suisses de Chocolat v. Cadbury Ltd, The Times*, November 25, 1997.
[62] *Erven Warnink B.V. v. J. Townsend & Sons (Hull) Ltd* [1979] 2 All E.R. 927.
[63] *Hodge Clemco Ltd v. Airblast Ltd* [1995] F.S.R. 806.
[64] *Re Dr Barnardo's Homes, National Incorporated Association v. Barnardo Amalgamated Industries Ltd and Benardout* (1949) 66 R.P.C. 103.
[65] *Lagos Chamber of Commerce Inc v. Registrar of Companies and Association of Merchants and Industrialists* (1955) 72 R.P.C. 263, P.C.
[66] *Marengo v. Daily Sketch and Sunday Graphic Ltd* (1948) 65 R.P.C. 242.
[67] *Lord Byron v. Johnston* (1816) 2 Mer. 29; *Clark v. Associated Newspapers Ltd* [1998] 1 All E.R. 959.
[68] *Joseph Rodgers & Sons Ltd v. W. N. Rodgers & Co.* (1924) 41 R.P.C. 277.
[69] *A. G. Spalding & Bros v. A. W. Gamage Ltd* (1915) 32 R.P.C. 273.
[70] *Morris Motors Ltd v. Lilley (trading as G. and L. Motors)* [1959] 3 All E.R. 737.
[71] *Harris v. Warren and Phillips* (1918) 35 R.P.C. 217.
[72] *Rolls-Royce Motors Ltd v. Zanelli* [1979] R.P.C. 148.

of control over the defendant's product.[73] This type of misrepresentation has arisen where the defendant suggests that he is authorised to act as an agent for the claimant,[74] or that a licence exists between the parties.[75]

Factors relevant to proving confusion or deception

6-27   In determining whether there has been a misrepresentation, the courts look at the facts of each case and many of the leading cases turn on their particular circumstances. The court, in making its decision, will consider factors such as the origin and nature of the goods or services, the market in which they are placed and the way in which they reach that market, the activities of competing traders and their use of marks, and the nature of the relevant customers.

The misrepresentation must occur at the point of sale. In *Bostik Ltd v. Sellotape G.B. Ltd*,[76] although the defendant's product was identical in colour to that of the claimant's Blu-Tack, the court held that the defendant's packaging was so different to the claimant's that the misrepresentation came too late (*i.e.* when the consumer had bought and opened the packet).

The likelihood of confusion will be assessed from the point of view of the average consumer. The court will have in mind, not a person who places the goods side by side and examines them in detail, but the impression created in the mind of the average consumer who may have an imperfect memory of the goods. This was seen in *Kimberley-Clark Ltd v. Fort Sterling Ltd*,[77] which involved a promotion by Kleenex of a range of tissues. The offer stated "softness guaranteed (or we'll exchange it for Andrex)", and contained a reference in small print to the effect that Andrex was a competing brand of tissues.[78] Despite the qualifying reference, it was held that a substantial number of normal but busy customers would think that the Kleenex tissues were produced by or in some way associated with the Andrex manufacturers.

In the "Penguin" case, the packaging and get-up of Asda's "Puffin" biscuits was so similar to McVities' "Penguin" biscuits that substantial numbers of the public would suppose that the two biscuits had the same manufacturer. The court held that the distinctiveness of the get-up placed a special obligation on Asda to avoid confusion.[79]

In the case of *Clark v. Associated Newspapers Ltd*,[80] *The Evening Standard* was found liable for passing off when it parodied the well-known published diaries of the Conservative politician, Alan Clark, in a series of articles. The choice of format, particularly the design of the heading ("Alan Clark's Secret

---

[73] See *Harrods Ltd v. Harrodian School Ltd* [1996] R.P.C. 697 and *United Biscuits (U.K.) Ltd v. Asda Stores Ltd* [1997] R.P.C. 513.

[74] *Wheeler and Wilson Manufacturing Co. v. Shakespear* (1869) 39 L.J. Ch. 36.

[75] *Mirage Studios v. Counter-Feat Clothing Ltd* [1991] F.S.R. 145.

[76] [1994] R.P.C. 556.

[77] [1997] F.S.R. 877

[78] Traders may seek to avoid confusion by the use of distinguishing elements which negate the effect of what would otherwise have been a misrepresentation, including disclaimers.

[79] *United Biscuits (U.K.) Ltd v. Asda Stores Ltd* [1997] R.P.C. 513.

[80] [1998] 1 All E.R. 959.

Election Diary" or "Alan Clark's Secret Political Diary"), was calculated to exploit Alan Clark's reputation as an author and the public interest in any diary written by him. Although the true author, Peter Bradshaw, was identified, its "neutralising" effect was not sufficient to prevent a substantial number of readers being deceived into thinking that the claimant was the author of the articles.

However, the heavy burden on a claimant to show likelihood of confusion is borne out by cases in which that likelihood was not proved on the balance of probabilities. So it has been held that members of the public would not be confused between Ford's Granada car model and the Granada television company,[81] that they would not be likely to associate McCain's "Stringfellow" frozen oven chips with the nightclub owner, Peter Stringfellow[82] nor would they be deceived into thinking that there was an association between the pink business pages of *The Evening Standard* and those of the *Financial Times*.[83]

Common field of activity

One issue that the courts have frequently had to consider is whether, in order for confusion to be likely, the claimant and defendant must have a common field of activity.

6-28

In *Harrods Ltd v. Harrodian School Ltd*, the famous London department store sued a school which had taken over the store's old sports ground and called itself the Harrodian School.[84] The Court of Appeal held that it was unlikely that the parents of children would send their children to the Harrodian School thinking that Harrods was responsible for the quality of the school's teaching. The fact that there was no common field of activity was a conclusive factor.

In *Lego System A/S v. Lego M. Lemelstrich Ltd*,[85] the absence of a common field of activity was not held to be conclusive. The claimant succeeded in showing a likelihood of confusion, despite the fact that it manufactured the famous children's toys and the defendant manufactured irrigation equipment (albeit equipment consisting of coloured plastic material).

This issue has arisen particularly in the context of advertising, merchandising and sponsorship where the names or images of celebrities or cartoon characters have been used without permission. Traditionally, the courts have adopted a strict approach. This can be seen in the *Kojak* decision made in the mid-1970s. This was a case brought by the makers of *Kojak*, a well-known television programme in which the lead character—a police detective—was often seen sucking on a lollipop. They sought to prevent the defendant manufacturing lollipops called "Kojakpops". Their application failed on the basis that

[81] *Granada Group v. Ford Motor Co. Ltd* [1972] F.S.R. 103.
[82] *Stringfellow v. McCain Foods (G.B.) Ltd* [1984] R.P.C. 501.
[83] *Financial Times Ltd v. Evening Standard Co. Ltd* [1991] F.S.R. 7.
[84] [1996] R.P.C. 697. See also *Stringfellow v. McCain Foods (G.B.) Ltd* [1984] R.P.C. 501.
[85] [1983] F.S.R. 155.

there was no common field of activity between the production of lollipops and the production of television programmes.[86]

With the growth of character merchandising and sponsorship in the intervening years, the courts have developed a less rigid approach. This perhaps reached its high water mark in the "Ninja Turtles" case[87] where the court rejected the strict approach previously adopted and agreed to grant relief to the rights owners of the Ninja Turtle cartoon characters against the distributors of goods in a different field of activity upon which the characters were being reproduced. The court paid particular attention to the fact that the public would believe or expect that a licence had been granted by the claimants to the defendants to sell the goods.

Whether this belief or expectation applies to a particular case will vary. In the more recent case of *Halliwell v. Panini*,[88] the unauthorised use of the Spice Girls' images on stickers was held, at the interlocutory stage, not to amount to passing off. It was not clear on the evidence that the absence of any disavowal of authorisation could reasonably lead the public to buy the defendant's product on the basis or in the belief that it was authorised by the plaintiffs.

In cases where celebrities appear in advertising without their permission, similar considerations will be applied.[89] This was seen in the Court of Appeal decision involving a British businessman who merchandised Elvis Presley products.[90] He opposed trade mark applications made in the United Kingdom by Elvis Presley Enterprises Inc. (based in Graceland) for the Elvis Presley name to be used in relation to toiletry products, because he ran a London shop which had been selling Elvis memorabilia for the last 20 years. Although it was dealing with trade mark proceedings, the Court of Appeal addressed the issue of character merchandising generally. It rejected the arguments of Elvis Presley Enterprises Inc. that the public would nowadays expect goods bearing the Elvis Presley name to be indorsed by the late singer's estate, and therefore that such goods had a distinctive source. It found instead that Elvis Presley products were not associated with any particular manufacturer and did not designate the origin of the goods.

---

[86] *Tavener Rutledge Ltd v. Trexapalm Ltd* [1977] R.P.C. 275. See also *Wombles Ltd v. Womble Skips Ltd* [1977] R.P.C. 99.

[87] *Mirage Studios v. Counter-Feat Clothing Ltd* [1991] F.S.R. 145.

[88] Lawtel, June 6, 1997.

[89] Well-known people, such as Eric Cantona, Paul Gascoigne, Damon Hill, Nigel Mansell and Jacques Villeneuve have registered as trade marks nicknames or likenesses. The Trade Marks Registry has now issued guidance on this practice following trade mark applications made by the Diana, Princess of Wales Memorial Fund: if the name or likeness is found not to be inherently distinctive, the applicant must prove that distinctiveness has been acquired through trading under that name or likeness (the Diana, Princess of Wales application failed on this ground because it was considered that there had already been widespread general use made of Diana's name and image). There is no "character right" as such under English law to bridge the gap between copyright, defamation and trade mark law. This is in contrast to the law in other jurisdictions, such as California and the Netherlands, which have introduced statutory protection of an individual's right to prevent unauthorised commercial use of their names and likenesses, without requiring that individual to prove the elements necessary for passing off.

[90] *Applications by Elvis Presley Enterprises Inc., The Times*, March 22, 1999, C.A.

In summary, therefore, the courts adopt a flexible approach to the issue of fields of activity and will be concerned to establish the expectations of the public in each case.

Using your own name

In certain circumstances, an individual may trade under his own name, despite   **6-29** someone else having goodwill in that name. Lord Simonds said in one case that "a man must be allowed to trade in his own name and if some confusion results, that is a lesser evil than that a man should be deprived of what would appear to be a natural and inherent right".[91] However, the use of the individual's own name must be done honestly and a person may not trade under his own name if it is deliberately adopted in order to benefit from the claimant's goodwill.[92] Nor is it a "defence", where a person is in fact misrepresenting the claimant's goods as his own, to claim that he is doing so only by using his own name.[93] Similarly this "exception" to passing off does not apply where a trader's claim is based on his forename or nickname.[94]

(4) DAMAGE

It is essential for a claimant to establish that his business or the goodwill   **6-30** attaching to it has suffered, or is likely to suffer, damage as a result of the misrepresentation. Damage takes a number of forms, including:

(a) loss of sales;

(b) loss of distinctiveness or dilution of goodwill;

(c) diminution of the value of the claimant's trade mark as a licensable or franchise commodity;

(d) restriction of the claimant's ability to expand his business.

Loss of sales is more likely to occur where the defendant is a direct competitor of the claimant's. Dilution of the claimant's reputation may occur where the defendant's goods are inferior to those of the claimant because the claimant no longer has control over the maintenance of his reputation. Associated with this is loss of distinctiveness, which has been successfully argued by claimants such as champagne producers and Swiss chocolate manufacturers who feared that their marks might become generic of goods to which they relate.

Sometimes damage can be inferred from the circumstances of the case. In these circumstances, proof of actual loss is not always required.

---

[91] *Marengo v. Daily Sketch and Sunday Graphic Ltd* (1948) 65 R.P.C. 242.
[92] *Joseph Rodgers & Sons v. W. N. Rodgers & Co.* (1924) 41 R.P.C. 277.
[93] *NAD Electronics Inc. v. NAD Computer Systems Ltd* [1997] F.S.R. 380.
[94] *Biba Group Ltd v. Biba Boutique* [1980] R.P.C. 413.

TRADE MARKS AND PASSING OFF

(5) REMEDIES

6-31 These are essentially the same as those available for infringement of copyright and registered trade mark. The most commonly sought are injunctions, search orders, orders for delivery up and damages or an account of profits.

124

Chapter 7

Breach of confidence

1. INTRODUCTION

The law of confidentiality can be used as a blunt instrument against the media. **7-01** Provided certain conditions are met, a claimant can prevent the public dissemination of truthful statements, or of information to which no intellectual property rights attach. There have been a number of high profile cases in the past decade or so, perhaps the most famous involving the Conservative Government when it chased Peter Wright, the former MI5 officer, around the globe in an ultimately futile attempt to prevent the publication of his book, *Spycatcher*.[1]

The media need to be particularly vigilant about the possibility of a claim arising. If confidential information has been imparted, the "confider" of the information may proceed against the person to whom the confidential information was initially confided ("the confidant"), as well as against third parties to whom the information may subsequently have been communicated. This could include journalists receiving information from their sources, and even extend to other media outlets which attempt to follow up the same story.

Until recently the threat of prior restraint in this area was particularly great. Journalists were sometimes reluctant to contact the subject of a story prior to publication for fear of triggering an injunction application based on breach of confidence. The Human Rights Act 1998 has however led to a greater emphasis on the protection of freedom of expression and it is likely to prove to be more difficult to obtain an injunction before trial.[2]

On the other hand, the Human Rights Act 1998 may encourage the development of the law of confidence in a number of ways. Some lawyers believe that the Convention right to respect for private and family life may lead to an expanded role for the tort of breach of confidence. Others have suggested that the Convention right could lead to the development of a separate new right to privacy broader in scope than confidence.[3]

Furthermore, there is a considerable body of media specific regulation dealing with the issue of privacy. This is referred to in Part II when examining

---

[1] See *Attorney-General v. Guardian Newspapers* (No 2) [1990] 1 A.C. 109; *Observer and Guardian v U.K.*; *Sunday Times v. UK (No 2)*, *The Times*, November 27, 1991.
[2] See 4(1) below.
[3] This approach could arguably be seen as consistent with the approach of the Court of Appeal in *R. v. BSC ex parte BBC* [2000] E.M.L.R. 587 (see Chapter 15 at para. 15-08).

the Codes of the various regulators, and journalists should be aware of the provisions for their own sake. However, in addition, the Human Rights Act now requires the court in the context of journalistic, literary or artistic material, in weighing the balance between free expression and privacy, to have regard to any relevant privacy code.

2. WHAT DOES A CLAIMANT NEED TO PROVE?

7-02   The requirements to be satisfied by a claimant are that the information must have the necessary quality of confidence (*i.e.* it must be secret), it must have been communicated in circumstances imparting an obligation of confidence, and there has to have been an unauthorised use of the information.[4] These broad requirements (considered in more detail below) allow the courts considerable latitude in interpretation.

(1) QUALITY OF CONFIDENCE

7-03   The courts will only find for a claimant if he can establish that the information in question has the necessary quality of confidence about it. This is a rather vague test, but the following criteria must be satisfied.[5]

(a) Information must not be in the public domain[6]

7-04   Information is in the public domain if it is generally accessible to the public.[7] This will be the case if it can be obtained from legitimate, non-confidential sources, even if it is not known to the public at large.[8] For instance, it was held in *Mustad v. Dosen* that information which had been published in a patent specification was not capable of protection by the court.[9] It follows that information is confidential if it is of limited public availability. Absolute secrecy is, therefore, not required: it is sufficient if relative secrecy remains (*i.e.* the secret is known to some, but not others). This is a matter of degree, depending on the facts of the case.[10] The fact that the confider intends to publish the infor-

---

[4]   *Coco v. A. N. Clark (Engineers) Limited* [1968] F.S.R. 415; *Attorney-General v. Guardian Newspapers (No. 2)* [1990] 1 A.C. 109.

[5]   If they are not met the information is not confidential, even if it is expressly stated to be so: *De Maudsley v. Palumbo* [1996] E.M.L.R. 460.

[6]   *Saltman Engineering Co. Ltd v. Campbell Engineering Co. Ltd* (1963) 65 R.P.C. 203; Bunn v. BBC [1998] 3 All E.R. 552.

[7]   Lord Goff in *Attorney-General v. Guardian Newspapers (No. 2)* [1990] 1 A.C. 109.

[8]   A third party, such a journalist, may be liable for breach of confidence if the material was obtained from a confidential source, even if the material *could* have been obtained from a non-confidential source. If such a journalist claims that the material was in the public domain, a court may have to take into account the skills and knowledge of that journalist in determining whether the material could have been gleaned from non-confidential sources.

[9]   [1963] R.P.C. 41.

[10]   *Franchi v. Franchi* [1967] R.P.C. 149. However, it has been recognised by the courts that the state of modern communications is such that what is known by some people is very quickly made known to others: *Attorney-General v. Guardian Newspapers* [1987] 1 W.L.R. 1248.

mation in the future does not prevent the information being confidential prior to publication.[11] Information which is required by law to be made public cannot be confidential.[12]

(b) Information must be significant and capable of being specified

Confidential information, even if it is not original, must be significant. Its sig- **7-05**
nificance may lie in its importance to the confider.[13] It cannot be trivial or useless information, so mere gossip or "tittle-tattle" would not be confidential unless its disclosure would be of substantial concern to the confider.[14]

Information must be capable of specification to be confidential, because the idea must be developed enough to demonstrate that it is not public knowledge. This may become an issue in a media context where a person is pitching an idea for a new television programme or film, or an innovative way of conducting an advertising campaign or a computer software program. This requirement does not mean that the idea must be original or in a certain form to be confidential, although its commercial value or significance may be heightened by its originality.[15]

While copyright may protect the idea once it has been reduced to writing, the necessary quality of confidence may arise before then if:

- there is a sufficiently original and identifiable concept; and

- it has commercial potential and can be realised in actuality.[16]

In *De Maudsley v. Palumbo*, an idea for an all-night dance club was held not to be confidential because it had not evolved beyond a desirable goal: a mental process in addition to the goal resulting in a definite product was needed before the idea can be protected.[17]

(2) OBLIGATION OF CONFIDENCE

An obligation of confidence arises when confidential information is commu- **7-06**
nicated by a confider to a recipient solely for a limited purpose. The recipient breaches that obligation by disclosing the information to a third party. However, the third party also comes under a duty of confidence to the confider if he receives information which he knows, or should have known, is to be used only for a limited purpose. The third party is, therefore, also liable for breach of confidence if he discloses that information.[18]

---

[11] *Times Newspapers Ltd v. MGN Ltd* [1993] E.M.L.R. 443. But this will be a factor against granting an injunction, as commercial interest in delaying publication will not necessarily be enough to confer confidentiality.
[12] *Initial Services Ltd v. Putterill* [1968] 1 Q.B. 396.
[13] *Moorgate Tobacco Co. Ltd v. Philip Morris Ltd (No. 2)* (1984) 156 C.L.R. 414.
[14] *Stephens v. Avery* [1988] 1 Ch. 449.
[15] *Saltman Engineering Co. Ltd v. Campbell Engineering Co. Ltd* (1963) 65 R.P.C. 203.
[16] See *Fraser v. Thames Television* [1983] 2 All E.R. 101.
[17] *De Maudsley v. Palumbo* [1996] E.M.L.R. 460
[18] *Prince Albert v. Strange* (1849) 1 Mac. & G. 25.

There are a number of well-established situations in which a duty of confidence arises.

(a) By contract

7-07   Contracts may include an express term that certain information cannot be disclosed without permission.[19] For example, an employment contract may contain a term restricting disclosure of trade secrets. Where a contract does not contain an express term, a court may nonetheless imply an obligation of confidentiality if information is disclosed only for a certain purpose and the implied term is necessary to give the agreement business efficacy.

(b) Special relationships

7-08   There are a wide range of relationships, occupations and offices which can give rise to a duty of confidentiality. The classic example is that of the confessions made to a priest, but the disclosures covered include those which arise out of relationships with doctors, counsellors, lawyers, mediators, bankers and teachers.

The relationship between a journalist and his source is not one of the relationships traditionally recognised by the courts as one of these special relationships, even though it is afforded certain protection under the Contempt of Court Act.[20] However, when orders are made requiring journalists to disclose their sources, the merits of their doing so in the public interest must be clearly demonstrated.[21]

The relationships covered by confidence may also be personal ones. Information imparted within a marriage gives rise to an obligation of confidence, even after divorce.[22] However, to the extent that spouses have previously written and talked in public about their relationship, the information is no longer confidential.[23] "Kiss and tell" revelations within other sexual relationships may also give rise to an obligation of confidence.[24] In *Barrymore v. News Group Newspapers*,[25] the entertainer, Michael Barrymore, obtained an injunction against the *Sun* and his former homosexual lover because an obligation of confidence arose in respect of information of a sexual nature because the information was for the relationship itself, and not for the wider purpose of publication.[26] However, the few "kiss and tell" cases decided relate to relatively long-term relationships: it is not clear whether more transient relationships would give rise to an obligation.

---

[19] Under Employment Rights Act 1996, s.43J as amended by the Public Interest Disclosure Act 1998, such a provision may be void in so far as it prevents an employee making a "protected disclosure": see Chap. 10 at 2.

[20] See Chap. 21 at 5.

[21] *John v. Express Newspapers*, [2000] E.M.L.R. 606.

[22] *Argyll v. Argyll* [1967] Ch. 302.

[23] *Lennon v. News Group Newspapers* [1978] F.S.R. 573.

[24] *Stephens v. Avery* [1988] Ch. 449.

[25] [1997] F.S.R. 600.

[26] It appears form the case law that the obligation arises in respect of information communicated between partners, as opposed to information about what they actually did together.

(c) Government secrets

If the Government wishes to prevent disclosure of certain information, it must **7-09** satisfy a court that the information is confidential, that it is in the public interest that its publication be restrained, and that there is no other public interest consideration more compelling than that in support of restraint.[27] Government secrets do not remain so indefinitely and will not remain confidential if the secrets are "stale". Although Cabinet discussions are normally confidential, in *Attorney-General v. Jonathan Cape* the meetings in question had taken place 10 years before publication and were found to be no longer confidential.[28]

Disclosure of confidential government information by civil servants such as security or intelligence officers can be restrained at any stage during that officer's lifetime if the information came into the officer's possession during the course of his work and if its disclosure would be damaging to national security.[29] In the case of the security services, this would cover all information except "trivia of the most humdrum kind".[30] Any third party to whom the officer has passed the confidential information may be liable to the same criminal or civil penalties, but an exception may be made in respect of breach of confidence if the confidential character of the information has been lost as a result of wide dissemination. This occurred in respect of allegations included in the memoirs of former MI5 officer Peter Wright, *Spycatcher*, publication of extracts of which by English newspapers the British Government sought to restrain: after publication of Wright's book in the United States and elsewhere the government's objections were largely groundless because the book was widely accessible.

(3) UNAUTHORISED USE

In order to prove breach of confidence, the confidential material must have **7-10** been, or threatened to be, used in a way not authorised when it was imparted. Such misuse may take a form other than public disclosure. For example, exploitation of commercial secrets by an employee for his own benefit could amount to a breach of confidence.[31] The misuse does not have to have been intentional for a breach to have occurred.[32] In some circumstances, it may need to be proved that the information used by the recipient or third party is the same as that disclosed by the confider, and that the information came (directly or indirectly) from the confider.

---

[27] *Attorney-General v. Jonathan Cape* [1976] Q.B. 752; *Attorney-General v. Guardian Newspapers (No. 2)* [1990] 1 A.C. 109.

[28] [1976] Q.B. 752.

[29] *Attorney-General v. Guardian Newspapers (No. 2)* [1990] 1 A.C. 109.

[30] *Attorney-General v. Guardian Newspapers (No. 2)* [1990] 1 A.C. 109. If the officer discloses such information he may also have committed criminal offences under the Official Secrets Acts. See Chap. 10 at 1.

[31] *Faccenda Chicken Ltd v. Fowler* [1987] 1 Ch. 117.

[32] *Saeger v. Copydex Ltd* [1967] 1 W.L.R. 923.

Although it has been suggested that the unauthorised disclosure should have resulted in detriment to the discloser in order to amount to breach of confidence, it is not clear whether this element is always necessary.[33] In any case, the threshold for establishing detriment is a low one. It is sufficient for the confider to prove that the information was being disclosed to people whom he would prefer not to have received it, even if the disclosure is to the confider's credit. There need be no financial loss or loss to the confider's reputation. In the case of government or public affairs, a higher standard of detriment is required: disclosure must be likely to damage the public interest.[34]

3. DEFENCES

(1) CONSENT

7-11 If the confider has consented to the use of confidential information, the confidant and any third party to whom it was subsequently disclosed may successfully defend a breach of confidence action. In *Mustad v. Dosen*,[35] the House of Lords held that a former employee could not be restrained from using the claimant's secret manufacturing process because the claimant had applied for a patent for the process, thereby waiving confidentiality by placing the information in the public domain.

(2) DISCLOSURE IN THE PUBLIC INTEREST

7-12 In considering breach of confidence claims, a court must balance two competing interests: the public interest of preserving confidences, and the public interest in making known to people matters of public concern. Three main issues need to be considered here:

(a) Scope of the wrongdoing being exposed

7-13 The public interest defence has developed from the earliest cases where it was held that confidentiality did not attach to revelations of iniquity or misconduct.[36] "Iniquity" covers crimes, fraud and other serious misdeeds (whether actually committed or merely contemplated) of such a nature that it is in the public interest that they be disclosed.[37] For example, the defendant in *Initial Services Ltd v. Putterill*[38] relied on the iniquity defence when he exposed that his former employer, a laundry, was part of a cartel operating in breach of the Restrictive Practices Act 1956.

---

[33] See Lord Goff in *Attorney-General v. Guardian Newspapers (No. 2)* [1990] 1 A.C. 109.
[34] *Attorney-General v. Guardian Newspapers (No. 2)* [1990] 1 A.C. 109.
[35] [1963] R.P.C. 41.
[36] *Gartside v. Outram* (1856) 26 L.J. Ch. 113.
[37] Lord Denning M.R. in *Initial Services Ltd v. Putterill* [1968] 1 Q.B. 396.
[38] [1968] 1 Q.B. 396.

More recently, the defence has been extended by the courts to include a broader range of matters, such as continuing threats to public health,[39] anti-social behaviour, hypocrisy, conduct likely to mislead the public (including gross immorality)[40] and the efficiency of public bodies or institutions.[41]

In *Lion Laboratories v. Evans*,[42] the court allowed publication of an article which cast doubt on the accuracy of the Lion Intoximeter, a device which measured the breath of suspected drink drivers for alcohol. It was held to be in the public interest that people who faced criminal prosecution based on such evidence knew of the Intoximeter's potential flaws. In another case, the court held that the defence applied to the disclosure of a printing company's management plan outlining a reduction in the workforce because the information was of significance not only to the industry but also to the local community.[43]

The defence has also been used to justify disclosures about the lives of public figures. *Woodward v. Hutchins*[44] concerned a breach of confidence by a former publicity agent of well-known singers, but the disclosure was found to be in the public interest because it corrected the misleading image as to their lifestyles which had been created by the publicity they had previously sought. This judgment, amongst others concerning celebrities and the entertainment industry, makes it clear that the defence does not apply only to serious wrongdoing.

(b) Quality of evidence to support the defence

A party relying on a public interest defence is not required to have full knowl- **7-14**
edge about the matters in question, or prove that the information is true, but the defence must be based on a well-founded suspicion rather than a mere allegation.[45] The media, particularly in investigating national security matters, should attempt to ensure that the information is obtained from a credible and accurate source, that allegations are sufficiently corroborated, and that the findings of any prior investigations into the matter are taken into account.[46]

(c) Extent of publication

To be successful, the defendant must show that the public interest justified not **7-15**
just the act but also the manner and extent, of publication. Publication of the

---

[39] *Hubbard v. Vosper* [1972] 2 Q.B. 84; *Church of Scientology of California v. Kaufman* [1973] R.P.C. 635; *W. v. Edgell* [1990] 1 All E.R. 835. As to the "continuing" nature of the risk, the defendant's public interest defence in *Schering Chemicals v. Falkman* [1982] 1 Q.B. 1 failed because the drug had been withdrawn from sale and those potentially affected had been alerted to its dangers.
[40] *Francome v. Mirror Group Newspapers* [1984] 1 W.L.R. 892; *Stephens v. Avery* [1988] Ch. 449.
[41] *Price Waterhouse v. BCCI Holdings (Luxembourg) S.A.* [1991] T.L.R. 478.
[42] [1985] Q.B. 526.
[43] *Sun Printers v. Westminster Press* [1982] I.R.L.R. 292.
[44] [1977] 1 W.L.R. 760.
[45] *Malone v. Metropolitan Police Commissioner* [1979] Ch. 344; *Attorney-General v. Guardian Newspapers Ltd (No. 2)* [1990] 1 A.C. 109.
[46] *Attorney-General v. Guardian Newspapers Ltd (No. 2)* [1990] 1 A.C. 109.

material must genuinely be in the public interest, and not merely in the interest of the media. In *Francome v. Mirror Group Newspapers*,[47] Sir John Donaldson would not allow publication of transcripts of the conversations of a leading jockey which appeared to show misconduct on his part: the judge considered that the public interest would be better served by passing the information to the police or the Jockey Club than by wider publication which, he said, could only serve the interests of the *Daily Mirror*.

Conversely, if there is imminent danger to the public, or a serious fraud is likely to impact on the public, wider disclosure in the press may be justified.[48] Part of the rationale for this is that the media is the quickest and most expedient way of informing the public of matters which affect it. Publication via the media may also be justified where the appropriate party to receive the information would be unlikely to act on it. The court in the *Lion Laboratories* case[49] acknowledged that wider publication was preferable in public interest terms than merely disclosing the information to the Home Office. The judge remarked that it was an essential function of a free press and beneficial for society that the media be permitted to campaign on certain issues in order to put pressure on the authorities to effect reform.

4. REMEDIES

7-16 Once confidential information has been published, there is often very little left to fight for. For this reason the most significant remedy in this context is an interim injunction restraining publication pending trial. The general description of the remedies available for copyright infringement is relevant to breach of confidence. This section focuses, however, on some of the particular issues which arise in the context of confidentiality.

(1) INJUNCTION

7-17 It is worth noting that the presumption against prior restraint in defamation cases[50] does not apply in confidence actions, and the assertion of a defence of public interest, unlike justification in defamation cases, will not necessarily lead to the grant of an injunction. Furthermore, it is likely that section 12 of the Human Rights Act 1998 will force the courts to give greater consideration to freedom of expression and the media's rights to publish expeditiously information in the public interest, particularly if the delay caused by an injunction would reduce the "news value" of the information. This represents a considerable shift in favour of media organisations resisting applications for injunctions in confidence cases.[51]

---

[47] [1984] 1 W.L.R. 892.
[48] *Initial Services Ltd v. Putterill* [1968] 1 Q.B. 396.
[49] [1985] Q.B. 526.
[50] Chap. 3 at 7.
[51] See Chap. 2, particularly at 2(4).

An interim injunction in a breach of confidence case can amount to a total ban on publication, even by publishers who are not parties to the case involving the injunction. Section 6(c) of the Contempt of Court Act has been interpreted to mean that a party which has "intended to impede or prejudice the administration of justice" may be guilty of contempt at common law.[52] It may therefore be a contempt for a third party publisher, knowing of an injunction against another publisher, to obtain and publish the same confidential information, thereby intentionally destroying the confidentiality which it was the object of the injunction to preserve.[53]

This occurred in relation to the publication of extracts from Peter Wright's book *Spycatcher* by *The Independent* and *The Sunday Times* when the editors of those papers knew that the extracts were the subject of injunctions against *The Observer* and *The Guardian*. The Court of Appeal ruled that it was irrelevant that *The Independent* and *The Sunday Times* considered publication to be in the public interest, and that they had not thought the publication would be in contempt.

A final injunction may be granted at the end of an action, regardless of whether disclosure has taken place or was restrained beforehand, to halt further misuse or unwarranted disclosure of confidential material. The court will take into account a number of factors, such as the claimant's conduct, the nature and importance of the material, the degree of confidentiality remaining in the material,[54] and the likelihood that the defendant will repeat the publication. Since it is a discretionary remedy, the court will also consider once more the adequacy of damages as a remedy for the claimant, and the harm to be suffered by the parties. The court may refuse to grant an injunction if it considers damages or another remedy to be adequate.

(2) SEARCH ORDER

As with copyright and other intellectual property claims, a claimant may apply for a search order to inspect premises on which he believes infringing activities to be taking place. Such an order will be made only if the claimant has a strong case, there is clear evidence that the defendant has incriminating material on the premises, and there is a real danger of such material being destroyed if the defendant is alerted.[55]   **7-18**

(3) DELIVERY UP

The court can order the delivery up or destruction of information obtained in breach of confidence. Where the items recording the confidential information are the claimant's property, delivery up will invariably be ordered[56];   **7-19**

---

[52] *Attorney-General v. News Group Newspapers Ltd* [1988] 2 All E.R. 906. See also Chap. 4 at 2(2).
[53] *Attorney-General v. Times Newspapers Ltd* [1992] 1 A.C. 191.
[54] *Coco v. A. N. Clark (Engineers) Limited* [1968] F.S.R. 415.
[55] See *Universal Thermosensors Ltd v. Hibben* [1992] F.S.R. 361.
[56] *Evitt v. Price* (1827) 1 Sim. 483.

destruction of the items will invariably be ordered where they are the property of the defendant.[57]

If a journalist is unwilling to deliver up material on the grounds that to do so would identify a source, he may rely on section 10 of the Contempt of Court Act.[58]

(4) DAMAGES OR AN ACCOUNT OF PROFITS

7-20 Claimants are generally more interested in stopping publication than they are in compensation. However, a claimant may be awarded damages as compensation for breach of confidentiality. It is often difficult to quantify such losses but a claim could include for example, loss of profits, loss of consultancy fees or the loss of a licence.

In the alternative, a claimant may elect to seek an account of profits. Where the confidential information only partially contributed to profits made, a claimant will commonly take damages because they are likely to exceed an account of profits. If the information was an essential factor in the profit made, an account of profits might yield greater returns than damages. If the information was essential to its operations, the defendant will have to account for its total profits.[59]

---

[57] *Peter Pan Corporation v. Corsets Silhouette Ltd* [1963] 3 All E.R. 402.
[58] See Chap. 21 at 5.
[59] *Peter Pan Corporation v. Corsets Silhouette Ltd* [1963] 3 All E.R. 402.

Chapter 8

Obscenity, blasphemy and race offences

1. INTRODUCTION

Almost everything covered in this text to date covers causes of action which **8-01** have their origins in civil law. It must not be forgotten, however, that there is a body of criminal law which can lead to prosecutions for content which is particularly offensive. There are a number of relevant statutory provisions, including those which outlaw material regarded as obscene, indecent, blasphemous or racist. These are considered in this chapter.

These provisions need to be borne in mind because, like contempt of court, they can attract serious penalties. More importantly, they may adversely affect the reputation of the publication concerned. It is true to say, however, that there have been few prosecutions in modern times. There are several reasons for this. The mainstream media is broadly sensitive to public sensitivities in this area. Furthermore, statutory and industry regulation impose obligations on the media which emphasise the importance of taste and decency and the need to avoid causing offence on religious or racial grounds. At the same time, where there have been prosecutions, the law can seem uncertain: much depends on contemporary moral standards, and these can change with time. Moreover, in the case of obscenity, a defendant will be acquitted if he can show that publication was "for the public good".

Considerable care is required in this area and the growth of the Internet has created new challenges for the existing law and for prosecutors. The Human Rights Act 1998 may also have an impact. The European Court of Human Rights has held that the right to free expression in Article 10 by the European Convention is applicable "not only to information or ideas that are favourably received or regarded as inoffensive . . . but also to those that offend, shock or disturb . . . any sector of the population.[1] Article 10 can, therefore, be relied on to protect the expression of ideas that offend most people.

---

[1] *Handyside v. U.K.*, 7 December 1976, Series A no. 24, p. 23.

2. OBSCENITY

(1) STATUTORY DEFINITION

8-02 Material which tends to deprave or corrupt may fall foul of the Obscene Publications Acts 1959 and 1964.[2] The legislation provides that an article is obscene if its effect (or the effect of any one of its items) is, if taken as a whole, such as to tend to deprave and corrupt persons who are likely, in the relevant circumstances, to read, see or hear the matter contained in it.[3]

The case law in this area has a somewhat Victorian air about it. "Deprave" means to make morally bad, pervert, debase or corrupt morally; "corrupt" means to defile or render morally unsound or rotten.[4] Material does not have to cause depraved or corrupt behaviour to be obscene: it merely has to have a tendency to debase morals.[5] The depravation and corruption need not be of a sexual nature; material may be obscene if it encourages extreme violence[6] or the taking of dangerous drugs.[7]

For journalists and those involved in the process of editing copy, it might seem at first sight that evaluating what this case law means is a complex task. However, the prosecuting authorities have met with little success[8] and prosecutions for obscenity are now largely directed at hardcore pornography.[9]

The courts take a fairly sanguine view of much material and it is clear that the publication must do more than merely shock or disgust readers, or mislead them morally. In determining the effect of an article, the court will consider only:

(i)   its impact on its likely audience (the "primary audience")[10]; and

(ii) whether the article would tend to deprave or corrupt a "significant proportion" of the primary audience.[11]

The court will not therefore take into account the effect of the article on those groups who are not within the article's target market such as, in the case of pornography, young children. This will be an even more powerful argument in the case of subscription-only services not accessible by children.

The court must also consider the article as a whole, and not merely isolated

---

[2] There are similar provisions in the Theatres Act 1968, which make it an offence to present or direct (subject to certain exceptions) an obscene performance of a play if its effect was such as to tend to deprave and corrupt persons who were likely to attend it: Theatres Act 1968, s.2.

[3] Obscene Publications Act 1959, s.1(1).

[4] *R. v. Penguin Books Ltd* [1961] Crim. L.R. 176.

[5] *DPP v. Whyte* [1972] A.C. 849.

[6] *DPP & A. and B. C. Chewing Gum Ltd* [1968] 1 Q.B. 159.

[7] See, *Calder v. Powell* [1965] 1 Q.B. 509; *R. v. Calder and Boyars Ltd* [1969] 1 Q.B. 151. In *R. v. Skirving*; *R. v. Grossman* [1985] 2 All E.R. 705: an article which described and promoted "free basing" as a method of taking cocaine was held to be obscene.

[8] Most famously failing to obtain a conviction against the publisher of *Lady Chatterley's Lover* in 1960: *R. v. Penguin Books Ltd* [1961] Crim. L.R. 176).

[9] See Chap. 25 at 6.

[10] *DPP v. Whyte* [1972] A.C. 849.

[11] *R. v. Calder and Boyars Ltd* [1969] 1 Q.B. 151.

passages which may not be obscene when viewed as part of a larger item. This factor may be relevant when looking at books, films or plays, but will be less so when considering newspapers and magazines: the latter are judged on an item-by-item basis, so one article may be obscene while the remainder of the newspaper or magazine is not.[12]

(2) WHAT ACTS ARE PROHIBITED?

The Obscene Publications Acts make it an offence either to publish or possess an obscene article.[13] The law governing each aspect is slightly different.

Publication

It is an offence to publish, whether for gain or not. This covers: **8-03**

(i)   distribution, circulation, sale, letting on hire, giving, lending, or offering for sale or hire;

(ii) showing, playing or projecting the article or, where data is stored electronically, the transmitting of that data.[14]

This provision of the 1959 Act was amended to include the transmission of electronically-stored data in order to keep pace with the capabilities of modern technology.[15] It was examined by the Court of Appeal in *R. v. Fellows; R. v. Arnold*, which concerned the use of a computer to store images in digital form in order that the user could display and print out indecent pictures of children.[16] The pictures could be accessed on the Internet by those who used a password and provided additional information for the database. However, the appellants submitted that some more "active" steps were needed to constitute publication. This argument was rejected, the Court finding that the data stored on the computer disc was "shown, played or projected" to those who gained access to the Internet archive of pictures built up by the appellant.

The more recent case of *R. v. Waddon* has established that the act of publication takes place when the data in question is transmitted by the defendant or his agent to an Internet service provider, and is still taking place when the data is received.[17] The Court of Appeal held that, although the material was uploaded to a United States website, the defendant continued to be responsible for its continuing publication when it was downloaded elsewhere.

---

[12] *R. v. Anderson* [1971] 3 All E.R. 1152.
[13] OPA 1959, s.2(1) as amended by OPA 1964, s.1(2).
[14] OPA, s.1(3). The developing and printing by the proprietor of a camera shop for a customer of a film containing photographs of a woman performing obscene acts was considered a "publication": *R. v. Taylor*, January 4, 1994, CA.
[15] See OPA, s.1(3) as amended by Sched. 9 to the Criminal Justice and Public Order Act 1994.
[16] [1997] 2 All E.R. 548.
[17] Unreported, April 6, 2000.

Including obscene matter in a broadcast or cable programme is also publication.[18]

Possession

8-04   Possession will only amount to an offence if the defendant had an obscene article intended for publication for gain, whether gain to himself or someone else.[19] A prosecution can be brought therefore against a defendant having the article in his ownership, possession, or control with a view to publication.[20] Money does not have to change hands: the exchange of one obscene article for another (for example, on the Internet) will be regarded as publication for gain.[21]

(3) WHAT IS AN ARTICLE?

8-05   An "article" is widely defined and means any article containing or embodying material to be read or looked at or both, any sound record, film, or other record of a picture or pictures.[22] It also includes anything used for the reproduction or manufacture of such articles, including photographic negatives, stencils and moulds.[23]

(4) INTENTION

8-06   If an article is obscene and published or possessed as described above, the person concerned is prima facie guilty of the offence regardless of intention. This was well illustrated by a case involving a book entitled *Last Exit to Brooklyn* which was held to be obscene for having encouraged drug-taking, even though its author claimed to have intended to discourage drug-taking by depicting vividly the degradation caused by such activities.[24] Another example which illustrates the strict liability aspect of these offences is the broadcasting of a live programme: both the person providing the obscene material on the programme as well as the broadcaster can be charged.[25]

(5) "DEFENCES"

Although there are no defences to strict liability offences *per se*, a court will not convict a person under the 1959 and 1964 Acts in the following circumstances.

---

[18] OPA 1959, s.1(4)–(6) as amended by the Broadcasting Act 1990.

[19] This includes obscene material kept with a view to including it in a television programme: Sched. 15 to the Broadcasting Act 1990.

[20] Obscene Publications Act 1959, s.2(1) as amended by OPA 1964, s.1.

[21] The 1959 Act applies to any publication for gain, whether the gain is by way of consideration or in any other way: OPA 1959, s.1(5). See *R. v. Fellows; R. v. Arnold* [1997] 2 All E.R. 548.

[22] OPA, s.1(2). A videocassette falls within this definition: *Attorney-General's Reference (No. 5 of 1980)* [1980] 3 All E.R. 816.

[23] OPA 1964, s.2.

[24] *R. v. Calder and Boyars Ltd* [1969] 1 Q.B. 151.

[25] Broadcasting Act 1990, Sched. 15.

(a) Innocent dissemination

If a person can establish that he had not examined the article in relation to   **8-07**
which he had been charged, and had no reasonable cause to suspect that its
publication would be unlawful under section 2 of the Obscene Publications
Act 1959, he will not be convicted.[26] The burden of proving this defence lies
with the defendant, who must show that he had no specific notice of the
offensive material.

In one case, the conviction of a director of a printing company was quashed
by the Court of Appeal because he had been absent at the time an order for
the relevant books was accepted and had no personal knowledge of the contents of the books.[27]

(b) Public good

A publisher of obscene material will not be convicted if he can prove that pub-   **8-08**
lication was justified as being for the public good.[28] Except in the case of plays,
films or film soundtracks, an article is in the public good if it is in the interests
of science, literature, art or learning,[29] or of other objects of general concern.[30]
The definition of "public good" is narrower in relation to plays, films or film
soundtracks: publication is justified as being for the public good only if it is in
the interests of drama, opera, ballet or any other art, or of literature or learning.[31] Television and radio programmes have the widest "defence" of public
good because in their case the defence combines both groups of interests outlined above.[32]

The onus of proving this defence is on the defendant. To do so, he may call
expert evidence as to the literary, artistic, scientific or other merits of the
article, as can the prosecution to show that the article lacks those merits.[33]

(c) "Aversion" defence

This defence is based on the proposition that material cannot tend to deprave   **8-09**
or corrupt if it is so lewd and unpleasant that it repels those who experience it
from indulging in the acts depicted.[34]

In the *Last Exit to Brooklyn* case, the failure of the trial judge to put the
defence to the jury was one of the main grounds for upsetting the conviction.

---

[26] OPA, s.2(5); Broadcasting Act 1990, Sched. 15.
[27] *R. v. Love* (1955) 39 Cr. App. R. 30.
[28] Nor will an order for forfeiture of the obscene material be made under OPA 1959, s.3.
[29] "Learning" has been interpreted to mean the product of some scholarly activity: *Attorney-General's Reference (No. 3 of 1977)* [1978] 3 All E.R. 1166.
[30] OPA 1959, s.4(1). "Other objects of general concern" is interpreted to be similar to art, litera-
ture or the other preceding categories in the list.
[31] Theatres Act 1968, s.3; OPA, s.4(1A).
[32] Broadcasting Act 1990, Sched. 15.
[33] OPA, s.4(2).
[34] This argument was relied on by the defence in the 1971 obscenity trial of those responsible for
the publication of a children's issue of *Oz* magazine, which contained articles and illustrations
of a sexual nature, including some famously featuring the cartoon character, Rupert the Bear:
R. v. Anderson [1971] 3 All E.R. 1152. See also *R. v. Elliott* [1996] 1 Cr. App. R. 432.

Last Exit to Brooklyn was a book which presented horrific pictures of homo-sexuality and drug-taking in New York. The book's only effect on any but a minute lunatic fringe of readers would be horror, revulsion and pity. It made readers share in the horror and thereby so disgusted, shocked and outraged them that, instead of tending to encourage anyone to homosexuality, drug-taking or brutal violence, it would have had precisely the reverse effect.[35]

(6) PROSECUTION AND PENALTIES

8-10 Obscenity is punishable in the magistrates' court by fines of up to £2,000 or six months' imprisonment and in the Crown Court by an unlimited fine or up to three years' imprisonment.

In addition to the normal criminal sanctions, the court can order seizure and forfeiture of the obscene material.[36] A warrant is required, and must be obtained from a justice of the peace by the police or the Director of Public Prosecutions (in the case of programme recordings or films). To grant a warrant, the justice of the peace must be satisfied that there is reasonable ground for suspecting that obscene articles are kept on premises or in vehicles within his jurisdiction for publication for gain or with a view to gain. The police can enter, seize and remove any such articles found. Any document relating to a trade or business related to those articles may also be seized. The occupier of the place searched, owner, author, maker, or other person through whose hands the articles passed before seizure may appear at court and present arguments as to why the articles should not be forfeited.

Forfeiture may be properly ordered of articles warehoused prior to export if they are obscene by normal standards, notwithstanding the absence of any intention to deprave or corrupt the British public by reason of the fact that they are destined only for export.[37]

3. INDECENCY[38]

There is no single offence of "indecency" but a number of disparate legislative provisions banning certain types of indecent material. The legislation does not define what is meant by "indecent" but it appears from case law to arise at a lower level of offensiveness than obscenity, particularly where children are con-cerned, and occurs if material is such as to shock or disgust the average person.[39]

(1) STATUTORY OFFENCES

It is beyond the scope of this text to examine all the relevant legislation in this area, and for the most part it is unlikely to affect the media, but the following are the most important.

---

[35] *R. v. Calder and Boyars Ltd* [1969] 1 Q.B. 151.
[36] OPA, s.3.
[37] *Gold Star Publications Ltd v. DPP* [1981] 2 All E.R. 257.
[38] See Pt. II in relation to the issue of taste and decency in statutory and industry codes.
[39] See *Knuller v. DPP* [1973] A.C. 435.

(a) Indecent photographs of children

The taking, making, publication or advertising of indecent photographs or **8-11** pseudo-photographs of children under 16 is an offence under the Protection of Children Act 1978.[40] The definition of "photograph" was extended by the Criminal Justice and Public Order Act 1994 to include data stored on a computer disk or by other electronic means which is capable of resolution into a photograph.[41] The Act also applies to negatives, films and videos.

The reproduction of indecent material to be found on the Internet has been held to be within the mischief aimed at by the 1978 Act because it was intended to target not just the creation of indecent material, but its proliferation. Therefore the definition of "making" has been given its natural meaning and interpreted to cover a person who downloads or prints indecent images, regardless of whether they originate outside the United Kingdom.[42]

A pseudo-photograph is a graphic image, whether made by computer or otherwise, which appears to be a photograph. If the impression created by a pseudo-photograph is one which cannot easily be identified as either an adult or a child but seems to be a child, it shall be classified as a child. It has been accepted that the Protection of Children Act 1978 covers a person involved in the creation of pseudo-photographs who may have had no contact with the subjects of the images.[43]

The Criminal Justice Act 1988 also creates the summary offence of possession of an indecent photograph of a child.[44]

(b) Importation of indecent material

The import into the United Kingdom of indecent or obscene material is pro- **8-12** hibited[45]. This provision was strictly interpreted for many years until it was established that the importation from the European Union (of a life-size sex doll) was permitted.[46] As a result, prosecutions are now largely restricted to hardcore pornography. European law recognises the validity of this prohibition on the grounds of public morality, even if the obscene material is for personal use only.[47] The public good defence under section 4 of the Obscene Publications Act 1959 does not apply in relation to this offence.[48]

---

[40] See Protection of Children Act 1978, s.1: the Act also applies to the distribution or showing, or having in one's possession for the purpose of showing or distributing, indecent photographs or pseudo-photographs.

[41] Protection of Children Act 1978, s.7(4)(b) as amended.

[42] *R. v. Bowden* [2000] 2 All E.R. 418.

[43] *ibid.*

[44] Criminal Justice Act 1988, s.160.

[45] Customs Consolidation Act 1876, s.42.

[46] *Conegate Ltd v. Customs and Excise Commissioners* [1986] 2 All E.R. 688.

[47] *Wright v. Commissioners of Customs and Excise, The Times*, February 23, 1998.

[48] *R. v. Bow Street Magistrates Court, ex p. Noncyp Ltd* (1989) 3 W.L.R. 467.

(c) Indecent telephone messages

8-13 Under the Telecommunications Act 1984, it is an offence to send by telephone any obscene, indecent, menacing or grossly offensive message originating in the United Kingdom.[49] This includes material sent over the Internet. However, the offence is committed by the originator of the message, rather than the carrier, and it is therefore unlikely that an Internet service provider would be at risk of prosecution.

(d) Indecent displays

8-14 According to the Indecent Displays (Control) Act 1981, it is an offence for a person to display or permit the displaying of indecent matter visible from a public place. A place is *not* public if it is closed to those under 18 years and:

- the public have to pay to see the display; or
- it is a shop and, in order to gain access to it, the public have to pass a signing warning them that they will see potentially indecent material.

The Act does not apply to television broadcasts, art galleries, museums, theatres, cinemas, Crown or local authority buildings. This offence might be committed, for example, by newsagents who display magazines with obscene covers in a position where they could be viewed from outside the shop.

(e) Indecent post

8-15 It is an offence to send indecent or obscene matter through the post, or to send or cause to be sent to any person any material describing or illustrating human sexual techniques which the sender knows or ought reasonably to know the recipient did not request.[50]

(f) Indecent comics

8-16 It is an offence to print, publish, sell, let for hire, or have for the purpose of selling or hiring it, a work likely to be read by those under 18 which consists of stories told mainly in pictures (with or without additional written material) which depicts crimes or acts of a violent, cruel, repulsive or horrible nature which would tend to corrupt the young reader.[51]

(2) COMMON LAW

(a) Corrupting public morals

8-17 In order to be guilty of the charge of conspiracy to corrupt public morals, the defendant must intend to corrupt public morals and have engaged in "conduct

---

[49] Telecommunications Act 1984, s.43.
[50] Post Office Act 1953, s.11; Unsolicited Goods and Services Act 1971, s.11.
[51] Children and Young Persons (Harmful Publications) Act 1955, s.1.

which the jury might find to be destructive of the very fabric of society" rather than merely leading people "morally astray".[52] Most prosecutions nowadays target the advertising of contact details for sexual liaisons.

(b) Outraging public decency

This offence may be applicable in circumstances where conduct outrages those **8-18** invited to see it. The "invitation" element of the offence means that there must have been "publicity" surrounding the indecent display. This element was satisfied in the case of *R. v. Gibson*, which involved the prosecution of the proprietor of an art gallery and an artist who had exhibited an artistic work featuring earrings made from freeze-dried human foetuses.[53] Unlike conspiracy to corrupt public morals, there is no requirement to prove an intention on the part of the defendant to outrage public decency.[54] The qualification in relation to the public good defence (see (a) above relating to corrupting public morals) also applies to this offence. However, it was held not to be a bar to conviction in the *Gibson* case.

4. BLASPHEMY

The offence of blasphemy or blasphemous libel is committed when material **8-19** which outrages and insults Christian religious feeling is published.[55] Whilst moderate and reasoned criticism of Christianity or expressions of anti-Christian feeling are not blasphemous, immoderate or offensive treatment of Christianity or Christian beliefs would render the publisher vulnerable to prosecution.[56]

The intention of the publisher is irrelevant: the prosecution merely has to prove that the material published was blasphemous.[57] Evidence as to the circumstances of publication and likely readership would be admissible on the question of whether the publication would cause public outrage. A defence is available to a publisher who can prove that the publication was made without his authority, consent or knowledge, and did not arise from lack of care or caution on his part.[58]

The leave of a High Court judge is required for a blasphemy prosecution against a newspaper without the leave of the court.[59] "Newspaper" is defined by the Newspaper Libel and Registration Act 1881 as one which contains public news, intelligence, occurrences, remarks or observations and is published not less than once every 26 days. In order for leave to be given, there

---

[52] *Knuller v. DPP* [1973] A.C. 435.
[53] *R. v. Gibson* [1991] 1 All E.R. 439.
[54] *ibid.*
[55] *R. v. Lemon* [1978] 3 All E.R. 175.
[56] *ibid.*
[57] *Whitehouse v. Lemon* [1979] 1 All E.R. 898.
[58] Libel Act 1843, s.7.
[59] Law of Libel Amendment Act 1888, s.8.

must be a prima facie case of blasphemy, the libel must be serious, and prosecution must be in the public interest.[60]

There have been calls for the offence to be extended or abolished[61] and prosecutions are extremely rare. There have been few this century, and the most recent was the controversial private prosecution in *Whitehouse v. Lemon* in 1978.[62] This concerned the publication of a poem and illustration about a homosexual's conversion to Christianity, which metaphorically attributed to Jesus Christ acts of sodomy and fellatio. Although that case resulted in the conviction of both the editor and publishing company of *Gay News*, it is regarded as unlikely that the Director of Public Prosecutions would now take action against any publication of artistic or literary worth.[63]

A Law Commission report three years after the case concluded that the offence of blasphemy had three fundamental flaws[64]:

(a) the ambit of the offence is so wide that it is difficult to assess in advance of publication whether the offence will be committed;

(b) the sincerity of the publisher is irrelevant;

(c) the offence protects only Christianity.

However, it also concluded that reform of the law to extend protection to all religions would serve no purpose in modern society.

The legitimacy of blasphemy law, in light of the European Convention on Human Rights, was tested in a 1996 case. The European Court of Human Rights held in *Nigel Wingrove v. U.K.* that the British Board of Film Classification (BBFC) was justified in refusing to grant a classification certificate to a film entitled *Visions of Ecstasy*.[65] The film centred on the life of a fifteenth-century Carmelite nun, St Teresa of Avila. The BBFC decided that the work, which included erotic scenes involving St Teresa and the crucified figure of Christ, would cause outrage at the unacceptable treatment of a sacred subject. The Board also concluded that a reasonable jury would find that the film breached the law of blasphemy. The European Court held the decision to be an infringement of the right to freedom of expression under Article 10 of the Convention, but that the BBFC decision was justifiable because the protection of Christians against serious offence was consistent with the right to

---

[60] *Goldsmith v. Pressdram Ltd* [1976] 3 W.L.R. 191 (a case of criminal libel).
[61] Blasphemy protects only the Christian religion. In *R. v. Bow Street Magistrates Court, ex p. Choudhury* [1991] 1 All E.R. 306 it was affirmed that a magistrate was correct in refusing to issue a summons in respect of Salman Rushdie's *The Satanic Verses* on the grounds that the offence of blasphemy applied only to Christianity. The court would not allow the extension of blasphemy to cover other religions because it would be virtually impossible for the courts to set sufficiently clear limits if the offence was to be extended.
[62] [1979] 1 All E.R. 898.
[63] G. Robertson and A. Nicol, *Media Law* (3rd ed.), p. 162: The authors note that the DPP declined to act in the cases of *Monty Python's Life of Brian* or Martin Scorsese's *The Last Temptation of Christ* despite some public pressure to do so.
[64] Law Commission, Working Paper No. 79: Offences against Religion and Public Worship (1981).
[65] *The Times*, December 5, 1996.

freedom of thought, conscience and religion under Article 9. The fact that English law protected only Christian faith did not detract from that aim. Nevertheless, the law in this area is likely to the subject to the scrutiny of the courts under the Human Rights Act 1998 to ensure that it does not interfere unnecessarily with freedom of expression.

Whilst the blasphemy laws are unlikely to be a matter of daily concern to anyone working in the media,[66] they are likely to survive in their present form for some time yet.

5. RACE OFFENCES

Whilst the laws of blasphemy may be seen as outmoded, laws aimed at banning the dissemination of racist material aim to tackle more pressing problems.[67] This should not be an area of great concern for mainstream publishers, unless they deliberately provide far right-wing groups or individuals with a platform for their views.[68] The key areas of law in this context are described below. **8-20**

(1) INCITING RACIAL HATRED

(a) Scope of the offence

Under the Public Order Act 1986 it is an offence for a person to **8-21**

- use words or behaviour;

- display written material;

- publish or distribute written material;

- distribute, show, or play a recording of visual images or sounds;

- broadcast material[69]; or

---

[66] As examined in Pt. II, the various regulators of content have included provisions in their Codes dealing with religious discrimination. It is noteworthy that ss.6(1)(d)(ii) and 90(2)(c)(ii) of the Broadcasting Act 1990 require the Independent Television and Radio Authority respectively to do all they can to ensure that their programmes do not involve abusive treatment of religious views and beliefs.

[67] Many regulators of content have Codes which reinforce the legal provisions, as well as preventing the use of racial stereotypes: see Part II of this text.

[68] However, the fact that any racially inflammatory publication subject to the Public Order Act 1986 (see below) will be viewed "having regard to all the circumstances" is of assistance to publishers. The European Court of Human Rights held in *Jersild v. Denmark* that the conviction of a Danish radio journalist for assisting in the dissemination of racist statements made by members of an extremist organisation in an interview violated his right to freedom of expression under Art. 10 of the Convention: *The Times*, October 20, 1994 (Case No. 36/1993/431/510).

[69] Public Order Act 1986, Pt. III as amended by the Broadcasting Act 1990, s.164.

- have in his possession written material or a recording of visual images or sounds with a view to its being displayed, published, distributed, shown, played or broadcast,

which is threatening, abusive or insulting, if he intends to stir up racial hatred or, having regard to all the circumstances, racial hatred is likely to be stirred up thereby.[70]

"Racial hatred" is hatred against a group of persons in the United Kingdom defined by reference to colour, race, nationality (including citizenship), or ethnic or national origins.[71] "Ethnic" has been construed by the House of Lords to mean a group which is regarded by its members and other people as a distinct community by virtue of certain characteristics, including a long shared history and a cultural tradition of its own.[72] Jews, Sikhs and Romany gypsies are considered ethnic groups,[73] but Muslims and Rastafarians[74] are not. The Act does not protect religious groups, per se.[75]

The words "threatening", "abusive" and "insulting" are not defined in the Act, so whether the material in question was of that nature would be an issue for the court to decide according to the ordinary usage of those words as applied to the facts of the case.[76]

(b) Exceptions

8-22 The Act does not apply to:

- a fair, accurate and contemporaneous report of proceedings in parliament; or

- a fair, accurate and contemporaneous report of public proceedings in a court or tribunal exercising judicial authority.[77]

(c) Defences

The available defences vary depending on whether the relevant material was broadcast or non-broadcast.

---

[70] Public Order Act 1986, Pt. III: ss.17 to 22.

[71] Public Order Act 1986, s.17.

[72] *Mandla v. Dowell Lee* [1983] 1 All E.R. 1062. Although the court was construing the word "ethnic" as contained in Race Relations Act 1976, it is thought that its interpretation would also apply to the Public Order Act 1986.

[73] "Travellers" *per se* are not an ethnic group: *Commission for Racial Equality v. Dutton* [1989] 1 All E.R. 306 (this case also involved interpretation of Race Relations Act 1976).

[74] *Crown Suppliers Property Services Agency v. Dawkins* [1993] I.C.R. 517.

[75] Leave to apply for a declaration that Muslims were covered by ss.17 and 19 of the Public Order Act 1986 was refused in *R. v. DPP, ex p. London Borough Council of Merton* (1999) C.O.D. 358.

[76] *Brutus v. Cozens* [1973] A.C. 854.

[77] Public Order Act 1986, s.26.

Non-broadcast material

A defence is provided to the use of words or behaviour or the display of **8-23**
written material in breach of the Act,[78] where it is not proved that the accused
intended to stir up racial hatred, if it can be shown that he did not intend his
behaviour to be threatening, abusive or insulting, and was not aware that it
might be.

A publisher will also have a defence to the following offences:

- publishing or distributing written material,[79]

- distributing, showing, or playing a recording of visual images or sounds,[80]

- having in his possession written material or a recording of visual images
  or sounds (with a view to its being displayed, published, distributed,
  shown, played or broadcast),[81]

provided he is not shown to have intended to stir up racial hatred, if he can
prove he was not aware of the content of the material, and did not suspect and
had no reason to suspect that it was threatening, abusive or insulting.

Broadcast material

A broadcaster, producer or director has a defence if he is not shown to have **8-24**
intended to stir up racial hatred, he did not know and had no reason to suspect
that the programme would be threatening, abusive or insulting, and it was not
reasonably practical for him to secure the removal of that material.[82]

A producer or director will have a further defence if he is shown not to have
intended to stir up racial hatred and where he had no reason to suspect that
the programme would be included in a programme service, or that the circumstances in which the programme would be so included would be such that
racial hatred would be likely to be stirred up.

(d) Prosecution and penalties

Individual journalists, editors, and a company and its officers can be prose- **8-25**
cuted for offences under the Act, subject to the Attorney-General's consent.
In considering his decision, the Attorney-General will take into account the
nature of the publication, its circulation, its target market, public sensitivities
at the time of publication, and the public interest in a prosecution.[83]

Following conviction in a Crown Court, the maximum penalty under the
Act is two years' imprisonment or a fine, or both. The maximum penalty in

---

[78] s.18.
[79] s.19.
[80] s.21.
[81] s.23.
[82] s.22.
[83] See Attorney-General's reply to parliamentary question on January 12, 1987.

the magistrates' court is six months' imprisonment or a fine, or both. The court also has the power to order forfeiture of any written material or recording to which the Act relates.[84] The provisions of the Police and Criminal Evidence Act 1984 for search and seizure also apply.

(2) RACIALLY AGGRAVATED HARASSMENT AND OTHER OFFENCES

8-26   Under section 31 of the Crime and Disorder Act 1998 a person is guilty of an offence if he commits an offence

(a)   under section 4 of the Public Order 1986 (fear or provocation of violence), or

(b)   under section 4A of the Public Order Act 1986 (intentional harassment, alarm or distress), or

(c)   under section 5 of the Public Order Act 1986 (harassment, alarm or distress),

and his actions were racially aggravated.[85]

Under section 32 of the Crime and Disorder Act 1998 a person is guilty of an offence if he commits an offence under section 2 of the Protection from Harassment Act 1997 and his actions were racially motivated.[86]

(3) DISCRIMINATORY ADVERTISEMENTS

It is an offence under section 29 of the Race Relations Act 1976 to publish an advertisement indicating an intention to discriminate on racial grounds. The test for whether an advertisement indicates such an intention is whether a reasonable person would understand that to be the natural and ordinary meaning of the words.[87]

A publisher has a defence if he can show that:

•   the advertisement was published in reliance on a statement made to him by the person who placed it that it would not be unlawful (by virtue of s.29(2) or (3))[88]; and

•   it was reasonable for the publisher to rely on the statement.

Proceedings under this section may be brought only by the Commission for Racial Equality.[89]

---

[84] Public Order Act 1986, s.25.
[85] The offences under the Public Order Act 1986 are set out in Chap. 10 at 4.
[86] The offence under the Protection from Harassment Act 1997 is set out in Chap. 10 at 4.
[87] *Race Relations Board v. Associated Newspapers Group Ltd* [1978] 1 W.L.R. 905.
[88] Knowingly or recklessly making such a statement, which is false or misleading in a material respect, is an offence under s.29(5).
[89] *Cardiff Women's Aid v. Hartup* [1994] I.R.L.R. 390.

Chapter 9

Data Protection Act 1998

1. INTRODUCTION

The Data Protection Act 1998 came into force on March 1, 2000 to comply **9-01** with the Data Protection Directive.[1] The purpose of the legislation is to provide a framework for the protection of individuals with regard to the processing of personal data and the free movement of such data.

In the context of this book, it is most relevant to those involved in direct marketing activities.[2] It is unlikely to affect journalists to a significant degree: their notebooks are merely a collection of papers which only incidentally contain personal information.[3] There are also exemptions available from the full rigour of the Act for certain journalistic activities.[4] However, publishers may become data controllers as a result of the personal data which they process. The Act may also hinder news and information gathering from organisations which are prevented from releasing individuals' personal data.

2. DEFINITIONS

The following key terminology is used in the Act.

DATA

This means information which: **9-02**

(a) is being processed by means of equipment operating automatically in response to instructions given for that purpose;

(b) is recorded with the intention that it should be processed by means of such equipment; or

---

[1] European Directive 95/46. The 1998 Act repealed the Data Protection Act 1984.
[2] See the Sales Promotion Code issued by CAP: see Chap. 17 at 3.
[3] See T. Welsh and W. Greenwood, *McNae's Essential Law for Journalists*, (15th ed., 1999) at p. 322.
[4] See 6 below.

(c)   is recorded as part of a relevant filing system or with the intention that it should form part of a relevant filing system.[5]

DATA CONTROLLER

9-03   This is a person who (either alone or jointly or in common with other persons) determines the purposes for which and the manner in which any personal data are, or are to be, processed.[6]

DATA SUBJECT

9-04   This means an individual who is the subject of personal data.[7]

PERSONAL DATA

9-05   This means data which relate to a living individual who can be identified:

(a)   from those data, or

(b)   from those data and other information which is in the possession of, or is likely to come into the possession of the data controller.[8]

PROCESSING

9-06   This includes the obtaining, recording or holding of information, or carrying out any operation or set of operations on the information or data.[9]

RELEVANT FILING SYSTEM

9-07   This means any set of information relating to individuals that is structured, either by reference to individuals or by reference to criteria relating to individuals, in such a way that specific information relating to a particular individual is readily accessible.[10] It is intended to include manual records.

---

[5] s.1(1) of the Act. It also applies to certain health and educational records: *ibid.*, s.68.
[6] *ibid.*, s.1(1).
[7] *ibid.*, s.1(1).
[8] *ibid.*, s.1(1),.
[9] *ibid.*, s.1(1).
[10] *ibid.*, s.1(1). The 1984 Act applied only to computer records.

SENSITIVE PERSONAL DATA

This means personal data consisting of information as to: **9-08**

(a)   the racial or ethnic origin of the data subject;

(b)   his political opinions;

(c)   his religious beliefs or other beliefs of a similar nature;

(d)   whether he is a member of a trade union;

(e)   his physical or mental health or condition;

(f)   his sexual life;

(g)   the commission or alleged commission by him of any offence; or

(h)   any proceedings for any offence committed or alleged to have been committed by him, the disposal of such proceedings or the sentence of any court in such proceedings.[11]

3. THE DATA PROTECTION PRINCIPLES

A data controller must comply with the data protection principles. In   **9-09**
summary, these are as follows:

1.   Personal data shall be processed fairly and lawfully. Personal data must
     not be processed unless it meets at least one of the conditions set out in
     Schedule 2 of the Act. These include the following:

     (1)   the data subject has given his consent to the processing[12];
     (2)   the processing is necessary (a) for the performance of a contract to
           which the data subject is a party, or (b) for the taking of steps at
           the request of the data subject with a view to entering into a con-
           tract;
     (3)   the processing is necessary for compliance with any legal obligation
           to which the data controller is subject, other than an obligation
           imposed by contract;
     (4)   the processing is necessary in order to protect the vital interests of
           the data subject;
     (5)   the processing is necessary for the administration of justice or for
           other functions of a public nature.

Sensitive personal data must not be processed unless it meets one of the even
more stringent conditions set out in Schedule 3.

---

[11] s.2 of the Act.
[12] Consent is not defined in the Act, but the European Directive indicates that consent must be
actively communicated between the parties. Consent cannot therefore be inferred from silence,
such as failure to return or respond to a leaflet.

2. Personal data shall be obtained only for one or more specified and lawful purposes, and shall not be further processed in any manner incompatible with that purpose or those purposes.

3. Personal data shall be adequate, relevant and not excessive in relation to the purpose or purposes for which they are processed.

4. Personal data shall be accurate and, where necessary, kept up to date.

5. Personal data processed for any purpose or purposes shall not be kept for longer than is necessary for that purpose or those purposes.

6. Personal data shall be processed in accordance with the rights of data subjects under the Act.

7. Appropriate technical and organisational measures shall be taken against unauthorised or unlawful processing of personal data and against accidental loss or destruction of, or damage to, personal data.

8. Personal data shall not be transferred to a country or territory outside the European Economic Area unless that country or territory ensures an adequate level of protection for the rights and freedoms of data subjects in relation to the processing of personal data.

4. RIGHTS OF DATA SUBJECTS

In summary, the rights of a data subject under the Act include the following:

(1) RIGHT OF ACCESS TO PERSONAL DATA

9-10 An individual is entitled[13]:

(a) to be informed by any data controller whether personal data of which that individual is the data subject are being processed by or on behalf of that data controller;

(b) if (a) is the case, to be given by the data controller a description of the personal data, the purposes for which they are being processed, and the recipients or classes to recipients to whom they are or may be disclosed;

(c) to have communicated to him in an intelligible form the information constituting any personal data, and any information held as to the source of that information;

---

[13] s.7(1) of the Act. A data controller is not obliged to comply with the data subject's request unless he has been received a request in writing and any fee he may require: s.7(2).

(d) where the processing by automatic means of personal data is for the purpose of evaluating matters relating to him (*e.g.* performance at work or creditworthiness), and has constituted or is likely to constitute the sole basis for any decision significantly affecting him, to be informed of the logic involved in that decision-taking.

Where a data controller cannot comply with the request without disclosing information relating to another individual who can be identified from that information, he is not obliged to comply with the request unless:

(a) the other individual has consented to the disclosure of the information to the person making the request; or

(b) it is reasonable in all the circumstances to comply with the request without the consent of the other individual.[14]

In determining "reasonableness" in this situation, the court should consider any duty of confidentiality owed to the other individual, any steps taken by the data controller with a view to seeking the consent of the other individual, whether the other individual is capable of giving consent, and any express refusal of consent by the other individual.[15]

(2) Right to prevent processing likely to cause damage or distress

An individual is entitled at any time by notice in writing to require the data controller to cease, or not to begin, processing any personal data of which he is the data subject, on the ground that: **9-11**

(a) the processing is causing or is likely to cause substantial and unwarranted damage or distress to the data subject or another person, and

(b) that damage or distress is or would be unwarranted.[16]

(3) Right to prevent processing for purposes of direct marketing

An individual is entitled at any time by notice in writing to require the data controller to cease, or not to begin, processing for the purposes of direct marketing personal data of which he is the data subject.[17] **9-12**

---

[14] s.7(4) of the Act.
[15] *ibid.*, s.7(6).
[16] *ibid.*, s.10.
[17] *ibid.*, s.11.

(4) RIGHT IN RELATION TO AUTOMATED DECISION-TAKING

9-13   An individual is entitled at any time by notice in writing to require the data controller to ensure that no decision which significantly affects that individual is made by him or on behalf of him which is based solely on the processing by computer of that individual's personal data.[18]

5. RESPONSIBILITIES OF DATA CONTROLLERS

9-14   A data controller has two main duties: to comply with the data protection principles and not to process personal data without having been registered by the Data Protection Commissioner.[19]

In registering, a data controller must notify the Commissioner of certain "registrable particulars", including a description of the personal data being processed, the category or categories of data subject to which they relate, and the purpose or purposes for which the data is to be processed.[20] He must also notify the Commissioner of the measures to be taken for the purpose of complying with the seventh data protection principle.[21]

6. EXEMPTION FOR THE PURPOSE OF JOURNALISM

9-15   Part IV of the Act sets out certain exemptions from the requirements of the Act. These relate to, for example, national security, crime and taxation, health and education and regulatory activity. Of particular interest is the exemption for "the special purposes", defined to mean the purposes of journalism, artistic purposes or literary purposes.[22]

Personal data which is processed only for the special purposes enjoy certain exemptions if:

(a)   the processing is undertaken with a view to the publication by any person of any journalistic, literary or artistic material[23];

(b)   the data controller reasonably believes that, having regard in particular to the special importance of the public interest in freedom of expression, publication would be in the public interest; and

(c)   the data controller reasonably believes that, in all the circumstances, compliance is incompatible with the special purposes.

---

[18]   s.12 of the Act.

[19]   The obligation to register may not apply in all cases: see *ibid.*, s.17.

[20]   *ibid.*, s.16(1).

[21]   *ibid.*, s.18.

[22]   *ibid.*, ss.3 and 32. This mirrors the language used in section 12 of the Human Rights Act 1998: see Chap. 2.

[23]   "Publish" in this context means make available to the public, or any section of the public: *ibid.*, s.32(6).

In determining whether the belief of the data controller that publication would be in the public interest was or is a reasonable one, regard may be had to his compliance with any code of practice which is relevant to the publication in question and which has been designated by the Secretary of State. In this regard, the Data Protection (Designated Codes of Practice) Order 2000 has designated the following Codes for the purpose of this section: the Broadcasting Standards Commission's Code on Fairness and Privacy, the Independent Television Commission's Programme Code, the Press Complaints Commission's Code of Practice, the BBC's Producers' Guidelines; and the Programme Code issued by the Radio Authority.[24]

If the processing is done for "special purposes", publishers will be exempt from the following provisions under the Act:

(a)   the data protection principles, save for the seventh principle;

(b)   section 7 (right of access to personal data);

(c)   section 10 (right to prevent processing likely to cause damage or distress);

(d)   section 12 (rights in relation to automated decision-taking); and

(e)   section 14(1) to (3) (rectification, blocking, erasure and destruction).

If a data subject makes an application to a court for an order in relation to any of these exempted circumstances, the court may stay such proceedings if it is satisfied that the data is being processed (a) only for the special purposes and (b) with a view to the publication by any person of any journalistic, literary or artistic material which, at the time 24 hours prior to the application, had not previously been published by the data controller.

This means that an order cannot be obtained under the Act to restrain the publication of a story. However, once the story has been published, the subject access provisions will apply.

Publishers should furthermore be aware that much of the personal data they process, such as data regarding subscribers or employees, is not collected with a view to publication for special purposes: such data is therefore not exempt.

7. REMEDIES

The remedies available under the Act include the following: **9-16**

(1)   A court may order the data controller's compliance if a data subject has been denied one of his rights.

---

[24]   S.I. 2000 No. 418. It came into force on March 1, 2000. These Codes are described in Pt. II and appear in full in the CD ROM accompanying this text.

(2) An individual may seek compensation from the data controller for damage or distress caused by contravention of the requirements of the Act.[25]

(3) If a court is satisfied on an application by a data subject that personal data are inaccurate, it may order the data controller to rectify, block, erase or destroy those data and any other personal data which contain an expression of opinion which appears to the court to be based on inaccurate data.[26]

The Act also creates offences including the following:

(1) Failure to register when required is an offence under the Act.[27]

(2) If the Commissioner believes that a data controller is breaching the Act, he may issue an enforcement notice requiring compliance.[28] Failure to comply with the notice is an offence.[29] The Act also contains powers of entry and inspection, exercisable on the grant of a warrant by a circuit judge.[30]

(3) Subject to certain exemptions, a person must not knowingly or recklessly, without the consent of the data controller (a) obtain or disclose personal data or the information contained in personal data, or (b) procure the disclosure to another person of the information contained in personal data.[31]

---

[25] s.13 of the Act. It is a defence to this provision if the data controller took such care as in all the circumstances was reasonably required to comply with the relevant requirement: *ibid.*, s.13(3).
[26] *ibid.*, s.14.
[27] *ibid.*, s.21.
[28] *ibid.*, s.40.
[29] *ibid.*, s.47.
[30] *ibid.*, Sched. 9.
[31] *ibid.*, s.55.

Chapter 10

Miscellaneous legal issues

1. NATIONAL SECURITY

(1) INTRODUCTION

The Official Secrets Acts 1911, 1920 and 1989 create a number of offences **10-01** which may be committed by the media in reporting government activities. A distinction can be made between those that may subsequently be offences committed by a person disclosing information and those committed by a person to whom the information has been disclosed. This section will broadly follow that demarcation.

Two points should be noted at the outset. First, prosecutions under the Acts will be not be instituted unless the Attorney-General has given approval.[1] Consequently, the decision whether to prosecute is likely to be influenced by political considerations.

The second point is that the government may also choose to pursue civil remedies against those who have contravened the Official Secrets Acts. This could involve claims for breach of confidence, breach of contract or copyright infringement.

(2) SPYING AND SABOTAGE

Before looking at the offences specifically concerned with disclosure, it is appro- **10-02** priate to note the more general offence relating to spying and sabotage created by section 1(1) of the Official Secrets Act 1911. This provides as follows:

"If any person for any purpose prejudicial to the safety or interests of the State:

    (a) approaches, inspects, passes over or is in the neighbourhood of, or enters any prohibited place[2]; or

---

[1] OSA 1911, s.8 (as amended by s.14(5) of the Criminal Jurisdiction Act 1975); OSA 1989, s.9(1). The exception is in respect of an offence under OSA 1989, s.4(2): see (3)(d) below. A prosecution in respect of such an offence cannot be instituted without the permission of the Director of Public Prosecutions OSA 1989, s. 9(2)).

[2] OSA 1911, s.3 contains the definition of "prohibited place": it includes a wide range of military and communications sites, munitions stores, transport networks, energy and fuel works and areas declared to be prohibited by the Secretary of State.

(b) makes any sketch, plan, model, or note which is calculated to be, or might be, or is intended to be, directly or indirectly useful to an enemy; or

(c) obtains, collects, records, or publishes, or communicates to any other person any secret official code word, or password, or any sketch, plan, model, article, or note, or other document or information which is calculated to be, or might be, directly or indirectly useful to an enemy,

he is guilty of an offence and liable on conviction on indictment to imprisonment for a term not exceeding 14 years.[3]"

This section is aimed principally at the spying activities of enemy agents[4] and, indeed, it would be rare for information obtained from spying to come into the media's possession. It is more likely that a journalist could commit an offence under section 7 of the Official Secrets Act 1920. This provides that any person who attempts to commit any offence under the Official Secrets Acts, or solicits or incites or endeavours to persuade another to commit an offence, or aids or abets and does any act preparatory to the commission of any offence under the Acts, is guilty of an offence. Arranging a meeting with a source who intends to commit an offence under section 1 of the 1911 Act could in certain circumstances amount to an offence under section 7.

The 1989 Act also makes it an offence for a person to disclose any information, document or article which he knows, or has reasonable cause to believe, to have come into his possession as a result of a contravention of section 1 of the Official Secrets Act 1911.[5]

(3) OFFENCES COMMITTED BY PERSONS DISCLOSING INFORMATION

The 1989 Act creates a number of offences relating to the disclosure of information.[6] These are considered below.

(a) Security and intelligence (section 1)

10-03 A person who is or has been a member of the security and intelligence services, or a person who has been notified that he is subject to the provisions of this

---

[3] The offence is laid down by OSA 1920, s.8(1).

[4] It has, however, been applied in other circumstances. For example, the House of Lords applied the section to nuclear disarmament demonstrators protesting at an airbase which was a prohibited place: *Chandler v. DPP* [1964] A.C. 763.

[5] OSA 1989, s.5(6).

[6] The penalty for summary conviction under the 1989 Act is a fine or imprisonment not exceeding six months, or both; on indictment the penalty is a fine and maximum imprisonment of two years, or both: OSA 1989, s.10. However, offences under ss.8(1),(4) and (5) relating to the safekeeping of information carry a maximum prison sentence on summary conviction of three months.

section, commits an offence if he discloses without lawful authority any information, document or other article relating to security and intelligence which is or has been in his possession by virtue of that position.[7]

A person who is or has been a Crown servant or government contractor[8] commits an offence if without lawful authority he makes a damaging disclosure of any information, document or other article relating to security and intelligence which is or has been in his possession by virtue of that position.[9]

A disclosure is damaging if (a) it causes damage to the work of, or any part of, the security and intelligence services; or (b) it is of information or a document or other article which is such that its unauthorised disclosure would be likely to cause such damage or which falls within a class or description of information, documents or articles the unauthorised disclosure of which would be likely to have that effect.[10]

It is a defence to a charge under this section that at the time of the alleged offence the defendant did not know, and had no reasonable cause to believe, that the information, document or article in question related to security or intelligence or, in the case of an offence under section 1(3), that the disclosure would be damaging.[11]

(b) Defence (section 2)

A person who is or has been a Crown servant or government contractor **10-04** commits an offence if without lawful authority he makes a damaging disclosure of any information, document or other article relating to defence[12] which is or has been in his possession by virtue of that position.

A disclosure is damaging if:

(a) it damages the capability of the armed forces, or any part of the armed forces, to carry out their tasks or leads to loss of life or injury to members of those forces or serious damage to the equipment or installations of those forces; or

(b) otherwise than as mentioned in (a), it endangers the interests of the United Kingdom abroad, seriously obstructs the promotion or protection by the United Kingdom of those interests or endangers the safety of British citizens abroad; or

---

[7] The reference to disclosure of information includes the making of statements which purport to be a disclosure of such information: OSA 1989, s.1(2).

[8] "Crown servant" and "government contractor" are defined as including civil servants, members of the armed forces, and the police: see OSA 1989, s.12.

[9] *ibid.*, s.1(3).

[10] *ibid.*, s.1(4).

[11] *ibid.*, s.1(5).

[12] "Defence" includes information as to the operations of the armed forces, weapons or equipment, policy and planning, and the maintenance of essential supplies and services needed in time of war: see *ibid.*, s.2(4).

(c) it is of information or of a document or article which is such that its unauthorised disclosure would be likely to have any of those effects.[13]

It is a defence to a charge under this section that at the time of the alleged offence the defendant did not know, and had no reasonable cause to believe, that the information, document or article in question related to defence or that its disclosure would be damaging.[14]

(c) International relations (section 3)

10-05 A person who is or has been a Crown servant or government contractor commits an offence if without lawful authority he makes a damaging disclosure of

(a) any information, document or other article relating to international relations,[15] or

(b) any confidential information, document or other article obtained from another State or an international organisation

which is or has been in his possession by virtue of that position.
   A disclosure is damaging if:

(a) it endangers the interests of the United Kingdom abroad, seriously obstructs the promotion or protection by the United Kingdom of those interests or endangers the safety of British citizens abroad; or

(b) it is of information or of a document or article which is such that its unauthorised disclosure would be likely to have any of those effects.[16]

It is a defence to a charge under this section that at the time of the alleged offence the defendant did not know, and had no reasonable cause to believe, that the information, document or article in question was such as is mentioned in section 3(1) or that its disclosure would be damaging.[17]

(d) Crime and special investigation powers (section 4)

10-06 A person who is or has been a Crown servant or government contractor is guilty of an offence if without lawful authority he discloses any information,

---

[13] OSA 1989, s.2(2).

[14] *ibid.*, s.2(3).

[15] The definition of "international relations" includes relations between states or between international organisations, and any matter relating to a state other than the U.K. or to an international organisation capable of affecting the U.K.'s international relations: see OSA 1989, s.3(5).

[16] *ibid.*, s.3(2). See also s.3(3).

[17] *ibid.*, s.3(4).

document or other article which is or has been in his possession by virtue of that position.

This section applies to any information, document or other article:

(a) the disclosure of which:

    (i) results in the commission of an offence; or

    (ii) facilitates an escape from legal custody or the doing of any other act prejudicial to the safekeeping of persons in legal custody; or

    (iii) impedes the prevention or detection of offences or the apprehension or prosecution of suspected offenders; or

(b) which is such that its unauthorised disclosure would be likely to have any of those effects.[18]

It is a defence to a charge in respect of a disclosure under section 4(2)(a) to prove that at the time of the alleged offence the defendant did not know, and had no reasonable cause to believe, that the disclosure would have any of the effects mentioned there.[19]

It is a defence to a charge in respect of any other disclosure to prove that at the time of the alleged offence the defendant did not know, and had no reasonable cause to believe, that the information, document or article in question was one to which section 4 applied.[20]

(e) Safekeeping of information (section 8)

A number of offences are created by this section, including the following[21]:   **10-07**

(i) a Crown servant or government contractor who fails to take reasonable care to prevent the unauthorised disclosure of any document or other article which it would be an offence to disclose under sections 1 to 4 above is guilty of an offence;

(ii) it is an offence for a Crown servant to retain the document or article contrary to his official duty. He will however have a defence if he believed he was acting in accordance with his official duty and had no reasonable cause to believe otherwise;

(iii) it is an offence for a government contractor, if he fails to comply with an official direction to return or dispose of such a document or article.

---

[18] OSA 1989, s.4(2).
[19] *ibid.*, s 4(4).
[20] *ibid.*, s.4(5).
[21] The offences created by this section that may be committed by journalists or other members of the public are dealt with below.

(4) OFFENCES COMMITTED BY THOSE TO WHOM INFORMATION IS DISCLOSED

(a) Information resulting from unauthorised disclosures or entrusted in confidence (section 5)

10-08 A person commits an offence if he discloses without lawful authority any information, document or article knowing, or having reasonable cause to believe, that it is protected from disclosure by sections 1 to 4 of the 1989 Act.[22]
An offence will only be committed where:

(a) the information, document or article came into the defendant's possession as a result of having been:

(i) disclosed by a Crown servant or government contractor without lawful authority;

(ii) entrusted to him by a Crown servant or government contractor on terms requiring it to be held in confidence or in circumstances in which the Crown servant or government contractor could reasonably expect that it would be so held; or

(iii) disclosed without lawful authority by a person to whom it was entrusted as mentioned in (ii); and

(b) the disclosure by the person into whose possession it has come is not an offence under sections 1 to 4.[23]

If the disclosure relates to security and intelligence, defence or international relations, the person does not commit an offence unless the disclosure is damaging and he makes it knowing, or having reasonable cause to believe, that it would be damaging. Crucially, at least from the media's point of view, there is no public interest defence under the 1989 Act nor a defence that the material disclosed is is already in the public domain. These factors may, however, be relevant to the question of whether the disclosure is damaging.
No offence is committed if the disclosure is made under section 5(1)(a) (i) or (iii) above unless the disclosure was by a British citizen or took place in the United Kingdom, Channel Islands, Isle of Man or a colony.[24]

(b) Information entrusted in confidence to other states or international organisations (section 6)

10-09 There is a separate offence which applies to:

(a) any information, document or article which:

(i) relates to security and intelligence, defence or international relations; and

---

[22] OSA 1989, s 5(2).
[23] *ibid.*, s.5(1).
[24] *ibid.*, s.5(4).

(ii)   has been communicated in confidence by or on behalf of the United Kingdom to another state or an international organisation,

has come into a person's possession as a result of having been disclosed without authority; and

(b)   the disclosure is not an offence under sections 1 to 5 of the 1989 Act.[25]

The offence will be committed where the person in possession of the information, document or article makes a damaging disclosure of it knowing, or having reasonable cause to believe, that the nature of the information is as described above, and that its disclosure would be damaging. Unlike section 5, there is a defence where the information has previously been made available to the public with the authority of the relevant state or international organisation.[26]

(c) Safekeeping of information (section 8)

A person who has in his possession or control any document or other article   **10-10**
which it would be an offence to disclose under section 5 commits an offence if (a) he fails to comply with an official direction to return or dispose of it; or (b) where he obtained it from a Crown servant or government contractor in confidence, or in circumstances in which the servant or contractor could reasonably expect it to be confidential, he fails to take reasonable care to prevent its unauthorised disclosure.[27]

It is also an offence for any person to disclose any official information, document or article which can be used for the purpose of gaining access to any information, document or article protected against disclosure under sections 1 to 6 of the 1989 Act in circumstances where it would be reasonable to expect that it might be used for that purpose without authority.[28] Journalists could be at risk of committing this offence in certain circumstances.

(5) DEFENCE ADVISORY NOTICES

Defence advisory notices (DA notices) are the basis for a voluntary system set   **10-11**
up between government and the media to issue guidance on matters which affect national security. The guidance is given by the Defence, Press and Broadcasting Advisory Committee (DPBAC). DPBAC is composed of senior staff from the Ministry of Defence and the Home and Foreign Offices, and representatives from the press and broadcasters.

The permanent secretary of the Committee is the point of day-to-day contact for members of the media who seek advice under the system. Any advice given is merely that, and cannot be legally enforced under the Official

---

[25] OSA 1989, s 6(1).
[26] *ibid.*, s.6(3).
[27] *ibid.*, s.8(4). There is a comparable provision concerning disclosures under s.6: see s.8(6).
[28] *ibid.*, s.8(6).

Secrets Acts or otherwise. Similarly, taking advice does not necessarily protect a publisher from prosecution under the Official Secrets Acts. The final decision as to whether to accept or reject any advice obtained lies with editors.

Advice is generally sought where the material in question falls within the areas which are the subject of DA notices. Copies of the notices are distributed by DPBAC to newspaper editors and their broadcasting equivalents. Each notice lists specific categories of information within the area of the Notice disclosure of which would put national security at risk, and seeks to explain the rationale for the restrictions.

The notices cover the following areas:

(1) defence and counter-terrorism;

(2) operations, plans and capabilities;

(3) non-nuclear weapons and operational equipment;

(4) nuclear weapons and equipment;

(5) ciphers and secure communications;

(6) identification of specific installations;

(7) United Kingdom security and intelligence services.

Further information may be obtained from DPBAC, Room 2235, Ministry of Defence, Main Building, Whitehall, London SW1A 2HB (tel: 020 7218 2206).

2. PUBLIC INTEREST DISCLOSURE ("WHISTLE-BLOWING")

10-12   Employees "blowing the whistle" on unscrupulous activities in the workplace acquired greater protection under the Public Interest Disclosure Act 1998 than existed previously.[29]

A worker has the right not to be subjected to any detriment by any act, or any deliberate failure to act, by his employer on the ground that he has made a protected disclosure.[30]

If the reason (or, if more than one, the principal reason) for an employee's dismissal is the making of a protected disclosure, it will be regarded as unfair dismissal and the employee will be entitled to compensation.[31]

A disclosure is "protected" where it tends to show one or more of the following:

(a) that a criminal offence has been committed is being committed or is likely to be committed;

---

[29] The Public Interest Disclosure Act 1998 came into force on July 2, 1999, and amends the Employment Rights Act 1996.
[30] Employment Rights Act 1996, s.47B(1).
[31] *ibid.*, S103A.

(b) that a person has failed, is failing or is likely to fail to comply with any legal obligation to which he is subject;

(c) that a miscarriage of justice has occurred, is occurring or is likely to occur;

(d) that the health and safety of any individual has been, is being or is likely to be endangered;

(e) that the environment has been, is being or is likely to be damaged; or

(f) that information tending to show that any matter falling within one of the preceding categories has been, is, or is likely to be deliberately concealed.[32]

A disclosure is not protected if the person making it commits an offence by making it.[33] A disclosure in breach of the Official Secrets Act 1989 would therefore not be protected.

In addition, the disclosure must have been in good faith to certain categories of people. The prescribed person depends on the circumstances of the case, but they include an employer (or other person with legal responsibility for the relevant failure), a legal adviser and a minister of the Crown.[34]

A disclosure may be made by a worker to other persons, such as the media, if:

(a) the disclosure is made in good faith;

(b) he reasonably believes that the information disclosed, and any allegations contained in it, are substantially true;

(c) he does not make the disclosure for reasons of personal gain;

(d) he reasonably believes he will be subjected to a detriment by his employer if he makes the disclosure, or (in certain prescribed circumstances) he reasonably believes that evidence will be concealed or destroyed, or he has disclosed the same information to his employer previously (or to other prescribed persons); and

(e) in all the circumstances of the case, it is reasonable for him to make the disclosure.[35]

It is not yet known how the provisions of the Act will be interpreted. In many cases, whether a disclosure is protected will depend on whether the discloser's belief was reasonable and if the disclosure was made to the appropriate person.

---

[32] Employment Rights Act 1996, s 43B (1).

[33] ibid., s 43B (3).

[34] ibid., ss 43C, D and E.

[35] ibid., s.43G(1). Factors to be considered in assessing whether disclosure is reasonable include the identity of the person to whom disclosure is made, the seriousness of the relevant failure, whether the relevant failure is continuing or likely to continue, and whether disclosure is made in breach of confidentiality: ibid., s.43G(3).

3. TELEPHONE TAPPING AND EAVESDROPPING

10-13   Telephone tapping and eavesdropping by radio and other means may be offences under one of three statutes.

It is an offence under the Wireless Telegraphy Act 1949 to use a wireless apparatus to obtain information about any message which the user is not authorised to receive. The disclosure of any information obtained from telephone tapping is also an offence, save in the context of legal proceedings.[36]

Separate offences apply to the interception of public telecommunications systems. Under the Interception of Communications Act 1985, a person who intentionally intercepts a communication in the course of its transmission by post or by means of a public telecommunications system is guilty of an offence.[37]

The Telecommunications Act 1984 also makes it an offence for any person engaged in running a public telecommunications system intentionally to disclose, otherwise than in the course of his duty, (a) the contents of any message intercepted in the course of its transmission, or (b) information concerning the use made of telecommunications services provided for any other person by means of that system.[38]

It is not an offence to tape record one's own telephone conversations. There are, however, provisions in many of the Codes described in Part II dealing with this issue.[39]

4. TRESPASS, NUISANCE AND HARASSMENT

If a journalist is on or around private property, or he pursues the subject of his story in a persistent manner, he needs to be aware of potential legal pitfalls. These are considered in this section. He should also bear in mind similar provisions contained in many of the Codes described in Part II.[40]

TRESPASS

10-14   A civil action for trespass lies against a person who enters private property when he knows, or ought to know, that he has been forbidden to enter. There is a normally an implied licence to enter private property, for example, to request an interview. If, however a journalist is asked to leave private property but refuses to do so, he becomes a trespasser. He will also be a trespasser, even if he is given licence to enter, if he obtains permission by fraud or does things while on the property for which he was not given licence.

---

[36] s.5.
[37] s.1.
[38] s.45.
[39] See the BBC's Producers' Guidelines (Chap. 12 at 2(3)), the ITC Programme Code (Chap. 13 at 2(3)), the Radio Authority Programme Code (Chap. 14 at 2(3)), the Broadcasting Standards Commission Code on Fairness and Privacy (Chap. 15 at 2) and the Press Complaints Commission Code of Practice (Chap. 16 at 3)
[40] See the references in the previous footnote.

An injunction and damages can be sought against the trespasser by the occupier of the land, who can also use reasonable force to eject the trespasser.[41]

Trespass may also amount to a crime if violence is used or threatened to secure entry.[42] In addition the offence of aggravated trespass was created by the Criminal Justice and Public Order Act 1994. It was originally aimed at hunt saboteurs and environmental activists. It arises where a person trespasses on land in the open air and, in relation to any lawful activity which persons are engaging in or about to engage in on that or adjoining land in the open air, does there anything which is intended by him to have the effect (1) of intimidating those persons to deter them from engaging in that activity, (2) of obstructing that activity or (3) of disrupting that activity.[43]

The senior police officer at the scene can order a person (or persons, if they have a common purpose) to leave if he reasonably believes that person to have committed, be committing, or be intending to commit aggravated trespass. If a person fails to leave as soon as practicable, or returns as a trespasser within the next three months, it is an offence punishable on summary conviction by three months' imprisonment, a fine, or both.

NUISANCE

Private nuisance gives rise to a civil claim where interference takes place with a person's use or enjoyment of his land. The making of persistent telephone calls can amount to a nuisance. Any claim must be brought, however, by a person who has a right to the land affected.[44] The key remedies are an injunction and damages.   **10-15**

A public nuisance occurs where a person unlawfully damages the public as a whole, or all the members of a class who come within the sphere of its operation. This is an offence at common law.[45] Moreover, if an individual has suffered special damage over and above that inflicted on the community at large, he may bring a civil claim.

HARASSMENT

An offence is committed by a person whose course of conduct[46] causes another person to fear that violence will be used against him, and that person knows or ought to know that his conduct will cause such a fear.[47] The offence   **10-16**

---

[41] *Hall v. Davis* (1825) 2 C.&P. 33.
[42] Criminal Law Act 1977, s.6.
[43] Criminal Justice and Public Order Act 1994, s.68(1).
[44] *Hunter v. Canary Wharf Ltd* [1997] A.C. 655.
[45] In *R. v. Johnson* [1997] 1 W.L.R. 367, the Court of Appeal found that the making of obscene telephone calls to at least 13 women amounted to a public nuisance.
[46] A "course of conduct" must involve conduct on at least two occasions. "Conduct" includes speech: Protection from Harassment Act 1997, s.7.
[47] Protection from Harassment Act 1997, s.4. There is a defence if the accused's course of conduct was pursued to prevent or detect crime or to comply with a legal requirement, or was reasonable for the protection of himself, another person, or property.

is punishable on indictment by a sentence of up to five years' imprisonment, a fine, or both, and on summary conviction up to six months' imprisonment, a fine, or both.

A lesser offence takes place where a person pursues a course of conduct which amounts to harassment, and that person knows or ought to know that his conduct amounts to harassment.[48] The Act states that references to harassing a person include alarming the person or causing the person distress.[49] The penalty for this offence on summary conviction is six months' imprisonment, a fine, or both. In addition, a restraining order can be imposed on the offender for a specified period or until further order.[50] It is a further offence to breach the terms of such an order without reasonable excuse.

A victim of harassment can bring civil proceedings under the Protection from Harassment Act 1997, seeking damages for anxiety and financial loss and an injunction.[51] The subject of the injunction will be guilty of an offence if he does without reasonable excuse anything he is forbidden to do under the terms of the injunction. An injunction could be sought under this provision to prevent persistent telephone calls.

Three offences under the Public Order Act 1986 should also be noted in this context.

SECTION 4 (FEAR OR PROVOCATION OF VIOLENCE)

10-17 This provides that a person is guilty of an offence if he

(a) uses towards another person threatening, abusive or insulting words or behaviour, or

(b) distributes or displays to another person any writing, sign or other visible representation which is threatening, abusive or insulting,

with intent to cause that person to believe that immediate unlawful violence will be used against him or another by any person, or to provoke the immediate use of unlawful violence by that person or another, or whereby that person is likely to believe that such violence will be used or it is likely that such violence will be provoked. Summary conviction can lead to up to six months' imprisonment or a fine.[52]

SECTION 4A (INTENTIONAL HARASSMENT, ALARM OR DISTRESS)

10-18 A person will be guilty of an offence if, with intent to cause a person harassment, alarm or distress, he:

---

[48] Protection from Harassment Act 1997, s.1. There is a defence if the accused's course of conduct was pursued to prevent or detect crime or to comply with a legal requirement, or was reasonable in the particular circumstances.
[49] *ibid.*, s.7.
[50] *ibid.*, s.5.
[51] *ibid.*, s.3.
[52] Public Order Act 1986, s.4(4).

(a) uses threatening, abusive or insulting words or behaviour, or disorderly behaviour, or

(b) displays any writing, sign or other visible representation which is threatening, abusive or insulting,

thereby causing that or another person harassment, alarm or distress.

It is a defence for the defendant to prove that he was inside a dwelling and had no reason to believe that the offending matter would be heard or seen by a person outside the dwelling, or that his conduct was reasonable.[53] Conviction can attract a six-month prison sentence or a fine.[54]

SECTION 5 (HARASSMENT, ALARM OR DISTRESS)

A person is guilty of an offence if he uses threatening, abusive or insulting **10-19** words or behaviour, or disorderly behaviour within the hearing or sight of a person likely to be caused harassment, alarm or distress thereby.[55] Summary conviction can lead to a fine.[56]

5. MEDIA COVERAGE DURING ELECTIONS

The Representation of the People Act 1983 is the principal piece of legislation **10-20** regulating the conduct of parliamentary and local government elections. There are a number of provisions dealing with media coverage, which are summarised in this section.[57]

FALSE STATEMENTS AS TO CANDIDATES

A person who, or any director of any body or association corporate which **10-21**

(a) before or during an election, or

(b) for the purpose of affecting the return of any candidate at the election,

makes or publishes any false statement of fact in relation to a candidate's personal character or conduct is guilty of an illegal practice, unless he can show that he had reasonable grounds for believing, and did believe, the statement to

---

[53] Public Order Act 1986, s.4A(3).
[54] *ibid.*, s.4A(5).
[55] *ibid.*, s.5(1).
[56] *ibid.*, s.5(6).
[57] There are provisions dealing with election coverage in the BBC Producers' Guidelines and the Codes of the ITC and Radio Authority which are reproduced in the CD ROM accompanying this text. Election advertising is excluded from CAP's Advertising Code: see Chap. 17.

be true.[58] Publication of the statement may be restrained by an application for an injunction to the High Court or county court.[59]

The false statement must be as to fact, and not an expression of opinion. The statement must also relate to the candidate's personal character rather than to his politics. It has been held, for example, that calling someone a Communist does not amount to a false statement about his personal character.[60]

It is also an illegal practice to, before or during an election, knowingly publish a false statement of a candidate's withdrawal from the election for the purpose of promoting or procuring the election of another candidate.[61]

A person found guilty of an illegal practice is liable to be fined on summary conviction and disqualified as an elector for five years.[62]

PROHIBITION OF EXPENSES NOT AUTHORISED BY ELECTION AGENT

10-22 It is an illegal practice for any person other than the agent to incur expense with a view to promoting or procuring the election of a candidate.[63] By accepting an advertisement from such a person, a newspaper publisher might be liable for aiding and abetting the commission of the offence.[64]

These restrictions do not apply to editorial comment regarding a candidate or election, or other published material which is not paid for. For example, the publication of an article provided by a candidate would not breach the Act.

BROADCASTING DURING ELECTIONS

10-23 In relation to a parliamentary or local government election, pending such election it is not lawful for any item about the constituency or electoral area to be broadcast if any candidate taking part in the item does not consent.[65] Furthermore, where the item is broadcast before the latest time for delivery of nomination papers, or is made after that time but without the consent of any candidate remaining validly nominated, any person taking part for the purpose of promoting or procuring his election is guilty of an illegal practice, unless the broadcast is made without his consent.[66]

---

[58] Representation of the People Act 1983, s.106(1). The statement does not need to be defamatory. The candidate would be free to resort to defamation or malicious falsehood proceedings if he wished: see chap. 3.

[59] *ibid.*, s.106(3).

[60] *Burns v. Associated Newspapers Ltd* (1925) 89 J.P. 205.

[61] *ibid.*, s.106(5).

[62] *ibid.*, ss.160 and 169.

[63] *ibid.*, s.75(1).

[64] *ibid.*, s.75(5).

[65] *ibid.*, s.93(1)(a).

[66] *ibid.*, s.93(1)(b).

6. ADVERTISING LAWS

Because advertising and other marketing activities often seek to change con-   **10-24**
sumers' behaviour, and in particular to persuade them part with their money,
freedom of expression tends to be more restricted in this context than is the
case with purely editorial content.

Indeed, there is a very substantial body of law dealing with various aspects
of advertising . This includes the generalised protection offered to the consumer against false trade descriptions,[67] as well as more industry-specific issues,
such as the regulation of advertising by the professions.[68] It is beyond the
scope of this text to explore this aspect in any detail.[69] Part II does, however,
examine the codes of the BBC, the Independent Television Commission, the
Radio Authority and the Committee of Advertising Practice, all of which
contain material of day-to-day concern in this area.[70]

Two areas which should be mentioned here—because of their relevance to
many forms of sales promotion—are lotteries and competitions.

The general rule is that lotteries are unlawful, save for a number of categories such as the National Lottery and certain local lotteries[71] and certain exceptions which do not generally relate to the media. Section 2 of the Lotteries and
Amusements Act 1976 makes it an offence in relation to a lottery (*inter alia*):

(1)   to advertise for sale or distribution any tickets for the lottery;

(2)   to print, publish, distribute or have in one's possession for the purpose of
      publication or distribution any advertisement of the lottery.

The penalty for these offences is a fine in the magistrates' court or, in the
Crown Court, a fine or a maximum of two years' imprisonment.[72]

A promotion will generally amount to a lottery if three elements are present:

(i)   prizes are distributed;

(ii)   the distribution is by means of chance; and

(iii) each participant, or a substantial number of them, makes a payment or
       contribution in return for the chance of a prize.[73]

---

[67] Trade Descriptions Act 1968.
[68] Many professional bodies, such as the Law Society, the Institute of Chartered Accountants and
the General Optical Council, have their own rules regarding acceptable advertising by their
members.
[69] See G. Crown., *Advertising Law and Regulation* (Butterworths, 1998) for a full survey of the
law. There is also a useful appendix in the CAP Codes which identifies the main statutory provisions affecting advertising.
[70] The Codes are reproduced in full in the CD ROM accompanying this text.
[71] Lotteries and Amusements Act 1976, s.1; National Lottery, etc. Act 1993. A lottery is not unlawful if it is a small lottery incidental to exempt entertainments (such as fairs and fêtes), private
lotteries, societies' lotteries and local lotteries: see Lotteries and Amusements Act 1976, ss.3–6.
[72] Lotteries and Amusements Act 1976, s.20.
[73] *See Readers' Digest Association Ltd v. Williams* [1976] 3 All E.R. 737: *Imperial Tobacco Ltd v.
Attorney-General* (1980) 2 W.L.R. 466.

Promotions invariably rely for their effectiveness on the distribution of prizes, so efforts to avoid a promotion being regarded as a lottery tend to focus on circumventing the second and third factors.

The chance distribution of prizes can be avoided if prizes are distributed according to merit or based on the exercise of skill. This may be achieved, for example, by asking participants to answer questions or perform a task (such as completing a slogan). The exercise of skill must, however, be genuine.[74] It should also extend throughout the game and not be confined to only one stage of it.[75]

The absence of payment or other contribution can be achieved by providing free entry. The free entry must be genuine and easily accessible. Minimal incidental costs such as postage or the cost of a phone call are unlikely to be regarded as a contribution.

It should also be noted that it is unlawful to conduct in or through any newspaper[76] or in connection with any trade or business or the sale of any article to the public:

(a) any competition in which prizes are offered for forecasts of the result either:

  (i) of a future event; or
  (ii) of a past event the result of which is not yet ascertained, or not yet generally known, or

(b) any other competition in which success does not depend to a substantial degree on the exercise of skill.[77]

The penalties for committing an offence under this section are the same as those for running an illegal lottery.[78]

In *News of the World Ltd v. Friend* a "spot the ball" competition was run in which participants had to pick the spot from which a football was kicked.[79] The person who picked the spot closest to the point chosen by the newspaper's panel of experts as the most likely was the winner. The scheme was found to be lawful because the spot chosen by the experts was not necessarily the spot from which the ball was kicked, and was therefore not forecasting. Furthermore, the experts' decision was not a future event within the meaning of the provision.

---

[74] There must be more than a scintilla of skill: *Moore v. Elphick* [1945] 2 All E.R. 155.

[75] *News of the World v. Friend* [1973] 1 All E.R. 422.

[76] "Newspaper" includes any journal, magazine or other periodical publication: Lotteries and Amusements Act 1976, s.23(1).

[77] Lotteries and Amusements Act 1976, s.14(1).

[78] See Lotteries and Amusements Act 1976, s.14(3).

[79] [1973] 1 All E.R. 422.

Part II

STATUTORY AND INDUSTRY REGULATION

Chapter 11

Introduction

1. REGULATION IN CONTEXT

In Part I we looked at the causes of action most relevant to those publishing **11-01** contentious material. We now examine the key planks of regulation which affect various media sectors. To complicate matters, these planks are not hewn from the same tree. Instead, they have their own histories, borne of particular political circumstances or the development of a new technology.

The most obvious distinction is between those regulators created by, and operating within, a statutory framework on the one hand and those devised and managed by a particular industry on the other. The former group includes the governors of the BBC (who are responsible for the BBC's content),[1] the Independent Television Commission (ITC) (with responsibility for the cable, satellite, the ITV companies, Channel 4 and Channel 5) and the Radio Authority (which supervises commercial radio stations). Each of these regulators (or their forebears) had their genesis in the birth of new forms of communication, which were often seen as having great power that needed to be kept in check.

We shall look at each of these regulators, as well as at another statutory regulator, the Broadcasting Standards Commission (BSC). As we shall see, the BSC's history is complex, being a statutory body which incorporates two previous bodies, only one of which had its origins in statute. To add to the regulatory melting pot, the BSC's role (which is to ensure fairness, privacy and respect for taste and decency) extends across a very wide range of broadcast media, including BBC television and radio, independent television and radio, cable and satellite.

There is therefore overlap between the BSC's work and that of the regulators already identified. This is nowhere more true than in the crossover

---

[1] The BBC's governors are described in this text as regulators in recognition of the fact that they enforce a statutory-based framework on those involved in publishing contentious material, the subject of this text. We acknowledge, however, that their role does differ from that of other organisations identified in this Part. The governors are political appointees and are not detached from the programme-makers in the same way that the ITC is separated from its licensees. Furthermore, the sanctions which can be imposed by the governors have little or no commercial impact. The governors are primarily concerned with ensuring that the BBC meets its obligations under its Charter.

175

between the BSC and the ITC. The ITC's role is more commercial in that one of its primary (though by no means only) interests is to ensure that ITV licensees comply with the terms of their licences. The BSC's concern with fairness and privacy is necessarily narrower, but perhaps more focused on viewer protection.

We will also review the operation of several regulators that owe their existence to structures set up by particular industries. They are:

(a)   the PCC (which maintains the professional and ethical standards of most newspapers and magazines);

(b)   the ASA (which regulates standards in non-broadcast advertising);

(c)   the Independent Committee for the Supervision of Standards of Telephone Information Services (which regulates the content and promotion of premium rate telephone services);

(d)   the Video Standards Council (which runs a scheme to classify computer games);

(e)   the Internet Watch Foundation (which adopts a "notify and remove" strategy in relation to offensive material on the Internet); and

(f)   the Internet Corporation for Assigned Names and Numbers (which supervises the allocation of domain names).

In addition, we will look at the role played by the British Board of Film Classification. This is something of a hybrid organisation. It is a non-governmental body, yet certain of its activities are defined in legislation. It is responsible for classifying films, videos and computer games.[2]

Ironically, the Internet, perhaps the most powerful new technology of all, has not spawned its own super-regulator to match the likes of the BSC or the ITC. Indeed, given the almost unbounded ability to communicate globally, it is unlikely to do so. Furthermore, digital technology is increasingly permitting the convergence of existing forms of communication. This means that it will become increasingly difficult for audiences to know whether the programming they are watching is broadcast or received through the Internet. Where this leaves existing regulators is hard to say and each regulator will need to keep its thinking in touch with these developments.[3] In time we may see the Internet and digital convergence acting as catalysts for changing the current "regulator per medium" approach with a measure of consolidation taking place. It is also likely that there will be an increasing role for industry self-regulation and for co-regulation between industry and the state.

---

[2] The BBFC's relationship to the Video Standards Council is described in Chap. 19.
[3] To date, the ITC has shown little appetite for regulating the Internet, whereas the ASA will adjudicate on "non-broadcast" advertising, including that which appears on websites (see Chap. 17 below). On the other hand, the ITC has granted licences for ADSL delivery.

2. CONSISTENCY BETWEEN REGULATORS

It is unsurprising to learn that the various regulators grapple with common **11-02** issues—privacy, fairness, accuracy or the right of reply, for example—and that there are some common themes to their responses.[4] Most accept the over-riding general principle that content should be legal, decent, honest and truth-ful. However, agreement at that high level ignores differences in detail and it is important for those working in this area to consult the relevant Codes for precise guidance.

To avoid inconsistency in approach in the broadcasting context, the Broadcasting Act 1996 requires each broadcasting or regulatory body (which includes the BBC, the ITC and the Radio Authority) to "reflect the general effect" of the BSC's Codes when drawing up or revising any code relating to either (1) principles and practice in connection with programmes, or in connec-tion with the obtaining of material to be included in programmes, or (2) stan-dards and practice relating to programmes.[5] In order to make this a two-way street, the BSC must consult these bodies when drawing up or revising its Codes.[6]

An important difference between the statutory and industry regulators is that the Codes of the industry bodies tend to be less detailed, but with state-ments to the effect that the spirit as well as the letter of the Codes must be respected. The sanctions that can be imposed by the PCC and the ASA are also less powerful. In practice, however, those dealing with the self-regulatory schemes are, and need to be, as vigilant as those operating within the statutory-based environments if they are to retain credibility.

3. APPROACH TAKEN TO EXAMINATION OF THE VARIOUS BROADCASTING CODES

Of the regulators to be considered in this text, the ITC and Radio Authority **11-03** have the most in common. They are both creatures of the Broadcasting Act 1990 and their functions are similar; namely, to issue and regulate licences that allow commercial television and radio companies respectively to broadcast in the United Kingdom. We are interested in the Codes which they produce to regulate content and, from this point of view at least, the BBC also has con-siderable similarities in approach.

Rather than reproducing the entirety of each organisation's Codes, the approach taken in this text has been to identify key areas of principle which

---

[4] It should be noted that the various regulations often set general criteria to ensure that the overall service offered by the publisher meets with public expectations. For instance, the BBC has undertaken to keep its services under review "with a view to the maintenance of high general standards in all respects (and in particular in respect of their content, quality and edi-torial integrity) and to their offering a wide range of subject-matter . . ." (clause 3.1 of the BBC's agreement with the Secretary of State referred to in Chap. 12 at 1(B). Such general cri-teria are beyond the scope of this text.
[5] Broadcasting Act 1996, ss.107(2) and 108(2).
[6] Broadcasting Act 1996, ss.107(4) and 108(4).

need to be addressed by each regulator and to see how each has done so. It will be noted that, because of the regulators' duty to consult one another, there are many occasions when the Codes adopt a similar approach. The Codes are reproduced in the CD ROM accompanying this text.[7]

The text therefore largely focuses on the following areas:

1. Statutory basis for regulator's functions.

2. Programme regulation, with particular emphasis on:

    (1) taste and decency;
    (2) accuracy and impartiality;
    (3) privacy and the gathering of information;
    (4) religious tolerance and the portrayal of minorities.

3. Advertising and sponsorship regulation, with particular emphasis on:

    (1) general principles;
    (2) misleadingness;
    (3) privacy;
    (4) pre-publication clearance.

4. Complaints procedures.

In so far as advertising and sponsorship are considered, our approach will be to focus on those areas which give rise to particular difficulty, namely the preservation of editorial integrity and ensuring that the public is not misled.

It is hoped that this template will aid easy comparison between the approach of the different regulators.

---

[7] All of the regulators have detailed rules on many issues which are beyond the scope of this text. These include such diverse topics as election coverage, the portrayal of smoking and the conduct of charitable appeals. The approach of the regulators to payments to witnesses and criminals is dealt with at 5 in Chap. 21.

Chapter 12

BBC television and radio

1. STATUTORY BASIS OF THE BBC

The BBC has 12 governors appointed by ministers, who must ensure that the **12-01** BBC's duties and responsibilities are complied with. These duties and responsibilities derive from two principal documents.[1]

(A) THE ROYAL CHARTER

The current Charter was granted for 10 years, expiring on December 31, 2006. It outlines the BBC's purposes and defines its constitution. The Charter states that the BBC must fulfil its legal and contractual obligations, particularly in relation to impartiality and standards of taste and decency, and that it complies with any directions given by the Broadcasting Standards Commission.[2]

(B) THE AGREEMENT BETWEEN THE BBC AND THE SECRETARY FOR STATE OF STATE FOR CULTURE, MEDIA AND SPORT

The Charter is accompanied by an Agreement between the BBC and the **12-02** Secretary for State of State for Culture, Media and Sport ("the Agreement"). The Agreement describes the services and standards expected of the BBC.

Under clause 5.1 of the Agreement, the BBC is required to "do all it can" to secure that all programmes broadcast or transmitted by or on behalf of or under licence from the BBC as part of the Home Services meet certain requirements. For our purposes, these include the BBC doing all it can to secure that programmes:

* serve the tastes and needs of different audiences and, in particular, in order to show concern for the young, are placed at appropriate times (cl. 5.1(b));

---

[1] The Charter and the Agreement, together with the Producers' Guidelines described below, can be downloaded from the BBC website at www.bbc.co.uk. The Producer's Guidelines are also reproduced in the CD Rom accompanying this text.
[2] The BSC is considered in Chap. 15.

- treat controversial subjects with due accuracy and impartiality, both in its news services and in the more general field of programmes dealing with matters of public policy or of political controversy, and do not contain any material expressing the opinion of the BBC on current affairs or matters of matters of public policy other than broadcasting and matter contained in programmes which consist of proceedings in either House of Parliament or proceedings of a local authority or a committee of two or more local authorities[3] (cl. 5.1(c));

- do not include anything which offends against good taste and decency or is likely to encourage or incite to crime or lead to disorder or to be offensive to public feeling (cl. 5.1(d));

- do not involve improper exploitation of any susceptibilities of those watching or listening to its religious programmes or any abusive treatment of the religious views and beliefs of those belonging to a particular religion or religious denomination (cl. 5.1(e));

- do not include any technical device which, by using images of very brief duration or by any other means, exploits the possibility of conveying a message to, or otherwise influencing the minds of, persons watching or listening to the programmes without their being aware, or fully aware, of what has occurred (cl. 5.1(f)).

In addition to the general provisions contained in the Charter and Agreement, the BBC has drawn up a code of ethics for programme-makers called the BBC Producers' Guidelines ("the Guidelines"). These begin with a short statement of the BBC's fundamental editorial principles — "the BBC's Editorial Values" — which are then followed with advice on a wide range of issues of concern to those involved in the broadcasting of contentious material.[4]

Programme makers should also be aware of the separate body of regulation issued by the Broadcasting Standards Commission touching on fairness, privacy, taste and decency. This overlaps with much that is contained in the Guidelines. The BSC's Codes are considered in detail in Chapter 15.

2. PROGRAMME REGULATION

(1) TASTE AND DECENCY

12-03 As we have seen, the Agreement provides that BBC programmes should not include anything which offends against good taste or decency. The BBC's

---

[3] The Guidelines include provisions relating to politics and politicians at Chaps. 18 to 20 which are beyond the scope of this text.

[4] The Guidelines are compendious in approach, addressing a multitude of subjects. Some of these are of only marginal concern to this text, such as Northern Ireland, broadcasting during elections and opinion polls. The approach of this text has been to highlight and summarise those of particular relevance. It should also be noted that the Guidelines contain very detailed provisions about consultation and referral to senior management. These appear in Chap. 1 of the Guidelines and there are further references throughout the Guidelines. These provisions are not reported in full in this text.

Editorial Values, which appear at the start of the Guidelines, deal with this issue:

> "Programme makers should be aware of and respect their audiences' often diverse views on what will and will not cause offence. Their right to challenge audience expectations in creative and surprising ways must be safeguarded but audiences should not be needlessly offended by what we broadcast and publish. It is vital to consider the expectations that audiences have of particular programmes, services and time slots. BBC television schedules must respect the 9 p.m. watershed."

The Guidelines then go on to offer further detailed guidance, though much that appears will be common sense to experienced programme-makers. The following are among some of the key provisions.

(a) General

There is a need to balance the right to challenge audience expectations in surprising and innovative ways with avoiding needless offence. Context is everything: scheduling can be vital in getting audiences to accept difficult material. It is also vital to consider the expectations that audiences have of particular programmes and timeslots.[5]   **12-04**

(b) The watershed[6]

The BBC has a policy of making 9 p.m. the pivotal point of the evening's television: a watershed before which, except in exceptional circumstances, all programmes should be suitable for a general audience.[7] The earlier in the evening a programme is placed, the more suitable it is likely to be for children to watch on their own.   **12-05**

The watershed reminds broadcasters that particular care should be taken over the inclusion of explicit scenes of sex and violence, and the use of strong language. However, it is important to avoid creating a "cascade" effect after the watershed.

A somewhat different approach applies to radio. Children do listen to Radio 1 and to sport on Radio 5 Live. They are less in evidence elsewhere and therefore a general watershed is inappropriate. However, scheduling considerations do apply, as do considerations of taste and decency. So songs played during the day on Radio 1 which feature strong language or explicit content dealing with drugs, violence and sex will normally be inappropriate.

With live radio programmes, producers must be aware of the possibility of contributors, phone-in guests and sometimes presenters themselves causing offence or even breaking the law. To minimise the risk, producers should

---

[5] Chap. 6, s.1 of the Guidelines
[6] *ibid.*, Chap. 6, ss.2 and 3.
[7] A similar approach is adopted by commercial television: see Chap. 13 at 2(1).

anticipate any potential problems and brief presenters before they go on air. Presenters of live programmes should be aware of how best to deal with a difficult situation.[8]

Separate guidance is given in relation to the BBC's international services which need to deal with different expectations of taste that operate in cultures across the world.[9]

(c) Signposts[10]

12-06 Audiences need to have enough information to judge if a programme is likely to be one they want to watch or listen to. The watershed may not be enough so whenever a programme contains material that might be offensive to significant numbers of viewers or listeners, specific signposting of the material or broadcasting a warning may be appropriate. Warnings should not usually be required for most pre-watershed programmes.

Channel controllers and departments responsible for scheduling or presentation need to be kept informed about potentially sensitive programmes to ensure they are correctly scheduled and signposted.

(d) Online[11]

12-07 General guidance here includes the fact that the BBC should never put anything on the Internet which it would not be prepared to broadcast. Pages carrying material linked to any broadcast programme must be appropriate to the programme and its likely audience. The use of certain, mainly four-letter, words in text on the Internet may be more offensive than using them on radio or television.

(e) Dealing with tragic events[12]

12-08 The aftermath of a tragic event may require scheduling changes. Every effort must be made to ensure that nothing that might cause widespread offence goes unscrutinised. Pre-recorded programmes should always be checked before first or repeat transmission, in case the content has been affected by intervening events.

(f) Language[13]

12-09 Strong language is one of the most frequent causes of popular complaint. It is more difficult to make judgments about the use of strong language in a pre-

---

[8] Live broadcasters may have a defence to defamation proceedings under Defamation Act 1996, s.1: see Chap. 3 at 5.
[9] Chap. 6, s.5 of the Guidelines.
[10] *ibid.*, Chap. 6, s.4.
[11] *ibid.*, Chap. 6, s.6.
[12] *ibid.*, Chap. 6, s.7.
[13] *ibid.*, Chap. 6, s.8.

watershed family serial or soap opera, seen or heard by large audiences composed of people from different ages and backgrounds. Common sense should enable producers to identify which words are questionable and when the use of them might be warranted. Programme-makers should be aware that terms of racist abuse are now considered to be offensive by all sections of the audience.

Offence is often caused by the casual use of names considered holy by believers, for example the use of "Jesus Christ" or "God", or of the names held holy by other faiths. While there is a wide range of attitudes to the use of these words, it is important for programme-makers to be satisfied that their inclusion can be justified despite the distress that may be caused.

The inclusion of strong language is a matter for judgment by individual producers, in consultation with heads of department or commissioning executives when necessary. The most offensive language should not be used on television before 9 p.m. After 9 p.m. it should only be used following careful consideration.

The practice on radio is different and the inclusion of sensitive topics and strong language depend less on time of day than on editorial merits and clear signposting of programme contents. On the music networks—and elsewhere —when substantial numbers of young people and families are listening, care is needed with regard to language and subject-matter.

Certain, mainly four-letter, words must not be used on television, radio or online without advance reference to and approval from designated senior management.

Deep offence will also be caused by profane references or disrespect directed at matters which are at the heart of various religions—for example, the Crucifixion, the Gospels, the Koran and the Jewish Sabbath. Particular care should be taken with programmes to be broadcast on the principal holy days of the main religions.[14]

(g) Sex[15]

Audiences in the United Kingdom have become more liberal but, even so, programme-makers broadcasting to diverse audiences in their homes are not as free as film-makers, theatre dramatists and novelists whose audiences are self-selected. Those watching with children before 9 p.m. expect programme-makers to honour the watershed by exercising appropriate restraint. Context, the intention of the production, the expectations of the audience, the watershed and signposting are all vital.   **12-10**

The BBC tries to operate by certain basic rules that apply to all programmes dealing with sexual activity:

- programmes should be adequately and clearly signposted;

- scenes should have a clear and legitimate editorial purpose and not be gratuitous;

---

[14] Chap. 6, s.9 of the Guidelines.
[15] *ibid.*, Chap. 6, s.10.

- sexually explicit material will not appear before the watershed, nor at inappropriate times too close to the watershed;

- there are limits to explicit portrayal at any time;

- material involving sexual violence or sadism will be treated with particular care and circumspection.

Sexual scenes that will disturb or shock should occur only for good dramatic reasons. In particular, viewers remain concerned about the depiction of sexual violence against women and sadistic sexual material. Such material demands careful consultation within departments and with channel controllers or, at their request, the Chief Adviser Editorial Policy.

Care should also be taken not to reflect in an unthinking way stereotypes of either male or female behaviour or apply different standards to male or female nudity. Sexuality is a universal human attribute: depiction of sex should not be linked solely or inevitably to the physical attractiveness of the characters involved.

(h) Comedy and entertainment[16]

12-11 Guidance is given about reference to stereotypes and religion and the need for particular care in this context.

(i) Acquired programmes[17]

12-12 The guidelines in relation to taste and decency apply equally to acquired programmes.

Some feature films, whether made in Britain or abroad, are suitable only for adult audiences. The British Board of Film Classification categorises every film for cinema or video release in the United Kingdom.[18] While these classifications offer some guidance to their suitability for showing on BBC television, they cannot be accepted without question. Tastes change and films once regarded as wholly unsuitable may become acceptable; but some films may never be acceptable on television. Special care must be taken over the acquisition of films which have an "18" certificate.

Acquired programmes need to be double-checked in detail prior to transmission to identify any need to edit, place the programme after the watershed, or issue a warning in the billings and/or on air.

(j) Violence[19]

12-13 Most audiences expect any violent scenes to serve a moral or a social point and context is important. Many of the general points considered in relation

---

[16] Chap. 6, s.11 of the Guidelines.
[17] *ibid.*, Chap. 6, s.12.
[18] See Chap. 15.
[19] Chap. 7 of the Guidelines.

to taste and decency (such as the importance of the watershed, signposting and context) are particularly relevant to the portrayal of violence.

There is very detailed guidance on the portrayal of violence and some of the key points include the following:

(1) Violence in the news and factual programmes: there is a balance to be struck between the demands of truth and the danger of desensitising people. The reporting of suffering and distress are given particular attention in the Guidelines.[20] In this context, news and factual programmes should follow some basic principles[21]:

- the dead should be treated with respect and not shown unless there are compelling reasons for doing so;
- close-ups of faces or serious injuries should be used very sparingly;
- the bloody consequences of an accident or terrorist attack should not be concentrated on unduly;
- violent material should not be used simply because it is available;
- the same value should be placed on human life and suffering whether it occurs in the United Kingdom or abroad;
- the time of transmission, whether pre or post-watershed, and the rest of the schedule should be taken into account.

(2) Violence involving animals: Audiences may be sensitive to violence involving animals. Such violent scenes must have a justified editorial purpose. Particular care must be taken in dealing with scenes in which humans appear to inflict violence on animals. It may sometimes be helpful to consider an on air announcement to make it clear that no harm was done.

(3) Adult drama: producers and directors should take particular care when violence involves:

- situations close to the audience's own experience, or which they perceive as being true to life;
- domestic and sexual violence;
- scenes where women and children are portrayed as victims;
- scenes of extreme or sustained violence of any sort;
- the context appearing to encourage approval of violence;
- suicide or attempted suicide.

It is important to take particular care when dealing with weapons that might encourage imitation, especially the use of easily accessible weapons such as knives, hammers or pokers, or methods that might suggest how violence can be made more effective.[22]

---

[20] Chap. 12 of the Guidelines.

[21] *ibid.*, Chap. 12, s.2.

[22] Further guidance appears in Chap. 8 of the Guidelines on "Imitative and anti-social behaviour". This chapter also includes sections dealing with drugs and the particular dangers of imitation by children. The BBC's Editorial Values at the start of the Guidelines make specific reference to the need to avoid the imitation of anti-social and criminal behaviour.

Violence is not always physical. Verbal aggression can be profoundly disturbing, particularly when the words used have sexual power. Care must be taken to ensure suitability for the intended time of transmission, particularly if audiences are likely to include children.

(4)   Children and violence: there is evidence that violence in circumstances resembling real life is more upsetting than violence in a fantasy setting. Children may feel particularly distressed when violence occurs in a familiar setting or between familiar figures. For instance, violence in the home between characters resembling their parents, or towards characters or pets, with which the child can sympathise, should be avoided.

The dangers of imitation are particularly real among children.[23] Extra care should be taken, for example, over karate chops or the use of weapons that are easily accessible such as ropes or knives or bottles. Criminal acts, if shown, should not become lessons in "how to do it". It is also important not to conceal the consequences of real-life violence.

(2) ACCURACY AND IMPARTIALITY

12-14   We have already seen that the Agreement requires the BBC to treat controversial subjects with due accuracy and impartiality.[24] The Agreement also requires the BBC to draw up a Code giving guidance as to the rules to be observed in complying with its obligations in this respect.[25] The BBC has issued rules in accordance with this requirement and they form part of the more wide-ranging guidance which appears in the Guidelines. Amongst the issues dealt with in this context are the following.

(a) Impartiality

12-15   The BBC's Editorial Values provide that:

"... due impartiality lies at the heart of the BBC. All BBC programmes and services should be open minded, fair and show a respect for truth. No significant strand of thought should go unreflected or under represented on the BBC."

There is also a great deal of further material in the Guidelines aimed at helping to achieve impartiality.[26] It is beyond this text to review the guidance in detail. However, it contains what would be regarded as common sense by experienced broadcasters. For instance:

•   all BBC programmes and services should be open-minded, fair and show a respect for truth;

---

[23] See previous footnote.
[24] cl.5.1(c) of the Agreement.
[25] cl.5.3 to 5.5 of the Agreement.
[26] Chap. 2, Pt. One of the Guidelines. Chap. 13 also deals with conflicts of interest.

- reporting should be dispassionate, wide-ranging and well-informed;

- a reporter may express a professional, journalistic judgment, but not a personal opinion;

- Whenever appropriate, persons portrayed in a drama or their surviving near relatives should be notified in advance and, where possible, their co-operation secured.

There is no right of reply as such. However, where a programme reveals evidence of iniquity or incompetence, or where a strong, damaging critique of an individual or institution is laid out, there is a presumption that those criticised be given a fair opportunity to respond. There may be occasions when this is inappropriate (usually for legal or overriding ethical reasons).

(b) Accuracy

The BBC's Editorial Values provide that the BBC: **12-16**

> ". . . must be accurate and must be prepared to check, cross-check and seek advice to ensure this. Wherever possible we should gather information first-hand by being there ourselves or, where that is not possible, by talking to those who were. But accuracy is often more than a question of getting the facts right. All relevant information should be weighed to get at the truth of what is reported or described."

The Guidelines then go on to give detailed advice which is beyond the scope of this text.[27] Key provisions include the following:

(1) General: the BBC must be accurate. Research for all programmes must be thorough. We must be prepared to check, cross-check and seek advice, to ensure this.

(2) Achieving accuracy: programmes should be reluctant to rely on only one source. Accuracy is often more than a question of getting the facts right. All the relevant facts should be weighed to get at the truth of what is reported or described. The Guidelines recognise that the reliability of news agency reports can vary.

(3) Correcting mistakes: when a serious factual error does occur it is important to admit it clearly and frankly. Saying what was wrong as well as putting it right can be an important element in making an effective correction.
     It is worth noting that Greg Dyke, in his first report in the BBC Programme Complaints Bulletin as Director-General, stated that "acknowledging important errors and putting them right is a sign of

---

[27] Principally to be found in Chap. 2, Pt. Two of the Guidelines.

strength, not weakness" . He conceded that the BBC had not always applied the Producers' Guidelines' in this respect.[28]

(4) Reconstruction: the reconstruction or restaging of events in factual programmes can be a great help in explaining an issue. It must always be done truthfully with an awareness of what is reliably known. Nothing significant which is not known should be invented without acknowledgement.

(5) Checking recorded or repeat programmes: programmes recorded some time before transmission or being repeated must be checked to make sure they have not been overtaken by events.

(3) PRIVACY AND THE GATHERING OF INFORMATION

12-17 The BBC's Editorial Values provide that the BBC:

". . . should respect the privacy of individuals, recognising that any intrusions have to be justified by serving a greater good. Private behaviour, correspondence and conversation should not be brought into the public domain unless there is a wider public interest."

The Guidelines then go on to provide further detailed provisions,[29] including the following key points.

1. Basic principles[30]

12-18 The right to privacy is qualified by:

- The public interest: people are less entitled to privacy when protection of privacy means concealing matters which are against the public interest.

- Behaviour: people are less entitled to privacy where their behaviour is criminal or seriously anti-social.

- Location: the right to privacy is clearly much greater in a place such as a private home than it is in a public place.

It is noted that, whilst there is no right to privacy in law as such, the European Convention on Human Rights (now enshrined in the Human Rights Act 1998) includes the right to privacy (Article 8) as well as free expression (Article 10).[31]

2. Private lives and public issues[32]

12-19 Public figures are in a special position, but they retain their rights to a private life. The public should be given the facts that bear upon the ability or the suit-

---

[28] BBC press release, May 3, 2000.
[29] Principally in Chaps. 4 and 5 of the Guidelines.
[30] *ibid.*, Chap. 4, s.1.
[31] See Chap. 2.
[32] *ibid.*, Chap. 4, s.2 of the Guidelines.

ability of public figures to attain or hold office or to perform their duties, but there is no general entitlement to know about their private behaviour provided that it is legal and does not raise important wider issues.

3. Operating on private property[33]

On most occasions programme-makers will seek permission before operating on private property. There are occasions where serious criminal or anti-social activity is being exposed when this may not be necessary. Activities are also subject to the law of trespass.[34] **12-20**

4. Doorstepping[35]

People who are currently in the news must expect to be questioned and recorded by the media. Questions asked by reporters as public figures come and go from buildings are usually part of legitimate newsgathering, even if the questions are sometimes unwelcome, and the rules on doorstepping are not intended to prevent this. **12-21**

In all other cases doorstepping should generally be a last resort. It needs to be approved in advance by the head of department who should do so only if:

*   the investigation involves crime or serious antisocial behaviour, and

*   the subject of the doorstep has failed to respond to a repeated request to be interviewed, refused an interview on unreasonable grounds, or if they have a history of such failure or refusal.

5. Media scrums[36]

When a person suddenly features in a news event it may be proper for representatives of many media organisations to go to a private home to try to secure pictures or interviews. **12-22**

In such cases, it is important that the combined effect of legitimate newsgathering by a number of organisations does not become intimidating or unreasonably intrusive. Journalists must not harass people unfairly with repeated telephone calls, or repeated knocks at the door, or by obstructing them as they come and go. It may be possible or appropriate for pooling arrangements to be reached, or for the BBC to withdraw altogether if it is clear that the subject does not intend to appear. BBC teams on the spot who are asked by the subject to leave should refer to editors for guidance.

---

[33] Chap. 4, s.3 of the Guidelines.
[34] See Chap. 7.
[35] Chap. 4, s.4 of the Guidelines.
[36] *ibid.*, Chap. 4, s.5.

6. Surreptitious recording[37]

12-23   There is detailed guidance on the use of surreptitious recording. The general principles for such recording are based on the overall approach to privacy and note that such recording should not be used as a routine production tool, nor should it be used simply to add drama to a report.[38] Wherever surreptitious recording is carried out it must be approved in advance by senior management and a record kept by the department concerned of how the recording satisfied the requirements of this chapter of the Guidelines, who authorised it, and brief details of who and what was recorded.[39] The key provisions in the chapter include the following.

(1) Surreptitious recording in public places[40]

12-24   People in a public place cannot expect the same degree of privacy as in their own homes. In general, however, journalists should operate openly in public where they can see and be seen. But sometimes it will be necessary for the safety of staff or for the style or content of the programme that recording takes place surreptitiously in public places. Programmes intending to do so must get approval in advance.

(2) Grief and distress[41]

12-25   Surreptitious recording of identifiable people in grief or under extremes of stress (for instance in hospitals) requires special consideration. Use of such material will usually be justified only if permission has been granted by the individuals concerned or by someone acting on their behalf. Heads of department must be consulted.

(3) Recording telephone calls[42]

12-26   The Guidelines provide that journalists should not record telephone conversations for broadcasting purposes to which they are not a party. This is illegal in the United Kingdom.[43]

   If a journalist wishes to record his own telephone call for possible broadcasting, he should normally seek the permission of the other party in advance. If he wishes to record without doing so, he must consult his head of department who should consult the Controller Editorial Policy. Recording will be authorised only if there is prime facie evidence of crime or serious wrongdoing and the programme-maker can show why an open approach would be unlikely to succeed.

---

[37] Chap. 5 of the Guidelines.
[38] *ibid.*, Chap. 5, s.1.
[39] *ibid.*, Chap. 5, s.2.
[40] *ibid.*, Chap. 5, s.3.
[41] *ibid.*, Chap. 5, s.4.
[42] *ibid.*, Chap. 5, s.7.
[43] See Chap. 7.

If, during a phone call, programme-makers take someone by surprise by saying, without warning, that they are recording a call for broadcasting purposes, this is the equivalent of " doorstepping".

It is permissible without prior referral for programme-makers to record their own telephone conversations for note-taking purposes, or to gather evidence to defend the BBC against possible legal action. Such recordings should not be broadcast. Only the Controller Editorial Policy can give retrospective permission to broadcast in exceptional circumstances.

(4) Secret recordings made by others[44]

When the BBC is offered material secretly recorded by others the test is whether, **12-27** under similar circumstances, the BBC would have felt it appropriate to conduct the recording. If there is a strong public interest in broadcasting the material irrespective of how it was obtained, programmes should refer to the relevant head of department who should consult the Controller Editorial Policy.

(5) Comedy and entertainment[45]

The specific guidelines prohibiting the planting of unattended recording **12-28** devices and the illegal recording of telephone conversations, also apply to comedy and light entertainment programmes. However, the other guidelines on secret recording are not intended to prevent recording for purposes of comedy or light entertainment. Here, different principles apply:

- people who feature prominently in the recordings should be asked to give their permission before the material is broadcast;

- the purpose should not be to expose people to hurtful ridicule or to exploit them;

- the journalist should respect the wishes of individuals who become aware of the recording and ask for it to stop;

- the journalist should give assurances about the destruction of any material recorded if asked for them;

- if permission has been obtained, the programme-makers must disguise any other recognisable bystander caught on camera whose permission has not been obtained, especially if the broadcasting of the recording might cause embarrassment.

7. Reporting suffering and distress

There are detailed provisions dealing with suffering and distress and the **12-29** emphasis of the Guidelines is on the importance of compassionate coverage.[46]

---

[44] Chap. 5, s.8 of the Guidelines.
[45] ibid., Chap. 5, s.9.
[46] ibid., Chap. 12.

For example, coverage should not add needlessly to the distress of people who already know of their loss; people in a state of distress should not be put under pressure to provide interviews against their wishes; and funerals should normally only be covered when the permission of the family has been obtained.

8. Fairness and straight dealing[47]

12-30   Programmes should be based on fairness, openness and straight dealing. This is important to everyone involved. It reflects concern for the interests of the programme, the interests of the people who appear in it and the interests of the audience.

The Guidelines pay particular attention to how contributors are dealt with. Unless there are special and legitimate considerations of confidentiality, programme-makers should be open about their plans, and honest with anyone taking part. Contributors ought to be able to assume that they will be treated in a fair way. In particular, they have a right to know:

*   what a programme is about;
*   what kind of contribution they are expected to make—an interview or a part in a discussion, for example;
*   whether their contribution is to be live or recorded; and, if recorded, whether it is likely to be edited. They should not be given a guarantee that their contribution will be broadcast, but nor should a substantial contribution be recorded unless it is expected to be used.

There is also detailed guidance about dealing with interviewees.[48] So, for example, it is important that interviewees understand why they are being invited for interview, what subjects they are going to be asked about, the context of the programme, and the sort of part they will play in it. It will not usually be proper to submit details of actual questions in advance, nor to give any undertaking about the precise form of questions.

9. Children

12-31   The Guidelines refer specifically to the issues surrounding the involvement of children in programmes.[49] It will normally be appropriate to seek the consent of parents or legal guardians before interviewing children or otherwise involving them in programmes, and the younger or more vulnerable the child, and the more sensitive the subject-matter, the more likely it is that consent will be essential. If children are to take part in programme-making during school hours it will normally be necessary to seek the consent of the school.

Where consent has been refused, reference should be made to the head of department before taking any decision to go ahead. This can normally be jus-

---

[47] Chap. 3 of the Guidelines.
[48] *ibid.*, Chap. 13.
[49] *ibid.*, Chap. 14.

tified only if the item is of sufficient public importance and the child's appearance is absolutely necessary.

Interviews with children need particular care. Children can be easily led in questioning and are often open to suggestion. Young children in particular may have difficulty in distinguishing between reality and fantasy. Programme-makers should be careful of prompting children and should allow them to speak for themselves.

(4) RELIGIOUS TOLERANCE AND THE PORTRAYAL OF MINORITIES[50]

The BBC's Editorial Values, in identifying the need to give a "full and fair view **12-32** of people and cultures in the U.K. and across the world", provide that:

> "BBC programmes and services should reflect and draw on this diversity to reflect life as it is. By doing so we introduce new talent, perspectives, faces and voices, enriching our programmes for our audiences. When portraying social groups, stereotypes should be avoided."

The Guidelines include reference to the following central issues:

(a) Hurtful or inaccurate stereotypes: people should appear in the full range of roles that reflect reality. Programmes should not categorise black people as criminals, women as housewives, disabled people as victims, gay people as ineffectual, old people as incapable, or people of any particular profession, vocation or walk of life as inevitable figures of fun.

(b) Religious tolerance: we have already seen that the Agreement includes a provision to ensure that there is no exploitation of those watching or listening to religious programmes.[51] In addition, the Guidelines contain more detailed provisions.[52] They note that people and countries should not be defined by their religion unless it is strictly relevant. Particular religious groups or factions should not be portrayed as speaking for their faith as a whole. Thoughtless portrayal can be offensive, especially if it implies that a particular faith is hostile or alien to all outside it. For example, footage of chanting crowds of Islamic activists should not be used to illustrate the whole Muslim world. Words such as "fundamentalist" and "militant" should be used with great care. What may be a fair description of one group may not be true of all similar groups.

(c) Portrayal of minorities and groups: the guidelines contain detailed advice about how to refer to various minorities or groups such as women, ethnic minorities, disabled people and the elderly.

---

[50] Chap. 9 of the Guidelines
[51] See 1(B) above.
[52] Chap. 9, s.6 of the Guidelines.

3. REGULATION OF COMMERCIAL ACTIVITIES

12-33 As we shall see, the ITC and the Radio Authority have detailed Codes regulating advertising and sponsorship, and particularly how and when they may encroach into programming. Until fairly recently, this was not a major concern for the BBC, which does not carry paid-for advertising (subject to the points made below). However, with the growing commercialisation of the Corporation, especially through BBC Worldwide, this has become an issue of greater concern and is addressed in the Guidelines.

The Editorial Values provide that:

> ". . . audiences must be able to trust the integrity of BBC programmes. They should be confident that decisions are made only for good editorial reasons, not as a result of improper pressure, be it political, commercial or special interest. The activities of programme makers must not be improperly influence BBC programmes."

The Guidelines then go on to provide very detailed guidance,[53] including the following:

(1) ADVERTISING AND SPONSORSHIP

12-34 No BBC service funded by the licence fee or other government funds may carry advertising or sponsored programming.[54] The BBC's international commercially funded channels and BBC Joint Venture channels are permitted to take advertising and some programme sponsorship in accordance with relevant guidelines and codes of practice.

BBC commercially funded television services from the United Kingdom are required to conform to all relevant ITC codes, as well as the Producer's Guidelines. The Producer's Guidelines tend to be stricter than the ITC codes. For example, the BBC will not carry religious advertising or take sponsorship for programming giving general consumer advice.

(2) COVERING OUTSIDE EVENTS[55]

12-35 The BBC covers a wide range of outside public events. As a general proposition all programming and broadcasting costs must be borne by the BBC or shared with other broadcasters. There are detailed rules covering such aspects as how to deal with sponsor's banners, on-air credits and advertising at outside events.

---

[53] This is to be found primarily in Chaps. 24 to 32 of the Guidelines. They are concerned with editorial issues, the BBC's programme-making activities and any on-air references to commercial products or organisations. Further advice on the BBC's commercial activities can be found in the BBC's Commercial Policy Guidelines. They cover questions such as the acceptability of BBC commercial ventures and how they should be undertaken, use of the BBC brand, promotional activities and fair trading.

[54] Chap. 24, ss.4 and 5 of the Guidelines.

[55] *ibid.*, Chap. 28.

For example, banners or placards should not come between the viewer and the action at sporting events. The number and type of banners acceptable will depend on the event and the size of the venue. They are unlikely to be appropriate during the coverage of arts events.[56]

If the BBC mounts an outside event, it may accept co-sponsorship from an outside body. Money from an outside sponsor can, however, only be used to enhance the event itself and must not be used to pay for any element of the broadcast coverage.

(3) PRODUCT PROMINENCE AND FREE OR REDUCED COST PRODUCTS AND FACILITIES[57]

From time to time reference will be made in programmes to commercial products, and commercial concerns, and there is detailed guidance on how to handle these references.   **12-36**

Programmes must never give the impression that they are indorsing or promoting any product, service or company. References in programmes to all products and services should be editorially justifiable and not promotional. A product or service must never be included in sound or vision in return for cash, services or any consideration in kind.

No BBC programme must ever accept free or reduced cost products or services in return for an on-air credit or any visual or verbal reference to the product or provider.

(4) GAME SHOWS AND COMPETITIONS[58]

Detailed rules are provided for the conduct of game shows and competitions. Game shows, quizzes and viewer or listener competitions should be conducted in a manner that is fair, honest, legal and decent. In quiz or game shows any significant prizes should be awarded on the basis of games or questions which are a test of skill, knowledge or judgement appropriate to the audience.[59]   **12-37**

There are also strict rules governing the prizes on offer. They should normally have been paid for, and programme-makers should aim for them to be original rather than expensive. The Guidelines state that it is "inappropriate to spend Licence Fee or Grant in Aid money on prizes of excessive value".

4. COMPLAINTS PROCEDURE

The BBC has a centralised Programme Complaints Unit (PCU). It can deal with any complaint arising from BBC licence-funded services on television,   **12-38**

---

[56] Chap. 28, s.2.2 of the Guidelines.
[57] *ibid.*, Chap. 25.
[58] *ibid.*, Chap. 22.
[59] See Chap. 7, which deals with lotteries.

radio and online. Complaints should be sent to the Head of Programme Complaints in the BBC Secretary's Department.[60] The PCU will consider complaints in the light of the BBC's obligations under the Charter and the advice contained in the Producer's Guidelines. Complaints can relate to matters including unfair treatment, bias, privacy or taste and decency. If the complainant is dissatisfied with the PCU findings, he can appeal to the Governors' Complaints Appeals Committee.

It must be noted, however, that the PCU has no power to award costs, damages or fines and relatively little weight appears to be given to the process of complaining. For example, the Producer's Guidelines contains little detail about the remit of the PCU and, unlike the BSC, it will not necessarily require its findings to be broadcast on air.[61] The PCU does, however, issue a periodical bulletin with details of complaints and particulars of those which have been upheld in whole or in part. Furthermore, it appears from the bulletin that the PCU, or programme-makers connected to a relevant programme, will give guidance to ensure that the same errors are not repeated. Adverse findings may of course also impact on a journalist's career.

---

[60] Complaints about the BBC's World Service are dealt with by the Chief Executive of the World Service. Complaints about the BBC's commercial and international television services are dealt with by the Head of Programming, International Networks, BBC Worldwide.

[61] See Chap. 12 at 4.

Chapter 13

Commercial television

1. STATUTORY BASIS OF THE INDEPENDENT TELEVISION COMMISSION

The Independent Television Commission (ITC) has a broad function in regu-   **13-01**
lating the provision of television programme services originating in the United
Kingdom.[1] This includes those broadcast on cable and satellite,[2] but excludes
those provided by the BBC and the Welsh Authority (*i.e.* S4C).[3] It was set up
by the Broadcasting Act 1990 and replaced two previous statutory bodies: the
Independent Broadcasting Authority and the Cable Authority.

The Broadcasting Act 1990 is the source for most of the Commission's
responsibilities and powers, including a number of general requirements as to
the content of television programmes. In this respect, section 6 (1) of the
Broadcasting Act 1990 ("the Act") states that the ITC:

"... shall do all that they can to secure that every licensed service complies with the following requirements, namely:

(a) that nothing is included in its programmes which offends against
     good taste or decency or is likely to encourage or incite to crime or
     to lead to disorder or to be offensive to public feeling;

(b) that any news given (in whatever form) in its programmes is pre-
     sented with due accuracy and impartiality;

(c) that due impartiality is preserved on the part of the person providing

---

[1] In certain circumstances—beyond the scope of this text—the ITC may have some jurisdiction
in respect of services originating outside the U.K. For example, if the ITC considers that a
foreign satellite service repeatedly includes matter which offends against good taste or decency
or is likely to encourage or incite to crime or to lead to disorder or to be offensive to public
feeling, it may recommend that the Secretary of State that the channel be proscribed:
Broadcasting Act 1990, s.177.
[2] Broadcasting Act 1990, s.2. There are some differences between the way satellite and cable are
regulated as opposed to terrestrial services (such as ITV licensees). For present purposes, the
key difference is that the 9 p.m. watershed that applies on ITV and Channels 4 and 5 is brought
forward to 8 p.m. on a subscription service available to satellite or cable viewers.
[3] The regulation of the BBC is described in Chap. 12. The functions and duties of the Welsh
Authority are similar to those imposed on the ITC and derive from ss.56–64 of the
Broadcasting Act 1990.

the service as respects matters of political or industrial controversy or relating to current public policy;

(d) that due responsibility is exercised with respect to the content of any of its programmes which are religious programmes, and that in particular any such programmes do not involve—

   (i) any improper exploitation of any susceptibilities of those watching the programmes; or

   (ii) any abusive treatment of the religious views and beliefs of those belonging to a particular religion or religious denomination; and

(e) that its programmes do not include any technical device which, by using images of very brief duration or by any other means, exploits the possibility of conveying a message to, or otherwise influencing the minds of, persons watching the programmes without being aware, or fully aware, of what has occurred."

The section states that the ITC:

". . . shall do all that they can to secure that there are excluded from the programmes included in a licensed service all expressions of the views and opinions of the person providing the service on matters (other than the provision of programme services) which are of political or industrial controversy or relate to current public policy" (s.6(4) of the Act).

These provisions are very similar, though not identical, to those imposed on the BBC in its Agreement with the Secretary of State and to those imposed on the Radio Authority.[4]

The Act requires the ITC to draw up and review codes giving guidance on:

(i) the requirement that due impartiality is preserved as regards matters of political or industrial controversy or relating to current public policy[5];

(ii) the portrayal of violence[6];

(iii) the inclusion of donations in programmes[7];

(iv) as to such other matters concerning standards and practice for such programmes as the ITC may consider suitable.[8]

The Act also deals with the ITC's obligations in relation to the regulation of advertising and sponsorship.[9] The ITC is required in particular to draw up and keep under review a code:

---

[4] See Chap. 14 at 1.
[5] Broadcasting Act 1990, s.6(3).
[6] *ibid.*, s.7(1)(a).
[7] *ibid.*, s.7(1)(b).
[8] *ibid.*, s.7(1)(c).
[9] *ibid.*, ss.8 and 9.

"(i) governing standards and practice in advertising and in the sponsor-
      ing of programmes, and

(ii) prescribing the advertisements and methods of advertising or spon-
      sorship to be prohibited, or to be prohibited in particular circum-
      stances . . .".[10]

The ITC is obliged to consult, amongst others, with the Radio Authority in
drawing up such a code.[11]

These general provisions are supplemented by the detailed codes which have
been drawn up by the ITC, including the Programme Code, the Code of
Advertising Standards and Practice and the Code of Programme Sponsorship.[12] In each instance, the Codes tend to contain specific rules fortified by
detailed notes on the relevant rule. It is worth noting that the ITC has no
authority to intervene before a programme has been shown, though it is a
licence requirement that licensees satisfy themselves prior to broadcast that
commercials comply with the Code of Advertising Standards and Practice.

Individual licensees need to ensure compliance with all of these obligations
which are binding on them as a matter of contract through their licence
arrangements with the ITC.[13]

The rest of this chapter looks at some of the key issues of principles to arise
from the various Codes.[14] Programme-makers should, however, also be aware
of the separate body of regulation issued by the Broadcasting Standards
Commission touching on fairness, privacy, taste and decency. This overlaps
with much that is contained in the ITC's Codes. The BSC's Codes are considered in detail in Chapter 15.

2. PROGRAMME REGULATION[15]

(1) TASTE AND DECENCY

We have already seen that the ITC must "do all they can" to secure that each   **13-02**
licensee complies with the requirement that nothing is included in its programmes which offends against good taste or decency or is likely to encourage or incite to crime or to lead to disorder or to be offensive to public
feeling.[16] The Programme Code includes further guidance[17], much of which
will be seen as common sense. Some key provisions appear below.

---

[10] Broadcasting Act 1990, s.9(1)(a).
[11] *ibid.*, s.9(2)(a).
[12] These appear in the CD ROM accompanying this text. There are a number of additional ITC
      codes which are beyond the scope of our subject-matter. These include the Code for Text
      Services (such as Teletext) which incorporates the Programming, Advertising and Sponsorship
      Codes with modifications.
[13] The approach of ITC licensees to compliance is described in more detail in Chap. 25 at 1.
[14] The approach adopted has been described in Chap. 11 at 3.
[15] The key principles are to be found in the ITC's Programme Code. In addition to the areas dealt
      with in this text, the Code addresses a number of other issues, including party political broad-
      casts (s.4), images of very brief duration (s.7) and charitable appeals (s.8).
[16] Broadcasting Act 1990, s.6(1)(a).
[17] s.1 of the Programme Code.

(a) Scheduling[18]

13-03 The ITC has a family viewing policy, the basis of which is that material unsuitable for children must not be broadcast at times when large numbers of children may be expected to be watching. The policy is pragmatic in that it assumes a progressive decline throughout the evening in the proportion of children present in the audience. It requires a similar progression in the successive programmes scheduled from early evening onwards: the earlier in the evening the more suitable, the later in the evening the less suitable. Within the progression, 9 p.m. is normally fixed as the time up to which licensees will regard themselves as responsible for ensuring that nothing is shown that is unsuitable for children. After 9 p.m. and until 5.30 a.m. progressively less suitable (ie more adult) material may be shown and it may be that a programme will be acceptable at, for example, 10.30 p.m. that would not be suitable at 9 p.m.

Where a programme service is only available to viewers on payment of a premium rate fee, its availability to children will be more restricted and the time at which parents may be expected to share responsibility for what is viewed may be shifted from 9 p.m. to as early as 8 p.m.

(b) Warnings[19]

13-04 Warnings are unlikely to be appropriate during family viewing time. The broadcaster, however, should consider whether any elements might disturb viewers, in particular younger children. Appropriate information should be provided at the start of programmes or, where necessary, prior to any news report which might disturb younger children.

At later times (*i.e.* after the watershed), clear and specific warnings should be employed where some viewers may find the programme disturbing. This does not diminish the broadcaster's responsibility for sensitive scheduling of programmes to reduce the risk of offence to the minimum.

(c) Language[20]

13-05 There is no absolute ban on the use of bad language. But it must be defensible in terms of context and authenticity, and should not be a frequent feature of the schedule. Bad language (including profanity) should not be used in programmes specially designed for children. The most offensive language should not be used before 9 p.m. Its use after that time must always be approved where practicable in advance by the licensee's most senior programme executive or the designated alternate.

---

[18] s.1.2 of the Programme Code.
[19] *ibid.*, s.1.3.
[20] *ibid.*, s.1.4.

(d) Sex and nudity[21]

Similar considerations apply here: the portrayal of sexual behaviour and of **13-06** nudity needs to be defensible in context and presented with tact and discretion. Of the greatest concern are scenes of non-consensual sexual activity, including rape, and particularly where there is graphic physical detail or the action is to any degree prolonged.

Representation of sexual intercourse should be postponed until after 9 p.m. Exceptions to this rule may be allowed in the case of nature films, programmes with a serious educational purpose, or where the representation is non-graphic, and must be approved in advance by the licensee's most senior programme executive.

(e) Violence[22]

The real world contains violence in many forms. Television has a duty to reflect this in news, drama, and other programmes. On the other hand, the portrayal of violence, whether physical, verbal or psychological, is an area of public concern. The Code contains detailed guidance, including the following.[23]

(i) The portrayal of violence in programmes

(a) Violence which is acceptable in one programme may become intolerable **13-07** over a period. Licensees should therefore avoid an undue concentration in the schedule of programmes containing violence.

(b) The time of screening of each programme is important. The ITC policy of "family viewing time" entails special concern for younger viewers.

(c) There is no evidence that the portrayal of violence for good or "legitimate" ends is likely to be less harmful to the individual, or to society, than the portrayal of violence for evil ends.

(d) There is no evidence that "sanitised" violence, in which the consequences are concealed, minimised or presented in a ritualistic way, is innocuous. Similarly, violence which is shown as happening long ago or far away may seem to have less impact on viewers, but it remains violence.

(e) Viewers are most likely to be offended by explicit images of distress and injury and of blood, particularly if they occur suddenly or unexpectedly.

(f) Dramatic truth may occasionally demand the portrayal of a sadistic character, but there can be no defence of violence shown or heard solely

---

[21] s.1.5 of the Programme Code.

[22] *ibid.*, s.1.6.

[23] Appendix 2 of the Programme Code includes a Statement of Common Principles on the Portrayal of Violence on Television. The Statement has been agreed by the ITC, BBC and BSC but does not supercede any of the organisation's own Codes. Its provisions appear in the CD ROM accompanying this text.

for its own sake, or of the gratuitous presentation of sadistic or other perverted practices.

(g) Ingenious and unfamiliar methods of inflicting pain or injury, which are capable of easy imitation, should not be included.

(h) Any programme item which on any reasonable judgment would be said to encourage or incite crime or lead to disorder is unacceptable.[24]

(i) Scenes which may unsettle young children need special care. Scenes of domestic friction, whether or not accompanied by physical violence, can easily cause particular fear and insecurity.

(j) Research evidence shows that the socially or emotionally insecure individual, particularly if adolescent, is specially vulnerable. Imagination, creativity or realism on television cannot be so constrained that the legitimate service of the majority is always subordinated to the limitations of a minority. But a civilised society pays special attention to its weaker members.

(ii) Suicide and suicide attempts

13-08 The evidence that television portrayal of a suicide attempt may be directly imitated by a viewer is inconclusive. The subject should nevertheless, as a matter of common sense, be handled with discretion and care, particularly in popular drama serials. There should be no detailed demonstration of the means or method of suicide.

(iii) Violence in the news

13-09 (a) News is subject, like any other programming, to the requirements of the family viewing policy.

(b) News footage of executions or other scenes in which people are clearly seen being killed or about to die require exceptional justification.

(c) Special consideration should be given to the possible effect of coverage of violent events in the United Kingdom upon local viewers for whom it might cause particular anxiety.

(f) Dangerous behaviour[25]

13-10 The portrayal of any dangerous behaviour easily imitated by children should be avoided, and must be excluded entirely at times when large numbers of children may be expected to be watching. This applies especially to the use in a manner likely to cause serious injury of knives and other offensive weapons, articles or substances which are readily accessible to children.

---

[24] This provision comes from s.5 of the Programme Code, a more general section dealing with terrorism, crime and antisocial behaviour.
[25] *ibid.*, s.1.7.

(g) Hanging scenes[26]

No film or programme including hanging or preparations for hanging capable   **13-11**
of easy imitation should be scheduled to start during family viewing time.

(h) Recorded programmes[27]

Programmes not used immediately should be checked before transmission to   **13-12**
ensure that any content is not rendered tasteless by intervening events, such as
death, injury or other misfortune.

(2) ACCURACY AND IMPARTIALITY

It has already been noted that news must be presented with due accuracy and   **13-13**
impartiality and that due impartiality is preserved as regards matters of political or industrial controversy or relating to current public policy.[28] Further
guidance on these and other matters relating to accuracy and impartiality in
this context are to be found in the Programme Code. It is not possible to reproduce all the very detailed guidance but it includes the following.

(a) General[29]

Licensees may make programmes about any issues they choose. This freedom   **13-14**
is limited only by the obligations of fairness and respect for truth, two qual-
ities which are essential to all factually-based programmes, whether on "controversial" topics or not.

Impartiality does not mean that broadcasters have to be absolutely neutral
on every controversial issue. However, they should deal even-handedly with
opposing points of view in the arena of democratic debate. Opinion should be
clearly distinguished from fact.

(b) Due impartiality[30]

While the requirement of due impartiality applies to all areas of controversy   **13-15**
covered by the Act, it does not mean that "balance" is required in any simple
mathematical sense or that equal time must be given to each opposing point
of view, nor does it require absolute neutrality on every issue. Judgment will
always be called for.

The provision that due impartiality must be preserved "on the part of the
person providing the service" is also significant. It puts the burden for compliance on licensees rather than individual programme-makers.

---

[26] s.1.8 of the Programme Code.
[27] *ibid.*, s.1.12.
[28] Broadcasting Act 1990, ss.6(1)(b) and(c). See 1 above.
[29] s.3.1 of the Programme Code.
[30] *ibid.*, s.3.2(i).

(c) Impartiality over time[31]

13-16   An impartial programme service does not necessarily have to ensure that in a single programme, or programme item, all sides have an opportunity to speak.

(d) Personal view programmes[32]

13-17   Personal view programmes on the controversial matters covered in the Act should respect the following principles:

*   Each programme must be clearly identified as giving a personal view both in advance announcements and at the start of the programme itself.

*   Facts must be respected, and licensees have an obligation to do what they can to ensure that the opinions expressed, however partial, do not rest upon false evidence.

*   A suitable opportunity for response to the programme should be provided, where appropriate, for example in a right to reply programme or in a pre-arranged discussion programme.

(e) Reconstructions[33]

13-18   Whenever a reconstruction is used in a documentary, current affairs or news programme it should be labelled so that the viewer is not misled. Conversely, any simulation of a television news bulletin or news flash to be included in any programme should either be subtitled or produced in such a way that there can be no reasonable possibility that it could be taken to be an actual news bulletin.

(f) Fairness in the conduct of interviews[34]

13-19   Interviewees should be made adequately aware of the format, subject-matter and purpose of the programme to which they have been invited to contribute, and the way in which their contribution is likely to be used. Written confirmation of these matters should be provided to the interviewee if requested.

For programmes dealing with political or industrial controversy or current public policy, interviewees should also be told the identity and intended role of other proposed participants in the programme, where this is known.

Sometimes, interviewees will seek to impose their own conditions on the conduct and use of their interview. Such requests are not improper, but care should be taken to ensure that what is included in the programme is determined by editorial criteria and not as the result of pressure. Licensees should

---

[31] s.3.3 of the Programme Code.
[32] *ibid.*, s.3.6.
[33] *ibid.*, s.3.7.
[34] *ibid.*, s.3.8.

consider whether, in the interests of due impartiality and fairness, they should disclose such agreements to viewers at the time of the broadcast.

(g) Politicians in programmes[35]

Because of the need to preserve due impartiality, no currently active politi- **13-20** cians should appear as newscasters, interviewers or reporters in any news programme, unless their use can be clearly justified, in which case their party allegiance should be clearly identified.

(3) PRIVACY AND THE GATHERING OF INFORMATION

(a) General[36]

There will be occasions when the individual's right to privacy must be bal- **13-21** anced against the public interest. Examples of how the public interest may be served include: (i) detecting or exposing crime or a serious misdemeanour; (ii) protecting public health or safety; (iii) preventing the public from being misled by some statement or action of an individual or organisation; and (iv) exposing significant incompetence in public office.

(b) Filming and recording of members of the public[37]

When coverage is being given to events in public places, editors and produc- **13-22** ers must satisfy themselves that words spoken or action taken by individuals are sufficiently in the public domain to justify their being communicated to the television audience without express permission being sought from the individuals concerned. This applies in particular to material from closed-circuit television cameras of which the individual is unlikely to have been aware. The Code gives a number of examples, including the following.

(i) Filming and recording in institutions, etc.

When permission is received to film or record material in an institution, such **13-23** as a hospital, factory, or department store, which has regular dealings with the public, but which would not normally be accessible to cameras without such permission, it is very likely that the material will include shots of individuals who are themselves incidental, rather than central, figures in the programme.

When their appearance is not incidental, where they are not random and anonymous or where, though unnamed, they are shown in particularly sensitive situations (for example as psychiatric or intensive care patients), individual consents to use this material should be sought. Any exceptions should be justifiable in the public interest.

---

[35] s.3.8(iii) of the Programme Code.
[36] *ibid.*, s.2.1.
[37] *ibid.*, s.2.2.

(ii) Filming on police operations[38]

13-24 When permission is given to film police or similar official operations of any kind involving members of the public in other than public places, it is the responsibility of the producer or senior crew member to make his position known to the members of the public involved and to identify the licensee or programme-maker for whom he or she is working as soon as practically possible. If asked to stop filming or to leave premises by the person responsible for the premises or police, they should normally comply. In such cases it must be recognised that there may have been a trespass. Therefore, reference should be made before transmission to the licensee's most senior programme executive or the designated alternate, who will need to be convinced that showing any of the material serves the public interest. Programme-makers should also make reasonable endeavours to inform innocent parties in advance of transmission of any material in which they are prominently featured.

(iii) Fairness to innocent parties

13-25 Where innocent parties are central figures in a serious crime, a tragic event or disaster, special care should be taken not to present them in an unfair light. Producers should, where practicable, contact them at an early stage and give due consideration to their perspectives. The same applies to members of the immediate family of central figures who have died. Producers should also, where practicable, inform such people of times of intended transmission of programmes and when programme trails will start to be transmitted.

Producers should assess the likelihood of personal distress arising from the programme, taking account of how recently the event took place, the nature and the extent of the presentation or portrayal of any innocent party, the extent to which the event continues to attract wider media attention, and the extent to which a clear public interest is to be served, as distinct from public curiosity. Arguments of public interest would be relevant, for example, where questions of a possible miscarriage of justice arise or where major legal, social or moral principles are at issue.

(c) Recorded telephone interviews[39]

13-26 Conversations conducted by telephone should not normally be recorded for inclusion in a programme unless the interviewer has identified himself or herself as speaking on behalf of a licensee, and has described the general purpose of the programme, and the interviewee has given consent to the use of the conversation in the programme.

There may be rare occasions, such as those involving investigation of allegedly criminal or otherwise disreputable behaviour, when these normal requirements cannot be observed. When, in the considered judgment of the producer,

---

[38] See also Chap 21 at 6.
[39] s.2.3 of the Programme Code.

such a case arises, he or she must obtain the explicit consent of the licensee's most senior programme executive or the designated alternate before such material is broadcast in a programme.

Companies should keep a log of all consents and be able to demonstrate that the procedures have been followed in case of a subsequent complaint.

(d) Hidden microphones and cameras[40]

The use of hidden microphones and cameras to record individuals who are unaware that they are being recorded is acceptable only when it is clear that the material so acquired is essential to establish the credibility and authority of a story, and where the story itself is equally clearly of important public interest. Consent of the licensee's most senior programme executive or the designated alternate must be obtained before such material is recorded (whether or not it is intended for transmission). Consent is required again before any such material is transmitted.

Licensees must keep full records of the consultation process followed in each case and of any material recorded and transmitted. The ITC will ask to see such records at regular intervals.

13-27

(e) Scenes of extreme suffering and distress[41]

Before presenting such scenes, a producer needs to balance the wish to serve the needs of truth and the desire for compassion against the risk of sensationalism and the possibility of an unwarranted invasion of privacy.

13-28

(f) Interviewing of children[42]

Any interviewing of children requires care. Children should not be questioned to elicit views on private family matters, nor asked for expressions of opinion on matters likely to be beyond their judgment. Later, the Code also refers to the need for consent from the local authority and parents.[43]

13-29

(g) Set-up situations[44]

Set-ups, where individuals are featured without their knowledge or without prior warning, are an established part of some entertainment programmes. Nevertheless, the use of such situations should always be carefully considered, and safeguards used to prevent unwarranted invasions of privacy.

Where material is recorded, the consent of the subjects should be obtained before transmission. In live situations, particular care should be taken to avoid

13-30

---

[40] See also Chap. 10 at 3 (Telephone Tapping and Eavesdropping) and Chap. 21 at 2 (Tape Recordings). s.2.4 of the Programme Code.
[41] *ibid.*, s.2.5.
[42] *ibid.*, s.2.6.
[43] *ibid.*, s.6.4.
[44] *ibid.*, s.2.8.

offence to the individuals concerned. Requests to leave private property or stop filming should be complied with promptly.

A different kind of set-up situation is one where the subject consents to being recorded for a different purpose from that covertly intended by the programme-makers. The use of such material without the subject's permission can only be justified if it is necessary in order to make an important point of public interest. Consent to proceed should, where practicable, be given before recording by the licensee's most senior programme executive or the designated alternate. Such consent is required again before transmission.

(h) Interviews without prior arrangement

13-31   Interviews sought on private property without the subject's prior agreement should not be included in a programme unless they have a public interest purpose. The same consideration applies to restaurants, churches and other places where the subject could reasonably expect personal privacy. Interviews in which criminal or other serious allegations are put to individuals should not be attempted without prior warning unless a previous request has been refused or received no response, or where there is good reason for not making a prior approach. Particular care needs to be taken where the person approached is not the subject of the allegations, for example a relative, friend or associate, to avoid the risk of unwarranted invasion of their privacy. Reporters and crews should leave "media scrums" unless there is a continuing public interest in their presence.

(4) RELIGIOUS TOLERANCE AND THE PORTRAYAL OF MINORITIES

There are several provisions explaining how licensees should portray minorities.[45] These include the following.

(a) Ethnic minorities[46]

13-32   Racist terms should be avoided. Their inclusion is acceptable only where it can be clearly justified within the context of the programme. Insensitive comment or stereotyped portrayal may also cause offence, however unintentional.

(b) People with disabilities[47]

13-33   There is a danger of offence in the use of humour based on physical or mental disability, even where no malice is present. Unnecessary reference to disability should be avoided and patronising expressions such as "crippled with", "victim", "handicapped" should where possible be replaced by more neutral forms such as "he/she is disabled" or "uses [not 'is confined to'] a wheelchair".

---

[45] See Chap. 8 on the law relating to obscenity and blasphemy and race offences.
[46] Programme Code, s.1.9.
[47] *ibid.*

Similar considerations apply to the treatment of other minorities including older people, homosexuals, and minority religious faiths or language groups.

(c) Religious tolerance[48]

We have already seen that the Broadcasting Act 1990 imposes obligations in relation to the exploitation of those watching religious programming and the denigration of any particular religion.[49] The Code includes further guidance. In particular, every attempt must be made to ensure that the beliefs and practices of religion are not misrepresented, and that programmes about religion are accurate and fair. Programmes must not denigrate others' beliefs.

13-34

3. ADVERTISING REGULATION[50]

(1) GENERAL PRINCIPLES

The Code of Advertising Standards and Practice begins with a general statement of principle,[51] including the following key points:

13-35

(i)   television advertising should be legal, decent, honest and truthful;

(ii)   advertisements must comply in every respect with the law, and licensees must make it a condition of acceptance that advertisements do so comply; and

(iii) the detailed rules set out in the Code are intended to be applied in the spirit as well as the letter.

Furthermore, no advertisement may offend against good taste or decency or be offensive to public feeling and no advertisement should prejudice respect for human dignity.[52] Along similar lines, advertisements must not without justifiable reason play on fear or exploit the superstitious.[53] There are also certain categories of products and services which may not be advertised.

The Code also contains some provisions dealing with political issues. No advertisements may be inserted by or on behalf of any body whose objects are

---

[48] s.9 of the Programme Code.

[49] See 1 above.

[50] The key principles are to be found in the ITC's Code of Advertising Standards and Practice. In addition to the areas dealt with in the text below, the Code addresses a number of other issues, including technical issues (noise and stridency: r.7; captions and superimposed text: r.8), health and safety (r.20) and specific advertising areas (such as religion and charities: r.11 and 12; lotteries: r.19; motorcars: r.21). There are also detailed appendices on topics including advertising and children (Appendix 1), financial advertising (Appendix 2) and medicines, treatments and health (Appendix 3).

[51] rr.1 to 4 of the Code of Advertising Standards and Practice.

[52] *ibid.*, r.13.

[53] *ibid.*, rr.16 and 17.

wholly or mainly of a political nature, and no advertisement may have any relation to any industrial dispute. No advertisement may show partiality as respects matters of political or industrial controversy or relating to current public policy.[54]

(2) MISLEADINGNESS

13-36 Several parts of the Code may be characterised as seeking to ensure that viewers are not misled by advertising. These are equivalent in certain respects to the provisions in the Programme Code dealing with accuracy and impartiality. They are of course particularly critical here because advertisements encourage the viewer to buy goods or service. Furthermore, ensuring programme integrity and separation of advertising from programme content are important policy objectives. The key provisions dealing with misleadingness include the following.

(a) Misleadingness: general provisions

13-37 Rule 24 provides as follows:

"(a) No advertisement may contain any descriptions, claims or illustrations which expressly or by implication mislead about the product or service advertised or about its suitability for the purpose recommended. In particular:

(i) no advertisement may misleadingly claim or imply that the product advertised, or an ingredient, has some special property or quality which is incapable of being established;

(ii) scientific terms, statistics, quotations from technical literature and the like must be used with a proper sense of responsibility to the ordinary viewer. Irrelevant data and scientific jargon must not be used to make claims appear to have a scientific basis they do not possess. Statistics of limited validity must not be presented in such a way as to make it appear that they are universally true. Advertisements must not seek to exploit public ignorance or to perpetuate popular misconceptions.

(b) Advertisements must make clear any important limitations or qualifications without which a misleading impression of a product or service might be given.

(c) Before accepting advertisements licensees must satisfy themselves that any descriptions, claims or illustrations have been adequately substantiated by the advertiser."

---

[54] r.10 of the Code of Advertising Standards and Practice. Public service advertisements are exempted from this provision under the Broadcasting Act 1990. See also Chap. 10 at 5 on election reporting.

(b) Separation of advertising from programming

A common theme running through the various regulatory codes is that the   **13-38**
viewer, listener or reader should be in no doubt as to whether he is experienc-
ing a programme or an advertisement. Rule 5 provides detailed guidance on
this issue, including the following:

> "(a) Advertisements and programme promotions must be clearly dis-
>   tinguishable as such and recognisably separate from the pro-
>   grammes.
> (b) Situations, performances and styles reminiscent of programmes
>   must not be used in such a way as to risk confusing viewers as to
>   whether they are watching a programme or an advertisement. In
>   marginal cases the acceptability of such an advertisement may
>   depend on positive indication that it is an advertisement. Where an
>   advertisement imitates or parodies a particular programme it must
>   not appear in the breaks in or adjacent to that programme.
> (c) Advertisements must not include extracts from recent or current
>   programme material, or incorporate programme titles, logos, sets or
>   theme music, except in the case of advertisements for products or
>   services which are based on the programme concerned, or advertise-
>   ments in which such products or services are offered as promotional
>   items . . ."

(c) Persons appearing in advertisements and in programmes

These provisions[55] are closely allied to those just described and serve a similar   **13-39**
purpose. They state as follows:

> "(a) In order to ensure that the purpose of the rules prohibiting certain
>   kinds of sponsorship is not circumvented, no advertisement may
>   feature a person who appears in any current programme which the
>   advertiser would be precluded from sponsoring by virtue of the ITC
>   Code of Programme Sponsorship.
> (b) No advertisement may feature, visually or orally, persons who regu-
>   larly present news or current affairs programmes on any U.K. tele-
>   vision service.
> (c) With limited exceptions, advertisements which include a person
>   who also appears, other than in a minor or incidental capacity, in a
>   programme may not be scheduled in breaks in or adjacent to that
>   programme. For the avoidance of doubt, a programme promotion
>   is deemed to be a programme for the purposes of this part of the
>   rule."

---

[55] Code of Advertising Standards and Practice, r.6.

(d) Comparisons[56]

13-40 Rule 26 provides as follows:

> "Advertisements containing comparisons with other advertisers, or other products or services, are permissible in the interest of vigorous competition and public information provided they comply with the terms of this rule and Rule 27.[57]
>
> (a) All comparative advertisements must respect the principles of fair competition and must be so designed that there is no likelihood of the consumer being misled as a result of the comparison, either about the product or service advertised or that with which it is compared.
>
> (b) The subject-matter of a comparison must not be chosen in such a way as to confer an artificial advantage upon the advertiser.
>
> (c) Points of comparison must be based on facts which can be substantiated and must not be unfairly selected.
>
> In particular:
>
> (i) the basis of comparison must be the same for all the products or services being compared and must be clearly established in the advertisement so that it can be seen that like is being compared with like;
>
> (ii) generalised superiority claims must not be made on the basis of selective comparisons."

(e) Denigration

13-41 Rule 27 provides that advertisements must not unfairly attack or discredit other products or services, advertisers or advertisements expressly or by implication.

(3) TASTE AND DECENCY

13-42 There is a general statement in the Code that no advertisement may offend against good taste or decency or be offensive to public feeling and no advertisement should prejudice respect for human dignity.[58] There are also a number of rules which recognise the importance of taste and decency. These include the following:

(a) particular care should be taken over advertising that is likely to be seen by large numbers of children[59];

---

[56] See Chap. 6 at 2(7) above for discussion of the Trade Marks Act 1994 and the likely impact of the Control of Misleading Advertisements (Comparative Advertising) (Amendment) Regulations 2000.

[57] See "denigration" at (e) below.

[58] Code of Advertising Standards and Practice, r.13.

[59] *ibid.*, r.41 and App.1.

(b) certain products cannot be advertised, such as guns, pornography and escort services.[60]

(4) PRIVACY

Individual living persons must not be portrayed or referred to without their express permission except in circumstances approved by the ITC.[61] A general exception is in advertisements for books, films, and particular editions of radio or television programmes, newspapers, magazines, etc., which feature the person referred to in the advertisement, provided the reference is neither offensive or defamatory.   **13-43**

In the case of advertising for news media outlets, licensees may also waive the requirement for prior permission if it seems to them reasonable that the individual concerned would have no reason to object. Such generic advertising must, however, be withdrawn immediately if individuals portrayed without their permission do object. This provision is perhaps more restrictive than the law of passing off.[62]

(5) PRE-PUBLICATION CLEARANCE

ITC licensees are required to ensure that any advertising which they transmit complies with the Advertising Code and to satisfy the ITC that they have adequate procedures in place to fulfil this requirement. All of the terrestrial channels and most of the main satellite and cable channels use the Broadcast Advertising Clearance Centre (BACC) to pre-clear commercials. The BACC has its own clearance guidelines, of which advertisers, agencies and broadcasters should be aware.[63] For national advertising campaigns, all scripts and finished tapes must be approved by the BACC. The BACC can ask for substantiating evidence in support of claims being made in advertising: advertisers should ensure that this material is available.   **13-44**

The ITC will not make rulings on the acceptability of particular advertisements in advance of their broadcast. Such requests should be directed to the relevant television company or, if appropriate, to the BACC.

4. SPONSORSHIP REGULATION

In addition to the Code on Advertising Standards and Practice, the ITC has a separate Code of Programme Sponsorship.[64] This Code concerns those   **13-45**

---

[60] At the time of writing, the ITC was conducting a public consultation which may lead to the removal or relaxation of some of these prohibitions. This move has been prompted by the provisions of the Human Rights Act 1998. r.18 Code of Advertising Standards and Practice.

[61] *ibid.*, r.15.

[62] See Chap. 6 at 3.

[63] Details can be obtained from BACC, 200 Gray's Inn Road, London WC1X 8HF. Tel: 020 7843 8265. Fax: 020 7843 8154.

[64] At the time of writing the ITC had issued a consultation paper which is likely to lead to a liberalisation of the Code.

aspects of television programme services which entail advertiser involvement in programming or promotional (rather than advertising) time. As was explained above in relation to the separation of advertisements and programmes, the ITC is concerned to ensure that the viewer is not misled, that the licensee remains independent and that any advertiser encroachment is kept within acceptable bounds.[65]

It is beyond the scope of this text to review the Code in full.[66] Amongst the key issues dealt with by the Code are the following.

(1) WHAT IS SPONSORSHIP?

13-46 The key principle to be derived from the Code is that a programme is deemed to be sponsored if "any part of its costs of production or transmission is met by an advertiser with a view to promoting its own or another's name, trademark, image, activities, products or other direct or indirect commercial interest."[67]

(2) PLACING OF SPONSORSHIP

13-47 Advertising which refers to sponsorship of a specific programme may not be transmitted in advertising breaks within or immediately adjacent to that programme.[68]

(3) PROGRAMME INTEGRITY[69]

13-48 A core principle of the Code is the preservation of programme integrity by not allowing programme agendas to be distorted for commercial purposes. No sponsor is permitted any influence on either the content or the scheduling of a programme in such a way as to affect the editorial independence and responsibility of the broadcaster.

In so far as promotional references are made, a number of important principles are enunciated,[70] including the following.

---

[65] It is worth noting that no sponsorship may breach the principles or spirit of the ITC Code of Advertising Standards and Practice.

[66] The Code appears in full in the CD ROM accompanying this text. There are other sections which deal with, for example, prohibited sponsors (such as political bodies and tobacco products: r. 4.1), restricted sponsors (such as prescription-only medicines and gaming: r.4.2), unsponsorable programmes (for example, the news: r.6), technical issues (like the placing and length of credits: r.8) and the use of sponsored programme support material (r.15).

[67] r.1.1 of the ITC Code of Programme Sponsorship

[68] *ibid.*, r.2.2. There are limits on the amount of advertising permitted in each hour (dealt with in the ITC Rules on Amount and Scheduling of Advertising): sponsorship cannot be used to circumvent those rules.

[69] *ibid.*, r.9.

[70] *ibid.*, r.10.

(i) Undue prominence

It is necessary at this point to refer back to the ITC Programme Code.[71] This **13-49** states that no undue prominence may be given in any programme to a commercial product or service. In particular, any reference to such a product or service must be limited to what can clearly be justified by the editorial requirements of the programme itself. An important practical yardstick is that no impression be created of external commercial influence on the editorial process. In no circumstances may the manner of appearance of a product be the subject of negotiation or agreement with the supplier. Branded products should not, as a general rule, be referred to in audio by brand name, or shown in close-up or from an angle which displays the branding to best advantage, or for any significant length of time.

It may be necessary in a news or factual programme to include a reference to or extract from a particular advertisement. This should, however, give it no greater prominence than is necessary to make the required point.

An entertainment programme may refer to or use extracts from advertisements providing the following conditions are fulfilled:

- No advertisement may be shown which has been transmitted in paid-for time in the United Kingdom within six weeks of the commencement of the programme or series.

- No advertisement may be shown for a product or service which appears in advertising during or around the programme or series.

- Product pack shots, brand names and logos should, so far as possible, be cut.

- The choice and range of advertisements may be subject only to the editorial requirements of the programme. In particular, they may in no circumstances be influenced by advertising, sales or marketing considerations.

(ii) Similarity between programmes and advertising[72]

Close similarity between a programme's content and an advertiser's advertising **13-50** might constitute grounds for regarding the programme as having an unacceptable promotional purpose. This is likely to be the case if a character created for advertising or marketing purposes is developed for use in a programme, regardless of whether the advertiser is involved in making the programme or not.

(iii) Sponsor references in programmes[73]

It is unlikely that any reference at all, whether visual or aural, to the sponsor **13-51** will be editorially justified.

---

[71] Detailed guidance can be found at s.10.6 of the Programme Code.
[72] cl.10.1(ii) of the Code of Programme Sponsorship.
[73] *ibid.*

(iv) Masthead programming[74]

13-52   Masthead programming is programming made or funded by periodical, news-paper, book or informational software publishers, which has the same name as or incorporates the name of the publisher's product in its title and which has editorial content similar to that of the publisher's product. An example of this has been the programme based on *OK* magazine.

Such sponsorship is permitted provided:

- programmes are not a television version of a specific edition of the parent publication;

- there are no references within the programme specifically to the parent publication or to any articles or other matter in that publication. Internal references to the programme title should be used only sparingly. Any visual references should be minimal.

(v) Promotions

13-53   Reference should be made again here to relevant provisions in the Programme Code.[75] Products or services may not be promoted in programme time. The only permitted exceptions to this rule are publications, off-air activities or recorded theme music available in support of actual programme content, though subject to certain conditions.

Announcements about material or activities that are clearly related to social action and educational programmes or programme items may, subject to certain provisos, be included within the programme itself.[76]

(4) PREMIUM RATE TELEPHONE SERVICES

13-54   In conclusion it is worth noting a further matter covered in the Programme Code, namely the use of premium rate telephone services in programmes.[77] This states that the licensee must retain control of and responsibility for the service arrangements and the premium line messages (including all matters relating to their content). In addition, any premium rate telephone service must comply with the Code of Practice issued by the Independent Committee for the Supervision of Standards of Telephone Information Services (ICSTIS).[78]

A premium rate message may only be used to convey information which is directly relevant to the programme with which it is associated, and which is of benefit to viewers. The call charge rate must be stated clearly and simultaneously with the premium rate number.

---

[74] cl.10.6 of the Code of Programme Sponsorship.
[75] Programme Code, s.10.3.
[76] *ibid.*, s.10.3 (v).
[77] This is covered in detail at s.10.4 of the Programme Code.
[78] See Chap. 18.

5. COMPLAINTS PROCEDURE

A complaint to the ITC about programming, advertising or sponsorship may **13-55** be generated by one of three main routes:

(1) Through the ITC Secretariat: the ITC is divided into regions, and its personnel monitor both local and network programming. It would not be feasible to monitor everything: personnel tend to focus on programmes which are likely to give rise to controversy.

(2) Through viewers' consultative councils: there are viewers consultative councils in each of the regions composed of a cross-section of viewers. Their task is to view programming and raise issues of interest or relating to regulation.

(3) Through the public: the ITC also considers complaints from the public, provided the complainant has seen the programme or advertisement in question.

The complaint will be investigated by the ITC Secretariat in London. If it considers that the complaint is entirely untenable, a reply is sent to the complainant to that effect. If, however, there appears to be some substance to the complaint, the ITC will write to the broadcaster asking for its views on how the programme or advertisement complies with the Codes. Should the response be inadequate, the ITC will issue a formal warning. This takes the form of a letter from the Chairman or Chief Executive of the ITC, identifying the error and stating that the ITC intends to publish the fact that it has issued a warning. The finding is issued in a press release and widely reported. It is unfortunate for broadcasters that the BSC and ITC can reach different conclusions: plainly, they have to live with the consequences of the most damning ruling.

Should the error be particularly serious, the ITC has the power to fine its licensee. The fine can be up to 3 per cent of qualifying revenue.[79] The ITC can also shorten or withdraw the licence. Significantly, unlike the BSC, the ITC has no power to require its adjudications to be broadcast by the offending licensee.[80] The ITC adjudications are subject to judicial review.[81]

It is worth noting that licensees must retain recordings of every broadcast programme for 90 days following transmission.[82]

---

[79] In a serious case against Granada in 1994, the company was fined £500,000 for product placement breach. Its *This Morning* programme invited viewers to enter a cookery competition, applications for which could be obtained from branches of Safeway or by buying *She* magazine. Competition prizes were groceries from Safeway. The competition was described as being "in conjunction" with *She* magazine and Safeway.

[80] See Chap. 15 at 4.

[81] *R. v. Independent Television Commission, ex p TV NI, Times Law Reports,* December 30, 1991.

[82] Broadcasting Act 1990, s.11(2)(a).

Chapter 14

Commercial Radio

14-01 ## 1. STATUTORY BASIS OF THE RADIO AUTHORITY

The Radio Authority ("the Authority") was created by the Broadcasting Act 1990. Its function is to regulate the provision in the United Kingdom of independent radio services[1]. As with the ITC, the 1990 Act is the source for most of the Authority's responsibilities and powers, including a number of general requirements as to the content of radio programmes.

(1) TYPES OF SERVICE

The obligations imposed by the Authority on its licensees will vary depending on the type of service involved. For present purposes, it is sufficient to be aware of the following categories of service:

National service

14-02 This is any sound broadcasting service which is provided on a frequency assigned to the Authority "for any such minimum area of the United Kingdom as the Authority may determine . . ."[2] A national service will in practice be one which tends to provide coverage to a large part of the United Kingdom.[3]

Local service

14-03 This covers any sound broadcasting service which is provided on a frequency assigned to the Authority "for a particular area or locality in the United Kingdom".[4]

---

[1] Broadcasting Act 1990, s.84(1). In certain circumstances—beyond the scope of this text—the Radio Authority may have some jurisdiction in respect of services originating outside the U.K. For example, if the Authority considers that a foreign satellite service repeatedly includes matter which offends against good taste or decency or is likely to encourage or incite to crime or to lead to disorder or to be offensive to public feeling, it may recommend to the Secretary of State that the station be proscribed: Broadcasting Act 1990, s.177.

[2] Broadcasting Act 1990, s.84(2)(a)(i).

[3] The criteria for determining the minimum area to be provided by a national service are set out at Broadcasting Act 1990, s.98(2).

[4] Broadcasting Act 1990, s.84(2)(a)(ii).

Restricted service

A restricted service is one which is provided on a frequency assigned to the **14-04** Authority "for a particular establishment or other defined location, or a particular event, in the United Kingdom".[5] A hospital radio service might fall within this category.

Satellite service

A satellite service consists of the transmission of sound programmes by satel- **14-05** lite either:

(i) from the United Kingdom for general reception in the United Kingdom; or

(ii) from outside the United Kingdom for general reception in the United Kingdom where the programmes consist of material provided by a person in the United Kingdom who is in a position to determine what is to be included in the service.[6]

Licensable sound programme service

This service covers sound programmes conveyed by a telecommunication **14-06** system for reception in the United Kingdom and otherwise than for the purpose of being received there by persons who have a business interest in receiving them.[7] The service is defined to exclude[8] the four types of service referred to above, a service where the running of the telecommunication system does not require to be licensed under Part II of the Telecommunications Act 1984, and a two-way service.[9]

Additional service

An additional service is one where telecommunication signals are sent by wire- **14-07** less telegraphy using "spare capacity within the signals".[10]

(2) GENERAL PROVISIONS RELATING TO CONTENT

Section 90(1) of the Broadcasting Act 1990 states that the Authority: **14-08**

". . . shall do all that they can to secure that every licensed service complies with the following requirements, namely:

---

[5] Broadcasting Act 1990, s.84(2)(a)(iii).
[6] Broadcasting Act 1990, ss.84(2)(b) and 84(3).
[7] Broadcasting Act 1990, s.112(1).
[8] Broadcasting Act 1990, s.112(2).
[9] A two-way service is defined by Broadcasting Act 1990, s.46(2)(c).
[10] Broadcasting Act 1990, s.114.

    (a)   that nothing is included in its programmes which offends against good taste or decency or is likely to encourage or incite to crime or to lead to disorder or to be offensive to public feeling;

    (b)   that any news given (in whatever form) in its programmes is presented with due accuracy and impartiality; and

    (c)   that its programmes do not include any technique which exploits the possibility of conveying a message to, or otherwise influencing the minds of, persons listening to the programmes without their being aware, or fully aware, of what has occurred."

Where the licensed service is a national, local, satellite or licensable sound programme service, the Authority must then also do all that it can to make sure the service complies with the following additional requirements in section 90(2) and (3) of the Act, namely:

(a)   that due impartiality is preserved on the part of the person providing the service as respects matters of political or industrial controversy or relating to current public policy (if a national service) or that undue prominence is not given in its programmes to the views and opinions of particular persons or bodies on such matters (if a local, satellite or licensable sound programme service);

(b)   that there are excluded from its programmes all expressions of the views and opinions of the person providing the service on matters (other than sound broadcasting) which are of political or industrial controversy or relate to current public policy; and

(c)   that due responsibility is exercised with respect to the content of any of its programmes which are religious programmes, and that in particular any such programmes do not involve—

    (i)   any improper exploitation of any susceptibilities of those listening to the programmes, or

    (ii)   any abusive treatment of the religious views and beliefs of those belonging to a particular religion or religious denomination.

These provisions are similar to the obligations imposed on the BBC and ITC.[11]

The Act requires the Authority to draw up and review codes giving guidance on:

(i)   the additional requirements in relation to due impartiality and undue prominence set out in section 90(2) and (3) above[12];

(ii)   the rules to be observed with respect to the inclusion in programmes of sounds suggestive of violence, particularly in circumstances such that

---

[11] See Chap. 12 at 1 and Chap. 13 at 1 respectively.
[12] Broadcasting Act 1990, s.90(5).

large numbers of children and young persons may be expected to be listening to the programmes[13];

(iii) the rules to be observed with respect to the inclusion in programmes of appeals for donations[14];

(iv) such other matters concerning standards and practice for programmes as the Authority may consider suitable.[15]

The Act also deals with the Authority's obligations in relation to the regulation of advertising and sponsorship.[16] The Authority is required in particular to draw up and keep under review a code:

"(i) governing standards and practice in advertising and in the sponsoring of programmes, and
(ii) prescribing the advertisements and methods of advertising or sponsorship to be prohibited, or to be prohibited in particular circumstances . . .".[17]

The Authority is obliged to consult, among others, the ITC in drawing up such a code.[18]

These general provisions have been supplemented by the detailed codes drawn up by the Authority, including the Programme Code, the Advertising and Sponsorship Code and the News and Current Affairs Code.[19] In each instance the Codes tend to contain specific rules fortified by detailed notes on each rule. It is worth noting that the Authority does not require programmes to be referred to it in advance of broadcast though licensees must satisfy themselves prior to broadcast that commercials comply with the Code of Advertising and Sponsorship.

The rest of this section looks at some of the key issues of principle to arise from the various Codes.[20] They tend to be briefer than those drawn up by the ITC or BBC, almost certainly because of the simplicity of the medium.

Programme-makers should also be aware of the separate body of regulation issued by the Broadcasting Standards Commission touching on fairness, privacy, taste and decency. This overlaps with much that is contained in the Radio Authority's Codes. The BSC's Codes are considered in detail in Chapter 15.

---

[13] Broadcasting Act 1990 s.91(1)(a).
[14] *ibid.*, s.91(1)(b).
[15] *ibid.*, s.91(1)(c).
[16] *ibid.*, ss.92 and 93.
[17] *ibid.*, ss.93(1)(a).
[18] *ibid.*, s.93(2)(a).
[19] These are reproduced in the CD ROM accompanying this text.
[20] The approach adopted in the text is described in Chap. 11 at 3.

2. PROGRAMME REGULATION

14-09   The Broadcasting Act imposes similar obligations about programme content on the Authority in respect of its licensees as are imposed on the ITC. Whilst the obligations are formally placed on the Authority, individual radio stations will need to comply with them under their licence arrangements.

(1) TASTE AND DECENCY

14-10   It has already been seen that the Authority must "do all they can" to secure that every licensed service complies with the requirement that nothing is included in its programmes which offends against good taste or decency or is likely to encourage or incite to crime or to lead to disorder or to be offensive to public feeling.[21]

The Programme Code contains further guidance, including the following.

(a) Protection of younger listeners[22]

14-11   When programming is specifically directed at a young audience, or there is evidence of a substantial young audience—and in particular if it includes pre-teenage children—care must be taken to avoid content such as: strong language, explicit news reports, discussion or phone-in programmes which cover explicit violent or sexual topics in a frank manner, musical items with violent or sexually explicit lyrics, and fictional material with strong language or violent scenarios.

The portrayal or description of dangerous behaviour, including the use of offensive weapons or articles readily accessible to them, must not be broadcast when children are likely to be listening.[23]

(b) Language[24]

14-12   The gratuitous use of offensive language must be avoided. It must not be used in programmes aimed at young listeners or when audience research indicates they might be expected to be listening in significant numbers. There is no absolute ban on the use of bad language, but its use must be defensible in terms of context and authenticity.

(c) Sexual matters[25]

14-13   The portrayal of, or allusion to, sexual behaviour must be defensible in context and presented with tact and discretion. Smut and crudity must be avoided. No

---

[21] Broadcasting Act 1990, s.90(1)(a).
[22] cl.1.2 of the Programme Code.
[23] *ibid.*, cl.1.7.
[24] *ibid.*, cl.1.3.
[25] *ibid.*, cl.1.4.

portrayal or description of sexual activity between humans and animals or between adults and children may be transmitted and these can be referred to in programmes only after consultation at senior radio station management level. Gratuitous sexual stereotyping must be avoided.

(d) Bad taste in humour[26]

There is a danger of offence in the use of humour based on particular charac-   **14-14**
teristics like race, gender or disability. Even where no malice is present, jokes can all too easily, and plausibly, exploit or humiliate for the purpose of entertainment. Items not used immediately must be checked before transmission to ensure that jokes or scenarios are not rendered tasteless by intervening events, such as death, injury or other misfortune.

(e) Portrayal of violence[27]

The Code contains fairly detailed guidance on the portrayal of violence   **14-15**
including the following:

*   violence must never be glorified or applauded;

*   the degree of violence portrayed or described must be essential to the integrity and completeness of the item;

*   methods of inflicting pain or injury, particularly if ingenious or unfamiliar or capable of easy imitation, must not be described or portrayed without the most careful consideration; and

*   the circumstances of the broadcast must be taken into account before broadcasting material which portrays violence, including the effects of natural disaster, accident, and suffering (for example, more detailed descriptions may be included in late news bulletins from those in earlier bulletins).

(f) Warnings[28]

Very occasionally, when material is broadcast that is likely to disturb in the   **14-16**
extreme, a short factual statement must be given about the nature of that material immediately in advance. However, the statement must be straightforward and must not invite listeners to be shocked.

(2) ACCURACY AND IMPARTIALITY

We have already noted the general obligations to ensure that news is presented   **14-17**
with due accuracy and impartiality and that due impartiality is preserved as

---

[26] cl.1.5 of the Programme Code.
[27] *ibid.*, cl.1.6.
[28] *ibid.*, cl.1.8.

regards matters of political or industrial controversy or relating to current public policy.[29] Further guidance on these and other matters relating to accuracy and impartiality are to be found in the Programme Code and the News and Current Affairs Code. Key points covered include the following.

(a) Recorded topical programmes[30]

14-18 Programmes not used immediately must be checked before transmission in order to ensure that none of the facts reported has been overtaken by intervening events.

(b) Reconstructions[31]

14-19 Reconstructions must be clearly described on air as such so that listeners are not misled. Programming intended to re-examine past events involving trauma, including crime, should take care to minimise the potential distress to surviving victims or surviving relatives in retelling the story.

(c) Simulated news broadcasts[32]

14-20 Simulations of radio news bulletins or news flashes may only be broadcast if the simulation is clearly obvious to listeners.

(d) Impartiality over time[33]

14-21 All news programmes, in whatever form, must be accurate and impartial. An appropriate range of views on controversial subjects should be reported either within a single news bulletin or in a series of news bulletins which are as adjacent as is reasonably possible.

For national licence-holders, each current affairs or documentary programme or series of programmes dealing with matters of political or industrial controversy or relating to current public policy on the same topic must be impartial. In the case of a series, the presentation of different points of view must be planned in advance with the intention to achieve impartiality in this way. Impartiality in a daily series must be achieved within a fortnight, in a weekly series within three weeks and in a monthly series within three months.

For other licence-holders, a particular view may be expressed in a current affairs or documentary programme or series of programmes. However, where alternative views on the matter exist, they must be reflected within a reasonable period of time following the broadcasts concerned, not exceeding three months.

---

[29] see 1 above.
[30] Programme Code, cl.2.3.
[31] *ibid.*, cl.2.4.
[32] *ibid.*, cl.2.5.
[33] News and Current Affairs Code, cl.1.2.

(e) Personal view programmes[34]

The "personal view" programmes referred to here are programmes or features **14-22** on matters of political or industrial controversy or relating to current public policy in which the presenter or central person presents his own view. Such programmes may be broadcast subject to the following safeguards:

(a) in billing and promotion, as well as within the programme or feature itself, it must be made clear that a personal view programme or feature is the expression of one person's view on matters about which other views exist;

(b) licence-holders must ensure that statements of fact in the programme or feature are accurate and that the opinions expressed, however partial, do not rest upon false evidence;

(c) the subject-matter must cover a wide range of relevant issues. They must include either a wide range of views or a response mechanism (*e.g.* a phone-in) which is broadcast within two hours of the view being expressed so that alternative views are exposed; and

(d) personal view programmes or features on political matters must not be scheduled at times when United Kingdom and European parliamentary or local government elections are pending.

(f) Conduct of interviews[35]

Licence-holders must ensure that: **14-23**

(a) an interviewee chosen as a representative of an organised group is in a position to speak on behalf of other members or supporters;

(b) where practicable, whether the interview is recorded or live, the interviewee has been made aware of the format, subject-matter and purpose of the programme and the way in which his contribution is likely to be used; and

(c) where practicable, the interviewee has been told the identity and intended role of any other proposed participants.

There is no general obligation to offer a pre-audition of the edited version to those whose contributions have been used.[36] On the other hand, it is possible that particular circumstances will make a pre-audition by an interviewee desirable or even essential, and producers, interviewers and/or managements should always give thought to this before completing their programme or

---

[34] News and Current Affairs Code, cl.1.4. Further rules apply to discussion and phone-in programmes (cl.1.5) and to dramas touching on political or industrial controversy (cl.1.11).
[35] *ibid.*, cl.1.7.
[36] *ibid.*, cl.1.8.

225

feature. To minimise the risk of misunderstanding, or even resentment, it may be helpful if the producer or interviewer tells the interviewee that the edited version of his words used in a programme or feature is likely to be shorter than the recording made at the time.

(g) Right of reply

14-24   Any mistakes should be corrected as quickly as possible and an apology broadcast where appropriate.[37] Moreover, a right of reply should be offered[38] if the licence-holder feels that fairness and impartiality and/or the need to avoid undue prominence merit such a step. A misstatement of fact can sometimes be simply corrected, particularly if the programme is live, since there is then the opportunity for a correction to be made within the programme itself. If this is not possible then, unless the need for correction is urgent, the licensee should, if the error has occurred in a regular bulletin, feature or programme, wait until the next relevant one.

(h) Politicians in programmes[39]

14-25   As regards appearances in programmes in a non-political role, it would be unduly oppressive to insist that every radio professional should cease to broadcast from the moment he starts to pursue a political career. Nevertheless care and discretion are required over the employment of such persons. The licence-holder must keep a written record of the appearances of M.P.s and MEPs in programmes.

(3) PRIVACY AND THE GATHERING OF INFORMATION

(a) General

14-26   The Programme Code includes a general statement that "the broadcasters' freedom of access to information and their freedom to publish are subject to certain limitations".[40] After reminding licensees of certain legal causes of action, the Code notes "each citizen's right to privacy", a right which must be balanced against the public interest. In fact, as was seen in Part I, no such right exists in English law (save for the provisions of the Human Rights Act 1998), nor is there a requirement under the Broadcasting Act for the Radio Authority to include provisions dealing with privacy. Broadcasters do, however, need to proceed with caution in this area: the key provisions touching on privacy are dealt with below, but they must be read in conjunction with the Broadcasting Standards Commission's Code on Fairness and Privacy.

---

[37] Programme Code, cl.2.1.
[38] *ibid.*, News and Current Affairs Code, cl.1.10.
[39] cl.3.1. This is rather more liberal than the equivalent provision in the ITC Programme Code.
[40] Programme Code, cl.3.

(b) Scenes of extreme suffering and distress[41]

Licensees must balance the wish to serve the needs of truth and the desire for **14-27** compassion against the risk of sensationalism and the possibility of unwarranted invasion of privacy. Great discretion should be used when interviewing or recording those directly affected by disaster, accident or crime, and efforts made to ensure that they are not caused any additional anxiety or distress.

(c) Interviews with members of the public[42]

When coverage is given to events in public places, licence-holders must satisfy **14-28** themselves that words spoken or actions taken by individuals are sufficiently in the public domain to justify their broadcast without express permission being sought.

(d) Telephone interviewees and participants[43]

Telephone interviewees and participants must have given consent to the use of **14-29** their contributions prior to broadcast, and telephone conversations may not be broadcast without the permission of the participants save in circumstances covered in (e) below.

There may be very rare cases, such as those involving the investigation of allegedly criminal or otherwise disreputable behaviour, in which these normal requirements cannot be observed. In such cases, permission to proceed with the broadcast or recording must be given by senior radio station management.

(e) Hidden microphones[44]

The use of hidden microphones to record or broadcast the words of people **14-30** who are unaware that they are being recorded or broadcast is acceptable only when it is clear that the material so acquired is essential to establish the credibility and authority of the story, and where the story itself is equally clearly of important public interest. In such cases, permission to proceed with the recording and broadcast must be given by senior radio station management.

(f) Interviewing of children[45]

All interviews with children require care. They must not be interrogated to **14-31** elicit views on private family matters, nor asked for expressions of opinion on matters likely to be beyond their judgment. The Code also refers to the need for consents from the local authority and parents.[46]

---

[41] Programme Code cl.3.1.
[42] *ibid.*, cl.3.2.
[43] *ibid.*, cl.3.3.
[44] *ibid.*, cl.3.4. See also Chap 10 at 3 (Telephone Tapping and Eavesdropping) and Chap 21 at 2 (Tape Recordings).
[45] *ibid.*, cl.3.5.
[46] *ibid.*, cl.5.5.

(g) Information about listeners[47]

14-32 There is detailed guidance to ensure that any information given by listeners is only passed to third parties with their consent. Licensees should err on the side of caution if there is the slightest doubt that the safety of a listener or listeners might be at risk. Information imparted with a view to a "blind date" occurring requires special care.

Licensees have adopted several methods of minimising risk. For example, the information that is passed on so that a meeting might take place is generally in a letter, vetted by the licensee, from the party being introduced. Advice is also regularly given that any first meeting should be in a well lit, public place known to the recipient of the information.

(4) RELIGIOUS TOLERANCE AND THE PORTRAYAL OF MINORITIES

14-33 It has already been noted that the Broadcasting Act 1990 imposes obligations on the Radio Authority to prevent the exploitation of those watching religious programming and the denigration of any particular religion.[48] These general provisions are fortified by further detailed guidance in the Programme Code, which is designed to safeguard listeners and their beliefs from abuse, exploitation or charlatanism.

For example, the belief and practice of religious groups must not be misrepresented,[49] programming broadcast to a particular geographical area must be sensitive to the religious make-up of the area served[50] and licence-holders must not broadcast programmes produced or provided by bodies who practise or advocate illegal behaviour.[51] There are also provisions dealing with other spiritual and ethereal matters such as the occult, exorcism and horoscopes.

Unlike the BBC and the ITC Codes, there are no detailed provisions dealing with the portrayal of minorities, race or disability, though we have seen that there are issues of taste and decency which do touch on this subject.[52] It is, however, likely that the Radio Authority would adopt a similar approach in dealing with complaints about the portrayal of any minority group and considering whether the spirit of its Codes had been breached.

3. ADVERTISING AND SPONSORSHIP REGULATION[53]

(1) GENERAL PRINCIPLES

14-34 Unlike the ITC, the Radio Authority has just one Code covering both advertising and sponsorship. The Authority's Advertising and Sponsorship Code

---

[47] Programme Code, cl.3.6.
[48] See 1 above.
[49] *ibid.*, cl.7.3.
[50] *ibid.*, cl.7.4.
[51] *ibid.*, cl.7.5.
[52] See 2(1)(d) above.
[53] The key principles are to be found in the Radio Authority's Advertising and Sponsorship

sets out a number of general principles to assist in determining whether intended advertising or sponsorship is acceptable.

The advertising principles are as follows:

(1) "Advertisement" refers to any item (other than a sponsor credit) which is broadcast in return for payment or other valuable consideration to a licensee or seeks to sell to a listener any product or service (excluding the promotion of unique station merchandising and tickets for station events principally designed to enhance local community involvement rather than to make an appreciable profit).

(2) Radio advertising should be legal, decent, honest and truthful.

(3) Advertisements must comply in every respect with the law, common or statute, and licensees must make it a condition of acceptance that advertisements do so comply.

(4) The advertising rules are intended to be applied in the spirit as well as the letter.

The sponsorship principles are as follows:

(1) "Sponsorship" refers to any item of publicity, other than an advertisement, broadcast in return for payment or other valuable consideration to a licensee.

(2) Editorial control of sponsored programmes must remain with the licensee.

(3) All sponsor involvement must be declared so that the listener knows who is paying/contributing and why.

(4) The sponsorship rules are intended to be applied in the spirit as well as the letter.

Certain specified types of advertising and sponsorship are expressly prohibited. They include any advertisement which is inserted by or on behalf of any body whose objects are wholly or mainly of a political nature, any advertisement which is directed towards any political end, or any advertisement which has any relation to any industrial dispute (other than an advertisement of a public service nature inserted by, or on behalf of, a government department).[54]

In the acceptance of advertisements for inclusion in a licensed service there must be no unreasonable discrimination either against or in favour of any particular advertiser.[55]

Code. In addition to the areas dealt with in this text, the Code addresses a number of other issues and includes a number of appendices covering the requirements for such areas as financial advertising (Appendix 1), advertising and children (Appendix 3) and medicines, treatments and health (Appendix 4).

[54] Broadcasting Act 1990, s.92(2)(a). See also Chap. 10 at 5 on election reporting.
[55] Broadcasting Act 1990, s. 92(2)(b).

(2) MISLEADINGNESS

Like the ITC Code of Advertising Standards and Practice, there are a number of provisions in the Authority's Code which aim in a general sense to protect the listener from being misled. They include the following.

(a) Identification

14-35 Advertising breaks must be clearly distinguishable from programming.[56] Licensees must ensure that the distinction between advertising and programming is not blurred and that listeners are not confused between the two. Advertisements which have a similar style and format to editorial must be separated from programming by other material such as a jingle/station ident or by scheduling in the middle of a break. Station presenters/newsreaders may voice commercials[57] provided that they do not:

(i) indorse, recommend, identify themselves with or personally testify about an advertiser's product or services (however, presenters may refer to their own appearance at an event run by an advertiser, provided that the words used do not indorse or recommend the product or service which the event is designed to promote);

(ii) make references to any specific advertisement (whether presenter-read or not) when in their presenter role.

A proper distinction should be made between programming material and advertising material. Particular care should be exercised where the product advertised by presenters/newsreaders may be seen to compromise the impartiality of their programming role. Product placement in programmes is prohibited.[58]

(b) Misleadingness[59]

14-36 Advertisements must not contain any descriptions, claims or other material which might, directly or by implication, mislead the listener about the product or service advertised or its suitability for the purpose recommended. They must clarify any important limitations or qualifications without which a misleading impression of a product or service might be given.

Before accepting advertisements, licensees must be satisfied that any descriptions and claims have been adequately substantiated by the advertiser.

---

[56] Advertising and Sponsorship Code, s.A, r.1.
[57] *ibid.*, s.A, r.4.
[58] *ibid.*, s.A, r.6.
[59] *ibid.*, s.A, r.8.

(c) Comparisons[60]

Advertisements containing comparisons with other advertisers, or other products, are permissible in the interest of vigorous competition and public information provided that (*inter alia*) the principles of fair competition are respected and the comparisons used are not likely to mislead the listener about either product, points of comparison are based on fairly selected facts which can be substantiated, and the comparisons chosen do not give an advertiser an artificial advantage over his competitor.

14-37

(d) Denigration[61]

Advertisements must not unfairly attack or discredit other products, advertisers or advertisements directly or by implication.

14-38

(3) Taste and Decency

There is a general exhortation in the Code that "advertisements must not offend against good taste or decency or be offensive to public feeling".[62] There is also further guidance including the following:

14-39

(a) Licensees must exercise responsible judgments when scheduling categories of advertisement which may be unsuitable for children and those listening to religious programmes.[63] Particular care is required in the following categories: sanitary protection products, family planning services, contraceptives, pregnancy-testing services/kits, anti-AIDS and anti-drugs messages and solvent abuse advice.

(b) Advertisements for alcoholic drinks, cigars, pipe tobacco, sensational newspapers/magazines or their content and violent or sexually explicit films must not be broadcast in or around religious programmes or programmes/features directed particularly at people under 18.[64]

(c) A sense of responsibility should be exercised where advertisements or their scheduling could be perceived as insensitive because of a tragedy currently in news or current affairs programmes, *e.g.* a commercial for an airline should be immediately withdrawn if a neighbouring news bulletin features details of a plane crash.[65]

---

[60] Advertising and Sponsorship Code, s.A, r.14. See Chap. 6 at 2(7) above for discussion of the Trade Marks Act 1994 and the likely impact of the Control of Misleading Advertisements (Comparative Advertising) (Amendment) Regulations 2000.

[61] *ibid.*, s.A, r.15.

[62] Advertising and Sponsorship Code, s.B, r.10.

[63] Advertising and Sponsorship Code, s.A, r.2.

[64] *ibid.*

[65] *ibid.*, Practice Note.

(d) Advertising in respect of a number of goods and services are explicitly proscribed by the Code. They include advertising for escort agencies, cigarettes and firearms.[66]

(4) PRIVACY

14-40 Individual living persons must not normally be portrayed or referred to in advertisements without their prior permission.[67] A general exception is in advertisements for books, films and particular editions of radio or television programmes, newspapers, magazines, etc. which feature the person referred to in the advertisement, provided that the reference is neither offensive or defamatory.

In the case of advertising for news media outlets, the requirement for prior permission may also be waived if licensees reasonably expect that the individual concerned would have no reason to object. Such generic advertising must, however, be withdrawn if individuals portrayed without their permission do object. It may be noted that this provision may be more restrictive than the law of passing off.

The Practice Notes state that if impersonations or celebrity soundalikes are to be used, it is strongly advisable to obtain advance permission.

(5) PROGRAMME SPONSORSHIP

14-41 The Code includes a specific section dealing with sponsorship. Amongst its key provisions are the following:

(a) All programmes may be sponsored, with the exception of news bulletins.[68] Certain categories of sponsor are prohibited.[69]

(b) Ultimate editorial control of sponsored programmes must remain with the licensee.[70]

(c) Sponsors may contribute to the editorial content of all sponsored programmes[71] except news features, news magazines, current affairs, business/financial news or comment, or programmes/documentary items addressing matters of political or industrial controversy or relating to current public policy. A contribution to editorial from a sponsor may be information, advice or ideas for a programme's content or presentation. The types of programme listed above may be sponsored, but sponsors may not contribute in any way to editorial content.

---

[66] Advertising and Sponsorship Code, r.3.
[67] *ibid.*, s.B, r.10.
[68] *ibid.*, s.C, r.2.
[69] *ibid.*, s.C, r.9.
[70] *ibid.*, s.C, r.4.
[71] *ibid.*, s.C, r.5.

(d) Indorsement of a sponsor's product or service within editorial is not permitted.[72]

(e) Sponsors may buy advertising spots in and around the programme they sponsor.[73]

The Code also states that product placement in programmes is prohibited.[74]

In addition to the Advertising and Sponsorship Code, the Programme Code contains provisions dealing with the conduct of competitions and premium rate telephone services. Of particular relevance in this context is the provision requiring licence-holders to retain responsibility for all competitions in programming time, whether or not commercial partners are involved. It is also worth noting that all premium rate telephone services must comply with the Code of Practice issued by ICSTIS.[75]

(6) ADVANCE CLEARANCE OF ADVERTISING[76]

14-42 The Code has identified certain "specified categories" of advertising which must be approved centrally prior to broadcast. Approval has to be sought through the Radio Advertising Clearance Centre (RACC).[77] The specified categories include alcoholic drink, food and nutrition claims and 18-certificate films and video.

The RACC has also assumed responsibility for the advance clearance of "national" and "regional" advertisements. "Local" advertisements (i.e. to be broadcast only by a station or stations servicing one particular locality) may be cleared by the relevant staff at the station concerned.

Pre-production scripts must be sent to the RACC at 46 Westbourne Grove, London W2 5SH or by fax to 020 7229 0352. The scripts must be accompanied by the following details:

• name of script submitter;

• advertiser;

• product/brand;

• title of script;

• length of script;

• radio station to broadcast material (if known); and

• supporting evidence for any factual claims.

---

[72] Advertising and Sponsorship Code, s.C, r.6.
[73] *ibid.*, s.C, r.8.
[74] *ibid.*, s.A, r.6.
[75] See Chap. 18.
[76] Guidance is contained in the Advertising and Sponsorship Code.
[77] The RACC has no statutory basis. It is owned and funded by licence-holders for whom it provides a convenient mechanism for weeding out problematic advertisements.

The Code states that licensees or their sales houses must hold a record of centrally-cleared scripts and the RACC clearance number (once approved). Sponsored programming does not need to be cleared in advance. The Authority's advertising staff can, however, offer general guidance.

4. COMPLAINTS PROCEDURE

14-43 The Programme Code contains detailed guidance for licence-holders about the handling of complaints from listeners.[78] Complainants should be encouraged to telephone or write, in the first instance, to the licence-holder. Licence-holders should deal promptly and thoroughly with complaints and must maintain their own internal complaints procedures and keep records of all written complaints received for at least 12 months. The Authority may ask to inspect these procedures. It may also ask for the submission of records. If listeners remain aggrieved, however, they must be told how to complain directly to the Radio Authority or the Broadcasting Standards Commission sufficiently promptly for them to conduct their own investigations, as appropriate. They must also be sent a copy of the leaflet "The Radio Authority and the Listener".

The Radio Authority can require a company to provide it with a tape or a transcript of broadcast material at any time up to 42 days after the broadcast was made.[79] A person or organisation who can establish a reasonable claim that a derogatory remark has been made about him on a licensed radio service, or who is affected by alleged strictures, unfairness or inaccuracies in matter broadcast by a licence-holder, should normally be provided with a transcript on request. If the company concerned proposes to withhold a recording or transcript, the Radio Authority must be told the reason. Tapes must be kept, if necessary beyond the 42 days, of all broadcasts in which licence-holders are aware of possible imminent complaints or problems.

If the Authority considers that a complaint is justified, it will take the matter up with the appropriate licensee. It may require the licensee to broadcast a correction or apology in such form and at such time as it may determine.[80]

In exceptional circumstances the Authority has additional sanctions at its disposal. However, it appears that the BSC is better geared up to dealing with complaints: the Authority does not appear to have a clear and detailed complaints procedure. Moreover, it cannot require its adjudications to be broadcast. Its most effective sanctions are imposing financial penalties and shortening or removing the offending station's licence.[81] These measures appear to be a more suitable means of achieving the delivery of a quality

---

[78] s.10 of the Programme Code; see also s.A, r.7 of the Advertising and Sponsorship Code.
[79] Broadcasting Act 1990, s.95.
[80] Broadcasting Act 1990, s.109(3).
[81] Broadcasting Act 1990, ss.110 and 111. In May 2000, the Authority imposed a fine of £75,000 on Virgin Radio when D.J. Chris Evans offered support on air to Ken Livingstone during the run up to the elections for London's mayor. This was a breach of the rules on political impartiality.

service overall rather than handling an individual's complaint. Adjudications are subject to judicial review.

The Code also contains provisions requiring licence-holders to promote the Radio Authority. For example, 25 announcements publicising the Authority's regulatory duties must be broadcast during daytime hours within a single three-week period each year by most licence-holders.

Chapter 15

Broadcasting Standards Commission

1. STATUTORY BASIS OF BROADCASTING STANDARDS COMMISSION

15-01   The Broadcasting Standards Commission (BSC) is responsible for dealing with complaints from the public about fairness and standards in broadcasting. It was created by the Broadcasting Act 1996 and provides a measure of streamlining to what had previously been a more cumbersome structure for handling such complaints.[1]

The BSC has the following main areas of interest:

(1)   unjust or unfair treatment in programmes;

(2)   unwarranted infringement of privacy in, or in connection with the obtaining of material included in, programmes;

(3)   the portrayal of violence in programmes;

(4)   the portrayal of sexual conduct in programmes; and

(5)   standards of taste and decency in programmes generally.

The BSC has three main tasks:

•   to produce codes of practice relating to standards and fairness;

•   to consider and adjudicate on complaints; and

•   to monitor, research and report on standards and fairness in broadcasting.

---

[1] The BSC replaced the Broadcasting Complaints Commission and the Broadcasting Standards Council, effectively merging the two bodies. The Broadcasting Complaints Commission had been created by the Broadcasting Act 1980 and dealt with complaints of unjust or unfair treatment, or unwarranted infringement of privacy, in radio or television programmes. The Broadcasting Standards Council began its existence as a non- statutory body but was given legislative recognition in the Broadcasting Act 1990. Its remit was to monitor the portrayal of violence and sex and matters of taste and decency.

It has been given a wide brief to cover programmes whether broadcast on radio or television, on the BBC or by a commercial broadcaster, on cable or by satellite.[2] Its remit also covers television commercials. For the first time, a single body regulates in all of these areas though, given the respective remits of the ITC and the Radio Authority, there is inevitably still a great deal of overlap.[3] Unlike these bodies, however, the BSC is less concerned with commercial issues and therefore perhaps represents the interests of the listener or viewer more directly. It can act in a more critical way than a court though, crucially, it cannot award compensation or grant pre-publication remedies.

The BSC consists of a chairman, one or two deputy chairmen and further members up to a total complement of 15. They are appointed by the Secretary of State for Culture, Media and Sport and serve for a period of three to five years.[4]

2. CODE ON FAIRNESS AND PRIVACY

The BSC is obliged by statute to draw up and review: **15-02**

> ". . . a code giving guidance as to principles to be observed, and practices to be followed, in connection with the avoidance of—
>
> (a)   unjust or unfair treatment in programmes . . .
> (b)   unwarranted infringement of privacy in, or in connection with the obtaining of material included in, such programmes."[5]

Broadcast regulators are obliged to reflect the general effect of the Code in their own Codes.[6] However, the guidance in any Codes issued by the BSC is not exhaustive. Whether the needs of fairness and privacy have been met can only be judged "by considering each particular case in the light of the information the broadcaster had available after diligent research at the time the programme was made or broadcast".[7]

We now look at the key provisions in the Code dealing with fairness and privacy in turn.[8]

FAIRNESS

The Code's key provisions relating to fairness are as follows:

---

[2] The programmes within the remit of the BSC are set out in ss.107(5) and 108(5) of the Broadcasting Act 1996
[3] This overlap has led many to question whether the BSC serves any useful purpose.
[4] Broadcasting Act 1996, s.106.
[5] Broadcasting Act 1996, s.107(1).
[6] Broadcasting Act 1996, s.107(2).
[7] Code on Fairness and Privacy, cl.1.
[8] The current Code is set out in the CD ROM accompanying this text.

(1) Dealing fairly with contributors

15-03   The Code contains detailed guidance on dealing with contributors. They must be dealt with in a straightforward and fair manner. They must be told, wherever practicable, of the nature of the programme and its purpose and, whenever appropriate, the nature of their contractual rights.[9]

Contributors should be informed about the areas of questioning and, wherever possible, the nature of other likely contributions.[10] They should not be coached or pushed or improperly induced into saying anything which they know not to be true or do not believe to be true.[11]

The Code recognises that news reports, which are often put together at great speed, are in a different category and it may not be possible to provide such detailed information to contributors. Even in these circumstances, however, contributors must be treated fairly.

All reasonable steps should be taken to ensure that guarantees given to contributors, whether as to content, confidentiality or anonymity, are honoured.[12]

The Code does, however recognise that deception can be used to obtain information where the disclosure is reasonably believed to serve an overriding public interest and the material cannot reasonably be obtained by any other means. Even then, the deception should be proportionate to the alleged wrongdoing and prior editorial approval at the most senior editorial levels should be sought.[13]

(2) Accuracy

15-04   Broadcasters have a general obligation to avoid unfairness through the use of inaccurate information or distortion, for example by the unfair selection or juxtaposition of material taken out of context.[14]

Broadcasters should take special care when programmes are capable of adversely affecting the reputation of individuals, companies or other organisations.[15] Particular care should be taken to deal with the danger of unsubstantiated allegations being made by participants during live programmes and to ensure that presenters are briefed accordingly.[16]

Contemporary drama which is based on the lives of and experience of real people should seek to convey them fairly. It should be made clear in advance to the audience whether the drama is loosely based on the events it describes or rather purports to be an accurate account.

---

[9] Code on Fairness and Privacy, cl.3.
[10] *ibid.*, cl.4(iv).
[11] *ibid.*, cl.4(vi).
[12] *ibid.*, cl.6.
[13] *ibid.*, cl.13.
[14] *ibid.*, cl.2.
[15] *ibid.*, cl.7.
[16] *ibid.*, cl.8.

(3) Correction and apology

Whenever the broadcaster recognises that a broadcast has been unfair, if the **15-05** person affected so wishes, it should be corrected promptly with due prominence unless there are compelling legal reasons not to do so. An apology should also be broadcast wherever appropriate.[17]

(4) Participation

Where a programme alleges wrongdoing or incompetence, or contains a dam- **15-06** aging critique of an individual or organisation, those criticised should normally be given an opportunity to reply. Equally, anyone has the right not to participate in a programme.[18]

PRIVACY

The Code includes the following key provisions relating to privacy.

(1) Public interest

The Code assumes that an infringement of privacy will not be acceptable **15-07** unless there is an overriding public interest in disclosing the information. This would include revealing or detecting a crime or disreputable behaviour, protecting public health or safety, exposing misleading claims or disclosing significant incompetence in public office. The means of obtaining the information must be proportionate to the matter under investigation[19] and an infringement can take place even if the material obtained is not broadcast.[20]

The Code states that the private lives of most people are of no legitimate public interest. It also gives a number of examples where an individual's consent should be obtained before filming. For instance, in obviously sensitive situations such as hospitals or police stations, an individual's consent should be obtained in addition to the consent of the relevant institution (unless their identity has been concealed).[21]

The Code recognises that individuals in the public eye are in a special position, though they do not forfeit the right to privacy in all situations.[22]

(2) Hidden microphones and cameras[23]

The Code assumes that broadcasters on location should only operate in public, **15-08** where they can be seen. Where recording takes place secretly in public, the

---

[17] Code on Fairness and Privacy, cl.10.
[18] *ibid.*, cll.11 and 12.
[19] *ibid.*, cl.14.
[20] *ibid.*, cl.15.
[21] *ibid.*, cl.16.
[22] *ibid.*, cl.17.
[23] *ibid.*, cll.18 to 21. See also Chap. 10 at 3 (Telephone Tapping and Eavesdropping) and Chap. 21 at 2 (Tape Recordings).

words or images recorded should serve an overriding public interest to justify the decision to gather the information, the actual recording and any broadcast.

The BSC's approach in this context was recently considered by the Court of Appeal.[24] The case concerned a complaint to the BSC by Dixons, the high street retailer, over secret filming in its stores by the BBC. The Corporation had secretly filmed several sales transactions in Dixons' stores to check whether Dixons had been selling secondhand goods as new. The filming revealed no wrongdoing and the footage was not broadcast by the BBC. Dixons complained that the BBC's actions had amounted to an unwarranted infringement of the company's privacy, and the BSC upheld the complaint. On an application for judicial review by the BBC, the court at first instance found that a body corporate did not enjoy a right to privacy. However, the Court of Appeal reversed this decision and ruled that the BSC had not exceeded its jurisdiction,[25] and that the Broadcasting Act 1996 made it clear that a company could complain about infringement of its privacy. Further, the secret filming by the BBC required justification because the fact that the film was secret prevented the company taking action to prevent it. Although the stores were public property, the invitation for the public to enter did not extend to secret filming.

An unattended recording device should not be left on private property without the full and informed consent of the occupiers or their agent unless seeking permission might frustrate the investigation by the programme-makers of matters of an overriding public interest.

(3) Doorstepping[26]

15-09 The Code recognises that surprise can be a legitimate device to elicit the truth where there is an overriding public interest. This may be the case where there has been repeated refusal to grant an interview or the risk exists that a protagonist might disappear. However, a careful balance must be struck: the Code acknowledges that repeated attempts to take pictures or to obtain an interview where consent has been refused can constitute an unwarranted infringement of privacy and unfairness.

The Code also contains similar provisions in relation to telephone calls. Broadcasters should normally identify themselves from the outset or seek agreement from the other party if they wish to use the recording. The Code treats the unsuspecting recording of a telephone call as the equivalent of doorstepping.[27]

(4) Suffering and distress[28]

15-10 Broadcasters should not add to the distress of people caught up in emergencies or suffering a personal tragedy. People in a state of distress should not be

---

[24] *R. v. BSC, ex parte BBC* [2000] E.M.L.R. 587. See 4 below.
[25] See *R. v. BSC ex parte Granada Television* [1995] E.M.L.R. 163.
[26] Code on Fairness and Privacy cll.25 to 27.
[27] *ibid.*, cll.22 to 24.
[28] *ibid.*, cll.28 to 30.

put under any pressure to provide interviews. For instance, programme-makers should obtain a family's consent before filming at a funeral.

(5) Children[29]

Children's vulnerability is a prime concern for broadcasters. They do not lose their rights to privacy because they have famous parents or because of events at their schools.   **15-11**

They should not be questioned about private family matters or asked for views on matters likely to be beyond their capacity to answer properly. Consent should normally be obtained from parents or those *in loco parentis* before interviewing those under 16 on matters of significance. If no consent has been obtained, the decision to go ahead can only be justified if the item is of overriding public interest and the child's appearance is absolutely necessary.

Similarly, children under 16 involved in police inquiries or court proceedings relating to sexual offences should not be identified or identifiable in news or other programmes.[30]

(6) Working with the police and others[31]

Broadcasters should be concerned about the terms on which they are granted access to police operations and other agencies, emergency services or bodies working with vulnerable people. When accompanying such operations, crews should identify as soon as reasonably practicable for whom they are working and what they are doing. If asked to leave or stop filming on private property, they should do so unless there is an overriding public interest.   **15-12**

3. CODE OF PRACTICE ON BROADCASTING STANDARDS

The BSC is obliged to draw up and review   **15-13**

". . . a code giving guidance as to:

(a) practices to be followed in connection with the portrayal of violence in programmes . . .

(b) practices to be followed in connection with the portrayal of sexual conduct in such programmes, and

(c) standards of taste and decency for such programmes generally."[32]

The current Code is based on the Code of the former Broadcasting Standards Council but has been subject to amendments following consultation. It applies

---

[29] *ibid.*, cl.32.
[30] See Chap. 4 for restrictions on court reporting.
[31] *ibid.*, cl.33.
[32] Broadcasting Act 1996, s.108(1),.

to radio and all forms of television, including satellite and cable channels, and to broadcast advertisements, unless otherwise stated. It begins with general issues of scheduling, taste and decency, then focuses on violence and sexual content. Its key areas of concern are summarised below, but reference should be made to the full text of the Code.[33]

Reference should also be made here to the BSC's research papers. These include practical guidance on the acceptability of content, such as the portrayal of sex and violence and the use of swear words. The research reveals how what is acceptable changes over time. They can be a useful source of information for those involved in compliance issues.

(1) SCHEDULING[34]

The Code includes reference to the following issues:

(a) Audience composition[35]

15-14   The composition of audiences to open access channels changes throughout the day and the content of broadcasts reflects this. For example, at certain times, parents will want to be confident that their children can watch or listen to programmes without the risk of being exposed to disturbing material.

Broadcasters have a clear duty to give enough information about the nature and content of programmes so as to allow parents to make an informed judgment as to whether a programme is suitable for their children to see and hear.

(b) The watershed[36]

15-15   The television watershed starts at 9 p.m. and ends at 5.30 a.m. It is well established as a scheduling marker to distinguish between programmes intended mainly for family viewing and those intended for adults. It should not be an abrupt change from family viewing to adult programming. But it is a signal to parents to exercise increasing control over their children's viewing.

Pay-per-view services give subscribers greater choice over what is available. Given their stricter security systems, the watershed does not apply in the same way. Similarly, there is no watershed for radio, but care should be taken at times when children tend to listen.

(c) Repeats, trailers and advertisements[37]

15-16   Broadcasters need to assess the suitability of material for its time slot. Repeats rescheduled from evening to day slots require particular care. Advertisements also appear without warning and audiences cannot selectively screen them out.

---

[33] This appears in the CD ROM accompanying this text.
[34] Code on Standards, cll.2–14.
[35] *ibid.*, cll.3 and 4.
[36] *ibid.*, cll.6 to 10.
[37] *ibid.*, cll.11 to 13.

(d) Labelling and warnings

Breaches of taste and decency can cause particular offence if they are encoun-   **15-17**
tered with little or no warning. Providing advance information is desirable.

(2) TASTE AND DECENCY[38]

The Code addresses many points dealing with taste and decency. It notes that   **15-18**
matters of taste shift quite quickly and vary from one age or social group to
another. They often relate to subjects which can cause embarrassment or upset.
Matters of decency, however, are based on deeper, more fundamental values
and emotions: respect to the bereaved at a funeral is an example. Offence to
decency is more likely to give rise to significant difficulty to a broadcaster. The
Code goes on to refer to a number of issues, including the following:

(a)   Respect and dignity[39]: the line between the public's right to information
      and the citizen's right to privacy can be fine and difficult to draw. See also
      the provisions in the Code on Fairness and Privacy.

(b)   Occasions of grief and bereavement[40]: care must be taken not to take
      advantage of people in deep shock, or persuade them into an expression
      of their emotions or views which they may later regret.

(c)   Scheduling[41]: careful scheduling is required where the subject-matter is
      very close to that of a tragic event or on its anniversary.

(d)   Swearing[42]: the Code does not contain a list of banned words. But words
      and phrases with sexual origins or applications cause particular offence.
      The abusive use of any of the synonyms for the female genitalia should
      be referred to senior management prior to broadcast. There is also hardly
      ever any justification for the use on television of offensive language before
      the watershed and certainly not without reference to senior management.

(e)   Offence to religion, race or people with disabilities.[43]

(f)   Drugs, alcohol and smoking.[44]

(3) PORTRAYAL OF VIOLENCE

The Code includes a long description of issues to be borne in mind in relation   **15-19**
to the portrayal of violence.[45] This includes the following:

---

[38] Code on Standards cll.15 to 47.
[39] *ibid.*, cll.17 and 18.
[40] *ibid.*, cll.19 to 21.
[41] *ibid.*, cl.22.
[42] cll.23–30
[43] cll.31, 36 to 43
[44] cll.34 and 35
[45] cll.48–78. The BSC is also a party with the BBC and ITV to the Statement of Common
      Principles on the Portrayal of Violence on Television. This is reproduced in full in the CD ROM
      accompanying this text.

(a) General observations: there are significant concerns about the portrayal of violence. These include the fear that repeated exposure to violence desensitises audiences, making them apathetic towards increases in actual violence or indifferent to the plight of victims or the copycat effect which could be a consequence of showing it in detail.

(b) Explicitness: a balance needs to be struck between the demands of truth and the danger of desensitising people. Where scenes of violence are included in television news bulletins, the fact that violence has bloody consequences should not be glossed over. However, decency demands that people should normally be allowed to die in private. Neither explicit hangings nor other judicial executions should be shown before the watershed, except in the rarest of circumstances.

(c) Suicides.

(d) Reconstruction of violent crimes.

(e) Violence in drama.

(f) Children and drama.

(g) Imitation.

(h) Animals.

(4) PORTRAYAL OF SEXUAL CONDUCT[46]

15-20 Research shows that audiences have generally become more liberal and relaxed about the portrayal of sex, but broadcasters cannot assume a universal climate of tolerance towards sexually explicit material. Offence may be given by making public and explicit what many regard as private and exclusive. Areas covered by the Code include:

(a) Factual programmes: where a news story involves a sexual aspect, it should be presented without undue exploitation.

(b) Discussion and phone-in programmes: programmes need to be scheduled with care and labelled to give warning of their likely content.

(c) Fiction: broadcasters must ensure that actual sexual intercourse is not transmitted. The broadcast of sexually explicit scenes before the watershed should always be a matter for judgment at senior levels. On radio, broadcasters must take into account the likely composition of the audience before scheduling more explicit portrayals of sexual activity.

(d) Children: a sexual relationship between an adult and a child or between underage young people can be a legitimate theme for programmes. It is the treatment which may make it improper or even unlawful. Explicit sexual acts between adults and children should not be transmitted.

---

[46] Code on Standards, cll.79–94

(e) Incest and child abuse.

(f) Animals.

(g) Nudity.

(h) Innuendo.

4. COMPLAINTS PROCEDURE

The BSC is charged with considering and adjudicating on complaints in pro-   **15-21**
grammes relating to its areas of interest, namely:

(a) unjust or unfair treatment;

(b) unwarranted infringement of privacy;

(c) the portrayal of violence or sexual conduct; and

(d) the alleged failure to attain standards of taste and decency.

The BSC's Codes are taken into account when considering complaints.

A complaint should generally be in writing.[47] The BSC will not entertain a complaint which is the subject of United Kingdom court proceedings. Further, where the person affected has a remedy in the United Kingdom courts, the BSC may decline to hear the complaint if it considers it inappropriate in the particular circumstances. The BSC can also refuse to hear complaints which are frivolous or which for any other reason it regards as inappropriate for it to entertain.[48] Decisions of the BSC are subject to judicial review, though the courts will be slow to interfere with the Commission's findings.[49]

It is unfortunate for broadcasters that the BSC on the one hand and the ITC and Radio Authority on the other can reach different conclusions: plainly, broadcasters have to live with the consequences of the most damning ruling. To address this issue, the BSC and Radio Authority have recently signed a memorandum of understanding setting out how complaints will be dealt with in cases of overlap to avoid double jeopardy wherever possible.[50]

A complaint under (a) or (b) ("a fairness complaint") is treated slightly differently to a complaint under (c) or (d) ("a standards complaint").

FAIRNESS COMPLAINT

This may be made by an individual or by a body of persons, whether incorpo-   **15-22**
rated or not,[51] though normally the complaint should be made by the person

---

[47] Broadcasting Act 1996, s.114(1).
[48] Broadcasting Act 1996, s.114.
[49] *R. v. BSC, exp. BBC* [2000] E.M.L.R. 587.
[50] Radio Authority/BSC press release: June 6, 2000.
[51] Confirmed in *R. v. Broadcasting Standards Commission,, ex p. British Broadcasting Corporation, ibid.*

245

directly affected by the broadcast. The complaint can be continued after a complainant's death.[52]

A personal representative, such as a family member, may make a complaint on behalf of the person directly affected if he is unable to do so. In addition, if the person affected by the complaint has died within five years of the broadcast, a personal representative, family member or someone closely connected to them can make a complaint. In considering the complaint in these circumstances, the BSC would have to consider whether the connection is strong enough.

In cases of unjust or unfair treatment the complainant (or the person he represents) must have either taken part in the programme and been the subject of the alleged treatment or, whether taking part or not, had a sufficiently direct interest in the subject-matter of that treatment.

In a privacy complaint, the complainant's privacy (or the person on whose behalf he is complaining) must have been infringed.

The BSC may refuse to entertain a fairness complaint if it appears to them not to have been made within a reasonable time after the programme was last broadcast.[53] This will normally be three months (six weeks in the case of radio programmes). The BSC must refuse to proceed with a complaint if it relates to a programme broadcast more than five years after the death of the person affected by it.[54]

A fairness complaint must be dealt with at a hearing or, if the BSC thinks fit, without a hearing.[55] Hearings are held in private. The complainant, broadcaster, programme-maker and any other person who the BSC considers might be able to assist will be given an opportunity to attend and be heard at the hearing.[56]

STANDARDS COMPLAINT

15-23   Anyone is at liberty to make a standards complaint about a broadcast programme or advertisement. Complaints must be made within two months from the last broadcast of a television programme or three weeks in the case of a radio programme—a shorter period than is allowed for a fairness complaint[57].

The legislation presumes that determinations will be made on written evidence, but the BSC may hold a formal hearing if it sees fit. Should there be a hearing, it will be held in private.[58] The complainant, broadcaster, programme-maker or any other person whom the BSC considers of assistance may be given an opportunity to attend and be heard at the hearing.[59]

---

[52] Broadcasting Act 1996, s.111(1), (2) and (7).
[53] *ibid.*, s.111(5).
[54] *ibid.*, s.111(4).
[55] *ibid.*, s.115(1).
[56] *ibid.*, s.115(2).
[57] *ibid.*, s.113.
[58] *ibid.*, s.116(1).
[59] *ibid.*, s.116(2).

DUTY TO RETAIN RECORDINGS

Broadcasters must keep copies of television programmes for 90 days and radio **15-24** programmes for 42 days after the day of broadcast to enable the BSC to consider either fairness or standards complaints.[60]

PUBLICATION OF BSC FINDINGS

After considering a complaint, the BSC may direct that their findings are to **15-25** be published in a particular manner (on television or radio or in the press) and within a particular period by the offending broadcaster.[61] The matters to be published may include a summary of the complaint, the BSC's findings on the complaint (or a summary) and, in the case of a standards complaint, any observations by the BSC on the complaint (or a summary). In addition, the BSC publishes its own reports of its findings.

Being required to broadcast an adverse finding is viewed as a serious and potentially embarrassing penalty and, for this reason, broadcasters should be careful to ensure compliance with the BSC's Codes. The ITC and the Radio Authority do not have any comparable powers[62]. Having said that, the BSC has no power to make financial awards, to impose fines, or to order the publication of an apology or correction.

The broadcasting regulators are obliged to arrange for the publication by broadcasts or otherwise of regular announcements publicising the BSC.[63] The Radio Authority's Programme Code, for example, states that each national licence-holder must broadcast such announcements six times a year, three of which should be in daytime.

---

[60] Broadcasting Act 1996, s.117.
[61] *ibid.*, s.119.
[62] See Chap. 13 at 5 (ITC) and Chap. 14 at 4 (Radio Authority).
[63] Broadcasting Act 1996, s.124.

Chapter 16

Newspapers and magazines

---

1. INTRODUCTION

16-01   The United Kingdom enjoys a buoyant newspaper and magazine sector. Newspapers and magazines are popular, with a tremendous range of publications on offer. But, at the same time, the public and politicians are wary of the power that can be exercised by the press.

It is true that the legal restraints on the United Kingdom press are amongst the toughest in the developed world. This is due largely to the rigours of our laws of libel and contempt.[1] From time to time, however, these restraints have not been felt to be adequate, particularly when it comes to the protection of privacy. During these periods of heightened mistrust of the press, there have been calls for new legislation, and especially in relation to privacy. The industry's response at these difficult times has been to tighten its system of self-regulation.

Matters reached crisis point in about 1990 after a series of high profile tabloid newspaper articles were considered by many to have brought the self-regulatory system into disrepute. The government appointed a departmental committee under Sir David Calcutt, Q.C. to investigate whether legislation was needed to give further protection to individual privacy from the activities of the press. The report of the Calcutt Committee was published in June 1990. It recommended the setting up of a Press Complaints Commission (PCC) in place of the then Press Council. The PCC would have 18 months to prove that self-regulation could work, failing which it was recommended that a statutory scheme be introduced.

This body was set up in 1991 and remains in existence to this day. Despite further periods of mistrust in the meantime, the PCC has been largely effective in keeping politicians at bay (principally by taking action in very high profile cases) and, for the present at least, there seems to be no political appetite for reopening the debate in favour of privacy legislation. Whether the PCC has been as effective in protecting the interests of the public at large, however, is a different question and beyond the scope of this text.

Whilst libel and contempt are still the main legal areas of concern for the press, given past swings of public opinion in this area, it is important for those

---

[1] See Chaps. 3 and 4

in the press to be fully conversant with the terms of the PCC's Code of Practice. Indeed, there is a trend for publishers to include a provision in the contracts of their editors and journalists requiring them to observe the Code. It is not known whether disciplinary actions against those responsible for actions amounting to a breach of the Code have taken place, though the current mood suggested by the press is that this is a distinct possibility, at least in serious cases.

2. PCC ORGANISATIONAL STRUCTURE

The PCC's primary function is to hear complaints from members of the public **16-02** about possible breaches of the Code by magazines or newspapers. It will also give general advice to editors on ethical issues. To achieve these objectives (and in an attempt to balance the interests of the press and public) a number of separate bodies have been created under the umbrella of the PCC. The key components are the following:

- The Commission: this has 16 members drawn from the press and public, of whom a majority are independent of the press. The remaining seven members are representative of national, regional and local newspapers and the magazine industry. It is the Commission which adjudicates on complaints. The Chairman is appointed by the press, but he is not entitled to be connected with the industry.

- Appointments Commission: this body selects members of the Commission. It is made up of the Chairman of the PCC, the Chairman of the Press Standards Board of Finance ("Pressbof") and three independent members (the public nominees). There is therefore a majority of members on this body who are independent.

- Code of Practice Committee: the Code of Practice is kept under review by this Committee. It will consider suggested changes to the Code from members of the public, from individual members or from the industry reacting to changes. It is composed of a cross-section of members of the national, regional and local press.

- Pressbof: the funding of the PCC is arranged by Pressbof. This body is composed of chairmen of several related trade associations and collects registration fees from across the newspaper and magazine publishing industry. It is modelled on, ASBOF, the equivalent body which funds the advertising industry's self-regulatory system described below.

The PCC costs in excess of £1.2 million per annum to run.[2] It is considered to be effective for the funding and operational sides of the PCC to be kept separate in order to give greater impartiality to its decisions.

---

[2] PCC's 1998 Annual Report.

3. THE PCC CODE OF PRACTICE[3]

16-03 The PCC's Code of Practice begins with a number of statements of principle. These include the following:

- all members of the press have a duty to maintain the highest professional and ethical standards;

- the Code is the cornerstone of the system of self-regulation to which the industry has made a binding commitment;

- editors and publishers must ensure that the Code is observed rigorously not only by their staff but also by anyone who contributes to their publications; and

- it is essential to the workings of an agreed Code that it be honoured not only to the letter but in the full spirit.

Notwithstanding its genesis, the Code is concerned with far more than just privacy. It is worth mentioning the full range of topics covered by the Code:

Clause 1	Accuracy
Clause 2	Opportunity to reply
Clause 3	Privacy*
Clause 4	Harassment*
Clause 5	Intrusion into grief or shock
Clause 6	Children*
Clause 7	Children in sex cases
Clause 8	Listening devices*
Clause 9	Hospitals*
Clause 10	Innocent relatives and friends*
Clause 11	Misrepresentation*
Clause 12	Victims of sexual assault
Clause 13	Discrimination
Clause 14	Financial journalism
Clause 15	Confidential sources
Clause 16	Payment for articles

---

[3] The latest version of the PCC Code of Practice was ratified by the PCC on November 26, 1997 and appears in the CD ROM accompanying this text. It can also be downloaded from www.pcc.org.uk

Many of the more important provisions, particularly those concerned with privacy issues, are subject to exceptions where the publisher can show a public interest. The clauses which may be susceptible to a "public interest" defence are marked above with an asterisk.

The Code does not give an exhaustive definition of "public interest", but states that it includes:

(i)   detecting or preventing crime or a serious misdemeanour;

(ii) protecting public health and safety; and

(iii) preventing the public from being misled by some statement or action of an individual or organisation.

The Code also states that, in cases involving children, editors must demonstrate an exceptional public interest to override the normally paramount interests of the child.

Unlike the Codes seen so far (which all have a statutory origin), the PCC Code is a brief document. It is narrow in scope and imposes generalised obligations. This gives flexibility, as does the commitment for the Code to be honoured "not only to the letter but in the full spirit". We will see a similar approach in the advertising industry's self-regulatory scheme in Chapter 17.

4. COMPLAINTS PROCEDURE

Anyone can make a complaint about a breach of the Code and the first step **16-04** (considered initially by a member of the PCC's Secretariat) is to determine whether it falls within the PCC's remit.

If it does, the complaint is brought to the attention of the editor of the relevant publication. The editor is asked to investigate and resolve the complaint within a matter of days. This is the manner in which most complaints are resolved and can lead to the publication of an apology or correction, or for an opportunity for the complainant to reply.

If this does not lead to the satisfactory disposal of the complaint, the matter is referred to the Commission for adjudication. The Commission collects most of its evidence by correspondence with the complainant, the editor and sometimes third parties. Once it has collected all the material which it considers it needs, a dossier is put together and presented to the Commission at one of its monthly meetings. At the meeting the Commission decides whether to accept or reject the complaint.

Every critical adjudication must be published in full and with due prominence by the publication concerned. This often means publication in the news section, and generally within the first four or five pages of the newspaper. The PCC has, on occasion, required republication of an apology if it considers that the original apology was not given adequate prominence. A rejected complaint does not have to be published, although the editor will sometimes choose to publish the favourable outcome.

There is of course no statutory obligation to comply with the PCC's findings, though failure to do so would bring the voluntary regime into disrepute. Unlike its predecessor, the Press Council, there is no requirement for complainants to waive their right to sue in the courts before a complaint is heard.

It is worth noting that there is something of a tendency growing up for aggrieved parties to contact the PCC in advance of a publication if they consider that the Code is being broken. For example, the PCC may be contacted if a "media circus" has descended on the complainant's house. Sometimes the PCC will intervene by contacting the editors of known publications, though this procedure tends to be informal and inconsistently applied.

Unlike the voluntary regime operated by the advertising industry, there is no procedure in place for reviewing or appealing against PCC adjudications. It is also unclear whether adjudications are susceptible to judicial review. In 1996 Ian Brady, one of the Moors murderers, did seek leave to bring proceedings for judicial review of the Commission's decision to reject a complaint against *The Sun* newspaper.[4] The complaint concerned the publication of a photograph of Brady in Ashworth Special Hospital taken with a camera fitted with a telephoto lens. In finding against Brady, the Court of Appeal left open the question whether the PCC's adjudications could be challenged through the courts.

5. EFFECTIVENESS OF THE PCC

16-05   The death of Diana, Princess of Wales, in 1997 had a significant impact on the behaviour of the press. Although initial reports that the death had been caused by pursuing photographers are now accepted as having been unfounded, the PCC moved quickly to avoid long-term damage to the industry.

The provisions in the Code dealing with harassment were bolstered within weeks: they were specifically addressed to journalists and photographers, and "persistent pursuit" was added as a form of harassment that could not be undertaken unless it was in the public interest.

The PCC has also increasingly emphasised the importance of its previous decisions, which it hopes will become a growing body of case law for future complaints. This so-called body of case law was alluded to in considering how Prince William should be treated by the press during his time at Eton. Reliance was placed on the previous complaint concerning harassment of a schoolboy in Accrington.[5]

Against this, the wording of the Code is fairly loose and does allow a degree of flexibility in interpretation. This is particularly so in relation to what is to be regarded as in the public interest, which can be used as a defence to a

---

[4] *R. v. PCC, ex p. Stewart-Brady*, *Times Law Reports*, November 22, 1996.
[5] PCC Annual Report 1995, p. 10. There is now a specific provision in the Code stating that young people should be free to complete their time at school without unnecessary intrusion. Further guidance on coverage of Prince William's private life was given when he became 18 in June 2000.

number of charges of wrongdoing under the Code. The PCC's adjudications in this area will always be subject to careful scrutiny.

Another difficulty is that the Code normally acts only retrospectively. This allows for an element of cynicism on the part of editors which might be less apparent were there, for example, the prospect of contempt proceedings. Whilst the PCC has started to address this issue by acting on occasion before publication this is exceptional and editors may take advantage of this weakness. Other possible weaknesses are the lack of financial penalties, and the language of the Code, which leaves much to the judgment of the editor.

The PCC has a number of strengths too. It maintains that it deals with most complaints in less than two months and complainants incur no legal fees in the process. Most individuals who file complaints could not afford to sue, and they might not have a legal remedy or be entitled to legal aid even if they did sue. It is also likely that publications will co-operate with the PCC in ways which a court would be unlikely or unable to achieve.

In terms of statistics, the public does appear to be using the PCC. It dealt with 3,023 complaints in 1996, 2,944 in 1997 and 2,601 in 1998. Whether this decline in numbers is due to satisfaction or dissatisfaction with the service cannot be discerned from the figures alone. However, the PCC maintains that it was able to broker settlements of the complaints in the vast majority of cases, only needing to adjudicate on 81, 82 and 86 in each year respectively. It is worth noting that the majority of complaints are concerned with inaccuracy, with 10 to 15 per cent concerning privacy.

6. NATIONAL UNION OF JOURNALISTS' CODE OF CONDUCT

The National Union of Journalists is the largest trade union in this sector, representing some 25,000 journalists in the United Kingdom. It has issued a Code of Conduct which its members agree to honour.[6]   **16-06**

The Code of Conduct is less detailed than the PCC Code but touches on some similar areas. For example, it contains provisions dealing with accuracy, the making of apologies, intrusions into grief and distress and discrimination. But the provisions tend to be less robust or not present at all. For example, the NUJ Code has nothing which refers specifically to the use of listening devices[7] or inquiries at hospitals.[8] These are, however, arguably caught by a more generalised provision stating that information, photographs and illustrations should be obtained "only by straightforward means" unless there are "overriding considerations of the public interest".

Furthermore, when there are provisions dealing with the same subject-matter as the PCC Code they are sometimes dealt with in a less robust manner.

---

[6] This is reproduced in the CD ROM accompanying this text. It may also be downloaded from www.gn.apc.org/media/nujcode.html
[7] NUJ Code of Conduct cl.5.
[8] *ibid.*, cl.6.

For example, the PCC Code requires an opportunity to reply "when reasonably called for". The Code offers a right of reply "when the issue is of sufficient importance", arguably a lower standard.

It is the weakest of all the voluntary provisions set out in this text, and provides no mechanism for public complaint.

Chapter 17

Advertising

1. INTRODUCTION

Advertising operates in a complex legal and regulatory environment. It is **17-01** subject to the general laws described in Part I. For example, advertising should not be defamatory or infringe a third party's intellectual property rights.

It is also constrained by detailed regulation. That regulation is usually determined by the medium on which the advertising appears.[1] Our description of the various forms of regulation therefore appears in the overall context of reviewing the regulation of a particular medium. Advertising on the BBC, in so far as it is permitted, is considered in Chapter 12, advertising on commercial television in Chapter 13, and advertising on commercial radio in Chapter 14.

This approach does not work in the most important remaining area of regulation, namely advertising in non-broadcast media (which includes press, cinema and sales promotions), where legislation has not sought to impose a single overarching regulator.[2] In this context, regulation is left principally to the advertising industry itself. That is the subject of this chapter.

2. REGULATORY FRAMEWORK FOR NON-BROADCAST MEDIA

The advertising industry has created three related bodies which between them serve to regulate non-broadcast advertising. They are the Committee of Advertising Practice, the Advertising Standards Authority and the Advertising Standards Board of Finance.

COMMITTEE OF ADVERTISING PRACTICE

Just as the pressure for legislation led to the creation of the Press Complaints **17-02** Commission (PCC) and its forebears, similar pressures led to the now

---

[1] This is not always the case, particularly where there are strong public policy reasons for regulating a particular sector. For example, prescription medicines and financial services are subject to special regulations, irrespective of the medium where the advertising appears. Specialist regulations of this kind are beyond the scope of this text.

[2] The PCC, for example, regulates only editorial, not advertising, content.

well-regarded system championed by the advertising industry. Indeed, the origins of the Committee of Advertising Practice (CAP) go back much further than the PCC: the CAP was set up in 1961 following the launch of commercial television a few years before. Commercials on television had to comply with a single Code and this prompted the industry to create the CAP to regulate non-broadcast advertising.

Its members consist of the trade and professional bodies that make up the advertising business.[3] So advertisers, agencies, direct marketers and various platform owners (including cinemas, newspapers and poster site operators) are all represented. CAP's chairman is elected by its members and will usually be someone from a business with advertising interests.

CAP's functions include the following:

(a) devising and amending the British Codes of Advertising and Sales Promotion. CAP has issued codes addressing several key areas of advertising. The most important are the Advertising Code and the Sales Promotion Code. In addition, there is a Cigarette Code, as well as specific rules covering the following topics: alcoholic drinks, children, motoring, environmental claims, health and beauty products and therapies, slimming, distance selling, database practice, employment and business opportunities, financial services and products, betting and gaming. The Codes are described in more detail below;

(b) co-ordinating the implementation of sanctions by its members;

(c) providing free pre-publication advice (including the compulsory vetting of cigarette advertising); and

(d) issuing help notes and ad alerts on current topics of concern to the advertising industry and public.

CAP's detailed work is assisted by two standing panels, the General Media Panel and the Sales Promotion and Direct Response Panel. These panels provide advice for the industry and help interpret the Codes. They can be used as a forum to reassess recommendations given by the CAP Secretariat. They can also be asked to look at a complaint before the Advertising Standards Authority has adjudicated.

Advertising Standards Authority

17-03   Soon after CAP was set up it was realised that there needed to be independent supervision of the industry's self-regulatory arrangements. The ASA was accordingly set up in 1962 to fulfil this role and to ensure that advertising and sales promotions comply with the Codes.

---

[3] There are more than 20 members, including the Advertising Association, the Institute of Practitioners in Advertising, the Direct Marketing Association, the Newspaper Society, the Internet Advertising Bureau and the Royal Mail.

The ASA is a limited company independent of the advertising industry and the government. It operates through a Council of 12 members, of whom the majority — including the chairman—are from outside the world of advertising.

The ASA's functions include:

(a) investigating complaints against advertisements and promotions in non-broadcast media;

(b) researching and monitoring issues, advertisements and promotions of concern; and

(c) issuing educational materials and publicising its activities.

CAP and the ASA share a joint secretariat, but their respective functions have been devised with the aim of balancing the views of the industry and public.

ADVERTISING STANDARDS BOARD OF FINANCE

Initially the funding for the CAP and ASA system of regulation was furnished **17-04** by the Advertising Association, the trade association for the whole industry. However, in 1974 the government insisted that the system needed to be made tighter if statutory regulation was to be avoided. This necessitated significantly increased funding, and the Advertising Standards Board of Finance ("ASBOF") was accordingly set up the following year.

The funding of the scheme is now achieved through a levy on advertising and direct marketing revenues which is managed by ASBOF. ASBOF sets the framework for industry policy-making and is responsible for CAP. ASBOF's members are drawn from a similar industry constituency as CAP.

3. THE BRITISH CODES OF ADVERTISING AND SALES PROMOTION ("THE CODES")[4]

(1) PUBLICATIONS COVERED BY THE CODES

The Codes begin with an introduction stating that they apply to the follow- **17-05** ing[5]:

(a) advertisements in newspapers, magazines, brochures, leaflets, circulars, mailings, fax transmissions, catalogues, follow-up literature and other electronic and printed material;

---

[4] The Codes are reproduced in the CD ROM accompanying this text. The Codes can also be downloaded from the CAP website at www.cap.org.uk. The Codes are often referred to as "the CAP Codes".
[5] At cl.1.1 of the Codes.

257

(b) posters and other promotional media in public places;

(c) cinema and video commercials;

(d) advertisements in non-broadcast electronic media;

(e) viewdata services;

(f) marketing databases containing consumers" personal information;

(g) sales promotions;

(h) advertisement promotions; and

(i) advertisements and promotions covered by the Cigarette Code.

There is then a list of matters to which the Codes are expressly stated not to apply:

(a) broadcast commercials[6];

(b) the contents of premium rate telephone calls[7];

(c) advertisements in foreign media;

(d) health-related claims in advertisements and promotions addressed only to the medical, dental, veterinary and allied professions;

(e) classified private advertisements;

(f) statutory, public, police and other official notices;

(g) works of art exhibited in public or private;

(h) private correspondence;

(i) oral communications, including telephone calls;

(j) press releases and other public relations material;

(k) the content of books and editorial communications;

(l) regular competitions such as crosswords;

(m) flyposting;

(n) packages, wrappers, labels, tickets and price lists unless they advertise another product, a sales promotion or are visible in an advertisement;

(o) point of sale displays except those covered by the Sales Promotion Code and the Cigarette Code; and

(p) political advertisements.[8]

---

[6] They are the responsibility of the ITC and the Radio Authority: see Chaps. 13 and 14.
[7] This is the responsibility of the Independent Committee for the Supervision of Standards of Telephone Information Services ("ICSTIS"). See Chap. 18.
[8] As defined in cl.12.1 of the Advertising Code.

This statement of remit is deliberately wide in scope. For example, there is no definition of what amounts to an "advertisement". This gives the ASA the ability to look at the spirit of what an advertiser is doing as much as at the letter. This could be seen as a weakness as much as a strength in that arguably some of the provisions of the Codes lack precision, though in practice this is a charge seldom levelled by either advertiser or consumer.

On the other hand, this lack of rigidity does give flexibility and this has already been seen in the way the ASA has come to deal with complaints arising from Internet advertising. The ASA has already ruled that "non-broadcast electronic media" includes advertisements on websites. It did not require significant rule changes to do so.

(2) ADVERTISING CODE

(a) General principles

The Advertising Code begins at clause 2 with a statement of some general **17-06** principles governing advertisements. They include the following:

- all advertisements should be legal, decent, honest and truthful[9];

- all advertisements should be prepared with a sense of responsibility to consumers and to society[10];

- all advertisements should respect the principles of fair competition generally accepted in business[11];

- primary responsibility for observing the Code falls on advertisers, though others (such as agencies and publishers) must also accept an obligation to abide by the Codes[12];

- the Code must be obeyed in spirit as well as in the letter.[13]

(b) Specific provisions

It is worth highlighting here those provisions which tend to be encountered on a more regular basis by advertisers[14]:

Substantiation: clause 3

Before submitting an advertisement for publication, advertisers must hold **17-07** documentary evidence to prove all claims, whether direct or implied, that are

---

[9] Advertising Code, cl.2.1.
[10] *ibid.*, cl.2.2.
[11] *ibid.*, cl.2.3.
[12] *ibid.*, cl.2.5.
[13] *ibid.*, cl.2.8.
[14] The detailed provisions of the Advertising Code appear in the CD ROM accompanying in this text.

capable of objective substantiation.[15] The evidence must be sent without delay to the ASA if requested. If there is significant division of opinion about any claims, they should not be portrayed as universally agreed.[16]

Legality: clause 4

17-08   Advertisers have primary responsibility for ensuring that their advertisements are legal and do not incite anyone to break the law.

Decency: clause 5

17-09   Advertisements should contain nothing that is likely to cause serious or widespread offence. Particular care should be taken to avoid causing offence on the grounds of race, religion, sex, sexual orientation or disability.[17] It is worth noting that ageism is not mentioned in terms by the Code.

Compliance with the Codes will be judged on the context, medium, audience, product and prevailing standards of decency. So, for example, an advertisement may be acceptable if it is published in a men's magazine or at a cinema before an adult film, but not if it were to appear at a bus stop poster or in a religious newspaper. Context is critical and the Codes state that a distasteful advertisement will not necessarily fail the decency requirement.

Honesty: clause 6

17-10   Advertisers should not exploit the credulity, lack of knowledge or inexperience of consumers.

Truthfulness: clause 7

17-11   No advertisement should mislead by inaccuracy, ambiguity, exaggeration, omission or otherwise.

Fear and distress: clause 9

17-12   No advertisement should cause fear or distress without good reason.

Safety: clause 10

17-13   Advertisements should not show or encourage unsafe practices except in the context of promoting safety.

Violence and anti-social behaviour: clause 11.1

17-14   Advertisements should contain nothing that condones or is likely to provoke violence or antisocial behaviour.

---

[15] Advertising Code cl.3.1. cl.14 provides further guidance where advertisers are relying on testimonials.
[16] *ibid.*, cl.3.2.
[17] *ibid.*, cl.5.1.

Political advertising: clause 12

Any advertisement, whenever published, whose principal function is to influ- **17-15** ence voters in elections or referendums is exempt from the Codes, but advertisers are urged to make their identity clear. However, advertisements concerning government policy as distinct from party policy are covered by the Codes.[18]

Protection of privacy: clause 13

Advertisers frequently use celebrities to help promote their campaigns. As **17-16** described elsewhere,[19] there may be a risk of a claim for passing off (unless prior consent is obtained) if the execution implies that the celebrity has indorsed the advertiser's product. The Advertising Code also contains provisions in this context which may limit an advertiser's ability to use an individual to promote their campaign without permission. It is worth setting out the key extracts in this context:

> "13.1 Advertisers should not unfairly portray or refer to people in adverse or offensive way. Advertisers are urged to obtain written permission before:
>
>> a. referring to or portraying members of the public or their identifiable possessions; the use of crowd scenes or general public locations may be acceptable without permission
>> b. referring to people with a public profile . . .
>> c. implying any personal approval of the advertised product; advertisers should recognise that those who do not wish to be associated with the product may have a legal claim.
>
> 13.2 Prior permission may not be needed when the advertisement contains nothing that is inconsistent with the position or views of the person featured.
> 13.3 References to anyone who is deceased should be handled with particular care to avoid causing offence or distress."

It will be apparent that the provisions in this clause in fact offer little in the way of protection of privacy. They are couched in terms which do no more than urge advertisers to behave in a particular fashion. Indeed, the key phrase in this section is that which reminds advertisers that they might be sued for passing off. In practice advertisers need to be aware of this section's provisions, but will find that it does not add significantly to their existing legal obligations.

---

[18] See also Chap. 10 at 5 on media coverage during elections.
[19] See Chap. 6 at 3 and Chap. 25 at 4.

Prices, free offers, availability of products and guarantees: clauses 15, 16, 17 and 18

17-17   The Advertising Code contains numerous provisions aimed at ensuring the honesty and legality of advertisements where products and terms of purchase feature prominently. These provisions offer some measure of consumer protection over and beyond that contained in legislation.

By way of example, clause 16.1 states that there is no objection to making a free offer conditional on the purchase of other items. But liability for any costs should be made clear in all material featuring the offer. An offer should only be described as free if consumers pay no more than:

(a)   the current public rates of postage;

(b)   the actual cost of freight or delivery;

(c)   the cost, including incidental expenses, of any travel involved if consumers collect the offer.[20]

The ASA is extremely active in this area of terms of purchase and has an important role to play.

Comparative advertising: clauses 19 to 22

17-18   The key provisions dealing with comparative advertising are as follows:

"Comparisons

19.1 Comparisons can be explicit or implied and can relate to advertisers' own products or to those of their competitors . . .

19.2 The comparisons should be clear and fair and not selected in a way that gives the advertiser an artificial advantage.

Denigration

20.1 Advertisers should not unfairly attack or discredit other businesses or their products.

20.2 The only acceptable use of another's broken or defaced products in advertisements is in the illustration of comparative tests, and the source, nature and results of these should be clear.

Exploitation of goodwill

21.1 Advertisers should not make unfair use of the goodwill attached to the trade mark, name, brand or the advertising campaign of any other organisation.

---

[20] Advertising Code cl.16.1.

Imitation

22.1 No advertisement should so closely resemble any other that it misleads or causes confusion."

In addition to these obligations, advertisers should be mindful of the provisions of the Trade Marks Act 1994 and the Control of Misleading Advertisements (Comparative Advertising) (Amendment) Regulations 2000.[21] This is reflected in Addendum 1 of the Code.

(3) SALES PROMOTION CODE

The Sales Promotion Code contains detailed and extremely helpful guidance **17-19** on the mechanics of how to run sales promotions. These promotions usually involve the provision of additional benefits designed to make goods or services more attractive to purchasers. Clearly, there is considerable scope for abuse and the Code aims to ensure that, throughout the lifetime of a campaign, promoters and consumers know exactly where they stand.

(a) General principles

As with the Advertising Code, the Sales Promotion Code begins with a state- **17-20** ment of some general principles. They are very similar to those which we have seen governing advertisements generally and include the following:

- all sales promotions should be legal, decent, honest and truthful[22];

- all sales promotions should be prepared with a sense of responsibility to consumers and to society. They should be conducted equitably, promptly and efficiently and should be seen to deal fairly and honourably with consumers. Promoters should avoid causing unnecessary disappointment[23];

- all sales promotions should respect the principles of fair competition generally accepted in business[24];

- primary responsibility for observing the Code falls on promoters, though others (such as intermediaries and agencies) also accept an obligation to abide by the Codes[25];

- the Code must be obeyed in spirit as well as in the letter.[26]

---

[21] see Chap. 6 at 2(7).
[22] Sales Promotion Code, cl.27.1.
[23] *ibid.*, cl.27.2.
[24] *ibid.*, cl.27.3.
[25] *ibid.*, cl.27.5.
[26] *ibid.*, cl.27.8.

(b) Specific provisions

Apart from the points just mentioned, the following provisions tend to be encountered on a more regular basis by promoters. Many of these mirror similar provisions in the Advertising Code.

Public interest: clause 28.1

17-21   Unlike the Advertising Code, there is a specific requirement that sales promotions should not be designed or conducted in a way that conflicts with the public interest. This reflects the particular risks, especially of direct economic loss, that can flow from promotions.

   Promotions should also contain nothing that condones or is likely to provoke violent or antisocial behaviour, nuisance, personal injury or damage to property.[27]

Substantiation: clause 29.1

17-22   Promoters must be able to demonstrate that they have complied with the Code by submitting documentary evidence without delay when asked by the ASA.

Legality: clause 30.1

17-23   Promoters have primary responsibility for ensuring that what they do is legal and that they do not incite anyone to break the law.

Honesty: clause 31.1

17-24   Promoters should not abuse consumers' trust or exploit their lack of knowledge or experience.

Truthfulness: clause 32.1

17-25   No sales promotion should mislead by inaccuracy, ambiguity, exaggeration, omission or otherwise.

Protection of consumers by promoters: clause 33

17-26   This clause includes provisions to the effect that promoters should make all reasonable efforts to ensure that their promotions, including product samples and adventurous activities, are safe. The Code states that particular care is required when sales promotions are addressed to children or when products intended for adults might fall into the hands of children.[28]

---

[27] Sales Promotion Code, cl.28.1.
[28] *ibid.*, cl.33.1.

Promotions should be designed and conducted in a way that respects the right of consumers to a reasonable degree of privacy and freedom from annoyance.[29]

Consumers should be told before entry if participants may be required to become involved in any of the promoters' publicity or advertising. Prizewinners should not be compromised by the publication of excessively detailed personal information.[30]

Availability: clause 35

This clause includes provisions requiring promoters to be able to demonstrate that they have made a reasonable estimate of likely response and that they are capable of meeting that response. This applies in all cases except prize promotions, where the minimum number of prizes available and any limitations should be made clear to participants. **17-27**

The mechanics of running a sales promotion: clauses 37 to 40

The provisions which appear in these clauses are critical to the running of many sales promotions. They can be summarised as follows[31]: **17-28**

- how to enter and what conditions, if any, apply to the promotion (participation: clause 37);

- how the sales promotion should be administered (administration: clause 38);

- any terms and conditions that may apply where consumers have to make a payment to participate (free offers and promotions where consumers pay: clause 39);

- how to enter a sales promotion with prizes and what conditions apply (promotions with prizes: clause 40)

These provisions are key to the running of sales promotion campaigns.

Advertisement promotions: clause 41

Advertisement promotions (or "advertorials") should be designed and presented in such a way that it is clear that they are advertisements. **17-29**

Charity-linked promotions: clause 42

The Code sets out detailed provisions covering the situation where a charity is to benefit from a promotion. In particular the promotion should identify the **17-30**

---

[29] Sales Promotion Code, cl.33.2.
[30] *ibid.*, cl.33.3.
[31] The provisions are reproduced in full in the CD ROM accompanying this text

charity and be able to demonstrate that the charity consents to the advertising or promotion.[32]

4. COMPLAINTS PROCEDURE

17-31 Complaints about matters falling within the scope of the Codes are made to the ASA Council. They should be put in writing, normally within three months of the advertisement's appearance, and accompanied by a copy of the advertisement or a note of where and when it appeared. If the complaint is also the subject of court proceedings, the ASA will normally decline to investigate.

If the complainant is a member of the public, the ASA will not disclose his identity without permission (unless subsequently required to do so by a court). On the other hand, pressure groups or industry competitors making complaints must be prepared for their identities to be disclosed in order for their complaint to proceed.

The fact-finding exercise necessary to deal with a complaint is conducted by the Secretariat. The Secretariat will then produce a report for the ASA Council with recommendations. The Secretariat may instruct advertisers or promoters to take interim action pending a Council ruling to avoid further harm. There is no provision for the Council or the Secretariat to hear oral evidence.

In exceptional circumstances, the ASA Council can be asked to reconsider its adjudication. Written requests for a review (they are not formal appeals as such) should be sent within 14 days of notification of the adjudication to the Independent Reviewer of ASA Adjudications, Bloomsbury House, 74–77 Great Russell Street, London WC1B 3DA. They should come only from the complainant or from the advertiser's or industry complainant's chairman, chief executive or equivalent.

A review can be made where additional evidence becomes available or where a substantial flaw was present in the ASA Council decision.

The independent reviewer will evaluate the request with two assessors, the chairman of ASBOF and the chairman of the ASA. He will then make recommendations to the ASA Council, which will then reconsider its earlier decision. The ASA's decision is final, though it may be possible in rare cases to seek a judicial review from the High Court on the basis of procedural unfairness.[33]

5. EFFECTIVENESS OF THE ASA

17-32 In determining the effectiveness of the ASA, similar considerations apply as apply to the PCC. The sanctions operated within the context of the advertis-

---

[32] The provisions are at cl.42.1 which appear in the appendix.
[33] This was first decided in *R. v. Advertising Standards Authority, ex p. Insurance Services PLC*, *Times Law Reports*, July 14, 1989. Successful challenges have been made on this basis, but the test to be satisfied is a high one.

ing industry's self-regulatory scheme are entirely unlike the blunt instruments of damages, costs, injunctions and fines that may be available from the courts. The industry relies on more commercially driven sanctions, although they stop short of making financial restitution. The sanctions available to the ASA include the following:

- The advertiser or promoter being banned from access to further advertising space.

- The ruling being published in the ASA's monthly report (including on the Internet). This may have some deterrent value, though in certain circumstances an advertiser may positively relish an adverse, controversial finding.

- Trading sanctions being invoked by a relevant trade body with which the advertiser or promoter is connected. This is a measure of last resort, and assumes that the advertiser in question actually belongs to a body which is a member of the CAP. If the advertiser is unwilling to comply with ASA rulings, it is less likely that he will be a member of a CAP association.

- If a misleading advertisement or promotion continues to be displayed after an ASA ruling, the council has the statutory power to refer the matter to the Director-General of Fair Trading.[34] The Director-General can then seek an injunction from the court to prohibit the further publication or dissemination of the offending advertisement. In practice, the Director-General seldom uses these powers, but they are an interesting example of "co-regulation", i.e. statutory and industry regulation working together.

Though these sanctions may lack real financial weight, there are a number of important advantages to the scheme. The Codes are observed in spirit as well as to the letter. Most complaints are resolved within four to eight weeks. The scheme is free, and complainants do not need to employ lawyers. It also has the support of the industry, which is therefore more likely to respond positively individually and as a group to adverse findings.

ASA statistics indicate a generally increasing level of complaints year on year. In 1980, there were 6,533 compared with 10,678 in 1997 and 12,217 in 1998. Most of these complaints are dealt with without the need for formal adjudications. For example, in 1996, of the total 12,217 complaints, 1,925 were upheld, 589 were not upheld, 673 were outstanding at the year end and the balance were either resolved informally or not investigated.[35]

Notwithstanding (or perhaps because of) these complaints,[36] there are currently no major threats to the system of industry self-regulation and the ASA's

---

[34] Control of Misleading Advertisements Regulations 1988, as amended by the Control of Misleading Advertisements (Amendment) Regulations 2000.

[35] Because they were either outside remit, not justified, there was no case to answer or they were withdrawn.

[36] They represent a tiny percentage of all paid-for advertising.

immediate future seems to be secure. It is true to say that the combined forces of the ASA and CAP have become established as a powerful and largely effective means of self-regulation for non-broadcast media. Indeed, so strong is their position that it has even been suggested that they should extend their influence into new areas like advertising on digital television, given its convergence with the Internet where the CAP already has a role.

Chapter 18

Premium rate telephone services

1. REGULATORY FRAMEWORK

Premium rate telephone services are charged on a different basis to ordinary telephone calls. The overall charge to customers is shared between the telephone company (for the carriage of the call) and the service provider (for the content). Such services are regulated by the Independent Committee for the Supervision of Standards of Telephone Information Services (ICSTIS).

18-01

ICSTIS is a non-profit-making limited company financed by the industry. It consists of around 10 members who are independent of the industry. The role of ICSTIS is to supervise both the content of and promotional material for premium rate services and to enforce its Codes of Practice.

2. THE CODES OF PRACTICE

ICSTIS has a Code of Practice which is similar in style and approach to the British Codes of Advertising and Sales Promotion.[1] It provides for such issues as:

18-02

- ICSTIS's terms of reference (clause 1);

- the placing of responsibility for compliance with the Code on the service provider (clause 2);

- the requirement to be legal, decent, honest and truthful (clause 3);

- the approach to specific services, such as children's services, competitions, virtual chat and services of a sexual nature (clause 4); and

- procedures and sanctions (clause 5).

In addition, ICSTIS has a Live Conversation Services Code of Practice which provides further regulation in respect of services involving two-way live

---

[1] Chap. 17.

speech. This Code and the general Code referred to above are reproduced in full in the CD ROM accompanying this text.[2] ICSTIS has also produced Guidelines on how it interprets and applies the provisions of the Code of Practice.

3. COMPLAINTS PROCEDURE

18-03 This is described in clause 5 of the Code of Practice. ICSTIS will investigate all complaints received within a reasonable period from the time when the call was made. The ICSTIS secretariat can itself initiate a complaint where there appears to be a breach of the Code.

If an apparent breach of the Code is of a minor nature, causing little consumer harm, the "informal procedure" may be used. In such cases:

(a) The service provider will be contacted and informed of the apparent breach.

(b) If the service provider agrees that a breach of the Code has taken place, the service provider will be required to remedy the breach. No other sanction will be imposed or any administrative charge levied.

(c) The service provider will be sent a letter confirming what has been agreed.

(d) If the service provider disputes the breach, the standard procedure may be invoked.

The standard procedure is more formal. The service provider will be given all the necessary information about the complaint and will be given a reasonable time in which to respond. In the absence of any special circumstances, this response will be required within five working days. In special circumstances, a shorter time limit may be set—but this will be no less than 24 hours.[3]

The committee may request an oral hearing if it wishes. It will then decide whether there has been a breach of the Code. ICSTIS may, at its discretion, review adjudications and/or sanctions in the light of new information. The sanctions that ICSTIS may impose include:

• requiring the service provider to remedy the breach;

• requiring an assurance from the service provider, or any associated individual, relating to future behaviour;

• requiring pre-vetting of material by the service provider;

---

[2] They may also be downloaded from the ICSTIS website at www.icstis.org.uk or obtained from ICSTIS, Third Floor, Alton House, 177 High Holborn, London WC1V 7AA (tel: 020 7240 5511).
[3] Where it appears to the secretariat that a breach of the Code has taken place which is serious and requires urgent remedy, the "emergency procedure" will be invoked: cl.5.5

- recommending to any relevant network operator that access to some or all of the numbers allocated to the service provider should be barred;

- recommending to all network operators that the service provider and/or any associated individual should be prohibited from providing a particular service;

- imposing an appropriate fine on the service provider to be collected by ICSTIS. Non-payment of a fine will be considered to be a breach of the Code;

- recommending to all network operators that the service provider and/or any associated individual should no longer be permitted to provide any premium rate services;

- requiring, in the case of virtual chat services, that service providers pay reasonable and valid claims for compensation.

All service providers found to be in breach of the Code may be invoiced for the administrative and legal costs of the work undertaken by ICSTIS.

Chapter 19

Cinema, video and computer games

1. INTRODUCTION

19-01 This section considers the regulation of cinema, video and computer games. They are dealt with together because, in certain respects, they have a common regulator—the British Board of Film Classification (BBFC). However, the BBFC does not enjoy a monopoly: the Video Standards Council and the Cinema Advertising Association each have a role to play. As we shall see, regulation in this area is based on a somewhat complex mixture of statute and industry self-regulation.

2. BRITISH BOARD OF FILM CLASSIFICATION

The BBFC is an independent, non-governmental body. Its main function is the classification of films and videos. Classification for the two media is conducted on a slightly different legal basis.

(1) FILM CLASSIFICATION

19-02 The BBFC classifies films on behalf of local authorities which license premises for film exhibition under the Cinemas Act 1985. Local authorities could, if they wished, choose to carry out the classification themselves, though in practice this almost never happens. In this sense, the BBFC acts on a non-statutory footing and exhibition of a film not classified by them will not constitute an offence *per se* (though local authorities would be obliged to undertake their own classification).

(2) CLASSIFICATION OF VIDEOS AND DIGITAL GAMES

19-03 The position is somewhat different here in that the BBFC is acting with statutory authority. The Video Recordings Act 1984 creates a number of offences. They include the offence of supplying or offer to supply:

272

"a video recording containing a video work in respect of which no classification certificate has been issued [by the BBFC] unless:

(a) the supply is, or would if it took place be, an exempt supply or

(b) the video work is an exempted work."[1]

In the context of this offence the following should be noted.

Video work

A "video work" means   **19-04**

"any series of visual images (with or without sound):

(a) produced electronically by the use of information contained on any disc or magnetic tape, and

(b) shown as a moving image."[2]

This includes DVDs and computer games.

Exempted work

A work is an exempted work[3] if, taken as a whole: **19-05**

(a) it is designed to inform, educate or instruct;

(b) it is concerned with sport, religion or music; or

(c) is a video game.

It will not be an exempted work if to any significant extent it depicts:

(a) a human sexual activity or acts of force or restraint associated with such activity;

(b) mutilation or torture of, or other acts of gross, violence towards, humans or animals;

(c) human genitals or organs or human urinary or excretory functions,

or is designed to any significant extent to stimulate or encourage anything falling within (a) or, in the case of (b), is designed to any extent to do so.[4]

Video games will usually be exempted unless they fall into one of these three categories of non-exempt work.[5]

---

[1] Video Recordings Act 1984, s.9(1).

[2] *ibid.*, s.1(2).

[3] *ibid.*, s.2(1).

[4] *ibid.*, s.2(2).

[5] The BBFC classifies only about 20 video games per year.

Exempted supply

19-06   There are certain situations[6] where the "supply" in question means that it is not necessary to obtain a classification. These are situations where, for common sense or policy reasons, it would be pointless to require a classification to be obtained. Examples include supplies which is not for reward[7] or which are made for medical training.[8]

There are various other offences under the Act, including the supply of a video work in breach of classification.[9]

(3) CLASSIFICATION CRITERIA FOLLOWED BY BBFC

19-07   As far as its duties under the Video Recordings Act 1984 are concerned, the Act contains specific guidance as to how the BBFC should classify video works. In particular:

"the certificate must contain:

(a)   a statement that the video work concerned is suitable for general viewing and unrestricted supply (with or without advice as to the desirability of parental guidance with regard to the viewing of the work by young children or as to the particular suitability of the work for viewing by children); or

(b)   a statement that the video work concerned is suitable for viewing only by persons who have attained the age (not being more than eighteen years) specified in the certificate and that no video recording containing that work is to be supplied to any person who has not attained the age so specified; or

(c)   the statement mentioned in paragraph (b) above together with a statement that no video recording containing that work is to be supplied other than in a licensed sex shop."[10]

The 1984 Act was amended by the Criminal Justice and Public Order Act 1994. This inserted section 4A into the 1984 Act.

This provides that the BBFC shall:

"in making any determination as to the suitability of a video work, have special regard (among the other relevant factors) to any harm that may be caused to potential viewers or, through their behaviour, to society by the manner in which the work deals with —

(a)   criminal behaviour;

(b)   illegal drugs;

---

[6] Video Recordings Act, s.3.
[7] *ibid.*, s.3(2)(b).
[8] *ibid.*, s.3(10).
[9] *ibid.*, s.11(1).
[10] *ibid.*, s.7(2).

(c)   violent behaviour or incidents;

(d)   horrific behaviour or incidents; or

(e)   human sexual activity."[11]

For these purposes,

•   "potential viewer" means any person (including a child or young person) who is likely to view the video work in question if a certificate or a classification certificate of a particular description were issued;

•   "suitability" means suitability for the issue of a classification certificate or suitability for the issue of a certificate of a particular description;

•   "violent behaviour" includes any act inflicting or likely to result in the infliction of injury,

and any behaviour or activity referred to in (a) to (e) above shall be taken to include behaviour or activity likely to stimulate or encourage it[12].

In addition the BBFC has issued Classification Guidelines[13] explaining how they approach the process of classification. The Guidelines deal with specific areas (for example, drugs, violence and horror) and describe key elements that will affect which classification is awarded (for example, only rare use of mild swear words is permitted for "U" certificate video works).

Although the 1984 Act applies only to the classification of videos and digital media, the BBFC applies the same tests to its classification of cinema films.

The BBFC's approach to classification recently came under scrutiny by the courts when a judicial review was brought by the BBFC against its own Video Appeals Committee (VAC).[14] The VAC had overturned a previous decision of the BBFC and allowed seven videos to be given R18 certificates (i.e. only suitable for sale in a sex shop). The court found that the VAC had acted correctly in striking a balance between freedom of expression and the potential for harm to children. It is expected that the decision will lead to a more liberal approach being adopted by the BBFC, at least in relation to how it classifies material to be sold in sex shops.

(4) CINEMA AND VIDEO COMMERCIALS

Cinema commercials are generally classified by the BBFC if they are more than 30 seconds long. Cinema and video commercials and their scripts are also generally pre-cleared by the Cinema Advertising Association (CAA). The CAA carries out its clearance in light of the Committee of Advertising Practice's Advertising Code which was considered in Chapter 17.   **19-08**

---

[11] Video Recordings Act, s.4A(1).

[12] *ibid.*, s 4A (2).

[13] The Guidelines are in the CD ROM accompanying this text. They may also be obtained from BBFC, 3 Soho Square, London W1V 6HD or downloaded from www.bbfc.co.uk.

[14] *R. v. Video Appeals Committee of the British Board of Film Classification, ex p. The British Board of Film Classification and (1) Sheptonhurst Ltd; (2) Prime Time (Shifnal) Ltd*, Times Law Reports, June 7, 2000.

3. THE VIDEO STANDARDS COUNCIL

The Video Standards Council (VSC) was set up in 1989 as a non-profit-making body to develop and oversee a Code of Practice and Code of Practice Rules designed to promote high standards within the video industry. The Code and Rules have subsequently been expanded to promote high standards within the computer and video games industry.[15]

The VSC has 11 classes of membership—ranging from trade associations and independent retail dealers to wholesalers and mail order companies—and there are specific rules for each segment of membership. Its concerns are therefore more wide-ranging than are relevant to this text. One area, however, which is of particular interest is the VSC's role in classifying games.

As we have seen, the BBFC does have a statutory duty under the Video Recordings Act to classify computer games. In practice, however, it rarely does so, unless the game fails to fall within the category of exempted works because of its sexual or violent content. The VSC fills this void through the voluntary rating scheme which it administers on behalf of the European Leisure Software Publishers Association (ELSPA), the computer games industry's trade association.[16]

Software publishers classify a game according to whether the particular game is most suited to one of four age ranges: 3 to 10; 11 to 14; 15 to 17; and 18 plus. This is intended to give a guide to parents as to the suitability of the game. It also helps publishers or distributors decide whether the game should be submitted to the BBFC for legal classification. The central monitoring of exemption claims is undertaken by the VSC.

A form must be completed by ELSPA's members. It asks whether certain elements are present in the game—for example, whether there is any nudity, or tobacco is used. These are consistent with the BBFC's own guidelines, so that it will become apparent whether the game requires statutory approval. Even if it is not required (which is the usual position), by completing the form, the publisher/distributor should be able to determine which classification is appropriate.

The form is then submitted to the VSC for confirmation that it is in agreement with the classification. If it disagrees, it may ask to see the game. If after consideration the VSC is of the opinion that the game has been wrongly rated, it will consult with the publisher/distributor concerned and advise as to the correct category. Appeals are dealt with by an appeal committee.

---

[15] Full details about the VSC and its Code can be obtained from VSC, Kinetic Business Centre, Theobald Street, Borehamwood, Herts WD6 4PJ (tel: 0208 387 4020) or from the VSC's website at www.videostandards.org.uk

[16] The scheme appears in the CD ROM accompanying this book.

276

Chapter 20

Internet

1. INTRODUCTION

There is no single, overarching regulator for the Internet. This is unsurprising **20-01** given the global nature of the medium and the difficulties associated with enforcement. The Internet, however, does not operate outside the law. The legal provisions described in Part I apply with equal force to those publishing material on the Internet, assuming they are subject to the jurisdiction of the United Kingdom courts. Publishers of content on the Internet must ensure, for example, that nothing is published which is defamatory or obscene.

As far as regulation is concerned, it has been seen that the Advertising Standards Authority (ASA) will consider complaints in respect of advertising on the Internet.[1] The other regulators considered in this text, including the Independent Television Authority, do not regulate content on the Internet. The only significant entity in the United Kingdom seeking to impose some form of regulation in this context is the Internet Watch Foundation (IWF). This section considers its role.

We will also look at an international arbitration procedure to combat the problem of "cybersquatting": the practice of registering domain names which are the same or similar to a trade mark, or other famous name or mark, with the intention of profiting from the registration. This procedure has recently been set up by the Internet Corporation for Assigned Names and Numbers.[2]

2. INTERNET WATCH FOUNDATION

(1) CONSTITUTION

The IWF was set up in 1996 to address the problem of illegal material on the **20-02** Internet, with particular reference to child pornography. It is an independent body funded by the United Kingdom Internet industry on a subscription basis.

---

[1] The Internet Advertising Bureau representing the industry is a member of the Committee of Advertising Practice (CAP).
[2] This procedure does not prejudice the claimant's rights to sue for trade mark infringement or passing off: see Chap. 6.

It is controlled by a management board drawn from the subscribers and a policy board drawn from a wide range of stakeholders in the Internet, including industry, child and education, consumer, libertarian and other media organisations.[3]

(2) REMIT

20-03   The IWF seeks to enforce the recommendations originally proposed by certain parts of the Internet industry in 1996 in a document called "R3 Safety-Net: Rating, Reporting, Responsibility". These proposals, which have been subject to some changes, have been agreed with the government and the police. The proposals, aimed primarily at child pornography, set out five key principles which can be summarised as follows.

(i) The Internet is not a legal vacuum

20-04   In general, the law applies to activities on the Internet as it does to activity not on the Internet. Responsible service providers wish to see that the law can be upheld online as well as offline.

(ii) Free speech, not censorship

20-05   The issue addressed has nothing to do with censorship of legal material or free speech. The issue is how to deal with material or activity which society, through democratic process, has deemed to be unacceptable in law. The core issue is crime. Legal, but possibly offensive, material raises a quite separate issue. Here, consumers should have the technological means to tailor the nature of their, or their family's, experience on the Internet according to their individual standards, thus supporting both individual responsibility and the Internet's "traditions" of diversity and free speech.

(iii) Responsibility

20-06   Service providers need to implement reasonable, practicable and proportionate measures to hinder the use of the Internet for illegal purposes, and to provide a response mechanism in cases where illegal material or activity is identified. According to the IWF service providers should not be asked to take responsibility for enforcement of the law, end users should retain responsibility for the content they place on the Internet, (whether legal or illegal), and the police should retain responsibility for law enforcement.[4]

(iv) Self protection

20-07   By taking appropriate measures across the industry, service providers can offer protection to the end user and to themselves. All responsible service providers

---

[3] Further information can be obtained from the IWF's website at www.iwf.org.uk
[4] In relation to defamation, see Chap 3 at 5.

wish to hinder the availability of child pornography, and to see it removed from the Internet. This clearly protects the public. The IWF advises that establishing a common understanding of what steps constitute a reasonable, practicable and proportionate approach can also provide a defence for service providers against prosecution on charges of knowingly permitting services to be used for the distribution of illegal material.

(v) Establishment and Jurisdiction

The law that determines what material or activity is illegal is the law of the country in which the consumer is affected by that material or activity. These proposals relate to service providers offering access to the Internet in the United Kingdom. They are designed to avoid any extraterritorial effect. **20-08**

(3) ENFORCEMENT MECHANISMS

Compared with other regulators, the IWF is less formal. It does not seek to create regulation over and beyond that contained in the general law. Its role may develop in the future. **20-09**

At present the IWF operates a hotline to accept complaints about illegal material on the Internet. The IWF needs to know what the complainant has seen and where it appeared. Complaints can be made by email (to report@iwf.org.uk), by telephone (08456 008844) or by fax (01223 235921).

Once the complaint has been received, the IWF will assess whether it is potentially illegal. If it is, the IWF will attempt to trace the source and pass details to the police. Confirmation of action will be reported to the complainant. Where the material originates outside the United Kingdom, the IWF will pass available details to the foreign service provider, where they can be identified, and to the Police National Intelligence Service, who will liaise with the police force in the appropriate jurisdiction.

The IWF also works to develop effective rating of content on the Internet.

3. INTERNET CORPORATION FOR ASSIGNED NAMES AND NUMBERS (ICANN)

(1) CONSTITUTION AND REMIT

ICANN was formed in October 1998. It is a non-profit, private sector corporation formed by a coalition of the Internet's business, technical, academic and user communities. It is intended to put the technical management and policy development of the Internet on to a more professional footing. One of its functions, of particular relevance to this text, is its responsibility to co-ordinate the domain name system.[5] **20-10**

---

[5] Further information can be obtained from ICANN's website at www.icann.org

(2) Uniform Domain Name Dispute Resolution Policy

20-11   All of the registrars for the .com, .net, and .org top-level domains subscribe to the Uniform Domain Name Dispute Resolution Policy.[6] The Policy provides that the registrars will cancel, suspend or transfer a domain name following the resolution of a trade mark-type dispute either by agreement, court action, arbitration or by way of a complaint to an approved dispute resolution service provider.[7]

The Policy is incorporated into all registration agreements between registrars and domain-name holders: the latter are therefore bound by contract to submit to any proceedings brought under the Policy.

(3) Pre-conditions for using procedure

20-12   To commence ICANN proceedings, a disputed domain name must be registered with an ICANN-accredited registrar. An example of such a registrar is US Network Solutions Inc. (NSI), which administers .com domains.

A case will also need to satisfy the following criteria.

(a) The disputed domain name is identical or confusingly similar to the complainant's trade mark or service mark

20-13   The "trade mark" may include a complainant's personal name, and these have been the subject of many disputes so far.[8] *Jeanette Winterson v. Mark Hogarth*[9] involved the registration by the respondent of the domain names jeanettewinterson.com, jeanettewinterson.net and jeanettewinterson.org. Although the complainant had not registered her name as a trade mark, she brought the proceedings based on passing off. These arose from international recognition and critical acclaim she had earned from books, essays and screen plays she had written under that name, and the fact that the use of that mark had come to be recognised by the public as associated exclusively with her work. The respondent's registration agreement included a statement that the registration did not, to the best of his knowledge and belief, infringe the legal rights of a third party. The panel ruled that "legal rights" does not require a trade mark to be registered; under English law the fact that the complainant could have restrained unauthorised used of her name by way of a passing off action was sufficient to show that she had rights in the mark.[10]

---

[6] See www.icann.org/udrp/udrp.htm

[7] At the time of writing, these were the World Intellectual Property Organisation (WIPO), the CPR Institute for Dispute Resolution (CPR), Disputes.org/eResolution Consortium (DeC), and the National Arbitration Forum (NAF). Each provider follows the Rules for Uniform Domain Name Dispute Resolution Policy, in addition to its own supplemental rules.

[8] The Rules do not require that a complainant's trade mark be registered by a government authority or agency: see WIPO's Final Report on the Internet Domain Name Process, April 30, 1999, paras. 149–150.

[9] Case No. D2000-0235, May 22, 2000.

[10] A panel, in construing such terms, is permitted by the Rules to apply any rules and principles of law that it deems applicable: see para. 15(a) of the Rules.

(b) The respondent has no rights or legitimate interests in the disputed domain name

The Policy suggests that a respondent may be able to demonstrate rights to a **20-14** domain name if he has used a domain name in connection with the bona fide offering of goods or services, he or his business has commonly been known by that name (even if no trade or service mark rights have been obtained), or he is making a genuine non-commercial or fair use of the domain name without intent to make a commercial gain, mislead consumers, or "tarnish" the trade or service mark at issue.

The panel in the *Winterson* case concluded that the respondent did not come within any of these categories, nor had the complainant licensed or otherwise permitted the respondent to use her name.

(c) The disputed domain name has been registered and is being used in bad faith

The Policy sets out a number of circumstances which may be evidence of bad **20-15** faith, including that the domain name was acquired primarily for the purpose of selling, renting, or otherwise transferring the registration to someone who is the owner of that trade or service mark (or the owner's competitor) for valuable consideration.

In the *Winterson* case, the panel concluded that the domain names had been registered in bad faith even though the respondent claimed he had not known that the names were trade or service marks. It found that ignorance of the law is no excuse, and that the respondent's intention to auction the domain names while public interest in them was running high was evidence of his lack of bona fides. The domain names were also being used in bad faith because they were not used in relation to any active websites.

(4) MAKING A COMPLAINT

A complaint must be filed in hard copy and by email with one of the three **20-16** dispute resolution service providers currently approved by ICANN. It must address certain issues, as laid down in the Rules for Uniform Domain Name Dispute Resolution Policy, and the fee must be received within 10 days of the complaint having been received. The fee is fixed between about U.S.$750–$2000, depending on the number of domain names in dispute and the number of people on the panel deciding the case.

Once a complaint has been received and assessed for compliance with the Rules, the provider will notify the relevant registrar and the respondent. The respondent then has 20 days to submit a hard copy and email response to the complaint. The dispute will be decided by an administrative panel of one to three appropriately-qualified experts: the number of panellists may be determined by the parties.[11] The parties may also have a say about who sits on the panel.

---

[11] The fees for a single-member panel will be paid entirely by the complainant, but the fees for a three-member panel may be shared between the parties.

Once appointed, the panel may request further documents from the parties. It will then make a decision within 14 days based on the documents it has received: there will be no hearing unless the panel decides such a hearing is necessary to resolve the complaint. The decision will be in writing and contain reasons for the decision.

A complainant who is not successful is not prevented by the Rules from pursuing the complaint in court proceedings, such as for passing off or trade mark infringement. However, the ICANN procedure is designed to provide a faster, cheaper and more effective remedy.[12]

---

[12] The first case in which the dispute resolution procedure was used was *World Wrestling Federation Entertainment Inc v. Michael Bosman* (Case No. D99-0001), which began on December 9, 1999. Since that time, hundreds of complaints have been filed.

Part III

NEWS AND INFORMATION GATHERING

Chapter 21

News and information gathering

1. INTRODUCTION

GENERAL

Having described the legal and regulatory backdrop, we can now turn our attention to the publication itself. This chapter is concerned with the start of the process when the author is collecting information for an intended story or other draft publication. We shall be looking at some of the legal pitfalls that can arise during this phase and how to manage them. Part IV will then go on to deal with the legal risks arising in the course of editing the story.

21-01

It is recognised that these stages are not entirely discrete. The editor may have initiated the story, and he is likely to be kept involved by his reporter or producer as new lines of inquiry develop. Equally, an editor will need to be aware of the concerns highlighted in this chapter during the editing phase. This chapter will, however, concentrate on the issues which tend to be uncovered at the coalface of an investigation, rather than in the editing suite or at the sub-editor's desk.

The approach adopted in this chapter will be to identify problems which create primarily legal rather than ethical difficulties. That is not to say that journalists should ignore ethical concerns or that such concerns are not important. Indeed, it may be highly desirable for programme-makers to devise their own ethical guidelines, particularly if they are working on a large number of investigations. These could cover, for example, the rules for approaching a subject (providing an opportunity to answer questions, doorstepping, secret filming and so on). Such rules mean that an agreed line can be taken, and may be of use in defending any subsequent proceedings in showing that the publisher acted in accordance with reasonable standards.

It is not, however, the goal of this text to examine issues of principle (impartiality, independence and straight dealing, for example) for their own sake.[1]

---

[1] For those interested in such an approach, see John Wilson, *Understanding Journalism: A Guide to Issues* (Routledge, 1996) and David Spark, *Investigative Reporting: A Study in Technique* (Focal Press, 1999). Both texts provide useful insights into the matters covered in this chapter.

These topics have of course been covered in Parts I and II, in so far as they are relevant to the law and, more particularly, to the various regulatory Codes. We will also see in Part IV how what one might describe as an ethical approach to the editing process may have its rewards in any subsequent legal proceedings. But our primary concern here is to identify when an investigation might run into legal obstacles and how the journalist can keep within the law.

REYNOLDS V. TIMES NEWSPAPERS

21-02   The recent decision of the House of Lords in *Reynolds v. Times Newspaper*,[2] though concerned with libel and the scope of qualified privilege, identified some key factors which can be used as a benchmark in assessing the quality of an investigation. The Reynolds guidelines are set out in full in Chapter 3 but, for present purposes, they emphasise the importance of establishing what has been done to verify the allegations being made and the need to assess both the cogency of the evidence relied on and the way in which that evidence has been collected. The matters addressed in this Part and Part IV should provide some practical guidance on how to meet those standards.

CIVIL PROCEDURE RULES

21-03   The new Civil Procedure Rules governing the conduct of litigation ("the CPR") also encourage journalists to research their stories properly prior to publication, rather than after a complaint has been received. This can be seen, for example, in the following new approaches to litigation:

(a)   The overriding objective of the CPR is that cases are to be dealt with expeditiously.[3] The courts now have a duty to manage cases to cut down on cost and delay, and to deal with cases in ways which are proportionate to the importance and complexity of the cases. It is intended that cases will come to trial more quickly.

(b)   The CPR allows the court to order disclosure of documents before proceedings start.[4] The recently produced Pre-Action Protocol for defamation actions sets out a code of good practice which parties should follow both before and during litigation. It emphasises that time is "of the essence" in a defamation action and provides for the exchange of information at the time of, or soon after, a complaint is made. This will encourage the settlement of cases before proceedings are initiated. This "front-loading" of information will disadvantage defendants who do not have their evidence to hand at an early stage.[5]

---

[2] [1998] 3 All E.R. 961. The case is considered in more detail in Chap. 3 at 5(3)(b).

[3] CPR 1.

[4] It is not thought that advance disclosure will be ordered against a publisher defendant until it is known what defence, if any, is to be relied on: see *Granada v. NGN Ltd*, July 30, 1999, unreported, *per* Eady J.

[5] For example, the extent to which the protocol has been followed will be taken into account in costs and other orders.

(c) Some parts of a publisher's defence may be decided as preliminary issue. For example, a publisher's defence of qualified privilege in a defamation action may be accepted or rejected by the court at an interim hearing before the action even reaches trial.[6] Whilst litigants could previously bring such applications, the courts are now more likely to be proactive in this regard given their enhanced role in case management.

(d) The former practice of a publisher relying initially on a "holding defence" (whereby he simply denied liability without explaining the grounds for so doing) will no longer tolerated.[7]

(e) New provisions under the CPR and the Defamation Act 1996 allow a claimant to obtain summary judgment if it appears to a court that it has no realistic prospect of success and there is no reason why it should be tried.[8]

2. GATHERING QUALITY EVIDENCE

It is highly desirable for journalists to gather the best quality evidence available in support of their story. There are several obvious reasons for this. It will allow an informed decision to be taken by the journalist and his editor about whether a story can be published at all and, if it can, what line should be pursued in reporting on the story. Once the story has been published, it also ensures that the publisher can assert his claims with a high degree of confidence. The quality of evidence should be reflected in the level of authority borne by the article and ought to lessen the risks of a claim being brought.

21-04

Even if a claim is brought, evidence of a high quality should enhance the prospects of successfully defending the claim, or at least keeping the level of damages to a minimum. Apart from later reducing the costs of any litigation (and facilitating compliance with the CPR referred to above), another key driver for ensuring that stories are supported by proper evidence is that, without it, a publication's credibility and reputation for reliability could suffer. Ultimately, and if seriously or persistently questioned, this could spell disaster for its future.

Of course, deciding what amounts to "quality evidence", or evidence of sufficient quality, is not always easy. There are, however, certain factors which will tend to suggest a greater degree of reliability and the investigating journalist will need to take these into account.

(1) TYPES OF EVIDENCE

Evidence can come in many forms, some of which are more reliable than others. It is important for the journalist to be aware of the advantages and pitfalls of

---

[6] See *GKR Karate U.K. Ltd v. Yorkshire Post*, January 17, 2000, unreported, (per Sir Oliver Popplewell).

[7] CPR 16.5.

[8] See CPR 24.2 and Defamation Act 1996, ss.8–10. The latter (summary disposal of claim procedure) came into effect on February 28, 2000. This is dealt with in Chap. 3 at 7.

each type of evidence. Some of the more common forms of evidence are considered below.

Tape recordings

21-05 Tape recorded evidence—either on audio or video—is perhaps the most compelling evidence that can be obtained. If nothing else, it will allow those involved in the editing process to accept a journalist's line in a less ambiguous way. It will also obviously be difficult for the subject of the story to challenge at a later date. For these reasons it is now customary for journalists to tape record interviews. Indeed, tabloid newspapers may be particularly anxious to do so because their journalists are so vulnerable to having their credibility attacked.

Once made, a recording should be carefully labelled with all relevant details, including the name of the person being interviewed, the date, time and place of recording. In a lengthy investigation the number of tapes can quickly build up, so labelling will help later on should they be required. It is also advisable, once a critical tape has been recorded, to take steps to prevent it being recorded over (*e.g.* breaking the tabs) or lost. If a transcript is needed, it may be prudent to take this from a copy so as to avoid damaging the original in the transcription process.

It might be thought good manners to ask if someone objects to being taped but, in practice, consent is not generally sought nor does its absence affect the admissibility of the tape. On the other hand, this may have some bearing on the credibility of the tape, particularly if the journalist could be said to be "leading his subject on". It may also make the tape subject to the criticism that its recording amounted to an infringement of privacy. However, whilst this might amount to a breach of one of the Codes outlined in Part II, this is unlikely to carry much weight in a court of law, particularly if the recording discloses a matter of public interest.[9]

Attention should also be paid to the issue of copyright where the speaker's words recorded on tape are reproduced in a story, since the speaker may own the copyright in his words. However, surreptitious recording is not necessarily a copyright infringement, and may be covered by the defence relating to reports of spoken words or fair comment.[10] An action may also be avoided if the words used by the publisher do not amount to "substantial copying".[11] Breach of confidence, or infringement of the right to priority under Article 8 of the European Convention, should also be considered if a conversation is being secretly taped.[12]

---

[9] The most serious consequence in court proceedings would probably be that an unauthorised recording could have some influence on the level of damages to be awarded to a successful libel claimant: see libel damages in Chap. 3 at 7.

[10] Copyright, Designs and Patents Act 1988, s.58. See also Chap. 5 at 8.

[11] Although the publisher should bear in mind that the test for "substantial copying" is one of quality not quantity: see Chap. 5 at 7.

[12] See Chap. 7.

Film and CCTV footage

Even more compelling than tape recordings, film footage seldom lies. It was **21-06** relied on by the media, for example, in support of the accusations against those alleged to be responsible for the murder of Stephen Lawrence. Closed circuit television footage provided by the emergency services or other organisations can also make for good television. However, care does need to be taken because camera footage may create legal or regulatory problems of which the journalist needs to be aware. These might include concerns about libel, privacy or contempt.

Signed statements

If an allegation is particularly contentious it is prudent for a journalist to seek **21-07** a signed witness statement from the source. This practice is frequently followed by the national tabloids. Ultimately, however, if a journalist has a live witness, he and his editor will always need to assess their reliability. Does the source have an ulterior motive in bringing the story to the attention of the journalist? The journalist needs to be as clear as possible about what that motive might be.

This is perhaps the most important risk assessment exercise to be undertaken in researching a story, because a story is only as solid as the journalist's source. As noted by Lord Nicholls in *Reynolds v. Times Newspapers*,[13] some informants have no direct knowledge of events and some will have their own axe to grind. A publisher should be particularly aware of sources who are being paid for information (even by the publisher itself), as this is often a motive for exaggerating, omitting or otherwise altering the facts to fit what the source believes to be the most saleable element of his story.[14]

Notebooks

Notes taken by a journalist, though less definitive than a tape recording, can **21-08** play a key role in supporting a publisher's story. Ideally they should be explicit, comprehensive and unambiguous. Conversely, the absence of any notes, or the existence of notes which do not fully support the version of events advanced by the journalist, may weaken the journalist's credibility at trial.

Care should be taken to ensure that nothing embarrassing, compromising or irrelevant is written down which has no bearing on the story at hand: this may show the journalist in a bad light at any subsequent trial. By analogy, the same point applies to film rushes that have not been broadcast as part of a television programme. Having made a contemporaneous note, reporters should avoid the temptation to insert any material later. This may affect their credibility as witnesses and the later addition might become evident from a forensic examina-

---

[13] [1999] 3 W.L.R. 1010.
[14] See 5(4) below.

tion of the notebook. Afterthoughts should be added as separate notes, and be signed and dated as such.

As with tape recordings, notebooks should obviously be labelled with details such as the reporter's name, telephone number and newsroom address (unless he is undercover). Once it is known that a notebook has a crucial note in it, it should be kept safe from destruction and, ideally, not used again.

The importance of note taking was illustrated in the libel case brought by Richard Branson against his competitors for the licence to run the National Lottery.[15] The allegations—made at a lunch attended by Branson and Guy Snowden, head of GTech, a major shareholder in Camelot—involved the suggestion that Snowden had attempted to bribe Branson to withdraw his bid for the licence. After Snowden had made the relevant remarks, Branson went to the toilet and wrote a contemporaneous note of what had been said. The so-called "loo note" was critical at the subsequent trial in establishing the truth of Branson's claim regarding the bribe.

Documents

21-09   Authentic, original documents are the most desirable for a journalist to secure, though this will often not be possible. Copies are the next best option and will normally be accepted in evidence by a court. The absence of documents frequently makes a story too risky to publish.[16]

In a lengthy investigation, a journalist may get several copies of the same document from different sources. To avoid any confusion as to the provenance of the document, it is advisable to make an unobtrusive note (for example, in pencil on the back of the document) to indicate the source (unless this conflicts with a confidentiality issue). Alternatively, a filing system should be put in place which ensures that there can be no confusion over provenance.

Cuttings searches

21-10   Cuttings searches on the subject of an intended story are frequently the starting point for research and commonly provide useful background information. There is a risk, however, that cuttings searches (or footage from a T.V. library) can become a substitute for proper research. Cuttings may be out of date and, of greater concern, they may not indicate that a story was the subject of legal complaint. Furthermore, the mere fact that a story had not previously resulted in a legal complaint does not mean that the subject will not complain if it is republished.[17] This is particularly the case if the cutting is used inaccurately, for example, by taking a quotation from a cutting and changing it or reusing it in a different context in a later newspaper article.

---

[15] *Richard Branson v. (1) Guy Snowden; (2) GTech U.K. Corporation; (3) Robert Rendine*, 1998, unreported.

[16] See Chap. 24 at 1(3).

[17] There is no consent to publication if a defamatory claim has been made in the past and has not been challenged by the subject of that claim: *Associated Newspapers v. Dingle* [1964] A.C. 371.

In practice, cuttings are a factor to go into the equation when deciding whether to repeat an allegation. If they have not previously led to a complaint then that may well mean that repetition would constitute a reasonable business risk.

Certificates of conviction

Definitive evidence of a criminal conviction can often be obtained from the court which dealt with the relevant prosecution. It is, however, necessary to know the exact date and court of conviction to obtain a certificate of conviction. The court should be able to advise whether any appeal against conviction was launched. **21-11**

Access to the Criminal Records Office via the Police National Computer is unlawful so, in the absence of a certificate or a fruitful cuttings search, a fallback position may be to rely on police sources.

Use of documents from legal proceedings

Valuable information for a story can sometimes be obtained from court files, certain parts of which are available for public inspection. Part 5 of the CPR provides that any member of the public **21-12**

> "may, during office hours, search for, inspect and take a copy of the following documents, namely:
>
> (a)   a claim form which has been served;
> (b)   any judgement or order given or made in public;
> (c)   any other document if the court gives permission."[18]

An application for permission can be made without notice to any third party.

Where documents from court proceedings are made available to a journalist which are not open to public inspection, particular care is required. If the source of the material is a litigant to those proceedings, that person will be subject to an implied obligation not to disclose material made available on discovery for any ulterior purpose. Furthermore, and of particular relevance to the media company, if the document has not been referred to in open court or in publicly available court papers, it will be more difficult to defend any defamation proceedings on the basis of qualified privilege.[19]

(2) INDEPENDENT VERIFICATION AND FACT CHECKING

Wherever possible, independent verification of an allegation should be obtained, particularly if the source has an ulterior motive for making his claim or the information was provided to the journalist on an "off the record" or **21-13**

---

[18] CPR 5.4.
[19] See Chap. 3 at 5.

confidential basis. This is particularly important when unsolicited material is sent to a journalist from an unidentified source.

In reality, it may be too difficult, expensive or labour-intensive to obtain supporting evidence for a contentious story. At the very least, it may be worth having another person present when a source is being interviewed. Clearly, however, if the story is an important one, the publisher must decide to proceed only after having considered all the risks involved.

It is worth noting that, in the United States, fact checking is an important part of the investigative process, particularly for magazines and journals. Fact checkers will go back to primary sources, or as near to them as they can get, to seek confirmation of the allegations being made. The main reason for the difference in approach is probably the emphasis in the United States on free speech and the difficulty of successfully suing for libel unless it can can be shown that the publisher acted with "malice". Malice is broadly defined and could be inferred if the publisher failed to make adequate checks of the claims being made. Given the high level of awards in the United States, fact checking has become an important part of the risk management process.

It will be interesting to see whether the guidelines formulated by Lord Nicholls in the *Reynolds* case[20] opens the door to the need for similar checks to be carried out in this country. As matters currently stand, many publishers leave accuracy and the need for verification of key issues to the common sense of their journalists without imposing a more rigorous approach to the subject. In practical terms there is also often inadequate time to go back to all primary sources for publications which have a quick turnaround time.[21]

(3) COPY FROM THIRD PARTIES

Agencies and freelance journalists

21-14   Many newspapers rely on external agencies to some extent to provide copy. This may be to supplement their own copy or for stories that the newspaper does not have adequate resources to cover. These agencies perform a particularly important role in delivering coverage on local news such as reports of court proceedings. However, copy derived from agencies or freelancers is a not infrequent cause for claims being brought against media organisations.[22] Whilst there are many highly reputable and professional agencies, there is a risk that the agency in question may be over-reliant on inexperienced or careless journalists. There may also be a temptation for the agency to file copy which puts a particular spin on a story because it will sell. Another risk lies in copy received from overseas where it may be difficult to check on the quality of journalism and the copy may be written with different legal considerations in mind.

---

[20] See 1 above.
[21] The BBC Producers' Guidelines make explicit reference (in Chap. 2) to the need to check facts by gathering first-hand information "wherever possible".
[22] Managing contempt of court risks in this context is considered in Chap. 24 at 2.

This is a difficult problem to manage and, unless the media organisation feels able to take an indemnity from the agency in respect of any claims that may arise (this is fairly unusual, probably because the indemnity may be of no value), the best that can be done is to raise awareness of the issue. Independent checks should be made by the media organisations of any serious allegations wherever possible.

Public relations companies

Journalists writing stories are in the business of selling copy, not just to the public but also in a sense to their editor. Like many salesmen, however, some journalists may be vulnerable to a particular spin being advanced by a public relations company employed on behalf of an individual or company. These stories, presented by plausible middle men, can be the most dangerous stories to publish and considerable care must be taken when assessing the version of events being presented. **21-15**

A similar problem can arise in the context of broadcasting where video or audio press releases are provided which purport to cover stories from an objective standpoint, but which are slanted to promote the viewpoint of the supplier. The BBC's Producers' Guidelines provide detailed guidance[23] which is worth noting because the principles apply to all journalists receiving material of this sort. They are in the following terms:

> "We do not normally use any extracts from such releases if we are capable of gathering the material ourselves. If we do use such material for sound editorial reasons we should always ensure that it is clearly labelled on air. The following points should also be borne in mind:
>
> - we should not normally use video or audio releases of news events or news conferences from which the BBC has been deliberately excluded by the organisers. If, in exceptional cases, such material is used, its source and status should be made clear on air, as should the fact that we were prevented from gathering it ourselves;
> - we should not normally use any interviews or sound clips from such releases. When there are powerful reasons to do so the source of the material must be made clear on air;
> - we must be wary of using a news release to illustrate a story about the organisation which provided it, particularly if it gives an unrealistic or overly favourable impression of the organisation. We should normally use such material only to illustrate the way in which the company or organisation is promoting itself;
> - sequences which include incidental music or commentary provided by the supplier should be used only to show how the company or organisation tries to portray itself;

---

[23] Chap. 26 of the Guidelines. Similar, though less detailed advice, appears at s.2.10 of the ITC Programme Code.

293

- if we use video news release material to illustrate a more general story, we must try to select shots which do not promote the supplier or their products. We should try to use it in conjunction with other illustrative material;
- we should not accept any editorial restrictions which the supplier places on use of the material."

3. APPROACHING THE SUBJECT OF THE STORY

21-16   The person who should know most about a story is its subject. In this sense, he is an obvious person to speak to for further information. He may be able to shed light on an apparently suspicious point and avoid the publication of a serious and indefensible libel. The subject may even be persuaded to co-operate in writing the story to ensure its accuracy or to make admissions or reveal additional information which the journalist did not possess previously. Even if the subject will not go that far, including a denial or comment from the subject may add balance and avoid a successful claim being made.

There is of course a risk that contacting the subject in advance might lead to an application to the court for an injunction to prevent any story being published.[24] Alternatively, the subject might be encouraged to contact a competing media organisation with a view to the publication of a pre-emptive "spoiler". This may greatly lessen the impact of what would have been an exclusive story.

There have always been a number of common obstacles to securing an injunction. First, it is difficult to obtain an injunction unless the claimant knows the words intended to be published. The journalist should therefore attempt, if possible, to be circumspect about disclosing what he knows and what he intends to publish. The courts are very unlikely to grant injunctions if the publisher intends to justify the allegations.[25] Whilst this creates an inbuilt advantage for media companies, because of the speed with which injunctions are brought before the court, they may be forced to decide on their probable line of defence at an early stage. If they subsequently fail, they may be forced to pay enhanced damages because of the aggravating nature of the conduct of their defence.

For these reasons it often makes sense to contact the subject only once enough evidence has been gathered to afford such a defence. It may also be prudent to delay the contact until close to the publication deadline to reduce the time within which any injunction could be sought.

Whilst the obstacles above are useful to the media, pre-publication injunctions were until recently a realistic concern for publishers. There are now powerful reasons to regard the threat of injunctions, particularly in the context of defamation, as a relatively minor risk and to regard contacting the subject before publication as a desirable step. In this respect the following factors should be borne in mind:

---

[24] This is known as a *quia timet* injunction.
[25] As a result of the rule in *Bonnard v. Perryman* (1891) 2 Ch. 269; see Chap. 3 at 7.

(1) Human Rights Act 1998[26]: section 12(3) of the Act provides that an injunction before trial will only be granted if "the applicant is likely to establish that publication should not be allowed". The court will also consider whether it is, or would be, in the public interest for the material to be published,[27] though it will also have regard to any relevant privacy code.[28] Broadcasting Standards Commission: failure to allow the subject an opportunity to contribute to a broadcast programme may amount to a breach of Broadcasting Standards Commission's Codes.[29]

(2) *Reynolds* case: as we have seen, the defence of qualified privilege may stand or fall depending on what was done to verify the allegations being made.[30] It will be difficult, if not impossible, to rely on the defence if the subject was not contacted before publication. It is accepted that there will be difficulties when a journalist does approach the subject and is told that he will not be able to speak to that person for a few days or a week. It is unclear whether enough will have been done in these circumstances to verify the facts as required by *Reynolds*. Further case law is still needed to answer this question.

Notwithstanding the reduced risks, the dangers of an application for an interim injunction do remain, particularly in the context of breach of confidence. This was seen recently when Cherie Blair, the Prime Minister's wife, obtained an injunction to prevent publication of extracts from a book by her former nanny appearing in the national press.

It is worth noting that a dilemma inevitably arises where the subject refuses to comment or make any denials. His silence may indicate that the allegations are correct, or it could mean that he has chosen not to speak to the media because he fears exacerbating the situation or attracting even wider media interest. The decision whether to publish in these circumstances will depend on the facts of the case, but it is always risky to infer culpability from silence.[31]

4. PRESERVING EVIDENCE

Material obtained in the course of investigating a story should generally be retained after publication. However, deciding what should be retained and for how long is a somewhat subjective decision. Our research indicated that practice varied widely, with broadcast journalists and those working on national

21-17

---

[26] See Chap. 2 generally.

[27] s.12(4)(a) of the Act.

[28] *ibid.*, s.12(4)(b).

[29] cl.11 of the Code on Fairness and Privacy referred to in Chap. 15. There are similar provisions in the BBC Producers' Guidelines (see Chap. 12 at 2(2)), though they are less likely to be concerning in themselves.

[30] See 1 above and Chap. 3 at 5.

[31] Note that "no comment" from the subject of defamatory allegations does not amount to consent to publish the allegations in question: see Chap. 3 at 5(4).

newspapers tending to keep their notes for longer than those in other sectors. There are a number of factors to consider in making a decision.

(1) BEFORE PROCEEDINGS ARE THREATENED

Several statutes provide implicit guidance on the preservation of documents. The following are of particular relevance.

(a) Defamation Act 1996

21-18   The Defamation Act 1996 stipulates that defamation actions should be commenced within a year of publication.[32] The absence of documents once a complaint arrives may make it more difficult for the journalist to verify the basis on which his allegations were made. He should therefore retain all relevant papers for at least this period of time after the allegation was published. Given the discretion of the court to extend the limitation period, it is prudent to retain the papers for at least three years.[33]

(b) Broadcasting Acts 1990 and 1996

21-19   Television and radio broadcasters are required to keep recordings of their programmes for 90 and 42 days respectively after transmission in the event of difficulties with the Independent Television Commission, the Radio Authority or the Broadcasting Standards Commission.[34]

(2) AFTER PROCEEDINGS ARE ISSUED OR THREATENED

21-20   Once it becomes apparent that proceedings are possible, specific obligations are imposed on the parties to that litigation.[35] In particular, the parties will be required to make mutual disclosure of documents as part of the court's "cards on the table" approach to proceedings. The following points should be noted:

(i)   "Document" is given a wide meaning. It includes notebooks, tape recordings, emails, telephone bills, documents received from third parties, diaries, photographs, video tapes and computer discs. Particular care should be taken to ensure the preservation of emails.

(ii)   The documents to be disclosed are those which are relevant to the case and which are or have been in the control of the parties.[36] A document is

---

[32] Defamation Act 1996, s.5.

[33] Further detail on the limitation period for libel appears in Chap. 3 at 5(6).

[34] See Broadcasting Act 1990, ss.11 and 95 and Broadcasting Act 1996, s.117.

[35] Our principal concern is with civil proceedings but it should be noted that material subject to an application under the Police and Criminal Evidence Act 1984 cannot be altered or disposed of between the application being made and its being decided: Sched. 1 to the Police and Criminal Evidence Act 1984.

[36] CPR 31.

relevant if it is one on which a party relies in his case, or which either sup-ports his case or adversely affects his case. Documents in a party's "control" can include those held by an employee, bank, lawyer, accoun-tant or other agent.

(iii) A party will have to allow inspection or, more commonly, provide copies of all documents disclosed except those no longer under his control or which are "privileged" from disclosure. Privileged documents include correspondence passing between a publisher and its solicitor which contain or request legal advice and documents created for the purpose of litigation, such as witness statements.

(iv) Both the parties and their solicitors are under a duty to the court to make proper disclosure. As officers of the court, solicitors have a special responsibility to ensure that full disclosure of all relevant documents is made and that no relevant documents are destroyed.

(v) A disclosure obligation of particular relevance to media organisations is that they must not publish or use otherwise than for their defence any material contained in documents disclosed by their opponent during legal proceedings save in certain circumstances, such as where the docu-ment is read out in open court.[37] Failure to comply with this provision is a contempt of court.

Disclosure can be a crucial stage in any litigation and may reveal critical weak-nesses in a party's case. This is particularly true of publishers in cases involv-ing malice or exemplary damages, where the state of mind of the journalist who wrote the story may be revealed by disclosed documents. For this reason, it may be prudent for a television company to destroy all rushes before broad-cast (and before any threat of proceedings has been made) to avoid disclosing any potentially embarrassing but irrelevant footage. The same point will apply to any extraneous notes taken by a journalist. However, such action is highly dangerous (destruction of documents can amount to contempt of court if proceedings are anticipated) and should only be taken after receiving legal advice. This action might also inadvertently destroy material which is helpful to the media company or raise doubts in the mind of a judge or jury about the true nature of the material that was destroyed and the motive of the publisher in not retaining it.

5. DEALING WITH SOURCES

(1) GENERAL PRINCIPLES

Sources are the life-blood of journalism, and need to be treated with care. **21-21**
Some will not mind being identified as the source for a story; others may insist

---

[37] CPR 31.22.

on it. Either way, the reporter should do his utmost to comply with the demands made by his sources if he is to ensure a future flow of information and nurture a reputation as someone "to do business with".

The greatest single issue in this context is guaranteeing a source's request for anonymity. This request is far from unusual, particularly in the context of investigations making very serious allegations, where sources may be more at risk of some form of injury or retribution from people whose interests would be affected by publicity. If sources were not shielded from such damage, whistle-blowers would be discouraged from revealing information which it is in the public interest to disclose. For this reason, the media will often go to considerable lengths to protect their sources, even risking prison or heavy fines for being in contempt of court.

It is therefore a well-recognised journalistic principle that a journalist should not reveal the identity of a confidential source. It is a specific requirement of the National Union of Journalists' Code of Conduct and is echoed in the provisions of the Press Complaints Commission (PCC) which recognises that journalists have a "moral" obligation to protect sources.[38]

Some recognition of the principle is also contained in section 10 of the Contempt of Court Act 1981. This provides that:

> "No court may require a person to disclose, nor is any person guilty of contempt of court for refusing to disclose, the source of information contained in a publication for which he is responsible, unless it be established to the satisfaction of the court that disclosure is necessary in the interests of justice or national security or for the prevention of disorder or crime."

As is apparent from its wording, the protection afforded by the provision (unlike the journalistic principle) is qualified. Journalists have in the past tended to criticise the provision for its failure to shield journalists from the threat of contempt proceedings should they refuse to reveal their sources in court. However, the following decisions illustrate the trend over recent years for the courts to look more closely to European law and its more sympathetic attitude to the media.

Secretary of State for Defence v. Guardian Newspapers Ltd[39]

21-22 The national security exception was at issue in this case. It concerned the publication by *The Guardian* newspaper of a memorandum about cruise missiles leaked by an employee of the Foreign Secretary. It was held, in the Secretary of State's favour, that the necessity element in section 10 had been satisfied by the mere possibility that other classified documents could be leaked in a similar way in the future, rather than that the publication of the document actually leaked would threaten national security.

---

[38] cl.15 of the Code.
[39] [1985] A.C. 339.

Re an Inquiry under the Company Securities (Insider Dealing) Act 1985[40]

In this case, an equally wide construction was placed on the prevention of **21-23** crime exception. The court rejected the journalist's argument that "prevention of crime" related to particular identifiable future crime or crimes, and preferred the interpretation that the phrase referred to crime in general.

X Ltd v. Morgan-Grampian (Publishers) Ltd[41]

This decision concerned the interests of justice exception. A magazine jour- **21-24** nalist was fined for failing to disclose the source of an article concerning the financial difficulties of an engineering company. The House of Lords held that the interests of justice could be interpreted to include the wish of the engineering firm to discipline a disloyal employee, regardless of whether legal proceedings were pursued to that end.

The *Morgan-Grampian* decision was later found by the European Court of Human Rights to have contravened the European Convention on Human Rights by undermining the protection of journalistic sources, without which the media could not fulfil its public-watchdog role in society.[42] The guidance of the European Court has since been cited by English courts as helpful, and greater weight has been given in recent cases to press freedom and the need for proportionality in seeking a source disclosure order.[43] Furthermore, with the incorporation of the European Convention into domestic law under the Human Rights Act 1998, it is likely that the courts will adhere even more closely to the reasoning of the European Court in its future interpretation of section 10.

John v. Express Newspapers[44]

A more recent judgment indicates that the courts will now be careful not to grant orders requiring disclosure of sources unless a clear public interest has been demonstrated. The case concerned the disclosure to the defendant journalist of a discarded copy of a barrister's legal advice in proceedings brought against Elton John's accountants. The Court of Appeal held, in weighing the conflicting public interests of protection of confidential sources and legal privilege (to which the advice was subject), that the minimum requirement to make a disclosure order was that all other practicable means of identifying the source had been explored. On the facts, the court found that the chambers concerned had failed to conduct an internal investigation to identify the source. The disclosure was held to be a one-off infringement of confidentiality and

---

[40] [1988] A.C. 660.
[41] [1991] 1 A.C. 1.
[42] *Goodwin v. United Kingdom* (1996) 22 E.H.R.R. 123.
[43] *Chief Constable of Leicestershire v. Garavelli* [1997] E.M.L.R. 543. But compare *Camelot Group PLC v. Centaur Communications Limited*, where the Court of Appeal rejected an application that section 10 should allow a journalist to withhold disclosure of leaked company accounts [1998] 1 All E.R. 251.
[44] [2000] E.M.L.R. 606.

accordingly disclosure of the journalist's source had not been shown to be necessary in the interests of justice.

Notwithstanding this increased liberality, some journalists may consider it prudent to think carefully before agreeing to confidentiality at all, though this approach will often be impractical. Alternatively, it may suit them not to know the source of any documents which they receive, or to avoid disclosing the identity of the source to colleagues who might then also face the threat of contempt proceedings. Having said that, the cases of contempt in this context have been relatively rare over the years, with the exception of a handful of very high profile cases.

A final point worth mentioning in the context of disclosing sources is the impact of the *Reynolds* decision where qualified privilege is being run as a defence to a libel claim.[45] This decision emphasises the importance of the steps taken by a journalist to verify his evidence before publication. One factor which a court may well consider relevant is the extent to which interviews were conducted with third parties and how credible their evidence was. The desirability of disclosing these details for the purposes of the defence may, however, conflict with promises of confidentiality. Whilst failure to divulge the source's identity in these circumstances would be unlikely to lead to contempt proceedings, it may cause a plea of qualified privilege to fail (or give credence to a plea of malice).[46]

(2) IS ANONYMITY EXPECTED?

21-25 Although it may seem obvious, a journalist should be clear as to whether he is being asked to protect a source's anonymity. Unfortunately, explicit language is sometimes not used or, if it is, the language used may be imprecise. The journalist or his source may say that their discussion is "off the record". This probably means that the material cannot be used at all, other than to give the journalist a steer to another source. The term can however be taken to mean that the matters discussed may be used in a story by the journalist, but that the source should not be identified, directly or indirectly, as the source for the story.

Other terminology can also be unclear. Information given as "background", "deep background" or "unattributable" is generally taken to mean that the information can be used without identifying the source. Sometimes a journalist will be told that "this conversation did not take place". Of course such a statement has no real meaning or legal effect (it would not entitle a journalist to say on oath that it did not take place) other than to emphasise in a perhaps more emphatic way that the source must remain confidential. Matters become more complicated if the source moves from "off the record" mode to "on the record" in the same interview. If a comment can be included but not attributed to the source, care needs to be taken in reporting the relevant fact.

Context is everything, and the journalist needs to be as confident as he can

---

[45] See *Gaddafi v. Telegraph* [2000] E.M.L.R. 431.
[46] See 1 above and Chap. 3 at 5.

300

(without appearing overly pedantic) about what he is agreeing to. In assessing whether to run with a story it will need to be borne in mind that the source may never be prepared to put his head above the parapet if things go wrong. This can also be the case where a source has agreed to be identified in the story but does not want to become involved if litigation ensues.

In conclusion it is worth noting that a source will sometimes issue information (often in the form of a press release) with a statement to the effect that the information should not be publicised before a particular day and time. Such embargoes are usually respected by the media: dishonouring an embargo might be a breach of confidence but, more importantly, the media company could forsake the privilege of receiving future releases.

(3) COURT ORDERS REQUIRING DISCLOSURE OF SOURCES

A number of different court processes can lead to a journalist or publisher **21-26** being required to disclose the identity of a confidential source.[47] There is little preventative action that can be taken to avoid such applications but it is sensible for media companies to develop a consistent policy to be followed when confronted with such requests. Whilst the powers available to the courts can seem draconian, it must be emphasised that it is only in rare cases that orders are sought and obtained.

Having said that, we did detect a natural disquiet about these applications, particularly from the television lawyers whom we interviewed. They felt it was generally the case that, if there was reasonable evidence of an offence, the police were usually successful with their applications. On the other hand, publishers do not want to be seen as betraying confidences or acting as an adjunct to the law enforcement process. Equally, the disclosure of material could expose their journalists to recriminations from sources or potential sources on future occasions.

The approach often adopted by the media therefore is to require the police to obtain court orders before acceding to applications for disclosure. Notwithstanding the poor prospects of resisting these applications, it was regarded by the media as important to put the police to the trouble of filing detailed affidavit evidence to ensure that they asked properly for specific information. A more relaxed approach may be taken by broadcasters, however, where the police are trying to obtain footage that has already been broadcast and is therefore in the public domain.

A suggested precaution is that broadcasters, in particular, keep accurate filing systems for their unpublished material and detailed indices so that journalists can readily produce the material required, in order to prevent the relevant authorities from taking away a broader range of material than they are entitled to.[48]

Applications seeking disclosure of anonymous sources are most likely to arise from one of the following routes.

---

[47] This has already been considered in the context of a claim for breach of confidence: see Chap. 7 at 2(2)(b).
[48] Courtney, Newell and Rasaiah, *The Law of Journalism* (1995, Butterworths).

(a) The Police and Criminal Evidence Act 1984 (PACE)

21-27   In the course of their work, journalists can come into contact with criminal activities. They may have sources who are involved in or have knowledge of crimes, or they may tape, photograph or film incidents which could give rise to criminal prosecutions. This material could be of considerable value to the police in investigating crimes.

PACE creates procedures which permit the police to apply to the court for access (or production) of documents and to search and seize premises. These are considered below. Before describing the procedures, it is necessary to define some key terms:

- Journalistic material: journalistic material is material in the possession of someone who acquired or created it for the purposes of journalism.[49]

- Excluded material: in the present context, excluded material means "journalistic material which a person holds in confidence and which consists (i) of documents, or (ii) of records other than documents".[50] A person holds such material in confidence if he holds it subject to an express or implied undertaking, restriction or obligation to keep it in confidence and it has been continuously so held since it was first acquired or created for the purposes of journalism.[51] "Undertaking" is not defined but it has been suggested that this would include background or research material submitted or obtained on a "not for publication" basis, but not information to be published on an unattributable footing.[52]

- Special procedure material: in the present context, special procedure material means "journalistic material, other than excluded material" [53]: in other words, non-confidential, journalistic material. By its nature, it is less sensitive than excluded material and is therefore afforded less protection from access by the courts.

Production orders

21-28   PACE makes provision for a court to allow a constable to obtain access to material for the purposes of a criminal investigation.[54] The application must be made to a circuit judge and on notice to the person against whom the order is sought. A journalist who failed to comply with such an order would be in contempt of court.

The order will require the relevant material to be produced to the police to be taken away, or to give access to it, within seven days or such longer period

---

[49] PACE, s.13.
[50] *ibid.*, s.11(1)(c).
[51] *ibid.*, s.11(3).
[52] Courtney *et al.*, at p. 266.
[53] PACE, s.14
[54] *ibid.*, s.9(1) and Sched. 1. Provision is made for similar applications by Customs and Excise: PACE, s.114.

as shall be specified.[55] The only realistic means of challenging such orders is by judicial review.[56] The Guardian and Observer newspapers were recently successful in seeking judicial review of production orders. These had been sought by the Metropolitan Police in respect of journalists' email and note-books which contained allegations made by former MI5 officer, David Shayler.[57] These documents repeated allegations made on more than one occasion by Shayler, and it was held that compelling evidence would normally be needed to demonstrate that the public interest was served by seizing journalists' working papers before an order would be made.

A court will make an order if one of two sets of "access conditions" are satisfied. These are as follows.

First set of access conditions

In summary, an order may be granted in respect of non-confidential, journa- **21-29**
listic material (*i.e.* special procedure material) if the following conditions are satisfied:

(a) there are reasonable grounds for believing:

    (i)   that a serious arrestable offence has been committed[58];
    (ii) that there is special procedure material on specified premises;
    (iii) the material is likely to be of substantial value and relevant;

(b) other methods of obtaining the material have been tried without success or were bound to fail; and

(c) it is in the public interest, having regard

    (i)   to the benefit likely to accrue to the investigation if the material is obtained; and
    (ii) to the circumstances under which the person in possession of the material holds it,

that the material should be produced.[59]

It is worth noting that, once a judge has found that a serious arrestable offence has been committed and that the material would be of substantial value, it invariably follows that disclosure would be in the public interest.[60]

Second set of access conditions

These contemplate access to confidential or non-confidential journalistic **21-30**
material. The conditions are satisfied if:

[55] *ibid.*, cl.4, Sched. 1.
[56] This is usually difficult and requires establishing that the decision was wrong in law, procedurally unfair or irrational.
[57] *R v. Central Criminal Court, ex parte Bright and Others*, The Times, 26 July 2000.
[58] For a definition of "serious arrestable offence", see PACE, s.116.
[59] 1 PACE, cl.2, Sched. 1.
[60] *R. v. Northampton Crown Court, ex p. DPP* (1991) 93 Cr. App. Rep. 376.

(a)   there are reasonable grounds for believing that there is material which consists of or includes excluded material or special procedure material on specified premises;

(b)   a search of premises for that material could have been authorised by a search warrant under legislation enacted before PACE and would have been appropriate.[61] This was a rare power and, in practice, an order in respect of confidential, journalistic material (*i.e.* excluded material) will only rarely be granted: for example, where the material is stolen, a warrant under the Theft Act 1968 would have been available.

Entry and search of premises

21-31   In certain circumstances the police can apply to the court for a search warrant to obtain confidential and non-confidential material from the media.[62] The application must be made to a circuit judge. It can arise in two ways:

(1)   Either set of access conditions specified above are fulfilled and the judge is satisfied that any of the following further conditions is satisfied:

    (a)   it is not practicable to communicate with any person entitled to grant entry to the premises to which the application relates;

    (b)   it is practicable to communicate with a person entitled to grant entry to the premises but not with any person entitled to grant access to the material;

    (c)   service of notice of an application for a production order may seriously prejudice the investigation.

(2)   The second set of access conditions is fulfilled and a production order has not been complied with. This could arise where a journalist is in possession of stolen material given to him in confidence which he refuses to hand over to the police in compliance with a production order.

(b) Police Act 1997

21-32   The Police Act 1997 provides for the police[63] to obtain from specially appointed commissioners prior approval for the entry on to and bugging of premises which is likely to give the police knowledge of "confidential journalistic material".[64] "Confidential journalistic material" is defined in the same terms as "excluded material" in PACE.[65] Prior approval is where the police are

---

[61] PACE, cl.3, Sched. 1.

[62] *ibid.*, cl.12, Sched. 1.

[63] Application for authorisation can also be made by a customs office, a member of the National Criminal Intelligence Service, or a member of the National Crime Squad: Police Act 1997, s.93(3).

[64] Police Act 1997, s.97. Such approval is not required in cases of urgency.

[65] *ibid.* s.100.

likely to gain access to "confidential personal information"[66] or "matters subject to legal privilege".[67]

Authorisation will be given if the commissioner is persuaded that entry and bugging is necessary because:

- it is likely to be of substantial value in the prevention or detection of serious crime; and

- what is sought to be achieved cannot reasonably be achieved by other means.[68]

In summary, "serious crime" includes offences which involve the use of violence, involve a large number of people pursuing a common purpose, result in substantial financial gain, or could reasonably be expected to result in imprisonment for three years or more.[69]

(c) Prevention of Terrorism (Temporary Provisions) Act 1989

This Act gives the security forces in Northern Ireland powers to obtain from the media either information or excluded or special procedure material for the purposes of a terrorist investigation.[70] Two sets of provisions are of particular relevance to journalists.   **21-33**

Access to information

It is an offence for a person who has information (as opposed to documents or other records) which he knows or believes might be of material assistance,   **21-34**

- in preventing the commission by any other person of an act of terrorism connected with the affairs of Northern Ireland; or

- in securing the apprehension, prosecution or conviction of any other person for an offence involving the commission, preparation or instigation of such an act,

to fail without reasonable excuse to disclose that information as soon as reasonably practicable.[71]

It is also an offence to collect or record any information that is likely to be useful to terrorists in planning or carrying out any act of terrorism, or to have in one's possession any document or record containing such information.[72]

---

[66] *ibid.* s.99.
[67] *ibid.* s.98.
[68] *ibid.* s.93(2).
[69] *ibid.*, s.93(4).
[70] The relevant provisions derive from PACE. The definitions of excluded and special material are as described above.
[71] Prevention of Terrorism (Temporary Measures) Act 1989, s.18.
[72] *ibid.*

Access to excluded or special procedure material

21-35   The police may obtain an order for documents or other records which qualify as excluded or special procedure material to be produced if:

- a terrorist investigation is being carried out; and

- there are reasonable grounds to suspect that the material is likely to be of substantial value; and

- there are reasonable grounds for believing that it is in the public interest for the material to be produced.[73]

Failure to comply with such an order is a contempt of court. Channel 4 was the subject of contempt proceedings in 1992 when it failed to comply with an order requiring disclosure of documents gathered for a programme alleging widespread collusion in sectarian murders between the Royal Ulster Constabulary and loyalist terrorists.[74] The station was fined £75,000 for its contempt, despite having argued that to produce the sensitive material would endanger the lives of its confidential source and a Channel 4 researcher who had worked on the programme.

(d) Official Secrets Act 1920

21-36   The Official Secrets Act 1920 gives the police power to apply to the Home Secretary for authorisation to require a person to provide the police with information if there are reasonable grounds to suspect that an espionage offence has been committed under section 1 of the 1911 Act.[75]

(e) Civil Procedure Rules

21-37   The CPR contain recognition of the principle of confidentiality of sources. The CPR allow a party to ask his opponent for further information if sufficient information has not been disclosed in that party's statements of case.[76] Part 53 of the CPR, however, which relates specifically to defamation actions, provides that a court order is required if a party requires further information from the other about the identity of the defendant's sources of information.[77] It is not known how the courts will interpret this provision in practice.

(4) CHEQUEBOOK JOURNALISM

21-38   Chequebook journalism is a day-to-day reality in the media industry, particularly in the world of tabloid newspapers. However, payments to witnesses

---

[73] Prevention of Terrorism (Temporary Measures) Act 1989, Sched. 7.
[74] *DPP v. Channel Four Television Co. Ltd* [1993] 2 All E.R. 517.
[75] Official Secrets Act 1920, s.6. See Chap. 10 at 1 for a description of the various offences under the Official Secrets Act 1911.
[76] CPR, Pt. 18 provides for requests for further information.
[77] CPR 53.3.

involved in criminal trials is a branch of the practice which has attracted particular controversy and public concern over many years. The practice perhaps
reached its low point in the context of the murder trial of Rosemary West.
According to a consultation paper issued by the Lord Chancellor's Department
following the case,[78] 19 witnesses had received money from, or signed contracts
with, the media by the time the trial started.

The consultation paper identified some of the dangers of the practice:

- witnesses promised or hoping for payment might exaggerate or distort
  their evidence in court to make their stories more newsworthy, or omit to
  give part of their evidence in court to ensure that an exclusive angle
  remained marketable after the trial;

- the possibility of exaggeration, distortion or omission might be greater if
  the payment was made contingent on a guilty verdict;

- the mere act of a journalist interviewing a witness before trial might
  render the witness's trial evidence "unbalanced and misleading" if the
  rehearsal of events brought out the most sensational elements of the
  witness's story;

- the rehearsal might result in contamination of the witness's evidence if he
  or she is told something by the journalist that is beyond the witness's own
  knowledge of events;

- the rehearsal might lead to intransigence on the part of a witness: a
  witness who gives the same account of events to more than one party is
  more likely to hold fast to inaccurate evidence if later challenged in court,
  through fear of being discredited;

- conversely, the more often a witness tells his or her story, the greater the
  danger of inconsistencies appearing, thereby increasing the risk that that
  witness will be discredited;

- even in the absence of inconsistencies in a witness's story, it was considered that the revelation of media payments devalued witness evidence in
  any case in which one was disclosed to the court, and that it generally
  undermined public confidence in the legal system.

There is nothing unlawful in the media making payments to witnesses *per
se*. However, in the case of payments to witnesses to court proceedings, the
media needs to be wary about whether such payments might amount to a contempt of court at common law.[79] As explained in Chapter 4, common law

---

[78] Lord Chancellor's Department, "Payments to Witnesses—Consultation Paper", October
1996. The paper recommended legislation and in February 1998 the Lord Chancellor stated
that the Government had accepted in principle a recommendation of the National Heritage
Committee that there should be legislation to ban media payments to witnesses.

[79] A payment by the media to a witness cannot breach the Contempt of Court Act 1981, which
is specifically confined to "publications". In practice, the publication of witness interviews or
accounts is generally postponed until after the conclusion of proceedings to avoid any risk of
contempt.

contempt arises in the case of conduct intended to impede or prejudice the administration of justice. In extreme circumstances, such a payment might also constitute the common law offence of performing an act tending and intended to pervert the course of justice. However, the difficulty for the prosecution in both instances would be to prove beyond reasonable doubt that the media organisation concerned had the relevant intention. Indeed, as far as we are aware, no such charges have been brought against media companies in respect of payments to witnesses.

Another form of controversial chequebook journalism is payment by the media to criminals or their families or associates. Again, such payments are not unlawful *per se*.[80] The most notorious example of this form of chequebook journalism occurred in the case of the "Yorkshire Ripper", Peter Sutcliffe, in 1981. Much public indignation was expressed at the "blood money" paid by newspapers to Sutcliffe's friends and relatives, particularly his wife, who was offered five and six figure sums for her "exclusive" story.[81]

Despite the current absence of legislation aimed specifically at payments to witnesses or criminals, the various content regulators refer to the practice and fairly strict rules are applied. There is generally a distinction in approach between payments to witnesses and payments to criminals. The position of the various regulators can be summarised as follows.

Press Complaints Commission

21-39 The weakest approach appears to be taken by the PCC. Clause 16 of their Code of Practice provides as follows:

> "(i) Payment or offers of payment for stories or information must not be made directly or through agents to witnesses or potential witnesses in current criminal proceedings except where the material concerned ought to be published in the public interest and there is an overriding need to make or promise to make a payment for this to be done. Journalists must take every possible step to ensure that no financial dealings have influence on the evidence that those witnesses may give.
>
> (An editor authorising such a payment must be prepared to demonstrate that there is a legitimate public interest at stake involving matters that the public has a right to know. The payment or, where not accepted, the offer of payment to any witness who is actually cited to give evidence should be disclosed to the prosecution and the defence and the witness should be advised of this.)
>
> (ii) Payment or offers of payment for stories, pictures or information, must not be made directly or through agents to convicted or confessed criminals or to their associates—who may include family,

---

[80] In the case of a criminal on the run, it could be argued that such a payment amounts to the criminal offence of assisting a criminal (Criminal Justice Act 1961, s.22(2); Criminal Law Act 1967, s.4(1)). See 7 below.
[81] See Press Council Booklet No. 7: "Press Conduct in the Sutcliffe Case".

friends and colleagues—except where the material concerned ought to be published in the public interest and payment is necessary for this to be done."

BBC

The BBC's Producers' Guidelines[82] provide that programmes should not make **21-40** payments to criminals, to former criminals who are simply talking about their crimes, to their relatives or to people whose behaviour is either clearly antisocial or whose activities have attracted such notoriety that any payment would be inappropriate. Any exception must be referred through the head of department to the controller of editorial policy. Payment of a fee will be approved only for a contribution of remarkable importance with a clear public interest which could not be obtained without payment.

In preparing material related to a court case for post-trial transmission, no programme may pay or promise to pay any person who may reasonably be expected to be called as a witness (save for genuine expenses).[83] Any exception to this general principle must be approved in advance by the relevant chief executive of the directorate concerned in consultation with the controller of editorial policy. An exception will be considered only where:

- there is an overwhelming public interest, or

- the interviewee is an expert witness whose professional opinion is being sought, or

- payment is strictly in return for the provision not of an interview but of other programme material (such as photographs or documents).

Independent Television Commission

The ITC's approach is arguably even tougher than the BBC's.[84] This provides **21-41** that no payment can made to a criminal whose sentence has not yet been completed. Former criminals should not be paid for interviews about their crimes unless an important public interest is served. No payment should be made to individuals, convicted or otherwise, for interviews about acts committed by them of a seriously antisocial nature, unless an important public interest is served. No commitment should be made to pay any witness in a criminal trial before a verdict has been reached.

Radio Authority

The approach of the Radio Authority is similar to that of the ITC.[85] It requires **21-42** that no payment should be made to a criminal whose sentence has not yet been

---

[82] Chap. 15, s.2.2 of the Guidelines.
[83] *ibid.*, Chap. 15, s.3.2.
[84] ITC Programme Code, s.5.2.
[85] Radio Authority Programme Code, s.4.2

discharged. Former criminals should not be paid for interviews about their crimes, nor should payment be made to those, convicted or otherwise, for interviews about acts committed by them of a seriously antisocial nature. No commitment should be made to pay any witness in a trial before proceedings are fully concluded.

A final point to note in this context is that sometimes indemnities will be sought by a source to protect him in the event that he is sued as a result of publication of his story. Agreeing to give an indemnity is a fairly unusual step for a media company to take and the request may be a factor influencing the decision whether to rely on such evidence. Clearly a view would need to be formed on the facts of the particular case.

6. DEALINGS WITH THE POLICE

21-43 The media and police enjoy an ambiguous relationship. For most of the time, co-operation makes good sense for both sides. The police need help from the media in gaining publicity in their search for suspects, witnesses and missing persons. The police may also want to communicate public warnings or obtain media coverage for press conferences and successful operations. Alternatively, they may desire a news embargo in the event of a kidnapping or other emergency. For the media, the police can be an important source for crime stories, which remain the "bread and butter" of many media outlets. Despite these areas of common ground, there are a number of issues which may be a source of difficulty.

Police activities can form the basis for legitimate inquiry by the media, and stories critical of the police have not infrequently attracted libel claims from individual officers. The media should therefore be particularly diligent in researching stories about the police as this can affect the level of co-operation that the journalist enjoys with police forces or from individuals within those forces.

There are other occasions when the police will wish to impose a news embargo, where the media agree not to publish certain information until the police consider it operationally safe to do so. Even though there is no legal requirement for the media to comply with the embargo, there is a voluntary national agreement between the media and police in kidnap cases where a life may be at stake that such an embargo will be observed. The police may also request embargoes or news blackouts in other circumstances on the grounds of public safety or security. Media organisations will need to assess at the time of the police request whether it is legitimate, as the media will be reluctant to agree to such informal arrangements other than in extreme circumstances.

Journalists may also need police approval to gain access to an event with a large police presence, or they may wish to accompany the police on raids or other operational activities. It has become more common for the police to require the media to sign written contracts setting out an understanding as to the basis on which the media is being allowed to participate. These agreements may cover issues such as limits on access, advance viewing of film or insurance.

Such terms may cause problems for the media, particularly if they are being asked to give assurances which go beyond acknowledging their existing legal obligations or responsibility for their own actions. Indeed, there may be occasions on which the terms proposed compromise the journalists and the offer of co-operation will have to be declined. Clearly, great care should be taken before signing a binding agreement.[86] Signing these agreements will generally not affect third party rights so journalists should still be aware of issues such as trespass.

Another instance when a media organisation can become caught up in a police investigation is when it has interviewed people with knowledge of criminal matters or taken photographs which might assist the police with their inquiries. The media's response to such circumstances can vary. Sometimes they will wish to trumpet the fact that they have delivered a "dossier" to the police. On other occasions their paramount concern will be protecting their sources (see 5 above).

Ultimately, there is a careful balance to be struck between cultivating close links with the police to obtain help and information on the one hand and retaining a professional distance on the other.

7. MISCELLANEOUS OFFENCES RELEVANT TO THE INVESTIGATIVE JOURNALIST

The manner in which an investigative journalist gathers information may give **21-44** rise to difficulties under the criminal law.

Going undercover to detect criminal activities can give rise to a number of legal problems. The journalist needs to play his role convincingly but equally he must be careful not to become an actor in any wrongdoing himself. If he is investigating drug dealing, for example, he may find himself in a position where his credibility would be undermined if he does not purchase drugs. Whilst this should be avoided if possible, when drugs are bought, they should be sent for analysis with orders for the drugs to be sent directly to the police. It should also be noted that under PACE, a trial judge can exclude evidence if the defendant would not have committed the offence but for the activities of an agent provocateur.[87]

Working too closely with criminals has other risks. It is an offence to give to a person who has escaped from prison or is otherwise unlawfully at large any assistance with intent to prevent, hinder or interfere with his being taken into custody.[88] It is also an offence knowingly to do any act with intent to impede the apprehension or prosecution of a person who has committed an arrestable offence.[89] Assistance is difficult to define, but it might only be necessary to prove some element of encouragement. In the case of a criminal who has escaped

---

[86] The BBC Producers' Guidelines note that the BBC has a standard form of indemnity agreed with the Association of Chief Police Officers which it recommends should be followed (Chap. 16, s.4 of the Guidelines).

[87] PACE, s.78.

[88] Criminal Justice Act 1961, s.22.

[89] Criminal Law Act 1967, s.4(1).

from prison, there might be risks if, for example, a radio station conducted an interview unless everything possible was done to help secure the criminal's arrest.[90]

Taking a job to find out what is happening inside a company may produce useful information for a story but it is not as risk-free as it might sound. Taking paid work could amount to obtaining money by false pretences; making someone incur expenses, such as paying an airfare or losing business, could be regarded as deceit.[91]

Going through a subject's rubbish and removing his documents might amount to theft, whilst copying any paperwork found could be a copyright infringement. Unauthorised access to computer material ("computer hacking") might be an offence under the Computer Misuse Act 1990.[92]

It is also worth mentioning the issues relating to data protection (dealt with in Chap. 9) and national security, telephone tapping, trespass, nuisance and harassment (dealt with in Chap. 10).

Should journalists suspect that they may encounter any of the problems raised in this section, they should liaise with their editor and take legal advice at the earliest opportunity. It is also prudent to document fully the steps being taken to avoid committing an offence during an investigation. Even if an offence is later proved to have been committed, this may be useful evidence in mitigation of any penalty.

8. PRESENTATIONAL ISSUES

Sometimes the manner in which material is presented, rather than the material itself, can court controversy. It is beyond the scope of this text to examine the ethical issues arising from this issue in detail but a number of situations should be mentioned.

(1) COMMERCIAL INDEPENDENCE

21-45 Media companies should be careful to distance themselves from any suggestion that they have a commercial interest in the contents of a particular publication. If a piece is published which supports a particular company, product or commercial viewpoint it is important that the media company is seen either to be independent and that its own interests did not affect the contents of the piece or, alternatively, if it is being partial, that it is partial in a transparent way and declares its interest.

It is good practice, for example, where the owners of a newspaper have an interest in a company which is the subject of a piece for their interest to be disclosed in the body of a story. This issue attracted considerable publicity when

---

[90] Paying such a criminal might also be an offence: see 5(4) above.
[91] It could also be breach of confidence: see Chap. 7.
[92] ss.1–3 of the Act.

Piers Morgan, the editor of *The Daily Mirror*, and two of his journalists were found to have bought shares in a company that was to be tipped in the newspaper. This left a serious question mark over the partiality of the advice being offered.

Apart from laws which deal with trading on insider information, there are no legal provisions dealing with the issue of share purchases by journalists. A common sense approach would demand however that journalists should not be allowed to purchase shares which are to be tipped (or possibly any shares at all). Indeed, the PCC Code of Practice includes a provision that journalists "must not buy or sell . . . shares or securities about which they have written recently or about which they intend to write in the near future".[93]

A different conflict of interest arose in the case of a book being written by Chris Patten, the former Governor of Hong Kong. The book, *East and West: The Last Governor of Hong Kong*, was to have been published by HarperCollins but it withdrew because its proprietor, Rupert Murdoch, was concerned that its publication would have had a damaging impact on his relations with China. The furore attracted a great deal of adverse publicity for the publisher and has clearly had a longer-term impact on its reputation.

The BBC's Producers' Guidelines provide detailed advice about conflicts of interest.[94] In relation to people working in financial journalism, they state that such individuals should register their dealings and must ensure that any financial interest does not prejudice their programme work.[95] There are no express provisions in the ITC or Radio Authority Codes but it would be good practice for journalists in these media to operate under similar constraints.

We have seen in Part II that all of the Codes contain detailed provisions regarding product placement in the course of programming.

(2) DEMONSTRATION OF CRIMINAL TECHNIQUES

Considerable care needs to be taken by broadcasters in the way they describe **21-46** criminal techniques. As explained in the Radio Authority Programme Code

> "there may be conflict between the demands of accurate realism and the risk of unintentionally assisting the criminally inclined. A public-spirited warning to listeners against novel or ingenious criminal methods, for example, may defeat its own aims by giving those methods wider currency than they might otherwise have. Similar caution is needed in the representation of police techniques of crime prevention and detection."[96]

Guidance of a similar sort appears in the ITC Programme Code[97] and the BBC Producers' Guidelines.[98]

---

[93] cl.14 of the Code.
[94] Chap. 10 of the Guidelines.
[95] *ibid.*, Chap. 10, s.11.
[96] r.4.5.
[97] cl.5.5.
[98] Chap. 8, rr.2 and 3.

(3) PRESENCE OF CAMERAS AT DEMONSTRATIONS

21-47 It is well known that the presence of television cameras can have an effect on those being filmed.[99] They can create an artificial environment and the broadcaster must be aware of this.

(4) RECONSTRUCTIONS

21-48 It is often necessary to re-enact or dramatise events to give a sense of reality to television footage. However, if scenes are reconstructed, then this should be made clear.[1] If not, this might be damaging to the television company's reputation and affect credibility in any court proceedings that arise.

(5) PARTICIPANTS IN TELEVISION SHOWS

21-49 Considerable care needs to be taken by programme-makers to ensure that people featured in documentaries or light entertainment are who they say they are. This created considerable embarrassment for the BBC when participants in a programme hosted by Vanessa Feltz turned out to be actors. The BBC Producers' Guidelines have been tightened in this regard.[2] They state that advertising for contributors may be an appropriate way of finding contributors, but that such advertisements should be a last resort.

---

[99] This situation is referred to in the ITC's Programme Code at s.5.7 and in the BBC Producers' Guidelines at Chap. 16, s.6.

[1] This is dealt with in the BBC Producers' Guidelines (at Chap. 2, Pt. Two, s.6) and in the ITC Programme Code at s.3.7.

[2] Chap. 3, s.4 of the Guidelines.

Part IV

LEGAL EDITING

Chapter 22

Introduction

It's five minutes to midnight. A newspaper's about to go to print and its night **22-01** lawyer is told that there is a threat of legal proceedings over one of the stories from a litigious tycoon. The journalist is convinced that his source is reliable but, if he is wrong, the paper could be sued for substantial damages. What should the lawyer do? Support the journalist? Get his editor out of bed? Spike the story?

Of course, the answer will depend on a whole series of factors. Indeed, the answer may well vary from publisher to publisher. What this Part will aim to do, however, is assist media companies in setting up suitable systems to allow the night lawyer or other appropriate members of staff to act positively and with confidence. We will look in particular at the role of those who should be involved in the editing process and will identify techniques to assist with the identification and management of risk in the content that is to be published.

We have already seen in Part III how the process should begin in the context of conducting investigations for a story. Part IV will look above the coalface. It is divided into three main sections:

(a) the key elements that will help create a structured approach to legal editing across any media company. These elements include allocating responsibility to named individuals, staff training, and agreeing limits on risk-taking (Chap. 23);

(b) the practical issues that should be borne in mind when undertaking legal editing specifically for defamation and contempt issues (Chap. 24);

(c) the main industry sectors—including newspapers, television and advertising—and in each instance identifying the principal legal concerns, and describing how to plan the production process and manage relations with third party suppliers (Chap. 25).

It is also worth noting that the media company will need to ensure that it has a proper system in place for handling complaints after publication. The elements to be considered in creating such a system are dealt with in Chapter 26. The issues raised are similar to those reviewed here and, in practice, these distinct aspects of risk management—minimising the risks of claims arising and disposing of them effectively should they arise—should be implemented in a cohesive manner.

The term "legal editing" will be used in this context to identify the steps taken to shape copy into a legally acceptable form. It is perhaps more commonly referred to as "legalling" or "lawyering". Whilst the process described implies that legal editing should be carried out at a fairly senior level, in practice all those involved in preparation of copy—whether news reporter, television producer or advertising executive—should have these steps in mind.

Chapter 23

Creating a structured approach to legal editing

Whilst an awareness of risk management is important at all levels, it is at the **23-01** editorial phase where the greatest concentration of effort is required. At the sharp end of investigative journalism, a can-do, can-find attitude is often a prerequisite for good copy. Once the story develops, however, it is critical for the media organisation involved in its dissemination to have sound risk management procedures in place. This means that a publisher should have planned and implemented an appropriate structure to manage its output from a legal and regulatory point of view.

A media company will, therefore, need to address the following key questions:

- Who should be responsible for managing legal and compliance problems?

- What limits should be placed on their powers?

- How can awareness of these problems be raised across the company?

- Can systems be set up which give advance notice of problems on individual stories?

Our research left us in no doubt about the importance of a proper structure. We witnessed various instances of how easily a newsroom, for example, can become "politicised": a programme-maker seeking legal advice elsewhere when he did not agree with the opinion of an in-house lawyer; a journalist who is reluctant to consult in-house lawyers who handled their own litigation; lawyers within an organisation having different approaches, thereby encouraging journalists to seek advice from the most liberal minded. These instances were admittedly not the norm, but point to the need for organisations to build up expertise and ensure a broadly uniform approach to legal editing. Each organisation will have its own needs and resources but the fundamental approaches to these matters should be similar. So when the night lawyer is faced with problems at five minutes to midnight he knows what procedures are in place and how his company requires the risks involved to be weighed.

1. WHO HAS RESPONSIBILITY FOR LEGAL EDITING?

23-02   It is important that a media organisation clearly delineates who has primary responsibility for risk management of content. That person will generally be an editor or equivalent, often working in close contact with a lawyer, but who has overall say will depend on the particular organisation involved. With national newspapers, it is usually the editor (who may delegate particular responsibilities to colleagues, such as the editors responsible for certain sections of the newspaper or to sub-editors); with broadcasters' greater dependence on insurance cover, a lawyer or compliance officer is likely to exercise greater influence. But there are many variations that can apply: risk management officers, in-house lawyers, night lawyers, external solicitors and barristers might all have a role to play depending on the organisation concerned.

Our researches indicate a diversity of approach. Independent television stations were particularly astute to the need to have clear systems in place. Certain television stations had procedures requiring the involvement of senior programme executives (up to the level of chief executive) in particular circumstances, such as using particularly offensive language or secret cameras.

A senior executive in one company told us: "We have found that prevention is better than cure, so that we try to stop any mistakes as soon as possible before transmission. In terms of delicate decisions, they go . . . to the top of the organisation."

The guidelines at another station made clear that production staff had to refer cases of doubt to their editors, senior management, chief executive or director of broadcasting as final arbiter. In each case the person making the reference had to record the referral and response in the programme file. At this particular station, relevant heads or controllers viewed programming prior to transmission to decide whether editorial changes were needed, warnings required or legal advice should be sought.

At the BBC, as has been seen in the Producers' Guidelines identified in Chapter 12, there is a precise referral procedure that may need to be set in train.[1] If there is a particularly contentious programme, it may be referred from the Head of Programme Legal Advice to the Controller. From there, it can, in appropriate circumstances, be referred higher up the management chain to the Managing Director (as well as to the Legal Advisor). It would, however, be unusual for a programme to pass through each of these levels.

There is a marked difference in approach between television and print media in terms of who has the final say in allowing material to be published. With newspapers, the lawyer generally advises on whether the material constitutes a fair or reasonable business risk. Responsibility to act on that advice then usually falls to the editor. If the lawyer feels particularly concerned, he might suggest the involvement of the managing director or chief executive of the newspaper. Our research indicates, however, that the autonomy of editors has

---

[1] The Guidelines appear in full in the CD ROM accompanying this text.

increased over the years and it would generally be their decision whether to go ahead or to involve senior management. Having said that, editors would be expected to talk to management on a daily basis and contentious stories are likely to be discussed in any event.

With television, there was a readiness by several of the senior lawyers we interviewed to take responsibility for the ultimate decision, albeit after lengthy consultation with the programme makers. Whilst in practice the difference with newspapers may not be that great (the view of the paper's lawyer will usually carry considerable weight), such difference as there is can be attributed to the fact that television stations will often carry insurance *requiring* the insured's lawyer to take a particularly active responsibility in the legalling process.

The key message is that, whatever system is in place, that system should be known, followed and respected by those working within the organisation.

2. DO YOU NEED AN IN-HOUSE LAWYER?

Every media organisation would probably choose to have a lawyer on the spot   **23-03**
(or at least on the end of a telephone) to give instant advice, but whether it does so is usually a question of economics. Different approaches are adopted depending on the particular industry. Some media groups, for example, have a contractual arrangement with an "outside" firm of solicitors, generally specialists in media law, which allows journalists and editors from any of those media outlets to contact those solicitors for advice at any time via telephone, fax or email, or personally if the lawyer comes to the newsroom.

Our research indicated that even the largest media organisations with their own in-house lawyers will seek external advice on certain matters. This is particularly the case on difficult issues of contempt or where large-scale litigation needs to be defended. This approach is particularly well founded in relation to contempt where, even if the advice received is ultimately proved to be misguided, the courts may take account of any legal advice when considering penalties to be impressed on the publisher.

TELEVISION

As has been seen in Chapters 13 and 15, television is almost certainly the most   **23-04**
tightly regulated sector. Consequently many television companies—including Channel 4, Channel 5, the largest ITV stations[2] and BSkyB—employ in-house lawyers to ensure compliance with the various Codes, as well as guarding against other threats such as libel and contempt.

The BBC is slightly different to other broadcasters because of the sheer size of the organisation. It employs approximately 50 lawyers, divided into four

---

[2] The larger ITV companies employ legal and business affairs officers. All ITV companies employ company secretaries, who may deal with legal inquiries.

main departments: programme legal advice, litigation, statutory and commercial legal affairs; and copyright and artists' rights. Pre-publication advice at the BBC is dealt with specifically by the Programme Legal Advice Department. It has duty solicitors available to answer queries by telephone 24 hours a day. The Department seldom instructs external lawyers on clearance matters and will tend to instruct counsel directly on particularly controversial topics, such as serious contempt problems.

It should be noted that there is a requirement in the licence granted by the ITC that licensees have to satisfy the Commission that they have established arrangements within their company to ensure that the ITC's Codes and guidelines are complied with. Licensees must ensure that relevant employees and programme-makers understand the Codes' contents and significance. The ITC has expressed its preference for each of its licensees to appoint a separate compliance officer and in most cases this has been done.

However, licensees' approaches differ in relation to the appointment of compliance officers. Some appoint separate, non-legally qualified, officers who work on compliance issues full-time. Others have their in-house lawyers deal with compliance issues in addition to legal matters. Sometimes, though less usually, the compliance role is fulfilled by department heads (although here ultimate responsibility may extend to someone such as the Director of Broadcasting).

At least one ITV licensee we interviewed had taken the decision not to appoint a compliance officer. They had, however, developed compliance manuals, procedures and reporting channels which they felt were appropriate and placed a wider responsibility to ensure compliance across the whole of their organisation. These procedures made clear that there was a substantial responsibility on the programme-makers and producers to comply with the ITC Codes and, indeed, it was a term of their employees' contracts that they used reasonable endeavours to comply with the Codes. These obligations were fortified by the company's commitment to regular training to raise awareness of the Codes.

The view was expressed to us that lawyers did not necessarily make the best compliance officers on the basis that they might be unduly cautious. Our research did not support this view, however, and indeed using heads of department had the inherent disadvantage that they could be too close to the programmes.

At those television stations with in-house lawyers, we noticed that they regarded themselves (probably rightly) as best able to clear material and would go to external advisers only occasionally, for instance on particularly controversial programmes.

The large independent television companies are likely to employ one or more lawyers to work on programme clearance. The trend for the ITV licences to be controlled by a small number of large corporations has helped improve economies of scale so it is now more likely that most programme clearance takes place in-house within these larger groups. Even in the larger companies, however, it is probable that external solicitors would be instructed to handle litigation. This is because the scale of many claims demands that a sizeable team works on each matter.

In the case of one ITV franchisee, a freelance media lawyer had been hired to work solely on a particularly contentious television series in spite of the fact that in-house lawyers were employed there; the nature of the programme was such that it required the involvement of a lawyer from the early development of a programme to the end, and was therefore time-consuming.

Regional television companies without an in-house legal adviser may place greater reliance on producers to keep an eye on any legal problems. Our research indicated that producers will refer more difficult issues to outside specialist lawyers, or to the company secretary if the issue is a minor one. If external lawyers are involved, vetting is mainly done by scripts being faxed or read over the telephone. Tapes of whole news programmes are listened to or viewed only occasionally.

NEWSPAPERS, MAGAZINES AND NEWS AGENCIES

There is a clear difference in approach between the national newspaper **23-05** groups and those operating locally or regionally. Most national newspapers have one or more in-house lawyers to clear copy before publication. They also make use of "night lawyers" to check newspapers immediately before they go to press.

The night lawyers interviewed for the purposes of this research were junior criminal or libel barristers or full-time media lawyers doing freelance work. They were generally expected to work from about 5 or 6 p.m., or after in-house legal staff have left for the day, until the first edition goes to press. They must also be available to be contacted after that time if the news desk needs further advice, for example, on copy which is changed in later editions. In addition, some Sunday newspapers employ night lawyers on Saturdays to provide advice if needed and to legal material which may not have been looked at earlier in the week. The major national newspapers have up to 10 night lawyers who are assigned shifts on a rota basis.

Legal advice in the larger news groups is, however, underpinned by experienced full-time lawyers. One large group that we spoke to had four full-time lawyers, together with 20 rota lawyers covering at nights and weekends. Another had three lawyers supported by 10 night lawyers.

We were told the night lawyer system had some disadvantages. Although a night lawyer consults with the staff lawyer on arrival for his shift about the "problems of the day", he may not have the necessary knowledge or experience of the organisation, the foibles of its journalists or how "running" stories are progressing. Problems might also fall between the cracks of day and night lawyers. Night lawyers are, however, seen as a necessary evil given the long hours during which a lawyer needed to be on duty. Even then, it is sensible for the staff lawyers to be on call around the clock for any emergencies. They may also need to be contacted in the event that journalists or editors do not accept the advice of the night lawyer.

The largest newspaper groups also used their in-house lawyers to conduct litigation. This saved money and had the potential advantage that the in-house lawyer might have been involved in the development of the story (though clearly there are downsides to this too). It is the exception rather than the rule for national newspaper to go to outside counsel. For example, one major newspaper group we interviewed estimated that it had taken advice externally only six to 10 times in the preceding 12-month period. In the context of the huge numbers of words being published on a daily basis by the group, this figure was tiny and meant that advice was sought on only the most complex issues.

Regional and local newspapers seldom employ their own lawyers[3]. By and large they tend to rely on their internal expertise for routine legal inquiries. Our research indicated that an informal system of "checks and balances" often grows up: reporters should first be aware of the legal dangers of a story, then the news desk and finally sub-editors and production journalists. Regional newspapers often rely on someone (usually on the news desk) who emerges as the "newsroom lawyer" because "he usually gets it right". If the newspapers took legal advice, they either instructed solicitors or the Newspaper Society in London. The Newspaper Society is a trade association which represents regional newspapers and, as part of their membership, the newspapers are entitled to assistance in copy clearance (but not with litigation).

Some of the larger magazine groups employ in-house lawyers who clear copy before publication but seldom deal with any litigation that results. In other cases, magazines rely on external solicitors or the experience of staff. It is worth noting that in many national newspapers and magazines, sub-editors are often very experienced and can be an important last line of defence in detecting possible problems.

News agencies do not have in-house lawyers responsible for pre-publication vetting, though the Press Association has a lawyer who deals with contracts and internal legal and business affairs. It retains external solicitors who are consulted from time to time. Sub-editors conduct informal legal checks but the onus is placed on journalists who are personally responsible for ensuring that their copy is legally sound.

Smaller agencies tend to be more reliant on the expertise of staff or the occasional reference to external solicitors.

BOOK PUBLISHERS

23-06 Whilst the larger publishing companies employ in-house lawyers, they tend to be taken on for their commercial rather than media law skills. For example, the larger publishers are increasingly working with software developers and other content owners in rights and merchandising activities. So even if a publisher has an in-house lawyer, he will seldom undertake the task of reading

---

[3] We came across one regional newspaper which had appointed a head of content. His job included consideration of potential legal problems. Other regional and local newspapers are known to handle complaints through their managing editor.

entire manuscripts for libel. This assignment is usually handled by external solicitors or counsel.

Even then, our research indicates that the percentage of manuscripts sent out for legalling is relatively small and will of course depend on the type of book concerned. One of the large publishers we interviewed sent out less than 1 per cent of its annual output (*i.e.* about 20 titles). A great deal of responsibility therefore lies with the commissioning editor.

It is often a question of economics, even with the largest publishing houses, whether to instruct a lawyer to libel read a book, and many experienced publishers will develop a feel at an early stage as to whether a manuscript is likely to prove problematic. Book publishers work to much tighter budgetary restraints than, say, newspapers and will often find that their outside adviser takes on the project as a "loss leader", either hoping to deal with any claims or take on other work from the client.

ADVERTISING AGENCIES

Practice within agencies is similar to publishing houses. Only a handful **23-07** employ lawyers and even those tend to hire for commercial rather than media law skills. In-house lawyers will review advertising executions prior to publication but may equally refer this task to external counsel. Other agencies may use external solicitors or a trade association, like the Institute of Practitioners in Advertising (which represents most of the United Kingdom's leading agencies). Rather like the Newspaper Society in relation to regional newspapers, the IPA offers a free clearance service to its members.

In agencies, considerable reliance is placed on account executives and more senior colleagues to keep an eye out for potential legal problems. Should a problem arise, they will take advice.

Agencies working in the television field will also have television administration departments to manage legal and regulatory issues on television productions.

3. RELATIONSHIP BETWEEN LAWYER AND JOURNALIST

Part of the lawyer's assessment of the risk associated with a story is their **23-08** knowledge of a journalist's reporting style and practice, legal "track record" and general professionalism. For this reason, one in-house lawyer at a national broadsheet is opposed to lawyers clearing copy at a computer terminal. He explained:

> "When you are grilling a journalist, it's essential to be face-to-face. I can tell from a journalist's body language what is going on. Although a phone and a fax are the next best thing, you need eyeball-to-eyeball contact."

Building a personal relationship based on trust—remembering that a service, as well as a safety net, is being provided—is also important. Neither side ought to dominate. On the one hand, there is a danger that having a lawyer on duty might encourage a less challenging approach from the journalist: the journalist should not feel unable to defend his corner. Indeed, he should be encouraged to provide as much relevant information as possible. On the other hand, an irresponsible approach should not be allowed to flourish where the journalist will try to blame the lawyer for allowing his story to be published.

The relationship must be viewed beyond the particular story at hand. There will inevitably be a degree of conflict: journalists tend to want to make public as much information as possible; some lawyers may see their primary responsibility as guarding against legal action and protecting the purse of their organisation. It is important, however, for the journalist to feel the lawyer is looking to say yes to material, or at least to get a story out in a manner that meets the apparently conflicting interests of the journalist and his employer. The relationship will fail if the journalist feels that the lawyer is merely playing safe or protecting his own position. Ideally, this difference in focus should lead to a collaborative approach with, in effect, a negotiation over what can be published.

Lawyers working for media organisations, experienced in the methods of news gathering and the ethos of journalism, cater to that culture in their interpretation of the law. This is implicit in the risk management that they undertake. One night lawyer for a major newspaper group described it thus:

> "Lawyers in media organisations are not so much "lawyers" as "risk-assessors". They do not observe so much the letter of the law as the spirit of it. Newspapers commit libels and other breaches of the law every day, so all a lawyer can do is tell the editorial staff whether the legal risk is one that can justifiably be taken without greatly jeopardising its legal position."

The same lawyer explained that the nature of newspaper production also makes a newspaper lawyer a different animal to most solicitors and barristers, because of the speed with which decisions have to be made—there is no time to research or deliberate on problems which have been presented to them. This is confirmed by a television lawyer, who said that she rarely seeks "outside" pre-transmission advice from "outside" lawyers because it would be more cautious and less practical than the advice she would give herself.

4. TRAINING

23-09 It is clearly in the interests of media organisations to reduce the risks associated with a publication wherever possible, though not to the extent of utterly denuding their product of appeal. Getting this balance right cannot be achieved just in a dialogue between lawyers, or between the lawyers and editors. For risk management to work effectively across an organisation, all those involved in the production of content must participate in the management of risk, and this requires a commitment to training.

The focus of training should be to ensure that all staff understand what risks can arise from publishing contentious material. They should be given at least a basic understanding of the main legal and regulatory constraints and the consequences that can flow from each area of risk. According to one journalist, the well-known industry maxim "if in doubt, leave it out" fails where a journalist does not know enough to leave the material out. It is important that staff appreciate that substantial damages can result from defamatory allegations, or fines and even imprisonment from publications deemed to be in contempt of court. If the ITC and Radio Authority Codes are relevant, members of staff should appreciate that heavy fines can be levied, and that ultimately the licence to broadcast could be forfeit in the event of persistent breaches.

Staff should also be taught about techniques that can be employed to reduce risk. At the very least, staff should be encouraged to contact senior colleagues or a duty lawyer should they have any particular concerns. It may be considered appropriate by their employer to ensure that their contract of employment places them under a duty to use reasonable endeavours to comply with legal and regulatory obligations. It is also highly desirable for staff to be given training in the handling of complaints.[4] Another area that ought to be covered in training—mentioned at 3 above—is the relationship between the lawyer and journalist.

Training can best take the form of regular seminars and courses. These might be organised by the in-house lawyer if there is one. Staff should be kept aware on an ongoing basis of key changes to the legal and regulatory framework.

Our researches indicated that practice varies widely amongst media companies. Perhaps most impressive of all was the training programme run by the BBC. In one year, its Clearance Department conducted about 120 seminars, presentations and roadshows which were attended by all parts of the Corporation. In addition, the BBC holds refresher courses and has produced training videos.

Other television companies also appeared to take training seriously with a range of different schemes in operation. Carlton organised talks for its trainee producers, whilst Meridian ran training seminars for journalists and independent producers about three or four times a year.

The impression gained from our research was that newspapers tend to place less emphasis on training. There seemed to be a greater reliance in this sector on experienced journalists and sub-editors who were able to identify problem areas or, if time pressure was critical, to take defensive action if a lawyer was not around to clear copy. Surprisingly, one large newspaper group which we interviewed gave no such training to its journalists. These journalists were

---

[4] See Chap. 26.

expected to rely on a "basic understanding" gained from their journalism studies. Similarly, court reporters tended not to have any ongoing legal training but relied on practical experience.

Other training schemes included risk management seminars organised by insurance companies for their clients and continuing professional development courses attended by in-house lawyers.

5. EARLY WARNING SYSTEMS

23-10   It is clearly desirable for media organisations to have as much warning as possible about problematic content. Its journalists ideally want to know at the outset, before wasting time and effort, how likely it is that the subject of their piece might give rise to legal difficulties. One of the most useful ways of providing this information early is to develop a database of actual or threatened claims made by individuals or companies. Keeping such a database requires considerable effort and, ironically, a track record of having complaints made against your organisation. For these reasons it tends to be only the largest national newspaper groups and broadcasters that are geared up to retaining comprehensive records of this sort. Our research indicated that, in many organisations, if there is any advance warning scheme, this may be little more than chance word of mouth.

'Hard' press clippings are gradually giving way to electronic archives at major newspapers. The most systematic approach we came across was that of a national newspaper group which kept a database listing all warnings alphabetically under the name of the complainant. It included the allegation complained of, the name of the relevant publication, the date of publication and the status of the complaint (for example, whether a claim had been issued, if the litigation was active or dormant, whether an apology or clarification had been offered, and which lawyer was handling the matter). Additional information included whether proceedings had been brought against any other party, whether a complaint had been sent to the PCC (and with what result) and more general details, such as whether the complainant was particularly sensitive or litigious on particular matters.

Another newspaper group had developed a cross-referencing facility within their electronic bases, so that journalists seeking cuttings on a given subject are automatically referred to the legal warnings "cue" if the subject or person is listed there.

A useful database might also contain the following:

(1)   letters from solicitors giving details of claims made by their clients against other parts of the media;

(2)   injunctions, orders and claim forms received relating to specific individuals;

(3) relevant guidance notes issued by the courts[5]: these may be further circulated by press releases from the Press Association[6]; and

(4) warnings from other media organisations putting their rivals on notice
that they will be sued if they reproduce their copyright material.

Even if a media organisation has gone to the trouble of creating such a database,
our researches indicated that it can be extremely difficult to ensure that the
people who need to know about the files actually do. One of the most effective
ways is to link the database with any cuttings searches that are carried out, but
this is not foolproof. The further safeguard of ensuring that orders and other
warnings are generally circulated to relevant personnel at the time a complaint
is received is desirable, though clearly this step may have been taken long before
the information is needed (people may have forgotten or left the company)

It is also sometimes difficult to tie a story to a particular injunction that has
been received. Unfortunately, there is no central database of all court orders
and libel claims. This would be of considerable benefit to complainants and
the media alike.

It was noteworthy from our research that many regional newspapers also
had warning systems in place. One kept legal notes on cuttings in their library.
The same publication also issued memos to all senior staff, copied to the
library, when rulings or orders were received. The editor and other senior staff
kept files of these memos. It is possible that those outside London may have
had greater difficulty learning about court orders or complaints, partly
because they miss out on the legal grapevine based in the Capital. Indeed,
regional newspapers learned of certain court orders through UKPG, the main
trade paper of the newspaper industry.

6. SETTING GENERAL LIMITS ON RISK

It would seem sensible for media companies to devise a vetting system which **23-11**
differentiates between stories on the basis of the severity of risks which they
pose. This may be particularly useful in the fast-moving environment of
newspapers where an editor needs clear guidance on those pieces which are
particularly problematic. It may also ensure consistency and enable those
involved in the clearance process to understand how their company
approaches risk.[7]

---

[5] This can happen in particularly sensitive cases concerned with national security or cases of particular public interest.

[6] In this regard it is worth noting that the Press Association is particularly careful to ensure compliance with court orders, especially because it supplies copy for the rest of the media. It will
ensure, for example, that court stories are marked "embargoed" if there is some reason to delay
publication (*e.g.* a postponement order or provision of information by the police on the basis
of an agreement not to publish immediately.).

[7] It is understood that the BBC has developed a rating system to identify medium to high risk
content.

One approach[8] which may have some appeal is for those responsible for clearing copy to assign one of the following levels of severity of risk to the intended piece:

(1) Trivial risk: this is a risk which the organisation could withstand with no difficulty to its regular activities.

(2) Minor risk: this is a risk which can be borne in a single accounting period, provided the number of instances of such risk does not become excessive. It is a risk which a busy media organisation is likely to take on a regular basis and one which would not necessarily be the subject of great debate at senior management level.

(3) Major risk: such a risk would be too great to absorb in one accounting period but would be acceptable if the cost could be spread over a period of time. Dependent on the organisation, the decision to take this risk ought to involve due consideration at the highest levels.

(4) Catastrophic risk: the risks involved in publishing such material are such that its effects would be to destroy or seriously damage the organisation.

It is obvious that the severity of risk posed by a particular publication will vary between organisations, depending on their financial situation. It is also likely that most risks will be trivial or minor. It should only be in rare cases that a decision is taken not to publish at all. Risk can often be reduced by presenting the subject in a different way.[9]

One difficulty that could arise is that guidelines, if committed to writing, could be disclosable as part of the disclosure process should proceedings be commenced in respect of a particular publication. These guidelines might be used to indicate that inadequate safeguards were in place on the occasion in question. As well as potentially undermining a publisher's defence(s), any deviation from the guidelines could have an adverse impact on the level of damages to be awarded. On balance, however, our view is that an organisation is more likely to find that standards of assessment are a valuable tool in assessing risk.

It is worth mentioning that our research supported the conclusion that it was only in a small percentage of cases that a decision not to publish was taken. This view is supported by other writers.[10] This approach was also evident from the research we conducted in the United States. However, it is necessarily difficult to determine which stories are too dangerous to be published and a media organisation may not wish to show too much vulnerability.

Some insight into this subject has been gained by researchers posing the

---

[8] This is derived from an approach suggested by Neil Crockford in *Insurance Learners: Risk Management (Witherby & Co. Ltd)*, p. 29. At least one newspaper group which we interviewed had adopted a similar approach.

[9] See Chap. 24 at 1.

[10] See Weaver and Bennett, "*New York Times Co. v. Sullivan*: The Actual Malice, Standard and Editorial Decision Making", (1993) 14(1), *Media Law and Practice*, p. 7.

question whether British editors would have published the Watergate allegations.[11] The case developed gradually and was based on confidential sources who initially did not want to be revealed. In some cases, the identity of the sources was unknown to the journalists themselves. The researchers' findings were that British editors and defamation lawyers would not have felt able to publish. The United States media, which of course broke the story, had the advantage of being able to rely on the public figure defence which exonerates media companies sued for libel by public figures unless they have acted with malice. This defence is not available under United Kingdom law.[12]

---

[11] See Weaver and Bennett, *op. cit.*
[12] The recent decision in Reynolds might lead to different conclusions were similar research to be conducted now. See Chap. 3 at 5.

Chapter 24

How to edit copy

24-01   Chapter 23 looked at the structures which a media company must put in place to manage the risks of publishing contentious material. Our attention now turns from the structures to implementation and assessing the material itself. That material may take many forms: a news story being filed by a journalist; a manuscript being delivered to a book publisher; a television commercial ready to be sent to a broadcaster for transmission. What should the lawyer or other person with responsibility for legal editing do when they receive the material? How should they go about assessing the risks posed by the material?

The first and most obvious requirement is that the person with responsibility for legal editing should have a sound grasp of the legal and regulatory issues relevant to his business. These have been described in Parts I and II. However, it is his assessment of how the relevant law and regulation will be applied to the material at hand that is at the heart of his editing function.

In some areas of law and regulation, there is little scope for interpretation. This is perhaps more the case with respect to certain of the provisions in the Codes described in Part II. On the other hand, defamation and contempt can frequently give rise to serious issues of interpretation. It is worth noting in this context that the United Kingdom is almost unique[1] and the serious consequences which it attaches to breach of libel and contempt laws[2] are largely to blame. As described in Part I, an unjustifiable defamatory allegation can lead to substantial damages, whilst contempt may result in criminal sanctions, such as a fine or imprisonment. Inevitably, sophisticated systems for cleaning copy before publication have been developed in the United Kingdom to deal with these problems.

To reflect this situation, the approach taken in this chapter is firstly, to concentrate on specific editing concerns which arise in legalling for defamation and contempt problems for all medium. Chapter 25 will then go on to look at the handling of legal and regulatory issues more generally by reference to the main industry sectors.[3]

---

[1] A limited number of common law jurisdictions, like Australia, have similarly rigorous libel and contempt laws.

[2] This compares with the position in the U.S. where the media benefits from free speech guarantees. Only tabloids would routinely tend to check stories prior to publication. The U.S. approach to fact checking is referred to in Chap. 21 at 2(2).

[3] It is worth mentioning again that the legal editor should be aware of the issues dealt with in Chap. 21 regarding approaches to news and information gathering.

1. DEFAMATION ISSUES

In this section we consider some of the main questions that the legal editor must ask himself when reviewing the material before him.

(1) WHO MIGHT SUE?

As was seen in Chapter 3, the claimant in a libel action has to prove very little   **24-02**
initially, but one of the points he must establish is that he has been identified by the words complained of. In most cases this will not be a contentious issue: he will probably be mentioned by name in the copy. There are, however, a number of common pitfalls to be aware of.

Fictitious characters

The copy should, so far as possible, avoid inadvertently identifying uncon-   **24-03**
nected third parties. Considerable care therefore needs to be taken where a fictitious name is used in, for example, a book, a television programme or a commercial. If a real person has the same name, or is otherwise identifiable from the fictitious circumstances, and those circumstances portray him in a derogatory manner, he may have a claim for libel, even if the publisher did not intend to refer to him.[4] This is a common source of legal actions. Indeed, the lawyer or journalist may be concentrating so heavily on the principal villain that other complainants can creep in unnoticed.

There is something of a dilemma here. If a fictitious character with a bizarre name is chosen, there is a greater risk of identifying a real person with the same name. Using a more commonplace name (*e.g.* John Smith) tends to be safer, though any specific circumstances in common with that fictitious character could allow a real person with the same name to sue. If a commonplace name is used, the pool of real people with that same name may be more likely to be identified with any surrounding circumstances.

Television stations are particularly vigilant on this issue and, as part of their "negative checking system", will conduct searches against central registries to minimise the risk of claims. The BBC's Producers' Guidelines highlight this issue[5] and suggest searching against, for example, addresses, flight numbers, clubs, companies, products and trade names, dentists, doctors, lawyers, M.P.s, judges, schools, shops and ships. BBC searches are carried out by the Information Research Library and take about two weeks.

Clearly, there are many other areas that could give rise to the need for checks to be carried out, for any area of activity might lead to the identification of a claimant. Costly claims could arise and television companies will sometimes buy an off-the-shelf company and change its name for a drama series. Apart

---

[4] *Hulton v. Jones* (1910) A.C. 20. See Chap. 3 at 2(2).
[5] Chap. 38, s.3 of the Guidelines.

from claims for libel, use of a trade name or brand could lead to proceedings based on trade mark infringement or passing off.

It is common practice for films to carry a disclaimer during the credits to the effect that any similarity between characters in the film and real persons are entirely coincidental. Whilst such a disclaimer would be a factor to consider in assessing whether the particular claimant had been identifiable, it is most unlikely to be a determining factor in any court proceedings.

Misleading captions and film footage

24-04   A journalist's story does not exist independently of the rest of the publication in which it appears. It will invariably be packaged to help make it more attractive to readers or viewers. A newspaper article will be given one or more headlines to draw in the reader and will perhaps contain some photographs. It may also be placed in a part of the newspaper covering several items on a related theme. In the context of television reporting, the speech of a reporter will be supplemented by appropriate visual footage to create a more compelling statement. The legal editor must be aware of the danger that this packaging creates a different impression to that of the original material filed by the journalist.

Indeed, newspaper articles not infrequently give rise to libel claims caused solely by the use of inappropriate headlines. The legal editor may have taken considerable care in editing the copy to ensure that a particular meaning is not borne by the article: that effort should not be wasted by less circumspect headlines or photograph captions.

A related problem is the risk of using the photograph of the wrong person or, in the context of television, poorly juxtaposed library shots or crowd scenes. These situations, rather like the use of fictitious characters, can lead to the identification and libelling of innocent individuals.

Peripheral parties

24-05   The risks of libel claims can be so great that it may be sensible to try to exclude reference to individuals who are peripheral to the main story. The greater the number of individuals who are identifiable, the higher the risk of publishing. It is surprising how often a story generates a complaint from a party who had not been uppermost in the minds of those involved in the production of the story.

Along similar lines, care should be taken when writing about companies and their directors. Has the wrongdoing been perpetrated by an individual director, by the company itself through its board, or is it impossible to say precisely which party? Care needs to be taken when identifying the wrongdoer and the correct approach will vary depending on the circumstances of the case. It may be prudent, for example, to publish a story criticising the company rather than its directors. Whilst a company can sue for libel, it cannot have hurt feelings and would therefore recover less damages than an individual in the event of a successful claim. A company might also be less inclined to sue. On the other hand, a company director could argue that he is identifiable (albeit to a perhaps smaller readership) by mere reference to the company's name, and thereby bring an action in his own name.

(2) WHAT DOES THE COPY "MEAN"?

In defamation claims, a claimant must establish that the words complained **24-06** of carry a meaning which is defamatory. Whilst the parties to such proceedings may contend that the copy bears their own favoured meaning, it is for the court (and usually for a jury) to decide what meaning the copy actually carries.

The lawyer editing the copy prior to publication must therefore keep an open mind about the range of possible meanings that could be borne by the material. He will need to be satisfied that those meanings (or at least those which might reasonably be borne by the copy) could be defended by his company in the event of a claim being raised. There are a number of practical points which the legal editor should bear in mind:

- Consider the material in context, as well as individual sentences. It is the overall impression given by the piece that can determine its meaning as well as distinct passages. A kindly phrase to the claimant buried towards the end of the material may not be enough to exonerate the publisher.

- Is the copy ambiguous in its meaning? This is a matter requiring careful consideration. Whilst it will usually be desirable to remove highly dangerous meanings, subtle ambiguities can sometimes provide a safer, more coded means of imparting a message.

- Spend time with the journalist, clarifying anything which you don't understand. Don't be afraid to ask questions if you do not fully understand the factual background to the article. If you don't understand, there's a fair chance a jury would experience the same problems. Only by understanding the full background can an informed view be taken about what the material means.

- Don't forget accompanying captions, photographs or headlines. Any trailers should also be consistent with the main piece. Any of these can change the overall meaning borne by the material.

- There is a journalistic convention that speech marks can be used to convey the meaning that a particular statement has been alleged but has not been established. Whilst this convention will normally be recognised, considerable care should be taken as to what the statement might mean to a jury.

- Beware giving a piece the meaning you want it to have rather than its true meaning. It is worth playing devil's advocate and considering the most derogatory meaning that the piece can bear.

(3) WHAT EVIDENCE IS AVAILABLE?

24-07   Once the lawyer has reached a view about the most likely meaning or meanings borne by the copy, he will in most cases need to consider whether the journalist's evidence supports that meaning.[6] The various types of evidence that might be available were considered in Chapter 21. The lawyer will need to weigh up the overall quality of this material, how likely it is that a claim might be brought and, if so, whether the evidence would be available at trial.

For example, are the journalist's sources prepared to be identified now? Have they indicated that they would help prepare a defence if sued? Or will they require a witness summons to testify at the trial? All of these factors will have a bearing on the risks of publishing.

If there are serious doubts about the evidence it might be possible to run a "denial" story, including a quote from the subject stating that he denies the allegations. The journalist may not be keen on this approach: the copy may end up contradicting his own thesis about the story. More significantly from a legal point of view, running a denial story will not necessarily avoid a complaint from the same potential claimant: the provision of a quote by that person does not in itself amount to consent to publication. Furthermore, it is no defence to a libel claim that the publisher is merely repeating a rumour. Having said that, a denial story will often minimise the risk of a complaint being received and dampen down any damages that might be awarded.

Another approach which is occasionally employed is to seek out a friendly M.P. and ask him to raise a relevant question in the Houses of Parliament. By raising the matter in Parliament the M.P. allows the media to rely on the defence of privilege in reporting the question and answer. This can make up for any weaknesses in the ability to produce evidence. This approach is not without risk. Although there may be difficulties with the evidence, the media organisation will not wish to jeopardise its credibility or that of its friendly M.P. There is also the disadvantage that the parliamentary exchanges could mean the loss of the media organisation's "exclusive"; on the other hand, the exchanges could generate greater interest in the story.

As a last resort (and one which might only be considered if the publisher is concerned about losing an exclusive story) might be to run a sympathetic version of events as described by the subject. This is often far from ideal, but in any event an approach which is perhaps less likely after *Reynolds*.[7]

(4) OTHER FACTORS

24-08   Whilst a strict review of meaning and evidence are the starting points for legal editing, there will almost always be a range of other factors to go into the "melting pot". These may include the following:

---

[6] This will of course not always be the case. Sometimes an allegation may be protected by privilege.

[7] *Reynolds v. Times Newspapers* [1999] 3 W.L.R. 1010: see Chap. 3 at 5.

(a) The lawyer needs to develop an awareness for stories that tend to create greater risks. Our research indicated that these included consumer programmes, business stories, dramas based on real people, investigative documentaries and stories about the police.[8] Stories about sporting personalities are also risky. These may appear on the sporting pages of a newspaper which are not always routinely legalled.

In recent years television has seen a reduction in the number of early evening comedy and drama programmes. These have tended to be replaced by fly-on-the-wall documentaries which may feature suspects and alleged misdemeanours. These programmes can give rise to defamation, contempt and privacy issues.

Reviews of consumer products have also required careful handling in recent times. Since publications will often seek to characterise any criticisms of products as fair comment, lawyers will need to ensure that the review cannot be construed as written with malice.[9]

(b) High profile individuals are more likely to sue. Their targets are often diary columnists and satirical television shows or articles. Whether they are minded to sue will depend on their profile, wealth, the political weight of the story, the gravity of the libel, and their propensity to litigate generally. For example, the Prime Minister of the day and senior members of the Royal Family tend not to litigate. On the other hand, certain business people are known to sue at the slightest opportunity: Robert Maxwell was such a person.

(c) Is the subject of the piece dead? If so, libel proceedings cannot be brought by his estate.[10]

(d) Defamation cases are as much about impression as truth, so great care should be taken over the accuracy of all aspects of the published story, even those which have no legal relevance. Quotes used in a story can be "tidied up" within reason but they must stay within context. However, changes of too significant a nature could suggest dishonesty on the part of the journalist.

A jury hearing a libel case will frown on mistakes and will be more likely to make an adverse finding against a piece which is littered with inaccuracies. The jury may reason that, if the publisher failed to correct errors, it is more likely to have been inaccurate in its coverage of the main grievances as well. This can create a risk that any plea of justification will be disbelieved or jeopardise the prospects of a qualified privilege defence.[11] Furthermore, these weaknesses in the preparation of a story could fuel the

---

[8] In contrast, our research revealed that in the US greatest concern was felt in stories dealing with professionals like lawyers and doctors who were considered to have more economic clout to bring to proceedings.

[9] See the comments at (d) below and Chap. 3 at 5(2).

[10] But note that a claim for malicious falsehood might survive: See Chap. 3 at 8.

[11] *Reynolds v. Times Newspapers*, above.

basis for findings of malice and the award of aggravated or exemplary damages.

(e) In cases where qualified privilege could be run based on *Reynolds*[12] (*i.e.* where the matter being investigated is "in the public interest" or "of public concern"), it may be useful for the media organisation to make a note, at the time of publication, stating why it regarded the story as being in the public interest. Though this might have an air of unreality—particularly because in most cases the journalist will hope to run a justification plea—the note could be produced at trial as further evidence of the seriousness with which the investigation was undertaken.

(f) In a similar vein, it is necessary to bear in mind any relevant Codes (such as the ITC's Programme Code or the PCC's Code of Practice). If a publisher appears to be in breach of these standards, whilst they may not be of strict relevance to the libel case, a claimant might point to them as evidence of bad faith or incompetence.

(g) Some publishers will take a chance on a story to boost circulation, either because the public will want to read the story or because a high profile trial could itself attract publicity. Equally, other companies may spike a story if there is any hint of a significant legal problem.

Even if the media company does not have its own evidence, it may chose to publish an allegation if other media companies are doing so.[13] This path is not without risks (it may have little or no evidence to support the allegations) but there may be a commercial imperative in running the story. The standing of the company breaking the story will be a factor in deciding whether to publish. It may also be prudent to report on the allegations in a more circumspect way: this may minimise the risk of a claim or, alternatively, reduce the level of any damages awarded. It is also worth noting that the in-house lawyers for the major newspapers and broadcasters tend to know each other and may be willing to have informal discussions with each other to assist in an assessment of the risks involved.

(h) Sometimes a story will generate such strong feelings that it has a dramatic effect on the way in which the media company is regarded. The factors involved may have little to do with legal issues. There have been several well-known examples in recent years. In the case of Salman Rushdie's *Satanic Verses*, Penguin Books found itself at the centre of an international diplomatic crisis whose effects were felt for many years. It had to provide security to the author and its staff and the financial costs ran into millions of pounds.

The response to *The Sun* newspaper's coverage of the disaster at Hillsborough in 1989 had similarly far-reaching implications. Because it portrayed Liverpool fans as culprits rather than victims, sales of *The Sun*

---

[12] *Reynolds v. Times Newspapers*, above.
[13] The larger newspapers often keep a duty editor at work until he has seen the first editions of rival publications.

on Merseyside suffered afterwards. A more recent example of the political dimension arose from HarperCollins' decision not to publish Chris Patten's book about Hong Kong.[14]

These instances serve as a reminder that on occasion an assessment of the political dimension will be as important as the more usual legal review.

(i) Does the story feel right? Legal editing is an art, not a science, and the lawyer should not ignore his experience and instincts. Ideally, he will know the journalist responsible for the copy from previous dealings and have a feel for his approach. In practice this may be important: often the lawyer may not have immediate access either to the journalist or the underlying evidence when being asked to clear the material. Whilst this should be avoided wherever possible, it is not an unusual occurrence and the lawyer is left to rely on his common sense. Particular care should be taken where the journalist seems to be over-emotional about securing publication of the story. This could later be relevant as evidence of malice (should a defence of qualified privilege or fair comment be raised), as a factor in assessing damages, or simply in gaining a jury's sympathy.

2. CONTEMPT ISSUES

The anticipation of contempt problems can be one of the most difficult areas **24-09** in which to give advice and the risks entailed in publication can be high. Matters are not helped by the fact that the law is broadly framed. Further, the courts have power to take a tough line on copy which creates a risk of prejudice to court proceedings—the journalist, editor or publisher may be sent to jail and heavy fines imposed.

The last time the penalty of imprisonment was imposed was 1949, when the editor of *The Daily Mirror* was sent to jail for three months. During the intervening years, there has been a change in emphasis by the courts. In-house lawyers who we interviewed were almost unanimous in their view that in recent years Attorney-Generals have taken a more liberal approach to the prosecution of possible contempts. Indeed, it is highly arguable that imprisonment might now be contrary to the European Convention on Human Rights and the provisions of the Human Rights Act 1998.[15] No doubt a desire not to alienate powerful newspaper editors has also played its part in keeping this issue off the political agenda.

However, notwithstanding these changed circumstances, it is still vital for those clearing copy to have the serious penalties of contempt uppermost in their minds when clearing copy. Even if the risks of imprisonment are low, the prospect of contempt proceedings being invoked to secure criminal penalties should help focus the attention of those involved in the legalling process.

---

[14] See Chap. 21 at 8 which deals with presentational issues.
[15] See Chap. 2.

Moreover, any adverse publicity resulting from a contempt complaint will be deeply unattractive for most media companies.[16]

Counsel's opinion may be crucial and is probably sought more often than in relation to libel. Assuming the opinion is favourable, the media company may choose to waive legal privilege and rely on the opinion as a means of discouraging the commencement of proceedings or, at worst, in mitigation of penalty. Indeed, it is increasingly the practice for in-house lawyers to give evidence setting out the considerations that prompted publication of the offending article. This may allow the publisher to demonstrate that it did not act recklessly, that it took advice from a respected source and that it acted in good faith and in accordance with that advice.

It is important for the lawyers and others involved in this process to keep clear records of the advice sought and given. One in-house television lawyer suggested that counsel's opinion was more likely to be sought by senior management if they were particularly concerned about a programme.

In practice the desire to publish a great deal of background information about particular crimes, arrests and charges can create pressure between the editorial and legal functions. There is often a certain degree of ignorance about contempt amongst journalists. The reaction of some journalists may be that the law of contempt prevents them writing. In fact, it is often surprising how much can be published. So an informed discussion between lawyer and journalist is critical.

Once proceedings are active, a detailed account of the background to a case, particularly if it includes information seriously prejudicial to the defendant, is likely to be viewed by a court as creating a substantial risk of seriously prejudicing the course of the proceedings and, as such, a contempt. This is all the more likely if the publication speculates about the likely verdict or has the effect of undermining confidence in the judicial process during the course of the case. On the other hand, the practical effect of the "fade factor"[17] is that the courts have become more tolerant towards reports of criminal cases at the time of arrest. Although recent cases illustrate that the courts still take a strict view of prejudicial publicity at the time of trial, media outlets today are less constrained at the time of arrest in the material they publish and the way they publish it: stories now often contain simple factual reports of incidents without qualifying words such as "alleged", "claimed" or "suspected of" and background comments from witnesses or neighbours; headlines are bolder; and the use of inverted commas around words to show that they are merely allegations has decreased.

By contrast, all these mechanisms come back into play at or around the trial date, when it must be made clear that charges are merely alleged, witnesses are merely making claims, and headlines contain merely allegations or submis-

---

[16] Recent years have seen something of a trend for criminal trials to be stopped because of what the trial judge viewed as prejudicial coverage. The most notorious cases involved Geoff Knights (see *Attorney-General v. MGN Ltd* [1997] 1 All E.R. 456) and the Taylor sisters (see *R v. Taylor* 1994 Cr. App. R. 361). However, neither case led to findings of contempt against the media organisations concerned.

[17] See Chap. 4 at 2(1).

sions rather than proven facts. Furthermore, publishing interviews with likely witnesses before the trial has concluded should not take place, nor should relationships be developed with those witnesses which might be perceived to influence the manner in which they give their evidence.

The following practical points should be borne in mind when legally editing copy that may involve the risk of contempt:

(1) Only the reporter can know what was said in court by the judge about reporting restrictions (the terms of an order are often not reduced to writing). If criminal proceedings are involved, the police will often tell a reporter whether someone has been arrested or charged, whether they have previous convictions, or whether identification is likely to be in issue at trial. The lawyer clearing the copy should ask the reporter whether he has made this inquiry. Whilst there is no guarantee that the information being given is correct, a record of the inquiries should be kept since this may have a bearing on liability or penalty should contempt proceedings ever be brought.

(2) There is no central registry which gives details of the stage which proceedings have reached. It is worth noting, however, in the context of cases involving children, that the Official Solicitor keeps a list of telephone and fax numbers of media organisations to which he sends details of orders he has obtained in children's cases. It is unfortunate that a more general system is not in operation, particularly for smaller, less publicised cases, though with the increasing computerisation of the courts this may become a possibility.

(3) There may be situations in which regional variation in coverage of criminal proceedings could be appropriate. For example, if a case is being heard in London, it would probably be acceptable for less restricted coverage to take place in Newcastle since a jury would be unlikely to be prejudiced by material published on local radio, television and newspapers. Considerable care needs to be taken in this respect. Indeed, if the story is not a local one, then the relatively low interest to local people may make the risks of publishing seem to be disproportionate.

(4) Jigsaw identification: in certain types of case (such as rape, sexual offences and matters involving children) it may not be not legally permissible to identify witnesses or even the defendant as being involved in such cases.[18] The media is not generally otherwise prohibited from reporting on the proceedings. A particular danger can arise in these circumstances from what is known as jigsaw identification. This happens where the reader of material from a number of news sources can piece together the identity of the protected individual. No single piece identifies the individual, but each gives different information about the individual which, when pieced together, allows him to be identified.

---

[18] See Chap. 4 at 3(2) and 3(3).

The courts have shown that they may treat some or all of the various media as being in contempt. Accordingly, agreement has been reached between most branches of the media (including at national and local level, and in print and broadcast organisations) on a common approach to the problem. The approach agreed upon is that the media will name the defendant but not his relationship with the victim. If necessary, the media will have to describe the crime as "a serious sexual offence" rather than, say, incest, which would effectively identify the victim. This approach avoids the situation where the defendant is sent to prison and the media is unable to name that person for fear of inadvertently committing a contempt.

The problems of jigsaw identification are more acute with newspapers because there are so many of them. The television stations tend to act in a more unified way because they are often part of a network. There is also less competition for news: each broadcaster has its own stories and the ITV companies share news through ITN.

Notwithstanding the agreement reached by the media, it is conceivable that parts of the media may still give details of an offence. In these circumstances, great care must be taken and the best approach may be for fresh coverage by other parts of the media to take a similar line. If a story is to be a report of court proceedings and the copy is being telephoned in it is prudent to ensure that the copy does not contain background material until the trial is over.

(5) Agency copy: copy received from news agencies is not routinely legalled. This is principally because of time constraints and is perhaps based on an assumption that the copy has already been checked. Particular problems can arise where agencies are careless in their court reporting.

Our research indicated that the standard of court reporting in agencies was mixed. For example, some reporters attempted to cover a number of cases in different courts and did not listen to entire proceedings, or they lacked knowledge of court procedure and contempt law. This can place newspapers in an exposed position: for example, if they use background information not presented in court or evidence heard in the absence of the jury.

However, it is clearly unrealistic for all agency court reports to be checked. The best approach—suggested by one newspaper lawyer—is to find out which agency filed the copy and to treat the copy according to the reputation or standing of the agency within the organisation based on previous experience. One eye should also be kept on any elements in the copy which appear to be inappropriate.

It is worth mentioning the Press Association's procedures for managing copy at this juncture. They are of particular importance in anticipating contempt issues. The Press Association operates an advisory system with their stories, both to inform their own staff when stories should be sent out to subscribers, and to warn subscribers of the nature of a court or crime story. For example, court stories filed on the agency's directories may be embargoed until a certain time, such as the verdict or sentencing of the accused. In such cases, the story is not sent to subscribers by the sub-editors until that point.

Sometimes a story is marked with a note indicating that it should not be sent to subscribers until further information is provided by the court, or until someone has checked with the reporter who filed the story that it is "ready to go out". Court stories may also be marked at the top with notes that indicate to subscribers the reason for an embargo: for example, that the police have supplied pre-sentence information at briefings on the basis that there is an embargo on the story until sentence.

Some stories are labelled "background", in which case they often contain potentially prejudicial material. In general, embargoed stories are kept in the system until verdict or sentence, although they are sometimes sent out to subscribers with a note on them saying "advisory to CSE" (chief sub-editor) notifying them of the legal dangers of publishing prematurely.

Whilst the Press Association will inform subscribers of court orders and injunctions if they affect one of the stories that has been filed, it does not distribute them otherwise.

It should be appreciated that an editor can be summoned to appear before a judge hearing a criminal case to explain the contents of an article published during the course of a trial. Judges in these circumstances may understandably be more concerned to ensure that their cases can proceed to a satisfactory conclusion than to protect the public's right to know. The request to attend can come at short notice and it is important that the media organisation is prepared. Ideally, counsel should attend and the editor should have all the facts at his fingertips. If the judge is dissatisfied with the editor's explanation, he may choose to refer the matter to the Attorney-General to consider whether to institute contempt proceedings.

Chapter 25

Editing copy for specific media

25-01   This Chapter examines specific approaches to legal editing in the main indus-try sectors.[1] Each section begins with a brief checklist of the principal legal and regulatory concerns of the sector. This is followed by sections on plan-ning the production process and on managing relations with suppliers whose input becomes part of the published material (and may therefore expose the publisher to claims from third parties). The main focus of this chapter is on managing the specific material at hand: Chapter 19 has already examined the basic structures which need to be put in place to allow legal editing to take place.

1. TELEVISION AND RADIO

(1) CHECKLIST OF LEGAL AND REGULATORY ISSUES

25-02   • Principal legal issues

— Libel
— Contempt and other reporting restrictions
— Copyright
— Rights in performance

• Principal regulatory issues

— Independent Television Commission Codes   (commercial television only)

— Radio Authority Codes   (commercial radio only)
— BBC Charter and Producers' Guidelines   (BBC television and radio only)

— Broadcasting Standards Commission   (all broadcasters)

---

[1] Cinema is not dealt with specifically. However, the issues to be dealt with in this sector are broadly the same as those covered in the sections dealing with television and advertising pro-duction.

(2) PLANNING THE PRODUCTION PROCESS

General

Unlike most other forms of publication, broadcasting (particularly television)   **25-03**
can involve budgets of tens or hundreds of thousands of pounds with production lead times of weeks or even months. Planning the process from a risk
management perspective means identifying in advance those programmes
which will need to be legalled, getting legal input at an early stage and agreeing a plan of action for ongoing legal monitoring during the production
process. This may mean involving a lawyer before the programme is commissioned by an editor. As the time for transmission nears, lawyers will check
scripts and tapes.

Of course, much material may not need to lawyered at all but an informed
assessment of this is required before a project has progressed too far for
changes to be made. It can be extremely expensive to put something right after
the event, particularly with a drama series, so a system should be in place to
anticipate likely problems. An early discussion should take place as to the
nature and purpose of the programme and the subjects it will cover. It is often
the producer who will trigger the involvement of the lawyers.

Where a controversial programme is being made—for example, a fly on the
wall documentary about drugs—it would be common practice for a lawyer to
be consulted, even for an initial discussion, as the programme concept is being
fleshed out. He would also expect to have sight of the final script and a rough
cut of the programme. The rough cut may also be viewed by the commissioning editor and the executive producer.

The producer will also want to establish good lines of communication
with the police (if necessary) so as to be sure, when broadcasting takes place,
what stage any criminal prosecutions have reached. This will help avoid any
risk of contempt. Obscuring individuals or otherwise concealing identities
at the last minute can be done, but anticipating these issues is clearly desirable.

It is worth mentioning that regional stations often have fewer resources a-
vailable for building a thoroughgoing process for advance clearance of
content. This is particularly true of local radio where, as with local newspapers, clearance procedures may be more informal.

Many local television and radio companies tend to prefer using local
lawyers to clear programmes. Whilst these lawyers may have less experience of
media law, their local knowledge and proximity to the studios are often more
important concerns.

Problems with live programming

Live television and radio create particular hazards for broadcasters. Unlike   **25-04**
recorded programming, there is little or no time to manage unplanned

problems.[2] It is important therefore for the lawyer and programme-makers, so far as possible, to have anticipated likely areas of difficulty before the programme begins. This is not always possible, however, and in practice greater reliance may be placed on the experience of presenters and editors, particularly where local television and radio news programmes are concerned.

The following points are worth bearing in mind:

(a) The legal and production team should have a clear grasp of the subject-matter, know who will be interviewed (and have some idea of what they will say) and anticipate the likely composition of the studio audience.

(b) If the programme is likely to be contentious, it may well be worth having a lawyer on standby to give advice to the director and presenter on suitable interventions.

(c) It may be appropriate to record an interview, rather than broadcast live, if it is felt that the interview could give rise to legal problems. This will give time to edit out controversial references.

(f) If a live interview could trespass into dangerous legal territory, an experienced presenter should try to anticipate potential problems. It may be appropriate for him to ask an interviewee in advance not to refer to particular subjects or, alternatively, agree that they will be covered in a way which will be legally acceptable.

If it is too late and something problematic has been said, the presenter should try to distance himself and the broadcaster from what has been said. In some cases it might be appropriate to apologise during or shortly after the programme. This is a difficult decision to take. It involves admitting some form of liability even before any complaint has been received and may make a subsequent defence of any proceedings more difficult. On the other hand, where a manifest mistake has occurred such a step ought to deter a claim or, if one is launched, then it will allow the broadcaster to be presented in a better light in any subsequent proceedings. Much depends on how the courts interpret the innocent dissemination defence provided under section 1 of the Defamation Act: this may have the effect of making it less likely that broadcasters feel the need to make a rushed apology in the course of a programme, since they may not be liable if they have taken reasonable care.

(g) In programmes making very serious allegations, the researchers in conjunction with the legal team will need to be satisfied in advance that there will be sufficient evidence to justify any claims.

(h) Our research indicated that problems can arise with radio in the morning with early breaking stories when more junior reporters may be

---

[2] s.1 of the Defamation Act 1996 provides a defence in certain circumstances where a defamatory statement is made in a live programme and the broadcaster has no effective control over the maker of the statement: see Chap. 3 at 5(5).

covering until senior editors arrive. Care is therefore required in this area, though it is recognised that radio is perceived as a more transitory, lower profile medium and tends to attract considerably less complaints than television.

(h) Phone-ins are a popular form of programming, especially with local radio stations. They can be a source of particular problems. As well as relying on the skills of the presenter, researchers should already have made a careful assessment of the caller before allowing him to go on air. Some stations use a device to delay the transmission of the call by up to 10 seconds to allow time to edit out of any undesirable material.

(3) MANAGING RELATIONS WITH CONTENT SUPPLIERS

Broadcasters have two major suppliers of content, namely independent production companies commissioned to produce programming and suppliers of other copyright works.

Independent production companies

The procedures for clearing copy will be virtually the same whether the production is carried out in-house or by an independent production company. There are two issues, however, to which the broadcaster must pay particular attention: ensuring production company involvement in the clearance process; and reaching a satisfactory agreement with the production company over who should be responsible if any third party claims are raised as a result of the broadcast programme. These points are considered in turn. **25-05**

(a) Production company involvement

It was admitted by many in-house counsel whom we interviewed that, in practice, it was often more difficult to keep in touch with independent producers than with the broadcaster's own personnel. This is an area where holders of Independent Television Commission licences could be exposed since their responsibility for content is the same whether they produced the programming themselves or used independent contractor. **25-06**

The problem can be addressed in part by working hard at encouraging a close relationship with the producer and providing an understanding of the responsibilities imposed on the broadcaster. Some television companies invite their producers to training seminars and train them in compliance procedures to promote their awareness and expertise.

Producers will also often want to be proactive in involving the broadcaster's legal department and keeping it appraised of developments. It is not in their interest to have to re-shoot parts of their programme. They will also not want to run the risk of alienating the legal department and thereby risk not having its support should problems arise at a later stage.

(b) Contractual considerations

25-07 Apart from including measures to foster a partnership with independent producers, the contract between broadcaster and independent producer will delineate the legal obligations on each side. It is commonplace for a production agreement to require producers to give a series of warranties to the broadcaster, for example, that the programme is original, does not infringe copyright or other intellectual property rights, is not defamatory, does not constitute a breach of confidence and is not in breach of any relevant Codes.

Complying with these warranties may be extremely burdensome for the producer. Whereas the broadcaster is likely to have his own lawyer to advise on content, this is a rarity amongst producers. Moreover, the broadcaster will often be in a better position to insure than the producer, have deeper pockets to meet any claim and, provided the producer has behaved reasonably, the broadcaster may want to preserve an otherwise sound relationship in the event of a claim being made.

To reflect this a broadcaster will often give a reverse indemnity to his producer as part of their contract. This means that, provided the producer has cooperated with the broadcaster's clearance procedures, the broadcaster will indemnify him from any claims arising from the content. Producers are thereby given a further incentive to involve the broadcaster's legal department at the earliest opportunity, with reasonable security that this should be in their best interests should a claim arise.

Our research suggests that, whilst it is regarded as prudent to secure an indemnity from an independent producer, the indemnity would not be relied on unless the producer has been grossly negligent.

Suppliers of copyright material

25-08 Broadcast material often includes the copyright works of third parties. Apart from the work of independent production companies, programming may include, for example, original musical works or films. Whilst it is beyond the scope of this text to describe all the steps which need to be taken in this regard, it is essential that the broadcaster secures appropriate licences or assignments (together with a waiver of any moral rights claims if appropriate) to permit broadcast to take place. It should be borne in mind that the contract with the third party supplier may contain provisions specifying when the programme can first be shown.

2. NEWSPAPERS AND MAGAZINES

(1) CHECKLIST OF LEGAL AND REGULATORY ISSUES

25-09 • Principal legal issues

- — Libel
- — Contempt
- — Copyright

- Principal regulatory issues

  — The PCC's Code of Practice
  — Committee of Advertising Practice Codes

(2) PLANNING THE PRODUCTION PROCESS

General

Newspapers contain literally thousands of words. To cope with this volume, a **25-10** sophisticated and reliable pre-publication process must be put in place which can manage the variety of risks posed by publication. There is no single right way of addressing the demands and practice varies. What follows is a description of some of the best elements that we witnessed amongst the largest newspaper groups.

As we have seen in the context of television production, getting early input from the lawyers and senior management will ensure that the journalist does not expend energy on a story which will not see the light of day. Lawyers may take a particularly proactive role, reviewing the news schedule in the morning and looking out for stories which were likely to create difficulties. At some newspapers the lawyer will join the editorial conference to anticipate which stories are likely to appear later in the day. The conference gives the lawyer an initial opportunity to consider at an early stage whether, for example, there is likely to be enough evidence to support a story. Of course, where substantial resources are to be devoted to a major story, the lawyer should be brought in at an even earlier stage.

The actual mechanics of a lawyer coming to review the journalist's copy are fairly standard. The journalist writes his copy and then files it either from his desk or externally by modem. The copy is often reviewed first by the news editor or his deputy, and then forwarded to the sub-editor. The lawyer may see the copy for the first time at any point from filing by the journalist to consideration by the sub-editor. This is a matter of practicalities, though the sooner the lawyer sees the copy the better. Obviously the journalist should contact the lawyer himself at an early stage if he has a particular concern. If not, the lawyer will make suggested amendments to the copy on screen or, if there is any complication, will speak in person or by telephone to the journalist.

National newspapers have a system which allows copy to be placed in a "legal cue" on the newspaper's computer system. At some newspapers it is assumed that copy placed in this "cue" will automatically be legalled by staff lawyers; in others, the lawyers prefer to work from print-outs and hard copy. There is a risk that stories not placed in the legal cue may contain legal issues which are missed. The system is thus reliant on the experience and training of those involved in the production process to pick out these stories.

The danger with such systems is that journalists may become less vigilant about legal problems because they know their story is to be legalled. Rather than exercise caution, they may write an unexpurgated piece headed "legal must" and leave any problems to be picked up by the lawyer. This situation is to be guarded against. Indeed, the legalling process will work best when the lawyer and writer have a good understanding of each other's approach and copy can be produced which the writer can expect to be cleared with little or no changes. Co-operation at the early stages of a story's genesis will help achieve this.

If the lawyer has simply amended or cut out parts of the copy, this can be misleading. It is therefore best practice to highlight suggested changes or alternate wording, with a note explaining the basis for the change. If there are serious problems, then the lawyer may advise against publishing at all and clearly he must be prepared to explain this advice to the journalist and the editor.

Whilst this type of process is used at many of the large newspaper groups, it is not the only approach. Some lawyers prefer to walk the news floor and deal with the journalist face to face. This allows a closer relationship to develop. If the journalist has any supporting documents or notebooks to hand they can be seen. An internal meeting may be necessary, during which the individual journalist or the head of a department (such as news or features) and the lawyer discuss the story and the legal advice given. Sometimes the lawyer deals directly with the editor on more fundamental issues.

Problems can arise where the particular system does not allow the lawyer to make notes on screen. In such circumstances he must tell the editorial back bench of his advised change orally, and an error may occur if the alteration or cut is not then incorporated into the final version of a story. This may also occur where the lawyer is checking page proofs. More than one newspaper group we interviewed had attempted to improve their systems in this regard by requiring night lawyers, for instance, to fill in an "advice sheet" or checklist as they legal each page proof. This is a record of advice given or the lawyer's comments on serious issues which arise. In the case of one newspaper, the night lawyer is required to make his marks on each page proof he legals, attach them to the completed advice sheet, and hand both back to the legal department the next morning to ensure there is a record of advice given.

Once the lawyer has legalled the story, the copy will then be passed back to the journalist and on to the sub-editors.[3]

Other difficulties can arise where legalled versions of stories in the computer system are subbed or edited at the news desk without being sent back to a lawyer to be checked again, allowing "safe" stories to become risky once more. This may also be the case where stories are changed, moved or added after the first edition comes out: "late-breaking" stories may not be legalled if the night lawyer is not consulted at home after his shift ends. The lawyer should therefore insist on seeing the page proofs in their final form, particularly if the story is contentious.

It is a matter of routine at the larger newspapers that almost all stories are legalled. Feature items are generally legalled some time in advance of publication. On the other hand, some stories are filed late and will be legalled on

---

[3] This copy is legally privileged.

the page proof rather than in hard copy. Proofs are brought to the lawyer, principally to check headlines photographs and captions. Sometimes a story is not legalled due to oversight but this seems to be a fairly rare occurrence. Similarly the final proof may not have been shown to the lawyer and this can give rise to problems with headlines and the overall context of the story.[4]

Regional newspapers tend to have a less structured regime and practice varies considerably between papers. They tend to be more risk averse than their national cousins. It is unusual for advice to be taken other than over the most controversial of stories. Indeed, our research indicated that many regional papers only formally sought advice from a lawyer a few times each year. In those circumstances they may fax or email the story to their solicitor or just discuss the piece over the telephone. The approach may come from a reporter, the editor or one of the sub-editors.

The practice in magazines is similar to newspapers, with the same difference between the large groups and smaller operations. The larger magazine groups have an in-house lawyer who works in a similar way to the lawyers on the national newspapers. Smaller magazines have a less rigid system in place for copy clearance. All magazines have the advantage of operating to longer deadlines.

Overseas and internet editions

Whilst we are principally concerned with the risks associated with publishing material in England and Wales, it must not be forgotten that English newspapers are often sold in other countries. For many years newspapers have sold copies in Scotland and the Republic of Ireland, and there has been a trend for international editions to be published or for copies to be sold more widely around the world. More significantly, many newspapers now have Internet editions which can be read in almost any country. From a legal perspective, the consequence of this globalisation is that newspaper groups are exposing themselves to potential liabilities in an increasing number of jurisdictions.

Managing the risk of these publications is no small task. Some of the more common issues to be dealt with are now considered. Reference should also be made to the discussion on *forum non conveniens* in Chapter 3.[5]

(a) General observations

It would be impractical and enormously costly for a newspaper to seek legal advice from every jurisdiction where a claim might arise. Indeed, lawyers in some jurisdictions might be unable to provide definitive advice as to whether a claim could arise. A more pragmatic approach has been adopted by newspapers, namely to focus their energies on territories which have given rise to particular difficulties in the past. Moreover, some comfort can be derived from the fact that England and Wales have relatively strict laws on libel and con-

25-11

25-12

---

[4] See defamation section in Chap. 24.
[5] Chap. 3 at 6.

tempt. So if the article in question is acceptable for an English audience, it is likely to be legally acceptable in most other jurisdictions.

Another approach sometimes suggested in the context of Internet editions of newspapers is to include a statement on the site to the effect that the material is not intended to be published other than in specified countries. The effectiveness of this approach would depend on the law of the relevant country, but it must be seriously doubted whether a disclaimer of this type could succeed.

(b) Northern Ireland and Eire

25-13 The risk of claims arising from publication in Northern Ireland and Eire has proved to be a particular problem for several years. Defamation claims have been brought by individuals caught up in Ulster's political troubles and the problems for newspapers have been significant. Claims brought in Eire by Republican sympathisers may receive a more understanding response from a jury in Dublin than in London. Another issue is the differing court procedures in Ireland compared with England, which can make it more difficult to make a payment into court and thereby settle a claim.

Because of these very specific concerns, we found widespread evidence of newspapers making changes to the editions (usually the first edition) destined for Ireland. Indeed, it is not uncommon for national newspapers to have an editor responsible for the Irish edition who will have a brief to monitor risks. The changes to the copy usually arise from concerns over libel and contempt.

If a sanitisation process is undertaken, then it must be followed through to its logical conclusion. This may involve amending all versions of the newspapers which might be published in Ireland. This could include any Internet edition, syndicated copy, sales by subscription or back issues made available on CD ROM or elsewhere.

(c) France

25-14 France has a law of privacy which has been invoked on occasion by United Kingdom celebrities. Most famously, the Duchess of York secured damages in Paris in respect of the publication of her toe-sucking exploits in France. More recently (and in the context of television), the BBC was successfully sued in France by the Barclay brothers for invasion of privacy in respect of a television programme which could be received on the north coast of France.

(d) United States

25-15 Certain states within the United States also have privacy laws. To avoid the risk of complaint it may be desirable (subject to the importance of the story) to avoid any publication in the United States or, alternatively, to delete reference to United States residents in a particular story.

(3) Managing relations with third party suppliers

Newspapers and magazines may wish to publish material in which copyright **25-16** is owned by a third party.[6] They will need to ensure that they acquire an assignment or suitable licence for the intended use. The following points should be noted:

(a) Photographs: newspapers frequently use photographs supplied by picture libraries. The acquisition process tends to be handled on a day-to-day basis by the picture desk who are usually experienced in this area. Normally it is not a subject of great concern: a picture library will grant a standard form licence for use of an image in the newspaper. The library should indemnify the newspaper in the event of any claims being made.

(b) Freelance journalists and photographers: particular care is required in dealing with freelancers. It is important to ensure that they are granting adequate rights for the intended use. Normally this will be implied from the fact that the copy has been tendered in expectation of payment. However, it is prudent to ensure that a written licence is obtained if it is intended to use the copy for any specific purposes (*e.g.* in an Internet edition). In relation to photographs it will be necessary to consider whether the photographer has asserted any moral right to be identified as the author of the photograph in question.[7] In recent years it has become the custom of many newspapers to state the name of the author beside his photograph in any event.

(c) Copy from overseas: another specific risk arises when newspapers acquire material from overseas. It will be important in reviewing the copy to bear in mind that the person supplying the material may not be used to operating in the more restrictive environment of United Kingdom libel law. It may be appropriate to obtain an indemnity in respect of any claims that may arise.

(d) Book serialisation rights: when a book is being serialised, the newspaper or magazine will need a licence to reproduce the extracts, as well as an indemnity in respect of any claims by third parties for copyright infringement. If the extracts are potentially defamatory, an indemnity should also be sought in this respect.

(e) "Spoilers": one area of risk taking, generally restricted to Fleet Street, arises where one newspaper deliberately uses copy or a photograph from a rival newspaper. "Spoilers" have been run for years and often the only issue is the compensation that may have to be paid. Often these disputes take on a life of their own, with tit-for-tat copying leading to an eventual out of court settlement.

---

[6] This issue has been referred to in Chap. 21 at 2(3).
[7] See Chap. 5 at 10(2).

Another area that can be a source of difficulty is contractual arrangements with printers and distributors. It is commonplace for these parties to require indemnities from the publisher in the event that they are sued because the publication contains defamatory material. In practice, printers or distributors may want to settle threatened proceedings against them without reference to the newspaper or magazine in question. It is therefore prudent, wherever possible, for the publisher to agree that indemnities will only be honoured where the publisher has conduct of the defence.[8]

3. BOOK PUBLISHING

(1) CHECKLIST OF LEGAL AND REGULATORY ISSUES

25-17 • Principal legal issues

— Copyright
— Libel
— Contempt

• Principal regulatory issues

— None

(2) PLANNING THE PRODUCTION PROCESS

25-18 The process of getting a book published is quite different to that of a newspaper, and this is reflected in the respective approaches to legal editing. Whereas a newspaper consists of many stories supplied by many authors who work to timelines of days or hours, a book may be a single story, created by one author with a production process of months.

Our research made it clear that a much more focused cost-benefit analysis took place before deciding whether to publish a particular manuscript. This will often involve an analysis of the likely sales (or longer-term benefit to publishers) should a particular allegation or book be published as against a watered down version of the same title. The consequence of such an approach is that a publisher is more likely to turn down a high profile title if the risks of publishing were too high and it was felt that a less risky version would not sell. With newspapers it may be more difficult to assess the impact of a single story as distinct from a whole newspaper.

Linked to this is the fact that publishers are more exposed to the risk of retailers and distributors withdrawing books after a complaint has been received. Even one error in a manuscript can jeopardise a book's continued sale or lead to hefty reprinting costs. The damage may be less pronounced for

---

[8] In relation to defamation, printers and distributers may also be able to rely on the defence of innocent dissemination: see Chap. 3 at 5.

newspapers, which may no longer be on sale when a complaint is received (today's newspaper may be tomorrow's fish and chip wrapper; today's book is here tomorrow too).

A considerable amount of planning is therefore required from the outset by a publisher. The initial review of the author's work is often carried out by his own agent and, thereafter, by the editor at the publishing house. Consideration even if only in a broad way, should be given to potential legal problems at the earliest possible moment. This is more feasible, and indeed more desirable, if the work is being commissioned.

In practice, the editor has an important role in handling the manuscript. It is part of his function to spot potential libel problems. His tact and experience are critical in the production of a title which will balance the views of the author and the need to manage the risks of publication. It may be necessary to give the author some guidance on the legal issues. One major publishing house has published a booklet for their authors setting out some of the key legal pitfalls, especially related to libel.

Once written, if the manuscript remains contentious, most publishers will send a copy to a lawyer for a detailed libel report to be prepared. This report will often provide a page-by-page analysis of the likely areas of difficulty, raise possible lines of defence, suggest amendments to the text and invite the author to produce the evidence on which he would rely if a complaint were to be received. The lawyer and editor may require one or more meetings with the author to go through that evidence and work on any revisions to the text.

This is a more detailed and extended process than the approach needed in clearing stories for newspapers. The principles are, however, the same: a collaborative relationship between writer, editor and lawyer; and the search for wording that allows the writer to have his say but permits publication on the basis of a reasonable commercial risk.

In addition to considering libel issues, the editor and lawyer should carefully consider the use of quotations from third parties. Are the extracts copyright works? If so, might their use be permitted under of the defences considered in Chapter 5 (for example, for the purpose of criticism or review)? Or will it be necessary to secure permission for their use?[9]

The need for a detailed examination of the manuscript can consume a disproportionate part of the book's production costs. For many books, however, the examination is vital and our research indicates that many lawyers (both solicitors or barristers) will not charge their normal rates for libel reading to take account of the economics of book production. This situation may be contrasted with newspapers where individual articles are usually less likely to involve detailed examination and report writing.

The first signs of trouble can occur when proof copies of a book are sent out to journalists for review purposes. This often happens before the final proof-reading is complete. It can give some insight into how a book is likely to be received and may in some situations allow for last minute changes to be made. But it is worth noting that our researches indicated that it was when

---

[9] See (3) below.

publishers rushed to print a book (often admittedly involving a high profile subject) that they were more likely to receive a claim.

(3) MANAGING RELATIONS WITH THIRD PARTY SUPPLIERS

25-19 The issues to be considered here are very similar to those dealt with in relation to newspapers and magazines at 2(3) above. Because of the less transient nature of books, however, it is even more important for publishing rights to be secured in writing.

Furthermore, consideration should be given to asking an author for warranties and indemnities on a number of points, for example, that he is the copyright owner, that publication of the book will not violate any law and that its contents are not defamatory. Indeed, it is common for these provisions to appear in publisher's contracts with their authors, but in practice publishers tend not to enforce the provisions. This is principally because authors may not have the financial resources to be worth suing and partly because publishers will be reluctant to alienate their authors in general.

Particular issues can arise when rights are acquired in books previously published in the United States: different libel and copyright considerations may have allowed material to be published there that would not be permitted in the United Kingdom.

As with newspapers and magazines, book publishers should be careful in the indemnities which they give to printers and distributors.[10]

4. ADVERTISING

(1) CHECKLIST OF LEGAL AND REGULATORY ISSUES

Principal legal issues

25-20 Because advertising is so closely associated with selling products or services, the public interest requires that it is subject to a far wider range of legal constraints than other forms of content.[11]

- **Principal legal issues**

- Copyright

- Moral rights

- Rights in performance

- Trade marks

---

[10] See the points raised at 2(3) above.

[11] The British Codes of Advertising and Sales Promotion issued by the CAP include a detailed list of the main statutes and regulation affecting advertising. A copy appears in the CD ROM accompanying this text.

- Passing off
- Defamation

- **Principal regulatory issues**

• Independent Television Commission Codes	(commercial television)	**25-21**
• Radio Authority Codes	(commercial radio)	
• Broadcasting Standards Commission Codes	(commercial television and radio)	
• Committee of Advertising Practice Codes	(non-broadcast media)	
• British Board of Film Classification	(cinema and video advertising)	

(2) PLANNING THE PRODUCTION PROCESS

General

Advertising campaigns can vary enormously in terms of budget and media to   **25-22**
be employed. At its most basic, the proposition may be no more than a classified advertisement in a local newspaper; at its most epic, a campaign might
include a commercial scheduled to run on national television supported by
advertising on radio, posters and print. Because of this diversity, it is impossible to describe just one way of producing campaigns.

Whatever the campaign, it is important for legal input to be sought at the
earliest opportunity, ideally at concept stage before significant costs have been
incurred. This task normally falls to the account executive.

Passing off

Advertisers frequently wish to associate their products or services with sports-   **25-23**
men, actors, politicians or other celebrities. Sometimes the celebrity is used in
a teasing way; at other times he is there to lend his direct indorsement to a campaign.

If the advertiser has obtained the celebrity's permission to the use of his
name or image, then there can be no risk of proceedings from that quarter. It
may, however, be too expensive or inconvenient to seek permission in which
case the advertiser needs to be careful to avoid any suggestion that the celebrity is indorsing his product (and thereby trigger a claim for passing off).[12]

Various techniques can be employed to avoid the risk of such claims, including the following:

---

[12] The law of passing off is described in Chap. 6. The ITC Code of Advertising Standards and
Practice (r.15) and the CAP Advertising Code (cl.13) contain similar, arguably stricter, provisions: see Chaps. 13 at 3(2) and 17 at 3(2) respectively.

- Avoiding eye content between the celebrity and viewer/reader. By analogy, a campaign in the style of Lord Kitchener's finger-pointing "Your Country Needs You" would probably be seen as a direct exhortation supported by the personality.

- Humour can make it clear that the celebrity is being in an ironic way, rather than in such a way as to lend his direct indorsement to the campaign.

- A tactical campaign associated with a celebrity's recent appearance in the media can make it clear that the celebrity is not giving his direct indorsement.

Internet

25-24 It is worth mentioning that specific attention needs to be given to campaigns run on the Internet. In most cases it is likely that the regulation of Internet advertising will be the same as that for more traditional media. However, preparing for the consequences of campaigns in this environment is particularly important. In 1995 Virgin Atlantic was fined U.S. $14,000 in the United States for providing inaccurate pricing on its website about the cost of its airline tickets.[13] More recently, the United Kingdom retailer Argos found itself in legal difficulties when it mistakenly advertised television sets on its website for £3 each. These cases highlight the need for care in the management of websites and for keeping information up to date.

(3) MANAGING RELATIONS WITH THIRD PARTY SUPPLIERS

25-25 Advertisers and their agencies may well need to acquire rights from third parties to allow their advertisements to be published. The type of rights to be acquired will vary according to the commercial in question.

If a television commercial is being produced, the agency will usually commission a production company to shoot the commercial. In this situation similar considerations apply to those outlined above in relation to broadcasters and independent production companies.[14] In particular, the agency will need to ensure that it has a licence or assignment of relevant intellectual property rights from the production company and director. It should also obtain a series of warranties, for example, that the commercial does not infringe copyright, is not defamatory and is not in breach of any relevant Codes.[15] These warranties will not in themselves prevent the advertiser or agency being sued,

---

[13] *New York Times*, November 21, 1995.
[14] See 1 (3) above.
[15] Many of these transactions are conducted on standard industry contracts. For example, "Producing Advertising Commercials" is a standard contract agreed between the Advertising Film and Videotape Producers Association, the Institute of Practitioners in Advertising and the Incorporated Society of British Advertisers. It is widely used in the advertising business. Another example is the Agreement for the Production and Licensing of Original Musical Composition agreed between the IPA and the Society of Producers and Composers of Applied Music (PCAM).

but they will provide a remedy against the production company to recover any compensation which has to be paid.

Apart from properly documenting relations with independent production companies, it may be necessary to secure rights from other parties. These could include the following:

- a copyright licence from a photographic library to use a protected photograph;

- a copyright licence to use a piece of music with a commercial;

- permission from a celebrity to use his likeness if the execution could suggest his indorsement of the campaign;

- appropriate usage rights from the artists who appeared in an earlier commercial if it is intended to use the commercial for additional purposes;

- a licence for the use of any trade marks which are to be used in the campaign, including branded props and certain international flags (which are afforded certain protections by the Trade Marks Act 1994);

- permission to use quotes, poetry, uniforms or works of art.

Particular care is required if a campaign is to use representations of postage stamps, bank notes or coins, when permission may be needed from the Royal Mail, the Bank of England and HM Treasury respectively.[16]

Cost is a factor which may encourage advertisers and their agencies to avoid paying hefty usage fees and an agency may be asked to produce something in the style of an existing copyright work. For example, an agency may commission a new musical work to be written in a similar style to an existing composition.[17] This can give rise to difficult questions as to whether the new work is "original" or amounts to a substantial copy of the piece which was the source of inspiration. It may be appropriate to seek an opinion from one or more musicologists, though such an exercise can be fraught with problems.

5. INTERNET

(1) CHECKLIST OF LEGAL AND REGULATORY ISSUES FOR ISPs

- Principal legal issues   **25-26**

    — Libel

    — Laws dealing with offensive material[18]

---

[16] In addition to copyright concerns, use of bank notes without permission may give rise to offences under the Forgery and Counterfeiting Act 1981.

[17] The recent case of *Norowzian v. Arks Limited (No. 2)* [2000] E.M.L.R. 67 was an example where a commercial was shot using a similar editing technique: see Chap. 5 at 2(1).

[18] There are a number of disparate areas of law which may be relevant here: Chap. 8 deals with the most important.

- Principal regulatory issues

  — Committee of Advertising Practice Codes
  — Internet Watch Foundation guidance

(2) PLANNING THE PRODUCTION PROCESS

Introduction

25-27   The Internet permits companies and individuals to publish material using a variety of technologies across computer networks. The following are examples of potential publishers on the Internet:

- the internet service provider ("ISP") which provides access to the Internet;

- the systems operator of a computer bulletin board;

- the moderator of a computer chat room, who reads all material posted to the room;

- the proprietor of a website;

- the author of a web page;

- someone who sends or posts an email.

For the purpose of this text, and in particular describing best practice in approaching legal editing, two distinctions should be made.

(a) Active or passive?

25-28   Our primary focus in this section are those businesses concerned with facilitating the delivery of content using the Internet, namely ISPs. There are particular legal and regulatory issues faced by these businesses arising from the fact that often, though not always, they do not know whether the content being delivered is legally contentious. In this respect they may be seen to be in a similar position to the Post Office or a telephone company.

   The position of ISPs when they take a more active role is somewhat different. If they provide moderating facilities for discussion groups, it will be more difficult for them to claim that they are innocent disseminators. In these situations, they should heed the approach taken by television companies in clearing live programming.[19]

   Website proprietors are in a different position again, more akin to that of newspaper publishers. Their staff actively produce copy for inclusion in the website and, as such, they should follow the production processes described elsewhere in this text for those working in the newspaper industry. The legal

---

[19] See 1(3) above.

and regulatory issues are broadly the same[20] and, where the material to appear on the site is likely to be contentious, similar clearance procedures should be followed. Particular attention should be paid to jurisdictional issues.[21]

ISPs which provide assurances about the acceptability of content are in a similar position to wesite proprietors and should take similar steps in terms of clearance procedures.

(b) Mass communication or private correspondence?

Email is becoming increasingly commonplace within business. Unlike other forms of communication addressed in this text, it is generally not used as a mass broadcast medium. When it is (primarily in the context of direct marketing), then it should be cleared in a similar way to other forms of direct marketing material. Use in other contexts falls outside the scope of this text. **25-29**

The innocent ISP

Given that this section is therefore concerned with those occasions when an ISP acts merely as conduit to the Internet, it is something of a misnomer to refer to the production process. **25-30**

The critical issue for ISPs in this situation is to ensure that, once they are on notice about offensive material, they do something to prevent its further dissemination. The ISP should ensure that a suitable mechanism exists for receiving such notifications and that someone in their organisation is charged with responsibility for following through.

The relevant law is contained in section 1 of the Defamation Act 1996.[22] This allows an ISP to defend a claim on the basis that

"(a) he was not the author, editor or publisher of the statement complained of,
(b) he took reasonable care in relation to its publication, and
(c) he did not know, and had no reason to believe, that what he did caused or contributed to the publication of a defamatory statement."

In looking at (b) and (c), the court has regard to the extent of his responsibility for the content of the statement or the decision to publish it, the nature and circumstances of the publication, and the previous conduct or character of the author, editor or publisher.[23]

It would seem that the following may be appropriate steps for an ISP to take:

(i)   ensure there is an adequate procedure to permit complainants to reach the ISP with ease, whether by email, letter or telephone. It is vital that a complaint will reach the correct person in a timely manner;

---

[20] Though the website will in practice not need to follow the PCC's Code of Practice if it is not a newspaper. The position of Internet editions of newspapers is described at 2(2) above.
[21] See 2(4) above.
[22] A fuller discussion of the section appears in Chap. 3 at 5(5).
[23] Defamation Act 1996, s.1(6).

(ii)   ensure that its staff are aware of the steps that need to be taken in the event of a complaint;

(iii) be permitted under the contract it has with its subscribers to remove any material which it considers to be defamatory, racist, offensive or which in its opinion it considers otherwise inappropriate. This will be important where an ISP receives a complaint from a third party and has to decide whether to withdraw the offending material. The ISP may be in an uncomfortable position in having to remove material without checking how genuine the complaint may be but failure to act swiftly, as seen in *Godfrey* (see below), may have adverse consequences. A term in the contract with his subscriber permitting immediate removal will avoid any consequential claim being brought by the subscriber;

(iv)   be permitted under its subscriber contract to terminate the contract in the event that the subscriber posts, or persistently posts, any material which it consider to be defamatory, racist, offensive or which in its opinion it considers otherwise inappropriate;

(v)   having removed a subscriber, the ISP should, so far as possible, take steps to ensure that the person removed from access to the ISP's services cannot sign up again.

There has been little case law dealing with this provision. In *Godfrey v. Demon Internet Ltd*[24], an interlocutory decision of the court indicated that an ISP would not be able to rely on the defence under section 1 when it failed to remove a defamatory posting until 10 days after it had been received. This suggests that a tough approach will be taken by the courts.

In relation to material which may offend against the criminal law, the Internet Watch Foundation (IWF) has set up a telephone hotline to allow members of the public to draw the attention of ISPs to offensive material, such as child pornography or racist material. ISPs should ensure that immediate steps are taken to remove this material once they have notice of its presence.[25]

(3) MANAGING RELATIONS WITH THIRD PARTY SUPPLIERS

25-31   This section is of less relevance here than with other sectors given that our focus is on ISPs with no control over content prior to posting. ISPs will, however, have contracts with individuals and companies which use their services to run websites, send email or participate in user groups. As mentioned above, it is important that ISPs ensure that those contracts prohibit the posting of any defamatory, obscene or other inappropriate material and allow the ISP to remove any such offensive postings. In addition, the contract should contain a provision allowing the ISP to seek an indemnity in the event that a claim is made and allow ISP to remove links to any offensive sites.

---

[24] [1999] 4 All E.R. 342. See also in Chap. 3 at 5(5)
[25] The service is described in Chap. 20.

6. PORNOGRAPHY

(1) CHECKLIST OF LEGAL AND REGULATORY ISSUES

- Principal legal issues   **25-32**
  — Obscenity[26]

- Principal regulatory issues

  — British Board of Film Classification (cinema, video, computer games)
  — Video Standards Council/ELPSA rating scheme (computer games)

It should be noted that most of the regulators described in Part II also have provisions dealing with taste and decency. Advertising of pornography is specifically banned from television and radio.[27]

(2) PLANNING THE PRODUCTION PROCESS

One of the difficult issues for the legal editor is to ensure that a publication   **25-33** complies with the provisions of the Obscene Publications Act 1959.[28] This outlaws the publication of an article which is obscene. What is obscene can change with the times, but a number of practical ground rules are currently followed:

(1) The legislation has generally been interpreted to mean the showing of a full male erection or penetration cannot be shown, though a partially erect penis may not be objectionable.

(2) A woman cannot be shown performing oral sex to the extent that the penis is in her mouth, though the shot may be taken from such an angle as to suggest that this is happening. There may be greater latitude if the programme is being broadcast for educational purposes or can be considered to be artistic or aesthetically acceptable.

(3) The depiction of anal sex is forbidden.

In relation to the requirements of taste and decency under the various Codes, anything suggestive of non-consensual acts or humiliation would tend to be forbidden.

The BBFC's criterion for classifying films is described in Chapter 19. As described there, recent case law indicates that they may take a more liberal approach in relation to how it classifies material to be sold in sex shops.[29]

---

[26] See Chap. 8 for the various legal areas of concern.
[27] ITC Code of Advertising Standards and Practice, cl.18 and Radio Authority Advertising and Sponsorship Code, r.3 respectively.
[28] See Chap. 8.
[29] *R v. Video Appeals Committee of the British Board of Film Classification, exp. The British Board of Film Classification and others*, Times Law Reports, June 7, 2000. See Chapter 19 at 2 above.

(3) MANAGING RELATIONS WITH THIRD PARTY SUPPLIERS

25-34 Pornography can appear in any almost any of the media described in this chapter. The approach to dealing with third parties will depend on the medium concerned.

Part V

COMPLAINT HANDLING

Chapter 26

Complaint handling

1. CREATING A STRUCTURED APPROACH TO COMPLAINT HANDLING

Even the best laid plans can go awry and a publisher may find itself defend- **26-01** ing an unwelcome complaint. Regardless of whether the complaint comes as a complete surprise or is half-expected, the publisher should ensure that his risk management strategy includes a clear and efficient system for complaints handling. The strategy adopted should be capable of responding to a complaint from any quarter, whether in the form of a solicitor's letter threatening libel proceedings, a complaint made by a viewer to the ITC or a letter to the editor from a disenchanted reader. In each case, the media company should be confident that its chosen structure will ensure the efficient handling of the complaint.

In describing these issues, particular emphasis is placed on defamation complaints. That is not to say that other complaints are ignored. It is simply that defamation is the only cause of action where the manner in which a claim is defended may have a bearing on the level of damages should the claim ultimately succeed at trial.[1] Furthermore, there are generally more options available for settling a defamation claim.

The approach to complaint handling should complement structures in place for copy clearance.[2] Media companies should address the following.

WHO SHOULD BE RESPONSIBLE FOR MANAGING COMPLAINTS?

There should be a clear line of control in every media organisation for han- **26-02** dling complaints. Those involved will vary depending on the type and size of the relevant company. They may include the editor, a complaints manager, an in-house lawyer or an external firm of solicitors. It may also be appropriate in certain cases for the company's press office or P.R. agency to be notified if the claim could have an impact on the organisation's business reputation.

---

[1] See Chap. 3 at 7 for a description of how defamation damages are to be calculated.
[2] See Chap. 23.

Because of the terms of their licences, we noticed in our research that the independent television companies adopted a particularly rigorous approach to complaints management. One company has a director of public affairs responsible for logging complaints, which are then notified to the relevant producer.

Another television company which we interviewed has a centralised Viewer Complaints Unit through which all complaints are filtered and logged. In that case, even if a complaint arrives at a particular department, details are copied to the central Unit. The Unit also monitors all responses and ensures that a suitable reply is given within a reasonable time. The BBC also has a central Programme Complaints Unit.

In many newspapers, including nationals and the largest regional groups, the initial response to a complaint will often be through the editor or a managing editor.

In the context of complaints about television commercials, broadcasters, advertisers and their agencies tend to rely at the outset on the Broadcast Advertising Clearance Centre (BACC). The BACC will usually have pre-cleared the commercial and will seek to defend their corner in initial dealings with the ITC.

WHAT LIMITS SHOULD BE PLACED ON THEIR AUTHORITY?

26-03   As with legal editing, there should be clear limits set on the authority of the person handling the complaint. It may be acceptable for a newspaper editor to commit his company to publishing a correction (or even paying a complaint's legal fees and a small sum in damages); it may be quite another, however, for him to take the decision to pay substantial compensation without consulting senior colleagues or the company's Board.

EARLY WARNING SYSTEMS

26-04   It is vital that everyone working in the company can be alerted to the fact that a complaint has been received, the nature of the complaint and the identity of the person handling it in the company. This aspect can be incorporated into the early warning system described in Chapter 23 to alert journalists of problems with potential new stories.

TRAINING

26-05   The task of handling complaints is an important one. It requires an understanding of the legal issues posed by the complaint, the techniques available for dealing with complaints and the potential risks for the company which may be considerable. It is therefore essential that those assigned the task of handling complaints are given adequate training for the task and it is recommended that this should be tied in with the training programme described in Chapter 23 for those involved in legal editing.

2. HOW TO GO ABOUT COMPLAINT HANDLING

(1) INITIAL ASSESSMENT OF THE COMPLAINT

The approach to complaint handling to some extent mirrors the steps described in Chapter 24 when we looked at how to go about legal editing, particularly in the context of defamation. Whereas a major concern at that stage is trying to work out who might sue over an intended publication and what their complaint might be, the complaint handler now knows the identity of the complainant and should have a reasonable indication of what their complaint is about. In other respects, however, the complaint handler acts rather like a legal editor when the complaint is received. **26-06**

In essence he has to undertake a similar exercise to that which took place (or should have taken place) in determining risk at the pre-publication stage. He will therefore need to consider the meaning which is likely to be borne by the words which are the subject of complaint. In particular, are they likely to be regarded as defamatory by a jury? If so, what defences might be available? The complaint handler will require access to the journalist's evidence and any other materials that can be secured quickly to assist in forming a view as to the prospects of being able to defend the claim.

The journalist should also be reminded of the company's obligations in relation to the disclosure of documents and the need to ensure that they are not destroyed.[3] Care should taken when writing internal memoranda once a complaint has been received. Unless they are protected by legal privilege, the note may have to be disclosed in any subsequent court proceedings and could be embarrassing.

The importance of investing time and energy at this early stage cannot be overstated. The complaint handler will need to consider, and give advice, on the following matters:

- Is the complaint likely to be successful?

- Might it succeed on some other ground which the claimant has not yet considered?

- How likely is it that the claimant will fight all the way to trial? Is the claimant insured or does he have the benefit of a conditional fee arrangement with a firm of solicitors?

---

[3] This is discussed in Chap. 21 at 4.

- Is it important for the media organisation not to be seen as a soft touch, prepared to settle at the earliest sign of trouble?

- Should the media company be seen to be standing by its journalist?

- Is it important for the media company to be seen to be putting up a fight as a matter of principle against an undeserving or notorious claimant?

- Will the claimant attract sympathy even if he loses?

- What are the implications of a successful claim? Primarily this means assessing the likely costs and damages that would have to be paid out. But there may be other considerations, such as P.R. fall-out from a high profile defeat or the danger of creating an unwelcome legal precedent in a novel area.

- Could the claimant afford to pay to pay the media company's legal bill if he loses?

It is recognised that it may not be possible to answer all of these or similar questions at the outset. Some will be of greater importance than others, depending on the facts of the case. Furthermore, it does not follow that a decision taken at the outset on these issues will be irreversible. Even if a decision is made to rebut the claims and fight a law suit, litigation is costly and unpredictable and constant reference should be made to these considerations as the matter progresses. The critical factor for a media company, however, is conducting detailed investigations and assessing those findings. Only once this has been done should the initial response be sent to the claimant.

In practice the response of media organisations will vary. Some will move to extricate themselves from a claim at the earliest opportunity. This is particularly true of the economically weaker elements of the media or those which are uninsured. Local newspapers in particular may be concerned about the impact that just one claim could have on their continuing viability. They may also be less inclined to find themselves in an acrimonious dispute with a key local personality or company.

Perhaps not unsurprisingly, national newspapers and broadcasters, with deeper pockets or better insurance cover, may end up digging in for a long fight, even when their prospects of successfully defending proceedings are not high. They realise that complaints must make a significant commitment in terms of time and money if they are to go all the way to trial. Even then, national newspapers or broadcasters may take into account ongoing political or commercial relationships in deciding how to respond to a complaint.

(2) PSYCHOLOGY OF COMPLAINTS

26-07 We all know that a well handled complaint can affect a complainants' response. If a restaurant apologises for poor service and throws in a free bottle of wine, we are more likely to leave content and perhaps return again. A refusal to apologise, on the other hand, can make us more angry and we will certainly tell the story to friends: the damage to the restaurant will be disproportionate to the original harm.

The psychology of claimants in libel claims is often similar to people who have had poor service in a restaurant. They commonly start out looking for a quick apology and perhaps payment of their costs. However, if the media company allows matters to drag on, even for a short time, attitudes may become hardened. The claimant may become irritated at the attitude of the media company and press for compensation too. On the other hand a complainant will generally be compromising if he can see that the publisher is handling the complaint efficiently and professionally. The simple message here for media companies is not to lose the opportunity of a relatively cheap and good natured settlement by delay or unrealistic expectations. Early disposal of a claim will also reduce the amount of management time spent on the claim.[4]

(3) SPEED OF RESPONSE

As we have seen, there are clear advantages in being able to dispose of a claim speedily. **26-08**

Making amends in such a manner for an inaccurate story is particularly feasible in the context of television and radio. Indeed, a broadcaster can carry an apology, correction or clarification during or immediately after the programme containing the offending material. This may happen unilaterally if, for example, the presenter or producer realises a mistake has occurred; it can also happen in the less likely event of a complaint being received during the broadcast itself. Anticipating and managing complaints with such speed requires experience and effective systems.

It is also feasible for swift resolution of disputes to take place in the context of online services, such as websites or usenet groups. Systems should be created which allow for the speedy resolution of complaints: these could include a freephone telephone number or the option of complaining to an email address (which is frequently monitored). On receipt of a complaint, the complaint handler (perhaps a systems operator) should be able to take immediate action to withdraw offending material as soon as it is brought to his attention. In certain cases, where the operator has a responsibility for the original content,[5] it may also be appropriate for him to publish an immediate apology.

With national newspapers it may also be possible to take immediate avoiding action if it becomes apparent that a first edition contains material which proves to be too contentious. In these situations, if the newspaper takes any action at all, that will often consist of no more than withdrawing or amending the story in subsequent editions rather than publishing an apology. This

---

[4] This is particularly the case given the new methods for early settlement provided for under the Defamation Act 1996: see Chap. 3.

[5] See the section on defamation and the liability of service providers in Chap. 25 at 5.

approach is usually driven by a hope that the first edition may not be seen by the potential complainant or, if it is, that an apology would make it more difficult for the newspaper subsequently to advance a defence of justification.

It is worth mentioning that sometimes the media company will itself learn of an error in a previous story without being notified of a complaint. Under the PCC's Code of Practice newspapers are obliged to publish corrections in any event. It is doubted whether this requirement is generally complied with, particularly when the likelihood of being caught out is small and there is a risk that a premature correction may lead to further problems in any subsequent litigation. It is more likely that the newspaper will act, if at all, only after a complaint has been received.

Even if an immediate apology is neither appropriate nor possible because of time constraints, dealing with a complaint expeditiously is nonetheless desirable. It was noteworthy that one regional newspaper which we interviewed set itself a target of responding to all complaints within 24 hours (even if the first response was no more than a holding reply).

(4) TONE OF RESPONSE

26-09 Another factor to bear in mind is that a courteous response will not aggravate a complaint. It is obvious that a personal response from the editor's office (rather than a letter from the legal department) may placate the complainant and enable a dialogue to be commenced. Indeed, according to Newspaper Society research, face-to-face meetings and private correspondence between editors and those with a complaint were an integral and effective part of the complaint process at regional newspaper level.[6]

As well as the obvious point that causing needless pain to a claimant may make it more difficult to resolve matters with him later on, there is a legal issue to be noted in the context of defamation proceedings. A defendant in such proceedings will tend to increase the level of any damages award at trial if he has handled the complaint in such a way as to further hurt the complainant's feelings. With this point in mind, every letter to the claimant should be written on the basis that it may be seen by a jury hearing the case.

Defendants, or potential defendants, should therefore, at least in theory, handle their defence, including all correspondence, in a professional, non-hostile manner. This should apply even if they are intending to justify the allegations about which complaint is made. However, in the real world, it is obvious that many undeserving complainants raise objections which have no merit, or if they do, their intention to launch aggressive litigation. In these situations the media organisation will want to be seen to meet fire with fire. It may prefer to have correspondence from the claimant's solicitors dealt with by its own lawyers; if the complaint is entirely unjustified, the editor will want to stand by his journalists and respond in uncompromising terms.

---

[6] "Britain's press: in defence of self-regulation" (The Newspaper Society, September 1992).

3. ELEMENTS FOR SETTLING A CLAIM

Though the initial response to a complaint may have been uncompromising, **26-10** in reality few claims lead to proceedings, and even fewer to full-blooded trials. Either the claimant decides not to proceed at all or, if he does, it is often in the interests of both parties to reach a compromise at some point before trial.

This section looks at the elements which usually form part of a compromise settlement. The relevance of each will depend on the circumstances of the particular case. Our emphasis is on defamation cases, though several elements — damages, undertaking not to repeat the wrongful act, delivery up of offending material, confidentiality, and even the making of an apology — will be used to settle other civil claims.

What this section does not address specifically are complaints to the ITC, the Advertising Standards Authority (ASA) or other regulators. By their nature, these complaints are not susceptible to formal negotiation (though the offer of undertakings may be useful) and are broadly resolved by the relevant regulator reaching its decision.

(1) PUBLISHING AN APOLOGY

Apart from paying damages, publishing an apology — and the precise **26-11** wording of any apology — are the most contentious aspects of settlement discussions, most complainants want an apology in fulsome terms with a high degree of prominence, but publishers are generally reluctant to comply.

This is particularly so with broadcast media where an apology is so much more visible than a printed apology. It is obviously impossible to apologise on screen, even for a minor libel, without bringing the programming schedule to a standstill, even for a few moments.

In the book publishing context, it may be possible to provide an erratum slip, though this allows the original statement to remain and may draw undue attention to something that had been forgotten by many readers. It may be more appropriate for a claimant to destroy current editions altogether and amend any future editions of the publication.

What should not be forgotten, by those involved in the negotiations is that generally a court has no power to order the publication of an apology or a right to reply.[7] This means that the offer to publish an apology, even one which does not meet all of the complainant's concerns, may be something of tangible benefit to the claimant in settlement discussions: even if he goes to trial and wins, there would be no apology. Juries do not give reasons for their decisions, only verdicts in favour or against the claimant. They will usually go on to award damages which, if substantial, may by implication vindicate the claimant. However, such an award is not explicit in terms of setting out precisely

---

[7] The exception to this is the power under s.9(2) of the Defamation Act 1996 for the court, in dealing with a summary disposal, to direct the defendant to publish a summary of the court's judgement. See Chap. 3 at 7.

how the complainant has been libelled and an agreed apology as part of a settlement may be perceived as more valuable.

This argument is somewhat diluted in that there are several methods of complaint which will lead to the publication of some form of finding in the same medium as the original publication. For example, any publication which is criticised by the PCC is duty bound to print the adjudication which follows in full and with due prominence. Similarly, under clause 1 of the PCC's Code of Practice the publication should always report fairly and accurately the outcome of an action for defamation to which it has been a party. In the same way, adverse adjudications against media owners by the Broadcasting Standards Commission (BSC) will also be published.

What none of these publications do, however, is take the form of a direct apology in which the media company speaks in its own tongue to the complainant and the public at large to record its regret at what has happened. They merely take the form of a report of the findings on the relevant body.

Assuming therefore that the media company is prepared to consider publishing an apology, the two sides will then become locked into fairly predictable patterns of behaviour in negotiating its wording. The following issues are frequently encountered:

(a) The media company will not want to call the apology "an apology". They will prefer to call it a correction or clarification, or to have no heading at all above the statement.

(b) The claimant may want the publisher to apologise "unreservedly" and to state that the allegations are "totally" untrue. This will often be resisted and a subject of negotiation.

(c) The claimant may want the apology to have a high degree of prominence. If an article appeared on the front page of a newspaper, the claimant will want the apology to appear there too. This will usually be resisted by the newspaper.

(d) Along similar lines, arguments may take place over whether the apology appears above or below the fold, on an odd or even page, or in the same size typeface as the original article.

(e) If the original story was accompanied by a photograph of the claimant, the claimant may demand one in the apology.

(f) The claimant may wish to include reference to the size of any damages paid; the publisher will resist this.

This pattern will, of course, not always apply. Sometimes the complainant will be satisfied with something less than a full apology, particularly if he is being paid damages. Not infrequently, a complainant will prefer there to be no apology because this might remind readers of something long forgotten or barely noticed first time round. In these circumstances he may be satisfied with a positive follow-up story or interview which makes no mention of the original story and which may either directly or indirectly correct the impression given by the earlier piece.

Another way of achieving a similar objective may be for the media company to supply the complainant with a private letter of clarification or apology. This is something which the complainant may keep for future use (if the matter should ever be brought up) or distribute. Another approach is for a newspaper to publish a letter to the editor from the complainant which rectifies the original article.

Conversely, there will be occasions when a newspaper, usually a national tabloid, will pay damages in order to secure a new story, particularly where the complainant is a well-known celebrity. This may be a suitable device for demonstrating to the world that peace has broken out between the disputants. It may also allow a better public relations "spin" for both sides.

Whilst publishing some form of apology or correction is often used as part of a settlement, the media company should bear in mind that this publication will not be protected by privilege and could give rise to a separate claim by a third party.[8] This should be taken into account in the wording agreed upon in the apology. One way round this difficulty is for the parties to agree to reading a statement in open court which will be covered by privilege (see (2) below).

It should also be remembered that a media company may decide to publish a unilateral apology. This usually happens as part of a damage limitation exercise when the media company realises that either all or part of the original story was incorrect.[9] If published in a timely fashion, such an apology may help mitigate any damages claim by the claimant. In the context of negotiations, a claimant may be alarmed at the prospect of a unilateral apology which may not be quite as fulsome as he would like. The defendant will for this reason often let slip that such an apology is to appear as a way of forcing through an early settlement.

(2) READING A STATEMENT IN OPEN COURT

Sometimes a claimant will wish to have a statement read out in open court. **26-12** This is a formal hearing provided for by the rules of court.[10] In some ways, the procedure is old fashioned and the statement is often read out before the judge in an almost empty courtroom. The procedure does, however, have several benefits. The most important factor is that the reading of the statement is protected by absolute privilege, while those reporting on the statement can do so protected by qualified privilege. This compares with the situation described above for an apology which appears in the newspaper that could attract a claim for libel by a third party.[11] The procedure can only be invoked if there

---

[8] *Tracy v. Kemsley Newspapers, The Times*, April 9, 1954.
[9] Another possible alternative now is for the media company to make an offer of amends under s.2 Defamation Act 1996: See Chap. 3 at 7.
[10] CPR Pt. 53, r.6.
[11] For this reason a media company may agree to a statement being read in open court of which it will then be able to carry a fair and accurate report.

are proceedings in existence: if not, the parties may agree for proceedings to be issued solely to enable a statement to be read.

A statement in open court is not something that a claimant can demand as of right. The permission of the court is required to make the statement and it is submitted in advance to a judge for approval. Where a claimant has accepted money paid into court, he may apply to the court for permission to read a statement. Normally, leave will be granted unless the amount paid in is very small. In those circumstances, the court will consider whether the proposed statement should be permitted according to its assessment of the strength of the claimant's case.

Unilateral statements can be read in court, but a joint statement is far more common. This has the advantage for the claimant of having the defendant apologise publicly and in agreed terms. It also creates a climate in which hostilities between the parties can cease, and allows the defendant to recognise its errors in a "mature" context.

The statement involves a court hearing normally lasting no more than a few minutes at which both parties are present. The statement will usually contain a vindication for the claimant, and should not contain any reservation calculated to lessen that vindication. It is a vehicle whereby a public apology is uttered by the defendant, though it may well contain a face-saving intimation that the defendant acted in good faith and reasonably in reaching the settlement.

Whilst a defendant may be reluctant to join in a statement, negotiations over the wording may give an opportunity for the defendant to explain how the story came about. Furthermore, negotiations over wording and the level of damages may come together and allow the defendant to weigh one against the other. A claimant may feel concern about a unilateral statement, particularly against a media company which, at least in theory, has the means to publish future articles justifying its reasons for publishing in the first place. A full and final settlement which allows both sides to explain their positions is the ideal and is achieved surprisingly often.

The rest of the media frequently report on statements in open court. In the case of media defendants, it is usual for the settlement to include a term that they will report on the statement at the next available opportunity in a prominent position or at a certain time.[12]

(3) UNDERTAKING NOT TO REPEAT THE LIBEL

26-13   Apart from securing an apology, obtaining the defendant's promise not to repeat the allegation is a key element in most settlements. The undertaking should be given on behalf of the defendant and those over whom the defendant exercises control. The customary formula is for the undertaking to be given (if a company) on behalf of itself, its directors, officers, servants and agents or (if an individual) on behalf of himself, his servants and agents.

---

[12] It is a requirement of the PCC's Code of Practice that newspapers fairly and accurately report the outcome of an action for defamation to which it has been party: cl.1(v).

The undertaking may be given in one of two forms. First, the undertaking can be given as a contractual promise by the defendant to the claimant as part of the contract of compromise. Should the defendant subsequently repeat the allegation, it would be open to the claimant to commence proceedings for breach of contract. The second option, which is more effective, is for the undertaking to be given by the defendant to the court. In the event of breach, it would be open to the claimant to institute a claim for contempt of court against the defendant. Such proceedings are quasi-criminal in nature, with penalties including fines, sequestration of assets and, in severe cases, imprisonment.

It is the norm for a defamation claim form to seek from the court the two remedies of damages and an injunction. Accordingly, if a defendant wishes to settle a strong claim, it will be difficult to do so without agreeing to the undertaking being given to the court in lieu of an injunction. It is, of course, advisable for a defendant to avoid giving the undertaking to the court, if it can do so, because of the severe consequences for breach.[13]

Once an undertaking has been given, whether to the court or simply as a contractual term, the defendant must ensure that a system exists within its organisation which will ensure the avoidance of repetition. It is advisable to make arrangements for a memo to notify all relevant personnel immediately after the undertaking is given. A suitable reference should also be made in the organisation's central library or other repository for such matters. Furthermore, the article complained of should be removed from any cuttings library or from other similar databases, such as CD ROMs, and from the Internet versions of the relevant publication.

The wording of undertakings can vary. Frequently a claimant will ask that the defendant undertake not to repeat the same or any similar libel of and concerning the claimant; otherwise it may be to the effect that the defendant will not repeat the allegation complained of, or any similar allegation concerning the claimant.

It is also worth the media company attempting to limit the scope of any undertaking it gives so that it will, in future, be permitted to report on the allegation in circumstances where a defence of privilege would arise. The undertaking could be qualified, for example, by allowing the defendant to report on future court or parliamentary proceedings where the same or similar allegations are repeated.

(4) DAMAGES

In all but the most trivial of claims, a claimant is likely to obtain damages. In Chapter 3 we examined how the courts (often a jury) will approach the question of quantum. As part of a settlement, however, other factors will come into play. Securing a fulsome or speedy apology should be reasons to reduce the claimant's expectations of what he might be awarded at trial. Closer to

26-14

---

[13] These were illustrated in *Bentinck v. Associated Newspapers* [1999] E.M.L.R. 556, where the journalist was fined £10,000 and the newspaper £25,000.

trial, this factor will be less relevant. On the other hand, a defendant may be prepared to pay a premium, beyond what might be awarded at trial, if it wishes to avoid adverse publicity flowing from a public hearing.

Another way of helping to achieve a settlement, particularly at an early stage, can be to suggest that the damages will be paid to charity. The charity might be one of the claimant's choice or one agreed by both parties. Payments to charity do not necessarily lead to lower payments than would otherwise be the case, though that outcome is sometimes achieved. They can, however, have an important psychological impact. They may show the media organisation in a more human light. They can create a sense that some good can come out of a confrontational situation, with both sides participating in a benevolent act, possibly marking a new beginning in their relationship. Refusing such a proposal might also cause some claimants some embarrassment if they do not want to appear greedy or motivated solely by money.

The courts are keen to encourage settlements wherever possible. One device commonly used in this context is the making of a payment into court by the defendant.[14] It can be an effective means of putting real pressure on a claimant to settle. The claimant will have 21 days to accept the monies paid into court in satisfaction of his financial claims. If he does not take the money, and at trial is awarded the same amount or less money than the sum paid into court, he will generally have to pay the defendant's costs incurred after the latest date on which the offer could have been accepted.[15]

Conversely, if a payment into court is accepted, the defendant will also have to pay the claimant's costs. If the costs cannot be agreed, they will be assessed by the court. The assessment will be conducted on what is known as the standard basis. This is generally about two thirds of the amount charged by the claimant's solicitor to his client. Similarly, if a claimant is successful at trial (and there is no effective payment into court), the claimant will normally be awarded his costs, again on the standard basis.

In settlements reached before trial, particularly those which are for significant claims, it is common for the defendant to agree to pay the claimant his costs on the more generous indemnity basis. This is more likely to mean that the claimant will have all his costs reimbursed and, as such, provides another reason for him to try to settle his claim before trial.

It was noted at (3) above that a defamation claim form will normally seek relief for damages and an injunction not to repeat the words complained of. In *Roache v. Newsgroup Newspapers Limited*[16] the defendants made a payment into court of £50,000. The claimant equalled, but failed to beat, this sum at trial but argued that his second sought after remedy—the injunction—had not been satisfied. On this basis he should be awarded his costs. The Court of Appeal held, however, that it was obvious from the size of the payment in that the defendant was not intending to repeated the libel and that, accordingly, the

---

[14] CPR, Pt. 36.
[15] CPR, r.36.20. If the claimant manages to achieve an award of damages higher than the monies paid into court, the payment will be of no consequence.
[16] *Times Law Reports*, November 23, 1992.

payment in was effective to meet the claimant's concerns. Since the case, however, it has become customary for the defendant to combine his offer to settle with a letter confirming that he will undertake not to repeat the libel complained of if the claimant accepts the moneys paid into court.

(5) CONFIDENTIALITY OF SETTLEMENT TERMS

It may be desirable for the parties to keep some or all of the settlement terms **26-15** confidential. Even if the entire agreement is not confidential (and the publication of an apology or reading of a statement in open court are inconsistent with such an approach), it is frequently the case that the amount of damages is kept secret. This can suit both sides, each claiming victory. Some insight may, however, be gained from the language of any apology or statement read in open court as to the likely level of damages. Although it is by no means a rule the usual formulation of "substantial" compensation means at least £5,000 to £10,000. If the figure is less than this, the formula may be "suitable damages", "appropriate damages" or simply "damages".

It is worth noting that the practical consequences of either party breaching the confidentiality of an agreement are unclear (unless incorporated into a court order when breach may lead to contempt proceedings). There may be breach of confidence claim for an injunction and damages. However, as the government discovered in the *Spycatcher* case,[17] the injunction remedy may be to no avail if the matter has already seeped into the public domain. Similarly, it may be difficult to place a value on any damages.

(6) DELIVERY UP AND DESTRUCTION OF OFFENDING ITEMS

If a claimant is successful at trial, the court will normally grant an order for **26-16** delivery up of any material including the defamatory allegations. The claimant will then be free to destroy the offending material. This remedy, like an injunction, is a means of ensuring that the allegation is not repeated.

4. DEFENDING A THREATENED INJUNCTION

A complainant may apply to the court for an interim injunction before any **26-17** publication has taken place. This is most commonly the case with a threatened libel, breach of confidence or infringement of intellectual property rights. In such cases it is important for the media owner to have a system in place to respond swiftly to the need to attend at court.

This issue has already been covered in the context of investigating a story

---

[17] [1990] 1 A.C. 109.

and making an approach to its subject.[18] A number of further practical points can be made:

(1) The media company may be forced to go to court at very short notice. In cases of particular urgency, an injunction can be sought outside regular court hours, over a weekend or by telephone to a judge. It is recommended for media companies to have established relationships with a roster of lawyers who can go to court at short notice on their behalf. It should also be possible to contact the journalist and any key sources at short notice.

(2) Media companies should be alert to the possibility of complainants seeking to use the threat of an injunction as a way of seeing copy prior to publication. This is something which media companies will usually try to resist. Indeed, providing the copy prior to publication may give the complainant evidence of the content of the intended story and assist with the application for an injunction.

(3) It will be necessary in most cases for a claimant to give a cross-undertaking in damages. In other words, should it transpire at trial that the interim injunction should not have been granted, the claimant will have to compensate the defendant for the losses flowing from the injunction. An interim injunction will usually be refused if the court believes that the claimant would not be able to satisfy such a cross-undertaking at trial. In some cases this may be a real issue. If, for example, a claimant has found out about the intended publication of a book after the manuscript has been printed the losses to a publisher could be substantial.

(4) In cases alleging infringement of copyright or other intellectual property rights, the media owner should seek to ensure that it has an accessible and accurate record of the basis on which it claims to be able to exploit the relevant work, whether that be in the form of trade mark registrations or licences to use a copyright work.

5. CONTEMPT COMPLAINTS

26-18 The issues arising in connection with actual or threatened contempt proceedings are dealt with in Chapter 26 ("Editing copy").

6. ALTERNATIVES TO COURT PROCEEDINGS

26-19 The courts have been compared ironically to the Ritz Hotel in that it is theoretically open to anyone to bring proceedings, and it is true that bringing court proceedings can be seen as a rich man's sport. This is particularly so in the

---

[18] See Chap. 21 at 3.

context of defamation where legal aid is not available. There are strict legal aid criteria which mean that it is rarely granted for other media cases such as malicious falsehood or intellectual property claims. Furthermore the recent introduction of conditional fee arrangements has yet to be seen to make significant impact. All of this means that there are any number of reasons why the media might be sceptical about the ability of many individuals or companies to launch court proceedings.

Our research indicates, however, that this is merely one factor in determining how the media considers stories before publication and complaints afterwards. It is by no means the only factor and, provided they are not going to be punished by enormous awards of damages, our findings suggest that the media are prepared to consider ways of resolving disputes without a full trial. Even though they may have large resources, court cases are extremely costly and time-consuming. The public relations implications of an adverse finding are also a factor in encouraging the media to shy away from full-bloodied battle in the courts.

One way round the problem of expensive court cases may be to use an arbitrator. This can be quicker and less costly than court proceedings. There have been one or two reported instances of arbitrators being used in the context of defamation proceedings.[19] However, this option is often not desirable. Complainants may prefer to have their case heard in a blaze of publicity and before a jury which can award substantial damages.

Arbitration worked in the instances referred to because in one the complainant was a judge seeking minimal publicity and damages; in the other, the newspaper agreed that it would not seek a costs order against the charity (enabling the charity to move forward without seeking the permission of the Attorney-General and without risking public money) in return for the charity's agreement not seek any damages. These examples are clearly not the norm.

Arbitration is, however, frequently used in the context of business disputes between advertisers, agencies, production companies and others involved in the creation of advertising. These arbitrations are provided for in many of the standard industry contracts.[20] It is likely that other forms of alternative dispute resolution, including mediation, will become more popular.

Furthermore, and depending on the nature of the complaint concerned, it may be that the matter will be dealt with by a statutory body or industry created regulator. Such dispute vehicles usually have the advantage of speed and reduced costs to all sides. In some instances, complainants will use these vehicles even if they have a remedy through the courts simply because they cannot afford to sue.

---

[19] The CPR also encourages parties to consider ADR: see, for example, para. 3.7 of the Pre-Action Protocol for defamation, which states that parties will be expected by the court to provide evidence that alternative means of resolving their dispute were considered.

[20] See, for example, "Producing Advertising Commercials", a standard contract agreed between the Advertising Film and Videotape Producers Association, the Institute of Practitioners in Advertising and the Incorporated Society of British Advertisers; and the Agreement for the Production and Licensing of Original Musical Composition between the IPA and PCAM (the Society of Producers and Composers of Applied Music).

On the statutory side, complaints might be directed to the ITC, the Radio Authority or the BSC depending on the nature of the complaint. Self-regulatory complaints might be dealt with by the PCC or the ASA. The remit of these bodies has been considered in Part II.[21]

The notion of a readers' ombudsman became much in vogue within national newspapers at the beginning of the 1990s. This person, employed by the newspaper, was supposed to represent the interests of readers. The ombudsman was introduced in response to the threat of statutory regulation, particularly in the area of privacy. However, it now appears to have fallen into disuse. It is possible that this is because the ombudsmen were introduced as a gimmick, were seen as adding little to the everyday involvement of editors in resolving complaints and have perhaps had their role usurped by the PCC which, under Lord Wakeham, has been more effective in removing the immediate threat of statutory regulation.

It is worth noting that in the United States some newspapers have an ombudsman but they tend to deal with questions of fairness rather than law. This is a role which could be fulfilled in practice by the editor, the managing editor or someone in a similar position.

---

[21] There are many other bodies which could deal with content-related complaints—bodies like the Medicines Control Agency which regulates advertising of prescription medicines or the Law Society which regulates advertising by solicitors—but they fall outside the scope of this book.

Part VI

FINANCIAL ASPECTS OF CLAIMS MANAGEMENT

Chapter 27

Financial planning

1. GENERAL

Thus far we have examined risk management in terms of the editorial process   **27-01**
governing a particular publication, focusing on the division of labour and
respective responsibilities of those involved in the production of that publication. However, media companies are in the business of producing many publications and, from the point of view of the financial stability of a business, it
is not satisfactory to view risk management in such narrow terms.

It may be acceptable to publish one highly contentious story, but too many
may place too great a strain on the overall stability of a business. Management
therefore need to be aware of the total levels of risk in respect of all existing
and potential claims, and there is an important function to be filled in co-
ordinating the editorial and financial aspects of a business. This may be a role
to be filled by a finance director or other risk manager. In addition to reviewing the current level of complaints, this person should conduct a periodic
appraisal of complaints received to see if lessons can be learned and changes
made.

2. BUDGETING FOR CLAIMS

The finance director will need to ensure that the company can meet any liabil-   **27-02**
ities that may accrue from possible claims. This can be achieved in a number
of ways. The smallest losses may be met out of operating budgets (*i.e.* out of
cashflow). More serious losses may be met out of some form of internal contingency fund. This could involve the payment of regular sums into a central
pool to take account of future potential liabilities.

Along similar lines, the media company may choose to insure itself in
respect of certain losses. Whether it makes sense to insure for a particular
loss depends on all the circumstances. This is considered in detail in Chapter
28.

Our research indicates that most media companies give very serious consideration to the question of insurance. What is rather more surprising is the
apparently less rigid approach taken to the scrutiny of current claims and how
such claims affect a media owner's assessment of further risks from future

publications. There may be several reasons for this.[1] It is an area where a scientific approach is difficult: the weighing up of a large batch of stories in the context of a newspaper and assessing their overall impact on the business may be something of an artificial exercise. A more realistic approach is to "batten down the hatches" if it becomes apparent that the number of claims being received by the newspaper is being increased over a particular period of time. This may point to the need for greater training or caution. Monitoring of claims in this way by the finance director can make a significant contribution.

3. SPECIFIC MEDIA

NEWSPAPERS AND PERIODICALS

27-03   Recent research has indicated that financial considerations carry little weight in influencing national newspapers' output, notwithstanding the considerable trouble it takes to minimise libel risks.[2] However, our own research and experience suggests a rather more rigorous approach.

An interview which we conducted with the legal manager for one of the national broadsheets began with his assertion that his function was to protect the purse of the organisation. His company was a public company which must operate efficiently and make a profit, so any legal outlays must be kept to a minimum. He remarked that things had changed, particularly as result of the recession during the 1990s. He reported on the yearly grilling he was subjected to by his company auditors as to whether sufficient reserve had been allowed for legal claims.

It is accepted that such a conservative approach does not apply universally, particularly amongst the tabloid press where the highly competitive market-place may prompt editors to publish sensational stories to achieve short-term circulation gains.

Even among other areas of the media, a sensational story can still be published after a careful consideration of the legal risks. In 1997 *The Daily Mail* identified those alleged to have carried out the killing of Stephen Lawrence. On the face of it this was a risky story. But the newspaper must have calculated that the risks of a libel claim were small (particularly in the absence of legal aid) and that a contempt prosecution could not be brought, or would have been politically embarrassing to the government.

One national newspaper group which we researched prepared budgets for litigation, based principally on payments made for the past five years. They also prepare six-monthly reports for the board on all litigation. Another Group has to inform their accounts department once a claim comes in, but no long-term forecasting is required.

---

[1] We recognise that this is an area where media organisations were less keen to co-operate with us in interview.
[2] Barendt and others, *Libel and the Media: The Chilling Effect* (1997, Clarendon Press,), pp. 71 to 77.

There is a fairly widespread practice of providing monthly figures to the accounts department or to the Board of likely expenditure, but it is not scientific. At a minimum, such figures usually include estimates damages and costs (for both parties in each action). It should also be stated how far the claim is likely to progress and how much a trial would cost. At each year end, companies will have to give a statement in their accounts of contingent liabilities.

Our research indicated a similar approach by magazine publishers to that of the national newspapers.

TELEVISION

Barendt[3] notes that greater care is taken in television companies to budget for claims. This is almost certainly because broadcasters have insurance policies which create a climate in which a more commercial approach has to be taken to the financial assessment of risk.   **27-04**

Our researches indicated that at the BBC considerable effort is put into budgeting. Departmental heads provide monthly forecasts which are then worked into the Corporation's overall budgets. One television company we spoke to indicated that it undertook a detailed yearly review of potential claims as part of its budgeting process.

BOOK PUBLISHERS

Practice seems to vary considerably between book publishers. However, because each book is seen as a separate venture (unlike each article in a newspaper), that book will often generate a business plan with a line for libel reading or insurance. Claims tend to be fewer against publishers so there is probably less of a need for overall budgeting.   **27-05**

---

[3] See n.2, above.

Chapter 28

Insurance

1. WHY INSURE?

28-01   Our strategies for managing the risks of publishing contentious allegations have so far concentrated on risk avoidance (not publishing the allegation) and risk reduction (moderating the allegation). Insurance is about risk transfer, allowing a publisher to transfer some of the risks of publication to a third party.

The risks of publication are most often financial, but publishers will also act in response to other threats, such as the possible loss of credibility or reputation and possible disruption to ordinary business activity. Insurance cannot generally cover these non-financial losses. What it can do, however, is to replace the uncertainty of future financial claims with the certainty that any significant losses will be borne by a third party.

The existence of insurance will not of course absolve the insured from all responsibility. His insurer will not let him publish and be damned. But insurance can provide a reasonable level of security that a contentious story, published within the conditions laid down by an insurance policy, will not lead to claims that cause serious difficulties for the publisher's business, whether in terms of its profitability or ongoing stability.

But the potential benefits of insurance do not mean that it is right for all publishers. It is first necessary to identify what risks are faced by the particular company, the relative dangers posed by each risk and then to ascertain how much insurance cover would cost. This can be a lengthy and complex process, particularly where a company operates on a global basis.

The process of assessment is likely to establish that some risks will best be absorbed by the company itself. For example, the relatively trivial costs of having to rewrite a newspaper article in the light of a threatened injunction. What if, however, an article were to attract a libel suit? Should the damages and legal costs be borne by the newspaper, or should it try to pass on the financial costs of future claims to an insurer? All these questions will need to be considered. Insurance is, of course, always bad value for money until a claim arises. This is as true for libel as in other area. Even in today's more moderate climate, damages pay-outs can run to well over £100,000, whilst the costs of a trial can run to many more times that figure. Because of punitive damages awards, claims in the United States could of course run to many times these levels and appropriate cover is essential.

An insured in the media business will often be looking for a special breed of insurer, an insurer who understands that it is not desirable to settle all cases at the first sign of trouble and that funding complex and detailed investigations will sometimes be necessary (notwithstanding any prepublication inquiries) to ensure that a powerful defence can be sustained at trial. Similarly, a journalist may refuse to identify his source: the insured does not want this to place him in a position of conflict with his insurer. It was suggested to us in our research that there may be advantages in choosing United States insurers who will probably have greater experience in handling complex claims with potentially high settlement values.

Protecting free speech and sound management of insurance claims are perhaps unlikely bedfellows. However, the somewhat unusual circumstances and demands created by the media insurance marketplace mean that the two objectives will be amongst the stated goals of the better insurers. It is also true to say that insurers do not like to be seen as a soft touch: this should be reflected in their approach to claims management.

Furthermore, in the case of very large organisations, the cost of premiums over the years could well equal the likely settlement costs of claims made. For such companies, however, insurance has another important function: to allow the cost of claims to be spread over a number of years rather than expose the company to the risk of many claims accruing together.

Equally, it may be possible for very large companies to meet liabilities out of current year funds and, as such, there may be no point in taking out insurance which will merely increase costs. However, even companies in this position may well decide to secure catastrophe insurance to protect against perils which could cause massive disruption to the organisation or threaten its continued existence.

It is worth noting the growing trend in recent years for substantial corporations to use "captive" insurance subsidiaries to insure the group's risks and then to go directly to the reinsurance market for cheaper catastrophe cover. Such an approach will be chosen if it fits in with the corporation's overall strategy towards managing risk and can be achieved at cheaper cost than conventional insurance.[1] Such techniques are currently only relevant to the very largest media corporations and are beyond the scope of this text.

In summary, all media companies are different but each should examine its potential exposures, especially in financial terms, and decide how best to plan for them.

2. WHAT RISKS CAN BE INSURED AGAINST?

Content management has been the principal concern of this text and will continue to be our primary concern in the context of insurance. However, media   **28-02**

---

[1] Captives can be formed by two or more companies in the same industry. The Newspaper Mutual Insurance Society which insures a large number of regional newspapers can be seen in this light: see below.

companies will need to secure cover for claims arising from contingencies incidental to their normal activities. Whilst a detailed examination of these risks is beyond the scope of this text, it is worth noting that claims for personal injury or property damage caused at a photographic shoot could well be more important to insure against than the risks of publishing the photographs themselves. In similar vein, employers should obtain additional cover for journalists working in hazardous locations, who may be exposed to the risk of accidents, or even kidnapping and ransom demands.

Turning to content-related claims, Parts I and II have looked at potential liabilities from the perspective of English law. Media insurers are, however, very familiar with the broader range of torts emanating from developed legal systems, such as the United States or Australia, and policies will often provide protection against the possibility of claimants seeking to mimic such claims in the United Kingdom.

The areas which are frequently covered by insurance include claims for:

(a) Libel, slander or malicious falsehood.

(b) Interference with rights of privacy or publicity.

(c) Trade mark infringement or passing off.

(d) Copyright or moral rights infringement.

(e) Breach of contract.

(f) Negligent acts, omissions or statements.

(g) Trespass.

Policies will often cover claims for injunctive relief prior to publication. This can be important: in the context of film or television, an insured should generally aim to have cover in place by the first day of filming. This will provide cover if, for example, an injunction is sought alleging copyright infringement. The risks before the first camera day are often thought to be less significant.

It is the norm for policies to provide for reimbursement of all damages and the costs for both sides, subject to any excess or limit on liability as discussed below. Given the often disproportionate level of costs, this element of cover is important.

Another dimension that will often need to be considered is cover for claims made in other jurisdictions. In practice, and assuming that publication were to take place on a worldwide basis, cover is usually only required for the relatively small number of territories where significant claims in terms of damages and costs could arise. The most likely territories in this context are the United States, Canada, Australasia, France and Germany. However, it is the norm, where cover extends beyond the United Kingdom, for worldwide liabilities to be insured against.

3. WHAT RISKS MAY BE EXCLUDED?

Certain types of claim are often excluded by insurers. Exclusions will depend **28-03** on the wording of the policy but they will frequently relate to claims determined by the insured's state of mind or which are of a criminal or quasi-criminal nature. The main reason for this latter category is that it is regarded as being contrary to public policy to insure for actions which could amount to criminal behaviour.

The following are examples of claims that are often excluded:

(1) Intentional, fraudulent or dishonest acts: separate cover may be necessary for the dishonest actions of staff.

(2) Contempt of court: this will not be covered because it is quasi-criminal in nature.

(3) Actions by government or regulatory bodies: an example here might be a fine imposed by the Independent Television Commission (ITC) on one of its licensees or the costs of withdrawing a poster following a ruling by the Advertising Standards Authority (ASA).

(4) Exemplary damages: there may be some difference in policies on the question of exemplary damages (which are again punitive in nature). Some insurers will provide coverage, others not. However, it would always be advisable to ensure that a policy covers this element which can be a significant part of a damages award in a United Kingdom libel case, and even more so in the United States.

(5) Claims by employees.

(6) Claims for injury or death: whilst media policies do not usually cover such claims, it will often be important to secure separate cover for public liabilities of this sort. Publishers should also be concerned about liability for personal injury or other loss that could flow from reliance on "how-to" books or videos.

(7) Claims for loss of profit: the potential for loss is often too high for the insured to accept this kind of risk, or to do so without some financial cap. It may be possible to agree cover for specific types of loss of profit that may be seen by an insurer as being highly remote and therefore acceptable for insurance purposes.

(8) Claims for breach of contract.

(9) False advertising: most policies will cover claims involving false statements about third party products but will not usually extend to false claims made in the insured's own advertising material.

4. SPECIFIC TYPES OF POLICY

The types of cover available to media companies are many and varied. This **28-04** section will look at some of the most popular options.

The policies that we shall consider are generally schemes geared to providing cover to an insured on an ongoing basis (*i.e.* for what is usually at least a 12-month period), rather than to companies or individuals looking for one-off cover. From an insured's point of view, an organisation is likely to have a spread of activities which will in turn mean a balance of risks. It is of course possible to obtain one-off cover from the open market for specific programmes, films, books or other publications, if required, though this may prove to be proportionately more expensive.

Many of the policies have a more or less standard wording. However, with larger companies operating across a diverse range of activities, the policy may be "manuscripted". This means that specific conditions will be added to the schedule of the policy to take account of situations not normally covered by the policy. Manuscripted policies are in practice more likely to be issued to broadcasters or large film production companies with a substantial output. It would be more usual for only named perils to be covered where, say, only a single film production is to be insured.

Many media companies are constantly creating new treatments or products with associated legal rights and potential problems. An advertising agency, for example, may be developing new print campaigns on a daily basis whilst a television station may have a certain amount of live programming being broadcast each day. In such circumstances it is more practical for a blanket (*i.e.* non-specific) policy to be issued, at least for the relevant part of the insured's business. This will, however, only be done if the insurer is satisfied that the insured has adequate procedures in place to minimise risks.

It should also be borne in mind that most policies in the United Kingdom market have traditionally had to be made within the period of insurance ("claims made"). In the United States, many policies are "occurrence wording", *i.e.* claims are made on the policy which existed at the date of the occurrence (often the date of publication). From the insured's point of view it is not a matter of great significance, though for the insurer in the media sector, occurrence wording may be a more meaningful way of analysing risk, given that claims often arise from the same publication date.

Unfortunately the terminology applied to policies used in this area can be confusing and there is often a great deal of overlap between the different kinds of policies. This is particularly so in relation to cover for defamation. The confusion is partly the result of the differing approaches adopted by British and American insurance companies. In what is a competitive market, insurers are now having to provide similar policies, whatever those policies may be called. Furthermore, some terminology may have been used in historically different contexts, outside the field of media liability. The review which follows is therefore given by way of general guidance: the precise terms of the policies are more important than their names.

(1) ERRORS AND OMISSIONS POLICY

28-05   Errors and omissions cover ("E.&O.") plays a significant role in the United Kingdom media insurance scene, particularly where broadcasters and producers are concerned.[2] It developed originally to protect against losses arising from content which contained negligent elements or which had been negligently permitted to be published. This approach was too narrow for media companies which could, for example, be exposed to liability for defamation irrespective of whether there had been carelessness on the part of the producer or his advisers. E.&O. has therefore been extended in scope to deal with defamation claims. It is sometimes called editorial products liability or defective advice cover.

There is no industry standard wording for E.&O. policies, so care needs to be taken over precisely what is covered under a particular policy. However, the named perils in an E.&O. policy will usually including the following:

- libel, slander or other forms of defamation;

- copyright and trademark infringement;

- invasion of privacy or publicity.

Policies will generally cover the insured (including its employees, officers, directors and agents) and all those in the chain of distribution (*e.g.* licensees, distributors and exhibitors). It can cover independent contractors, freelance writers or authors but this may require naming an additional insured. A policy will usually cover each side's legal costs and any damages.

It may be possible to include additional perils. These can include claims relating to:

- merchandising or losses flowing from an injunction (such as print, advertising and promotional costs);

- trespass;

- breach of contract;

- passing off;

- negligent misstatement; and

- website damage.

E.&O. cover is similar to professional indemnity (P.I.) cover described below, save that the focus of E.&O. is more towards those involved in the dissemination of content; P.I. cover was traditionally more concerned with professional negligence. In practice, the distinction between E.&O. and P.I. has largely gone though, for historical reasons, E.&O. tends to be the preferred terminology in the United States.

---

[2] Film and television companies will also often require production insurance. This type of cover falls outside the strict concerns of this text but will provide cover for hazards such as financial loss caused by delays during filming, damaged equipment and injury or death.

(2) PROFESSIONAL INDEMNITY POLICY

28-06   Professional indemnity insurance ("PI", or professional liability insurance as it is sometimes called) provides a wide range of cover. It protects a company or firm against claims for negligence on the part of its directors, officers and employees. It has in effect been E.&O. insurance for the professions (doctors, lawyers, architects, etc.) and for others who owe a duty of care in respect of their actions, errors or omissions.

Traditionally cover was only available to professionals, and claims would only fall within the rubric of a policy if the insured failed to meet the standards that were generally expected within his profession. This approach did not quite fit the bill where defamation claims were concerned: there is no need to prove negligence for a defamation claim and often the intended insured was not a professional in the strict sense. Notwithstanding the terminology, insurers will now provide cover for libellous content, though they will be cautious of doing so if the insured's business is more than incidental broadcasting or publishing: in such cases a further policy will often be required.

This is often not ideal for many media companies, though it is generally suitable for advertising and P.R. agencies. P.I. would, for example, cover a media company for printing an error in a client's press pack.

PI policies should be contrasted with Directors' and Officers' cover ("D.&O."). With D.&O. the focus is on claims against directors and senior executives for wrongful acts or trading, and for defence costs. D.&O. policies usually have an exclusion for libel and slander.

(3) MEDIA LIABILITY POLICY

28-07   This is a separate category of policy to E.&O. but the two have much in common from the point of view of media companies. It will cover named perils, usually including libel and related torts, privacy, publicity and intellectual property. Whilst it does not provide cover for errors and omissions in the provision of services by the insured to third parties, the policy may be manuscripted to this effect.

(4) LIBEL POLICY

28-08   What is called a libel policy tends to be issued by Lloyd's underwriters or other United Kingdom insurers. In practice it will usually cover libel, slander, copyright, trade mark, breach of contract and an assortment of related torts (such as privacy and publicity). Cover for negligence in the content or provision of related services is usually not covered, though this may be agreed by way of indorsement on the policy.

(5) NEWSPAPER MUTUAL INSURANCE SOCIETY

28-09   It is worth mentioning the Newspaper Mutual Insurance Society (NMIS). NMIS had a particular niche in the United Kingdom regional newspaper market. It was set up in the 1930s to provide mutual insurance for the regional newspaper market. It covered most publishing risks including libel, malicious falsehood, intellectual property infringement, breach of confidence and negligent misstatement. In recent years, however, it had became less attractive as new players came into the market and ceased to write any new policies from about 1999. It is currently only dealing with claims under old policies.

(6) COMBINED (OR PACKAGED) INSURANCE POLICIES; COMPREHENSIVE INSURANCE POLICIES

The policies considered so far have provided protection for specific types of loss **28-10** with a media emphasis. However, individuals and companies often require cover for several different types of risk at the same time: a combined or commercial policy can provide such cover in one policy. As well as covering content-related claims, this type of policy can be devised to cover contingencies as diverse as property damage, professional indemnity and public liability.

One of the advantages of the policy is that it can allow a company to obtain global coverage for all of its subsidiaries for a wide variety of claims. Such policies tend therefore to be purchased by larger companies. The policy will, for example, usually cover death or injury (which E.&O. does not). However, a potential weakness for media companies is that the policy may not provide cover for certain media specific risks, such as a claim for copyright infringement. This could create the danger that the insurer might seek to avoid liability on a particularly large claim not specified under the policy. Particular care will therefore be needed with such policies to check their wording and to obtain indorsements where appropriate. Alternatively, it will often be the case that media companies with a comprehensive general liability policy will also purchase a more content-specific policy, such as E.&O.

(7) DEATH OR DISGRACE INSURANCE

This form of cover protects against the losses that can follow if, for example, **28-11** a celebrity involved in a film or television commercial dies, becomes terminally ill or disgraces himself. Disgrace in this context generally means that the celebrity commits a criminal act or otherwise offends against good taste and decency. The policy anticipates the contingency that the insured will need to replace the named celebrity and covers the costs of so doing.

(8) CANCELLATION AND NON-APPEARANCE COVER

This protects the insured should a scheduled event not take place. **28-12**

(9) CATASTROPHE COVER

As its name suggests, this policy will protect an insured against losses from a **28-13** major, specified calamity. A policy of this nature is useful to many organisations that consider day-to-day cover for all claims may be too costly but, at the same time, wish to have a long stop cover to prevent a meltdown claim being made against their business.

(10) COMPLETION BONDS

28-14   These policies offer a financial guarantee that a film will be made on time and within a budgeted figure. If the film comes in over budget, the completion bond covers the excess.

5. WILL INSURANCE BE ISSUED AND HOW MUCH WILL IT COST?

28-15   In other areas of insurance (such as motor accident or fire) there are often tariff rates because insurers can build up a detailed level of understanding of the likely risks. Their calculations can be made on an almost scientific basis. Prediction is more difficult with media publications. The number of claims and size of compensation awarded is likely to show a greater range of fluctuation.

   In practice, premiums will depend on three key factors: the size of risk; the insured's risk management expertise; and the level of risk to be shared by the insured. These factors are considered below.

   It is worth noting, however, that the cost of premiums has been subject to market fluctuations over the years. At present the market seems to be moving in favour of the insured with a number of factors, perhaps pointing towards a reduction of premiums in the short to medium term: the general downward trend in libel awards; the implementation of the Human Rights Act 1998 and its emphasis on free speech; the reduction of the limitation period in libel claims to one year; the Woolf reforms which appear to be leading to a reduction in the number of claims and trials.

(1) SIZE OF RISK

28-16   The size of risk can be influenced by a number of factors that can vary between media organisations operating in different spheres. The following factors may be of relevance in any particular situation:

(a)   The likely level of circulation of the insured publication: is the publication a village newsletter seen by a few hundred readers or a book purchased by several thousand? In the case of a broadcaster, how many hours' programming are to be shown each year? As audience figures increase, so will the level of risk.

(b)   The type of subject-matter generally appearing in the publication: is the publication of a type that aims to expose wrongdoing? If the insured is a broadcaster, what is the type and breakdown of its programmes? An insurer will want to know the balance as between, say, documentaries,

396

investigative programmes, drama and news. Similar considerations will apply to other types of publishers.

(c) Whether warranties and indemnities are to be obtained from third parties responsible for providing material for publication: it is standard practice to obtain warranties and indemnities from relevant third parties to the effect that the material supplied is not defamatory, an infringement of copyright or other intellectual property rights, or would otherwise give rise to any claim. The insurer will need to know however whether the insured would seek to rely on the assurances. There is often some reluctance to join a third party supplier unless that party has its own cover or is a substantial organisation well able to absorb the loss.

(d) In the case of television and radio, the amount of live programming. If there is a delay mechanism which can effectively minimise problems, this will be a factor in assessing the premium.

(e) The extent to which the insurance will include associated merchandising or publication by several distribution channels, such as CD ROM or the Internet.

(f) Whether the insurer will also be providing cover against non-content (*i.e.* potentially less risky) issues.

(2) INSURED'S RISK MANAGEMENT PROCEDURES

All companies operate in different ways, but the attention which they give to   **28-17** managing risk will be considered by their insurers when determining the cost of their premiums. In this context, it is often broadcasters and producers seeking E.&O. or similar cover who will face the most challenging inquiry and detailed application forms will have to be completed.

An insurer will be interested in a number of indicators, including the following:

(a) The insured's claims record: this will be regarded as an important means of assessing the likelihood of an insured being sued again in the future. Some E.&O. insurers express a preference for applicants who have been in operation for at least three years.

(b) The insured's clearance procedures: the insurer will want to know what steps the insured takes, for example, to minimise the risks that content contains libellous material or that satisfactory licences have been obtained to use copyright material.

(c) The insured's personnel: this is a particularly important consideration. The insurer must have confidence in the abilities of the in-house lawyer, head of compliance or external lawyers used by the insured. Ideally, the insurer will have worked with the individuals before. If not, the insurer may wish to see resumes of those with overall responsibility to ensure that they have the necessary academic and practical background to understand the legal and regulatory issues.

(d) The insured's training: do the relevant editors have any libel or legal training? If not, what practical experience do they have?

(e) The insured's experience: if the insured has no track record in the industry, or relevant part of it, the insurer will be wary of granting generous terms at an early stage.

(f) The number of programmes made in-house as against those commissioned. There may be less control over bought-in programmes.

(h) The authority of the insured's lawyers: an insurer will offer more competitive terms if it knows that the insured's lawyers will take a proactive stance, changing a programme or even preventing broadcast in the event of problems arising.

(3) INSURED'S SHARE OF RISK

28-18 It will usually make sense for the insured to accept at least a share of the risks of publication. This will make the insurance policy cheaper. It will also give the insurer the comfort of knowing that the insured has a direct financial stake in the possible risks (apart from an increased premium next year). This ought to incentivise the insured to pay greater attention to minimising those risks.

The insured's participation in the risk can be achieved in any or all of three ways, namely through the excess, the limit on liability and co-insurance.

(a) Through the excess

28-19 The excess (or deductible) is the amount of the first part of each and every claim (up to an agreed level) which will be borne by the insured. It may also be called the "self-insured retention". Such a provision is usual in most types of insurance. The possibility that the insured has something immediate to lose in the event of a claim should have the effect of putting some pressure on the insured to be more vigilant.

Of equal importance is the fact that the insurer will not incur disproportionately high administrative costs handling smaller claims.

The excess to be applied will to some extent be affected by the level of premium and the limit applied to the policy (see (b) below). Moreover, the insured will need to consider whether it can live with an excess set at a high level (say, £250,000) to achieve a lower premium or if such an excess would fail to provide the necessary level of security to the insured's business. This is clearly a commercial decision to be taken after discussions between the insurer, the insured and its broker. On occasion, a higher deductible might be agreed for specific programmes if they are felt to be higher risk.

One ITV company that we interviewed had an excess of £5,000, a figure which had been achieved after a reasonably good claims record over several years. For a new broadcaster with no track record, however, a minimum of £25,000 could be expected.[3] Similarly a relatively new cable station that we interviewed was saddled with an excess of £50,000, though a broker we interviewed considered that a figure of £10–25,000 would be a better reference point. On the other hand, the ITV Network Centre insists on a deductible of no greater than £10,000 for independent producers because they fear that many independents would not have sufficient resources to meet a higher deductible.[4]

The NMIS had excesses starting at around £500 to £1,000, though there were some insureds with excesses of around £25,000. A newspaper insured with an excess at such a high level will have decided to seek protection for only the most serious of claims that could otherwise place serious strains on the business.

(b) Through a limit on liability

This is the maximum amount that the insurer will pay out on any individual claim or aggregate of claims. It may be that the insured will be prepared to cover claims beyond the limit or will seek separate top-up or catastrophe cover. Unlike an excess or co-insurance, a limit is unlikely to have a significant impact on the insured's conduct prior to publication.   **28-20**

In the context of E.&O. cover for independent producers working for the ITV Network, for example, a standard policy would normally have limits of £1 million per claim or £3 million in aggregate.

(c) Through co-insurance

Co-insurance means that an agreed part of every claim will be borne by the insured himself. This was traditionally set at 10 per cent in the United Kingdom market. As well as impacting on the cost of the premium, the insured's participation in the risk will tend to make the insured more careful in assessing the risk of publication.   **28-21**

There is clearly a relationship between excess, limit and co-insurance. The ultimate cost of a premium will only be known after all these variables have been considered. Considering these variables will however be more straightforward for one-off policies, where the insured has a less complex business or wishes to obtain cover for only part of its activities. Co-insurance does not generally operate in the E.&O. market.

6. DO MEDIA COMPANIES USUALLY INSURE?

The use of insurance varies widely and often depends on the medium involved. We shall examine the traditional approach to insurance by a number of   **28-22**

---

[3] According to brokers in interview with the authors.
[4] Speech on media liability insurance by Don Christopher, *Celador*, September 27, 1999.

different media. This is an area of considerable change, however, with companies increasingly trading in many spheres, particularly with a multimedia flavour.

(1) FILMED ENTERTAINMENT

28-23   The most prevalent and developed market is for filmed entertainment (*i.e.* film and television) and E.&O. cover is the most common policy in this area for content-related claims.

Our research indicated that E.&O. was particularly popular with the ITV companies (which are obliged to under their licences to secure such cover) and with many independent producers (for whom it may be a contractual delivery requirement). The BBC, however, had an entirely different philosophy. It is such a large organisation, with so many differing activities, that it can sensibly self-insure for almost all contingencies. There were a number of exceptions to this strategy: cover was often obtained for independent productions and in respect of overseas sales. The BBC also maintained cover for catastrophic claims that could have a major impact on budgets. These were understood to be in respect of claims in excess of £1 million.

(2) NEWSPAPER AND MAGAZINE PUBLISHERS

28-24   It is ironic, but unsurprising, that the newspapers and magazines with the greatest exposure will often find it unrealistic to obtain insurance cover. In particular, almost all of the newspapers with substantial nationwide circulations are uninsured. Their approach will often be to rely on self-insurance or, occasionally, catastrophe cover to protect themselves against a long, drawn-out libel case.

There are two main reasons for this. First, the costs of insurance would in most cases be prohibitive. Secondly, any insurer wishing to offer cover in this market would require a similar clearance regime to that which applies to broadcasters with E.&O. cover. National newspapers operate in a far more competitive environment than broadcasters. With newspapers the emphasis on breaking a major story is considerably greater and catching up with rival publications can mean taking significant risks on short notice. The clearance procedures which insurers would require would be almost certainly be unacceptable to proprietors of such publications.[5]

Amongst the national press, it is only *The Financial Times* which is well known for being covered by insurance. This is explained by the generally cautious editorial style of the paper which may have made insurance a more realistic prospect than for other newspapers. Indeed, the paper is understood to have an excellent claims record. We are aware that one other newspaper group does retain catastrophe cover.

---

[5] The legal manager of one national newspaper whom we interviewed expressed relief that that his newspaper had no insurance cover. If it were insured, that would create cumbersome and inconvenient procedures which would obstruct the production process.

Research suggests that as many as half of all regional newspapers are insured[6]. These will tend to be regional or specialist publications with no inhouse lawyer and run on a fairly modest basis. Typically they will need to weigh carefully the costs of premiums against the possible size of any claims. To keep costs down, they may wish to agree to an excess of between, say, £5,000 to £10,000, leaving the insurer to bear the losses on any larger claims.

As far as magazines are concerned, it is common, though by no means universal, for insurance cover to be in place, though the trend may be for this to become more prevalent.[7]

(3) BOOK PUBLISHERS AND AUTHORS

Our research indicates that many of the larger book publishers are insured in respect of content-related claims. The publisher will often have the author added as an additional name. Traditionally, publishers have obtained libel insurance policies. **28-25**

In relation to libel, there will usually be a requirement to obtain a libel report from a lawyer confirming that publication would amount to a reasonable commercial risk. Where a manuscript involves particular problems, the insurer would expect to be kept fully advised of possible risks.

(4) INTERNET

The Internet is a relatively new area of activity for insurers, with little in the way of claims experience or legal precedent. With other areas of publication, an insurer can evaluate its likely exposure from experience of past claims within the relevant industry sector and from the insured's own claims record. However, with broad-based media organisations operating in this area there is already tremendous pressure to write insurance for Internet-related claims. **28-26**

Insurers will in one sense find this to be familiar territory: similar anxieties will have been felt with the advent of other technologies such television and video. Where the Internet creates the scope for seemingly limitless liabilities is in its invitation for claims to arise in any territory around the world. Unresolved questions relating to jurisdiction and intellectual property rights will give insurers particular difficulties in writing new business. Internet cover that does not protect against these possible claims, however, would seem to be seriously flawed.

At this stage in the Internet's development, therefore, a particularly collaborative approach will be required between the proposer and intended insurer. However, the approach to assessment of risk is likely to be no more than a modified version of current practice. This means that the insured will focus on the three factors described above: the size of risk, the insured's risk management expertise and the level of risk to be shared by the insured.

---

[6] See Barendt *et al.*, at p. 94.
[7] *ibid.* at p.156.

There are an increasing number of persons who may find themselves facing claims arising from publication on the Internet. Those responsible for creating the content include online newspapers, website publishers and those contributing copy or advertising material to such sites. As far as internet service providers (ISPs) are concerned, their legal position is not entirely clear and the recent decision in *Godfrey v. Demon Internet Ltd* may start alarm bells ringing amongst insurers.[8]

The following matters are likely to be of particular significance in the context of ISPs:

(a) The level of editorial control (actual or ostensible) exercised by the insured: this is an important consideration in view of the provisions of section 1 of the Defamation Act 1996 (and in light of United States case law). The effect of these provisions is that the ISP will have a defence where he took reasonable care and did not know and had no reason to believe that what he did caused publication.

   ISPs have come to grief where they have, however, held themselves out as exercising control (*e.g.* by advertising themselves as a family-type service). Accordingly, the insurer may require modifications as to the manner in which the proposer holds itself out.

(b) Procedures for the speedy resolution of complaints, including the removal of offending material. The *Godfrey* decision has highlighted the importance of this factor.

(c) The territories where the ISP's service is likely to be published. With the Internet, this will usually mean access on a global basis. It may be necessary for the website to contain a statement that e-commerce may only be conducted with certain countries, though the effectiveness of such a provision on certain tortious claims may be doubted.

(d) Whether those tendering content for publication provide written indemnities to hold the ISP harmless in the event of a claim.

(e) Whether Internet-literate counsel is retained by the ISP.

(f) Whether there is a warning on the site forbidding the posting of defamatory or otherwise offensive material. Again, the effectiveness of such a provision may be doubted.

Notwithstanding that this is new territory, it ought to be possible and sensible to obtain cover for ISPs. Indeed, insurers confidently advised us in the course of our researches that ISPs would tend to require a combined libel and professional indemnity policy to cover most media-related liabilities. There are also a number of insurers now offering specific cyberspace policies targeted at Internet access providers and commercial online services.[9]

---

[8] See Chap. 3 at 5(5) and Chap. 25 at 5.
[9] One insurer was offering £1 million cover with a minimum premium of £2,500 and an excess of £2,500. It preferred applicants who had been in operation at least three years and used standard contracts with third parties.

As far as the actual purveyors of content are concerned, the legal position is somewhat clearer and insurers will be able more readily to rely on existing criteria to determine the levels of risk involved. Even here, though, there will be new questions which arise: should the insured seek cover for claims arising in other jurisdictions when the insured's server is within the United Kingdom? What effect will this have on the premium?

Another area where cover will be required is in relation to intranets and emails. This ought to pose less difficulties for insurers. Cover is already available for claims arising from internal memorandum and other correspondence (under, for example, P.I. policies). The new modes of communication, whilst they will encourage a more global and less thoughtful form of communication, are unlikely to add very significantly to the volume of communications that might give rise to claims.

(5) ADVERTISING

It is commonplace for advertisers, advertising agencies and P.R. companies to have libel insurance in place. This normally takes the form of P.I. or E.&O. cover. **28-27**

Agencies frequently also take out an advertising agencies indemnity (AAI) policy which provides blanket cover for the production of television commercials. This will automatically cover death and disgrace for non-celebrity artists.

7. WHO ARE THE KEY PLAYERS?

The world's media insurance market is worth about U.S.$90 million and operates primarily from the United States. It is regarded by the insurance industry generally as a small market and the relatively modest revenues are a disincentive for new companies to compete. There is therefore currently a fairly small group of insurers offering cover for media-related liabilities. Typically, these insurers offer cover through brokers rather than directly to the public. **28-28**

Geographically the market is focused on activity in a few western countries, principally the United States, the United Kingdom, Canada, Australia and parts of the European Union.

Traditionally, media insurance has also been one of the more volatile markets. This is exemplified by *The Wall Street Journal* libel award in 1997 where the MMAR Group was awarded US$23 million in general damages and a staggering US$200 million in punitive damages by a jury.[10] However, apart from the threat posed by new claims based on a privacy right, the market in the United Kingdom is likely to become somewhat more stable after the Court of Appeal decision in the *Elton John* case.[11]

---

[10] The award was later reduced on appeal and a retrial ordered.
[11] *John v. MGN* [1997] Q.B. 536. See Chap. 3 at 7.

London is the world's leading market for many types of insurance. Whilst this supremacy does not extend into media, it still has the most significant market after the United States. Insurance in the United Kingdom is generally provided by a number of large corporations. In addition, cover is available through Lloyd's, an association of individual underwriters (or Names) who accept unlimited liability for the insurance which they write. The membership of Lloyd's consists of underwriters and intermediaries (Lloyd's brokers) who act as agents for insureds.

There has been a change in the United Kingdom in recent years with the arrival of the large United States insurers. The United States market is much larger and these insurers have the ability to cover United States risks as well, including punitive damages, an area traditionally avoided by Lloyd's.

The main underwriters at Lloyd's are Hiscox, R.E. Brown (part of Octavian Agency) and Denham Direct (part of Barber). In the company market, the key players include Chubb, AIG and Royal Sun Alliance.

In addition, there is a separate category of provider. Such a person can best be described as an underwriting manager and claims supervisor. Examples in the United Kingdom are Blanch Crawley Warren and Media/Professional Insurance (Media Pro). They allow insurers with less media expertise to enter the market. Typically, they will form a pool of non-media insurers and on their behalf conduct all marketing and claims management. The insured has no direct dealings with the pool, only their manager.

8. HOW CAN COVER BE OBTAINED?

28-29   Insurance can be obtained through an insurance intermediary, or sometimes directly from the underwriter. There are two main types of intermediary, brokers and Lloyd's brokers.

To call oneself a "broker", it is necessary to be registered with the Insurance Brokers Registration Council. As such, the broker must meet certain standards as to the manner in which he conducts business. He must be independent of the insurance companies and must not favour one unduly. Brokers are agents for the proposer (*i.e.* the intended insured) but are paid by the insurer. A Lloyd's broker is an insurance broker who is allowed to place business at Lloyd's. He must comply with the regulations of the Committee of Lloyd's. The best known brokers in the media field include Aon/Albert Ruben and C. Heath Lambert.

In practice, it makes better sense to go through a broker rather than an underwriter. The broker can advise on the most appropriate market, underwriter and terms for the insured. Whilst cost will always be important, the broker will be able to advise on those underwriters which will provide good service and sensible claims handling. He can also warn of any concerns as to the financial rating of the intended insurer. Guidance on such issues will be vital if the insured does not have its own in-house expert to advise on the types of claim, particularly those with a media flavour, that need to be covered.

It does not cost the insured any more to go through a broker (who earns commission or a fee) and the broker can act as a useful intermediary for the insured.

The broker will run through a detailed proposal form with the insured touching on all the issues which we have identified as being relevant to the ultimate cost of the premium.

It should be borne in mind that contracts of insurance are contracts "of the utmost good faith" (or *uberimae fidei*). This means that the insured must make full disclosure of all material matters which are known to him. What is material depends on whether the facts in question would influence the insurer in fixing the premium or deciding to take the risk at all. This is an ongoing obligation. Failure to make full disclosure may allow the insurer not to honour (avoid) the policy.

Particularly with E.&O. cover, and policies of a similar type, detailed proposal forms will need to be completed. These are usually reviewed by the insurer's own legal counsel. This may lead to further discussions about possible problem areas and there may need to be a period of negotiations over terms. This could take several months. However, one broker we spoke to claimed to represent large insurers who have paid out substantial claims under policies that have been under negotiation when a claim has been made. Such generosity can only be expected to be shown to the largest companies, and publishers should make sure that cover is in place at the earliest opportunity.

Assuming that the relationship with the insurer is successful, there will probably be an annual review meeting at which the broker and insured look back over the past year (the usual period of cover for anything more than a one-off policy) to help decide on the coverage terms for the year ahead. In the event of any claims, it will be the broker's job to represent the insured and assist in the satisfactory handling of the complaint.

9. PREPUBLICATION CLEARANCE PROCEDURES

We saw in Part IV that sensible management of content involves the setting up   **28-30** and operation of procedures that will minimise the risks of publication. Should a publisher wish to insure some or all of these risks, the potential insurer will require satisfaction that suitable procedures exist and work. What the insurer looks for was described at 5 above.

It follows, if insurance is issued, that the insured should continue to operate those procedures and that the insurer will continue to take an interest in how they operate. The insured will continue to have some financial interest in minimising risk: in addition to any share it may have in potential liabilities, it will want to ensure that future premiums are kept to a minimum.

Apart from the motivation of the potential financial or other fall-out from a claim, prepublication procedures of some sort will be required of the insured under his contract of insurance. The contractual obligations will vary and publishers, together with their broker and lawyers, should look carefully at the precise obligations.

Policies may provide:

- that all material should be vetted prior to publication (possibly by a named firm);
- that only material considered by an editor to be "likely to be contentious" need be vetted;
- that certain types of material should be vetted (*e.g.* television documentary dramas); and
- that any changes recommended by the lawyer, including advice not to publish, should be followed.

An indication of the steps that need to be taken by an insured can be seen in the clearance procedures which appear in the Appendix. These appear in the E.&O. policy for procedures operated through one of the leading underwriting groups. Similar guidance may well appear in other policies. It is not uncommon for risk management seminars to be offered to insureds and their brokers.

If the insured is a large media company with regular output, or has a lengthy claims record, the insurer will almost certainly require that satisfactory risk management procedures are in operation. Whether the insurer requires all programming to be vetted depends on the particular circumstances.

Policies covering book publishing may require the publisher to draw the insurer's attention to particular risks prior to publication. Equally, there may be a blanket policy with no requirements for vetting. However, if claims start to spiral, for example, the insurer may well take a more forceful approach.

Notwithstanding any provisions in the policies, our research indicates a remarkably close contact between the insured (perhaps through its lawyers) and the insurer. The relationship tends to work as a consensual one if it is to be successful on a long-term basis.

It is apparent that the lawyers, particularly those within large media organisations, are prudent in any event, even if cover is in place. Too many lapses will have an effect on next year's premium. Moreover, it is common sense, where the insured intends publishing a particularly controversial allegation, for the lawyer to involve the insured in the decision-making process at the earliest opportunity.

Equally, it will often make commercial sense for the insurer, so far as possible, to support and be seen to support the creativity of the insured. Our research is clear: insurers generally do not wish to be seen as acting as censors[12]; nor do they tend to interfere with the judgment of the insured's lawyer.

One anomaly thrown up by the contractual nature of the insurance is the question of where the loyalties of the lawyer vetting copy should lie. He may be the insured's external solicitor but his bills are being met by the insurer in the event of a claim. Whatever the strict legal position, however, the lawyer's function can only be performed if a collaborative approach is adopted.

---

[12] One even operates with the slogan, "We insure free speech worldwide".

10. INSURER'S ROLE IN HANDLING COMPLAINTS

If something goes wrong, the insurer needs to be notified at the earliest oppor-   **28-31**
tunity, even if the claim comes within the excess. Indeed, it is often a term of
the policy that the insured cannot take any step without insurer's approval. It
is particularly important that the insured does not bring in a new solicitor
without approval.

E.&O. insurance can tend to involve a close relationship between insurer,
insured and the solicitor. With other kinds of insurance there may be less need
for prepublication clearance under the policy and the solicitor accordingly has
a less close relationship with the insurer. In these cases, the insurer may allow
the insured to remain with its existing solicitor or may prefer the insured to
use one of the solicitors' firms on their panel. Ultimately, the insurer pays the
legal bills and will be able to insist on its choice of adviser. However, this is less
likely to be the case if there is a significant excess on the policy.

After the claim has been notified, there will then be a requirement to consult
with the insured during the conduct of any defence. This may be expressed in
the contract of insurance so that the publisher must act as a "prudent insured"
at all times.

The cases where the costs get completely out of hand and the insurer insists
on a settlement are rare. Insurers will so far as possible wish to take a sympathetic line, particularly where a long-term relationship exists or can develop.
This may encourage the insurer to fight a costly case if the insured reasonably
considers that its original programme was correct and feels obliged to stand
by its production team.

There may even be the occasional case where the insured would be inclined
to settle but the insurer tries to discourage this if it considers that there are, for
example, important freedom of speech issues involved or if to settle might
encourage other ongoing claims.

If an insurer wishes to settle, it will usually be able to rely on a buy-out
clause if the insured insists on fighting on. This will entail the insured being
given a sum of money to allow the insurer to drop out of the picture and
permit the insured to fight on. From this point on the insurer has no further
liability to the insured. Equally, it will not share in any payment that the
insured can secure as part of any subsequent settlement.

Appendix

CLEARANCE PROCEDURES

The Clearance Procedures below should not be construed as exhaustive and they do not cover all situations which may arise in any particular circumstance or any particular Production:

1. Applicant and its counsel should continually monitor the Production at all stages, from inception through final cut, with a view to eliminating material which could give rise to a claim.

2. The script should be read prior to commencement of Production to eliminate matter which is defamatory, invades privacy or is otherwise potentially actionable.

3. Unless work is an unpublished original not based on any other work, a copyright report must be obtained. Both domestic and foreign copyrights and renewal rights should be checked. If a completed film is being acquired, a similar review should be made of copyright and renewals on any copyrighted underlying property.

4. If the script is an unpublished original, the origins of the work should be ascertained – basic idea, sequence of events and characters. It should be ascertained if submissions or if any similar properties have been received by the Applicant and, if so, the circumstances as to why the submitting party may not claim theft or infringement should be described in detail.

5. Prior to final title selection, a Title report must be obtained.

6. Whether Production is fictional (and location is identifiable) or factual, it should be made certain that no names, faces or likenesses of any recognizable living persons are used unless written releases have been obtained. Release is unnecessary if person is part of a crowd scene or shown in a fleeting background. Telephone books or other sources should be checked when necessary. Releases can only be dispensed with if the Applicant provides Underwriters with specific reasons, in writing, as to why such releases are unnecessary and such reasons are accepted by Underwriters. The term "living person" includes thinly disguised versions

of living persons or living person who are readily identifiable because of identity of other characters or because of the factual, historic or geographic setting.

7. All releases must give the Applicant the right to edit, modify, add to and/or delete material, juxtapose any part of the film with any other film, change the sequence of events or of any questions posed and/or answers, fictionalise persons or events including the releasee and to make any other changes in the film that the Applicant deems appropriate. If a minor, consent has to be legally binding.

8. If music is used, the Applicant must obtain all necessary synchronisation and performance licenses from composers or copyright proprietors. Licenses must also be obtained on pre-recorded music.

9. Written agreements must exist between the Applicant and all creators, authors, writers, performers and any other persons providing material (including quotations from copyrighted works) or on-screen services.

10. If distinctive locations, buildings, businesses, personal property or products are filmed, written releases must be secured. This is not necessary if non-distinctive background use is made of real property.

11. If the Production involves actual events, it should be ascertained that the author's sources are independent and primary (contemporaneous newspaper reports, court transcripts, interviews with witnesses, etc) and not secondary (another author's copyrighted work, autobiographies, copyrighted magazine articles, etc).

12. Shooting script and rough cuts should be checked if possible, to assure compliance with all of the above. During photography, persons might be photographed on location, dialogue added or other matter included which was not originally contemplated.

13. If the intent is to use the Production to be insured on Videotapes, Videocassettes, Videodiscs or other technology, rights to manufacture, distribute and release the Production must be obtained, including the above rights, from all writers, directors, actors, musicians, composers and others necessary therefore, **including proprietors of underlying materials.**

14. Film clips are dangerous unless licenses and authorisations for the second use are obtained from the owner of the clip or party authorised to licence the same, as well as licenses from all persons rendering services in or supplying material contained in the film clip; e.g. underlying literacy rights, performances of actors or musicians. Special attention should be paid to music rights as publishers are taking the position that new synchronisation and performance licenses are required.

15. Aside from living persons, even dead persons (through their personal representatives or heirs) have a "right of publicity", especially where there is considerable fictionalisation. Clearances must be obtained where neces-

sary. Where the work is fictional in whole or in part, the names of all characters must be fictional. If for some special reason particular names need not be fictional, full details must be provided to Underwriters in an attatchement to the Application.

16. Consideration should be given to the likelihood of any claim or litigation. Is there a potential claimant portrayed in the Production who has sued before or is likely to sue again? Is there a close copyright or other legal issue? Is the subject matter of the Production such as to require difficult and extensive discovery in the event of necessity to defend? Are sources reliable? The above factors should be considered in your clearance procedures and recommendations.

Index

411

THE COMPANION CD

Instructions for Use

Introduction

These notes are provided for guidance only. They should be read and interpreted in the context of your own computer system and operational procedures. It is assumed that you have a basic knowledge of WINDOWS. However, if there is any problem please contact our help line on 020 7393 7266 who will be happy to help you.

CD Format and Contents

To run this CD you need at least:
- IBM compatible PC with Pentium processor
- 8MB RAM
- CD-ROM drive
- Microsoft Windows 95

The CD contains data files of the Appendices to the book, which are the Guidance Notes referred to throughout the text, together with relevant statutory material (see contents list on CD). It does not contain software or commentary.

Please refer to the "**Contents List**" document for the numbering of Appendices.

Installation

The following instructions make the assumption that you will copy the data files to a single directory on your hard disk (e.g. C:\Gallant), and that your CD-ROM drive is called D:\.

Please follow the instructions below for WordPerfect 9 and above

Using the materials with Microsoft Word

N.B. for other versions of Word, and other Windows word processors in general, the instructions will be similar, but if you are not sure refer to the documentation that came with your word processor.

To open a Gallant document in Word, select **File, Open** from the menu. Highlight the Gallant directory in the **Directories** list box. Select the desired document, e.g. "App3a" from the list and press **OK**.

LICENCE AGREEMENT

Definitions

1. The following terms will have the following meanings:

"The PUBLISHERS" means Sweet & Maxwell of 100 Avenue Road, London NW3 3PF (which expression shall, where the context admits, include the PUBLISHERS' assigns or successors in business as the case may be) of the other part on behalf of Thomson Books Limited of Cheriton House, North Way, Andover SP10 5BE.

"The LICENSEE" means the purchaser of the title containing the Licensed Material.

"Licenced Material" means the data included on the disk;

"Licence" means a single user licence;

"Computer" means an IBM-PC compatible computer.

Grant of Licence; Back-up Copies

2.(1) The PUBLISHERS hereby grant to the LICENSEE, a non-exclusive, non-transferable licence to use the Licensed Material in accordance with these terms and conditions.

(2) The LICENSEE may install the Licensed Material for use on one computer only at any one time.

(3) The LICENSEE may make one back-up copy of the Licensed Material only, to be kept in the LICENSEE's control and possession.

Proprietary Rights

3.(1) All rights not expressly granted herein are reserved.

(2) The Licensed Material is not sold to the LICENSEE who shall not acquire any right, title or interest in the Licensed Material or in the media upon which the Licensed Material is supplied.

(3) The LICENSEE shall not erase remove, deface or cover any trademark, copyright notice, guarantee or other statement on any media containing the Licensed Material.

(4) The LICENSEE shall only use the Licensed Material in the normal course of its business and shall not use the Licensed Material for the purpose of operating a bureau or similar service or any online service whatsoever.

(5) Permission is hereby granted to LICENSEES who are members of the legal profession (which expression does not include individuals or organisations engaged in the supply of services to the legal profession) to reproduce, transmit and store small quantities of text for the purpose of enabling them to provide legal advice to or to draft documents or conduct proceedings on behalf of their clients.

(6) The LICENSEE shall not sublicence the Licensed Material to others and this Licence Agreement may not be transferred, sublicensed, assigned or otherwise disposed of in whole or in part.

(7) The LICENSEE shall inform the PUBLISHERS on becoming aware of any unauthorised use of the Licensed Material.

Warranties

4.(1) The PUBLISHERS warrant that they have obtained all necessary rights to grant this licence.

(2) Whilst reasonable care is taken to ensure the accuracy and completeness of the Licensed Material supplied, the PUBLISHERS make no representations or warranties, express or implied, that the Licensed Material is free from errors or omissions.

(3) The Licensed Material is supplied to the LICENSEE on an "as is" basis and has not been supplied to meet the LICENSEE's individual requirements. It is the sole responsibility of the LICENSEE to satisfy itself prior to entering this Licence Agreement that the Licensed Material will meet the LICENSEE's requirements and be compatible with the LICENSEE's hardware/software configuration. No failure of any part of the Licensed Material to be suitable for the LICENSEE's requirements will give rise to any claim against the PUBLISHERS.

(4) In the event of any material inherent defects in the physical media on which the licensed material may be supplied, other than caused by accident abuse or misuse by the LICENSEE, the PUBLISHERS will replace the defective original media free of charge provided it is returned to the place of purchase within 90 days of the purchase date. The PUBLISHERS' entire liability and the LICENSEE's exclusive remedy shall be the replacement of such defective media.

(5) Whilst all reasonable care has been taken to exclude computer viruses, no warranty is made that the Licensed Material is virus free. The LICENSEE shall be responsible to ensure that no virus is introduced to any computer or network and shall not hold the PUBLISHERS responsible.

(6) The warranties set out herein are exclusive of and in lieu of all other conditions and warranties, either express or implied, statutory or otherwise.

(7) All other conditions and warranties, either express or implied, statutory or otherwise, which relate to the condition and fitness for any purpose of the Licensed Material are hereby excluded and the PUBLISHERS shall not be liable in contract or in tort for any loss of any kind suffered by reason of any defect in the Licensed Material (whether or not caused by the negligence of the PUBLISHERS).

Limitation of Liability and Indemnity

5.(1) The LICENSEE shall accept sole responsibility for and the PUBLISHERS shall not be liable for the use of the Licensed Material by the LICENSEE, its agents and employees and the LICENSEE shall hold the PUBLISHERS harmless and fully indemnified against any claims, costs, damages, loss and liabilities arising out of any such use.

(2) The PUBLISHERS shall not be liable for any indirect or consequential loss suffered by the LICENSEE (including without limitation loss of profits, goodwill or data) in connection with the Licensed Material howsoever arising.

(3) The PUBLISHERS will have no liability whatsoever for any liability of the LICENSEE to any third party which might arise.

(4) The LICENSEE hereby agrees that

(a) the LICENSEE is best placed to foresee and evaluate any loss that might be suffered in connection with this Licence Agreement,

(b) that the cost of supply of the Licensed Material has been calculated on the basis of the limitations and exclusions contained herein; and

(c) the LICENSEE will effect such insurance as is suitable having regard to the LICENSEE's circumstances.

(5) The aggregate maximum liability of the PUBLISHERS in respect of any direct loss or any other loss (to the extent that such loss is not excluded by this Licence Agreement or otherwise) whether such a claim arises is contract or tort shall not exceed a sum equal to that paid as the price for the title containing the Licensed Material.

Termination

6.(1) In the event of any breach of this Agreement including any violation of any copyright in the Licensed Material, whether held by the PUBLISHERS or others in the Licensed Material, the Licence Agreement shall automatically terminate immediately, without notice and without prejudice to any claim which the PUBLISHERS may have either for moneys due and/or damages and/or otherwise.

(2) Clauses 3 to 5 shall survive the termination for whatsoever reason of this Licence Agreement.

(3) In the event of termination of this Licence Agreement the LICENSEE will remove the Licensed Material.

Miscellaneous

7.(1) Any delay or forbearance by the PUBLISHERS in enforcing any provisions of this Licence Agreement shall not be construed as a waiver of such provision or an agreement thereafter not to enforce the said provision.

(2) This Licence Agreement shall be governed by the laws of England and Wales. If any difference shall arise between the Parties touching the meaning of this Licence Agreement or the rights and liabilities of the parties thereto, the same shall be referred to arbitration in accordance with the provisions of the Arbitration Act 1996, or any amending or substituting statute for the time being in force.